SECOND EDITION, REVISED AND EXPANDED

# TRADE,
# DEVELOPMENT
## AND
# FOREIGN DEBT

How trade and development
concentrate economic power
in the hands of dominant nations

# MICHAEL HUDSON

ISLET

First published 1992 by Pluto Press
345 Archway Road, London N6 5AA

British Library Cataloguing in Publication Data
Hudson, Michael
Trade, development and foreign debt.
I. Foreign trade. Theories
I. Title 382.104
ISBN 13: 9783949546013

Library of Congress Cataloging-in-Publication Data
Hudson, Michael, 1939-
Trade, development, and foreign debt: a history of theories of polarization and
convergence in the international economy / Michael Hudson.
p. cm.
Includes bibliographical references and index.
ISBN 13: 9783949546013
1. Protectionism – History. 2. International economic relations – History. I.
Title.
HF 1713.1483 1992
382-dc20

# Contents

## PART I  ORIGINS OF INTERNATIONAL ECONOMICS

*Scholastic views on trade accommodate gain-seeking—Monetization of Europe's economic life—Cosmopolitan Christendom gives way to national economies—Mercantilism as an economic system to create a surplus—Monetary preconditions for economic expansion—Shaping markets to serve the national interest.—Augmenting the nation's skilled labor and other vital economic inputs—The objectives and costs of colonialism.*

*How national endowments and cost structures evolved—The strategy of mercantile colonialism—Regional characteristics of imperial trade and payments.*

*The subordinate but critical role of money—The monetary dimension of foreign trade and payments—Monetary expansion increases employment before prices—Monetary theory and moral philosophy—Tucker's and Steuart's criticisms of Hume's adjustment mechanism.*

*How wealthy nations consolidated their head start—Would free trade lead to greater international equality, or polarization?—How rich nations might lose their economic lead—Anti-colonialist tendencies within mercantilism—Free trade as a strategy of English nationalism.*

## PART II  THE CREATION AND DIVISION OF WORLD PRODUCT AND INCOME

*Cost value, political institutions and the specialization of labor—The return to peace after the Napoleonic Wars spurs a tariff debate—International economics and domestic value theory—Arguments of the tariff debate, 1815–48—The methodology of comparative-cost doctrine—Constant returns to scale—The traded commodities are produced in both countries—No trade in common production inputs—Fully employed and domestically mobile labor and capital—No emigration or capital outflows; No imbalance in international trade and payments—No impact of domestic or foreign debtor monetary inflation or deflation on comparative costs—No conflict between private interests and social utility—Recasting Ricardo's free-trade assumptions dynamically.*

## PART III  THE IMPACT OF FOREIGN DEBT ON TRADE AND DEVELOPMENT

I dedicate this book to my mentor
Terence McCarthy (1909–1979)

# Acknowledgements

Teaching international economics from a historical perspective during 1969–72 was only the starting point for this book. During the 1960s and 1970s, Augustus M. Kelley and Garland Press enabled me to reprint many of the classics in international trade theory, and in many cases to publish introductions to them. In the late 1970s the United Nations Institute for Training and Research (UNITAR) provided an opportunity to develop a systems-analysis approach to juxtapose the reality of positive-feedback mechanisms in the world economy with the Chicago School's laissez faire equilibrium theorizing.

In the 1970s I was able to recast my critique of the International Monetary Fund's intellectual pedigree in reports for Canada's Science Council, the Minister of State for Science and Technology, the Department of State and the Institute for Research in Public Policy. A preliminary emphasis on polarization versus convergence mechanisms in these reports helped me focus the present book more along these tines.

Rik Davidson at the Toronto University Press provided support by obtaining Canadian government funding to publish this book in 1978. Although the university's economics faculty (free-market in trade theory but not in ideas) censored its publication, the Press's reader, Tom Naylor, subsequently became a good friend and has made many valuable suggestions. Joe Hollander of M. E. Sharpe also made many good editorial suggestions, as did Al Eichner and Lynn Yost.

Early intellectual support for this book came from Gunnar Myrdal and, most of all, Terence McCarthy, in showing me that most of today's issues and their intellectual responses were anticipated, often eloquently, in past debates about the workings of the international economy. It was at their urging that I studied England's mercantilist/free-trade debate of 1750–75, the bullion debate following the Napoleonic Wars, and the long debate over the Corn Laws and other protectionist issues throughout the nineteenth century.

In addition to doing a remarkable job of proofreading to catch innumerable errors from the scanned and amended version of the original London edition and draft of the present version, Keith Wilde has helped me clarify many difficult points left murky in my earlier draft of this book. Cornelia Wunsch has designed the book in a way that I think has made the ideas as visually accessible as one could wish. I am in debt to her editorial as well as aesthetic judgment.

It often happens that the universal belief of one age of mankind ... becomes to a subsequent age so palpable an absurdity, that the only difficulty then is to imagine how such a thing can ever have appeared credible. ... It looks like one of the crude fancies of childhood, instantly corrected by a word from any grown person.

John Stuart Mill, *Principles of Political Economy* (1848)
preliminary remarks

# Preface to the Second Edition (2009)

The past few years have shown how destructive are the trade and fiscal theories that lead countries to sacrifice their economic development and self-sufficiency in food and other basic needs while servicing unpayably high debts stemming from their legacy of trade and financial dependency. The result is a chronic balance-of-payments deficit, funded by foreign loans whose interest charges put even more downward pressure on exchange rates. Backed by the Chicago School's pro-creditor doctrines and International Monetary Fund (IMF) and World Bank "conditionalities," countries impose domestic austerity and shift resources to their export sectors rather than building up their domestic market. The promise is that this will maximize their economic growth and help them catch up with the United States. The actual result is deepening dependency.

These destructive policies have succeeded largely because students and politicians throughout the world have been indoctrinated with neoliberal models that ignore foreign trade and debt dependency except to deny that these phenomena pose a problem. The logic is that each country should make use of its natural endowments and "factor proportions" between labor and capital.

Historically, first England and later the United States endowed *themselves* with capital, by means of protectionist policies and their own credit creation. England put forth the argument for free trade to persuade other countries *not* to adopt the strategy that had enabled it to overtake Holland and France. English trade strategists recognized that under a regime of free trade, raw-materials suppliers would fall into in the Biblical position of "hewers of wood and drawers of water," becoming increasingly dependent on England as the workshop of the world.

Why teach a course in so doctrinaire a discipline? The answer is that there is a long classical tradition of international trade and financil principles other than those being taught today. But despite the growing awareness that IMF models have lost credibility, the early classical and later protectionist tradition has been all but forgotten, censored by the neoliberal historians of economic thought who have gained academic ascendancy in the United States and abroad. I therefore set out to provide an alternative. This history of theories of trade and foreign debt originated as the lectures for my graduate courses in international economics at the New School for Social Research during 1969–72.

Designing the course forced me to confront the problem of relevance. Free-trade orthodoxy ignores the widening global disparities in productivity and incomes, and its associated neoliberal financial theory endorses the IMF/Chicago prescription of financial austerity for debtor countries. Was it wasting the time of students, many of them from Third World countries, to tutor them in theories that deny the existence of structural trade and payments deficits by assuming that all such problems are automatically self-curing?

Robert Heilbroner, chairman of the Economics Department, explained that the course's task was to turn out professionals. Its objective should be that when the school's graduates met other economists at business or social functions, they would have a common vocabulary and point of reference so as not to embarrass the school or themselves. A working familiarity with orthodox theories would be their union card—and after all, students registered for these courses primarily to get good jobs. This usually meant working as public relations writers on behalf of large financial institutions and international agencies promoting laissez faire, deregulation of markets and a tax shift off finance and real estate onto consumers. And yet regardless of such personal-interest considerations, one-third of graduate students claimed to be there to learn how to help their countries develop instead of becoming more commercially and financially dependent.

The first question was how much room there was to fit the reality of global economic polarization into the curriculum. It seems that once economists get hired by universities or government agencies, they develop a tolerance for models describing a hypothetical "what if" world of trade and payments equilibrium, a world that supposedly promotes growing equality among nations. How best to ward off this unrealistic mirage?

My solution was to review the long history of more realistic economic theorizing. Economic analysis was not so wrongheaded at its inception. The mercantilists and early free traders—men such as David Hume and Josiah Tucker, James Steuart, Adam Smith and the many critics of David Ricardo—had few illusions that economic relations among nations (and persons) were converging rather than diverging. They were by no means so cut off from reality as to imagine that economies had fixed supplies of natural "endowments" of labor and capital of similar productivity. Nor did they have in mind an abstract world with no emigration, international investment and technological divergence among nations, as the factor proportions theory assumes. These early writers nonetheless have been misrepresented by the leading historians of economic thought, who depict their theories of international economics as being identical in content with today's free-trade orthodoxy. The result is an ideologically censored history of thought.

Earlier trade theorists did not share the unrealistic assumptions made by today's economists. Before there was an economics discipline as such, trade and financial theory dealt dynamically with the monetary, demographic, political and technological dimensions of international economics. Yet most modern histories of trade theory ignore—indeed, strip away—these contributions, trivializing the writings of Hume and his contemporaries as being more simple-minded and "modern" than they actually were with regard to international trade, prices, productivity and the effectiveness of government policy.

Since World War I international economics has gone so far as to define itself as a subdiscipline assuming no international migration of labor, no capital investment and no transfer problems resulting from foreign indebtedness. These assumptions rule out consideration of what should be at the center of a realistic curriculum.

To lock in this narrow-mindedness, conventional historians of international economics limit their scope to past anticipations of today's free-trade orthodoxy. If they deal with mercantilist writers at all, it is to harp on their most naïve errors. The result is like trying to reconstruct the writings of the early Christian Gnostics solely from the accusations of their persecutors. To help rectify this situation I undertook to write an alternative history of international trade and financial theories along more realistic and less anachronistic lines. Specifically, this book seeks to achieve four general objectives:

1. to trace the evolution of theories demonstrating how the world economy is characterized by polarization mechanisms. These mechanisms result from market forces favoring the lead nations and from the political diplomacy by which the governments of these nations have steered market forces over the past four hundred years;

2. to show why the world economy does not work in the way postulated by the so-called automatic adjustment mechanisms and financial austerity programs at the heart of today's laissez faire orthodoxy;

3. to explain why countries submitting to this orthodoxy suffer intensifying poverty and chronic instability; and

4. to demonstrate what assumptions must be changed and, above all, what "exogenous" factors not acknowledged by today's orthodoxy must be taken into account by a more realistic theory.

By emphasizing how the mercantilist, early "free-trade imperialist" and protectionist perspectives (that is, pre-Ricardian and anti-Ricardian theory) achieved greater realism than today's orthodoxy, I describe not only the enthronement of error but also the development of more dynamic and lifelike theories of the world economy. In particular I focus on the migration of capital and skilled labor across national boundaries, and how foreign debt and widening cost differentials lead to dependency relationships that exacerbate economic polarization.

In addition to surveying the history of international economics, this book lays the basis for a new theoretical perspective, the leading premises of which acknowledge

i. the numerous absolute elements of international cost structures based on common raw-materials and capital-goods prices. If economies pay the same dollar price for oil and other raw materials, capital equipment and services, how much effect does currency depreciation have on export pricing?

ii. the character of minimum necessary import needs, debt service and other constraints that are not price responsive. If countries need to import grain to eat, and oil to fuel their energy and heat their homes, how much "correction" of consumption can be expected to result from price changes?

iii. the ability of active policy-making to improve the quantity and quality of the various factors of production. If factor endowments are the product of policy, what effect does international diplomacy have on foreign investment and the migration of skilled and unskilled labor?

Taking Keynes's analysis of the German reparations problem in the 1920s as a model, I analyze structural limits to international trade and payments. The fact that I treat debt and other financial transfer payments as paramount gives structural analysis a different focus from that of the Latin American structuralist school. Debt service swamps the balance of payments of debtor countries, forcing reliance on the IMF and World Bank whose economic planners impose financial austerity that prevent debtor economies from achieving balanced growth and becoming self-supporting. Balance-of-payments deficits, aggravated by financial raids on their central banks, leads to currency depreciation that diverts domestic investment and output away from the home market to the export sector. This depresses the terms of trade, pushing the balance of trade even further into deficit. On the basis of these principles I find that structural limits exist for each country's balance-of-payments earning capacity, and hence the ability to service debts and otherwise subsist in today's world.

IMF austerity programs don't work because they impair productive powers by curtailing infrastructure spending, and advocate anti-labor income policies. What is called for is *more* infrastructure to lower economy-wide production and distribution costs, and higher incomes so as to raise labor productivity. What also is needed is to build up the domestic market rather than impoverishing labor in the belief that somehow this will make the economy more competitive.

Matters are aggravated when the leading financial nations use debt leverage to force economies to sell off the natural monopolies and other enterprises in the public domain, especially when many of the buyers are foreign. This leads to chronic balance-of-payments drains—"capital transfers" from debtor to creditor nations.

The result threatens to become a new financial road to serfdom. It is not the kind that Friedrich Hayek warned against, but the more classical debt-peonage resulting from dismantling government planning and regulatory power. It was precisely this planning and regulatory power that England, the United States, Germany and Japan used to acquire their international lead. Yet this is being denied to today's less developed countries, much as was the case in their earlier colonial phase. A false and anti-historical "Chicago School" line of theorizing strips away the study of how modern-day "endowments" of capital and productivity came to be put in place.

Focusing on the short run, today's laissez faire theorizing discourages infrastructure spending and currency stabilization, and takes productivity considerations for granted as being the result of allegedly natural endowments. This book emphasizes the history of theories as to how foreign trade transforms labor and capital productivity under conditions of increasing returns, at least for successful economies. The book's final section describes the negative impact of foreign debt on the terms of trade and explains the role of financial structures in determining competitive advantage.

With such questions, however, we leave the realm of what early theorizing had to offer. I therefore conclude by summarizing what is needed to reverse the narrowing scope of international economics so as to achieve a body of theory better able to deal with today's multilayered world economy.

* * *

I have taken the opportunity of preparing a Chinese translation of this book to edit these lectures into a more concise text, and to correct the myriad of misprints that marred the British 1992 edition. I find no need to update it, as the intervening years have not seen substantive progress in international economic theorizing, but only a consolidation of the narrow-mindedness underlying the neoliberal Washington Consensus.

China faces a set of problems remarkably similar to that of Britain in the 17th and 18th centuries, and the United States and Germany in the 19th century: In the domestic economy, how to achieve equal productivity of labor and capital with the leading nations; and how to avoid foreign debt, and in the international economy, how to create a national financial and monetary system independent of the credit creation of nations that already have established their currencies as international reserves. Both these aims require national independence from the neoliberal dictates of the World Bank, the International Monetary Fund and

International Trade Organization, whose policies seek to "pull up the ladder" to prevent governments from enacting the policies that nurtured the industrial development and financial systems of the world's leading nations.

Translation of this political system into a cosmopolitan ideology of international finance and trade is remarkably parallel to England's strategy of "free-trade imperialism" described in Chapter 4. Much as England promoted free trade and related economic liberalism as a means of consolidating its economic power globally—and post-colonially—in an epoch when it was the world's leading industrial nation, the United States adopted free trade and deregulation of international finance after World War II as a means of consolidating the system I have described in *Super Imperialism* (1972; 2nd ed. 2002) and its sequel *Global Fracture* (1979; 2nd ed. 2004), and what Henry Liu aptly calls Dollar Hegemony.

The basic question for China, as for post-Soviet economies and Third World countries, is what governments need to do to shape their economic environment and its "market incentives." The answer entails a body of economic and fiscal theory to counter the IMF and World Bank economic plans that lock client economies into dependency on a dollarized global economy polarizing between debtors and creditors, enabling foreign investors use debt leverage to pry away and privatize the natural monopolies and public enterprises of "host economies." This book seeks to provide an analytic basis for "steering mechanisms" for governments to regulate markets and establish an appropriate tax system to achieve the desired growth in wealth without the economic polarization between savers and debtors, *rentiers* and an increasingly dependent client population.

# INTRODUCTION

## The Political Context

Economics is not a "disinterested" science aiming objectively to describe how the world works, and debates over economic doctrine are not merely academic matters. Their inspiration is more policy-oriented and ideological than innocent, because the destiny of nations is at issue. Starting with an intent to either defend the status quo or change it, most theorists promote free trade or protectionism, and either creditor or debtor interests. And inevitably, the resulting policy conclusions favor either international dependency or national autonomy. Given this aim of creating a *doctrine* more than just a *theory*, the first task in constructing an economic model is to discover what assumptions, scope and methodology must be put in place to endorse the pre-determined policy, and to exclude considerations that would lead to other policy results.

Representing the interests of the industrial creditor nations over the past century, economic orthodoxy has been constrained by its need to promote creditor-oriented, free-trade results. This starting point is presented as an analytic conclusion, as if it were not cooked in advance. Empirical experience falls by the wayside as the basic premise of today's orthodoxy is that the world economy will work automatically to promote equality of incomes, if only governments refrain from intervening. Countries are told that all will work out for the best if only they refrain from interfering with "free markets," by which is meant markets shaped over many centuries by the industrial creditor nations. Assumptions, evidence and methodology that would produce policy conclusions contrary to free trade and unrestricted capital movements are ruled out, while the analysis of how national policy has transformed economic development over the past few centuries is discouraged by viewing trade and investment as resulting from differing natural "endowments" of labor and capital—or "factor proportions." Despite the widening disparity in international incomes and productivity, economists continue to speculate on the logical conditions necessary to produce convergence.

Orthodox theory assumes that productivity and institutional structures such as land tenure are given rather than being the proper subject of economic policy to transform. Rarely acknowledging a positive role for government policy or the effects of diplomatic coercion, laissez faire theory purports to demonstrate that the existing pattern of trade and investment is quite natural as between relatively self-sufficient and politically active industrial creditor nations on the one hand, and dependent, diplomatically passive debtor countries on the other. While governments in the industrial nations subsidize and otherwise promote their own technological innovation and productivity growth so as to prevent equilibrating tendencies, laissez faire models speculate on what *might* happen if all governments were to remain aloof from shaping the rules of trade and investment.

Endorsing the existing status quo and its dependency patterns, such models have become a tool to reinforce the advantages of these nations over their increasingly indebted raw-materials suppliers. Their formulators reason as if their carefully limited scope and methodology are the epitome of scientific method. Yet their methodology makes the unrealistic assumption of equal (or as modern jargon puts it, "homogeneous") labor and capital productivity throughout the world. Only on this assumption would international incomes become more equal through free trade and investment.

When such a body of theory continues to be applied despite the fact that the effects it predicts are the opposite from those visibly occurring, one must conclude that it has become more an exercise in public relations than scientific analysis. When a theory recommends that countries specialize in what they are "best" at producing at any given moment in time, it advises them to ignore the long-term gains from protectionism designed to maximize *future* wealth and well-being. Attributing the Ricardian "gains from trade" to productivity differentials becomes a political statement that protectionist moves to achieve self-dependency waste the opportunity to live relatively well in the present, regardless of the future. And by emphasizing pricing and distribution functions rather than production functions, orthodox trade theory ignores the extent to which production coefficients and technology can be altered—and the extent to which this requires public infrastructure spending, and hence national fiscal policy.

This line of speculation ignores the corrosive dependency effects of the monoculture syndrome—reliance on a few raw materials, leading to dual economies throughout the southern hemisphere. Presuming automatic tendencies to be at work within the world economy to promote equilibrium and even parity, such theorizing nurtures an unwarranted faith in processes that actually work to intensify international economic convergence.

The United Nations Conference on Trade and Development (UNCTAD) has shared this narrow scope of viewing Third World trade problems in terms of prices that reflect existing production and trade relations. Instead of urging Third World countries to improve food self-sufficiency by shifting land and capital from plantation crop exports to domestic production, UNCTAD urges industrial nations to subsidize prices of raw materials imports by means of an income transfer to governments that are controlled by *rentier* oligarchies and their foreign creditors. While this would raise Third World export levels and thus *seem* to reduce its chronic balance-of-payments deficits, it would exacerbate long-term problems by financing the failure to diversify.

The problem is that higher export prices for raw materials are a disincentive to modernizing domestic agriculture and industry. Instead of broadening and upgrading the national economic base, they subsidize the status quo, encouraging the perpetuation of monocultures. Modest improvements to the commodity terms of trade are depicted as enabling the exporting countries to continue exchanging their primary commodities and low-wage manufactures for food and high-technology imports from the industrial nation. The result is growing economic dependency and widening trade deficits. The principal beneficiaries of such a policy end up being the world minerals cartel and foreign creditors to Third World governments.

Quite a different policy was followed in past centuries by England, the United States, Germany and Japan. A satisfactory explanation for the success of these nations would acknowledge the linkages among international trade, investment, finance and diplomatic leverage. It would describe how the leading industrial nations have monopolized the gains from trade and parlayed them into an investment position that has consolidated their control over world resources. It would trace how international credit has been extended far in excess of debtors' capacity to pay, keeping them on a tight debt leash. It would demonstrate how the attempt to transfer the requisite foreign exchange depresses debtors' terms of trade, to the benefit of creditor-investor nations. Finally, it would acknowledge that "market" tendencies are shaped by a visible political hand. The conditions imposed on Third World countries for obtaining World Bank, IMF and commercial bank credit and foreign aid subordinate their development to serve interests of the industrial creditor nations. These requirements include the imposition of austerity programs that shrink the domestic market, a tax shift off of real estate and monopolies onto domestic labor, and sell-offs of the public domain and natural monopolies to foreign investors, capped by the pursuit of much "freer" trade policies than the United States, Europe and other nations themselves pursue. The net result of these policies is to promote even higher concentration on raw-materials exports at the expense of domestic production.

It should be clear enough by now that no invisible hand guides world market forces to serve the interests of all trading parties symmetrically. At no time during the past two centuries has the world economy operated in the benign manner believed by today's laissez faire proponents. Early free traders were anything but benign, as reflected by Bernard Semmel's term "free-trade imperialism." The gains from industrial and agricultural technology have been concentrated in the industrial nations and converted into an international creditor position. Third World investment has been applied one-sidedly to export sectors, warping domestic sectors into a monoculture syndrome from which countries today are trying to escape.

The great question today concerns the character of future national planning in the face of the financial and technological transformations of the 1990s. Reversing the wave of privatization, deregulation and anti-government ideology that occurred in the 1980s, the consequence of today's global financial crisis probably will be to see governments intervening to restore their more traditional role. Dissolution of centralized Soviet planning principles may even have helped clear the way for a re-examination of effective versus ineffective planning principles, the terms on which mutual checks and balances can best be achieved between the public and private sectors, and the role of market feedback. Every economy is planned, and the main question today is whether this planning will be done mainly by governments or by the international financial institutions that have moved in to fill the vacuum created by the disparagement of governments and dilution of their powers in favor of central bank independence.

Meaningful national trade policy requires a broad scope and long-term time frame capable of relating economic, financial, technological, ecological, demographic, international, military, social, political and cultural functions into an integrated overall view. For this reason alone a re-examination of mercantilist and protectionist theories of trade and development is justified, for they sought to develop just such a comprehensive worldview.

The founders of economic policy in Britain, continental Europe, the United States and Japan created a broad scope for their theorizing at the outset of their moves toward international power. Comprehensive protectionist theories underlay the policies they followed during their formative period when they sought to catch up with and overtake the lead nations of their day—the Netherlands and France in the seventeenth and eighteenth centuries, and Britain in the nineteenth century.

My objective in this book is to re-integrate trade theory with "development" theory—if we can call predecessors of Adam Smith such as James Steuart "development" theorists, along with early English free-trade strategists and foreign protectionists. Like today's free-trade logic, the monetarist orthodoxy employed by the International Monetary Fund and World Bank (spiced with some Keynesian income theory but lacking any hint of Keynes's writings on the transfer problem) rejects the long-run context. The models of price formation and income distribution underlying austerity plans and comparative advantage take productive powers for granted, or at least assume that they will become more similar internationally over time. These models need to be replaced by a more production-oriented body of theory based on the perception that the dynamics of today's market-oriented trade and finance (reinforced by the hand of governments) are largely responsible for widening disparities of international productive powers and incomes. Such models would be able to explain why physical productivity and balance-of-payments earning power have been retarded for less developed countries, pushing their international payments into structural deficits in a polarizing world economy. It is to pave the way for such a body of theory and to defend active public policy that I have written this book.

I wrote it in the process of searching through the literature to see how economic theorists in earlier times conceptualized the problem. This history of trade, development and capital-transfer doctrines accordingly focuses on the key ideas and debates over underlying assumptions. I trace the pedigree of free-trade orthodoxy to the Ricardian position in Britain's Corn Law debates, and the pedigree of today's monetarist orthodoxy back to the "losing" Ricardian position in England's bullion debate after the Napoleonic Wars. Instead of attempting a comprehensive survey of every writer on international economics and its many sub-categories, I focus on the major concepts that have shaped the discipline since its inception in the mercantilist epoch. The common issue spanning these two and a half centuries of theorizing is whether the international economy, when left to "free market" principles, promotes economic convergence or polarization between lead nations and latecomers.

I have not devoted space to the elaboration of trade theory since 1960. Although the literature is abundant, it applies only a limited scope and number of concepts. This book emphasizes general principles, not subsequent restatements. The constraints of modern book length also dictate this summary treatment. The aim of these lecture notes is to provide a syllabus for teaching international trade and financial theory in its historical context, not as a set of timeless abstractions separated from policy interests.

# PART I

## Origins of International Economics

… the most elaborate treatises on the subject [of political economy are] found wanting. To all of them, perhaps, it may be objected, that they attempt to construct a permanent fabric out of transitory materials; that they take for granted the immutability of arrangements of society, many of which are in their nature fluctuating or progressive; and enunciate with as little qualification as if they were universal and absolute truths, propositions which are perhaps applicable to no state of society except the particular one in which the writer happened to live …

But it is, when not duly guarded against, an almost irresistible tendency of the human mind to become the slave of its own hypotheses; and when it has once habituated itself to reason, feel, and conceive, under certain arbitrary conditions, at length to mistake these convictions for laws of nature … (And this, we may observe, *en passant*, is one of the reasons why a literal understanding cannot be a good understanding, and why the greatest powers of reasoning, when connected with a sluggish imagination, are no safeguard against the poorest slavery—that of subjection to mere accidental habits of thought.) It is in this manner that in all countries the lawyer, from the habit of making the existing system his standard of comparison … becomes usually a sworn foe to all reform, merely because he cannot, for the life of him, realize the conception of any other system, or fancy what it could be like. And we think there is some danger of a similar result in the case of the English political economists.

John Stuart Mill, "Miss Martineau's Summary of Political Economy" [1834],
*Works* (Toronto: 1963), IV, pp. 225ff.

# 1

## Early European Commercial Strategy

During the eleventh, twelfth and thirteenth centuries two types of worldliness transformed Europe's economies: commerce from the Levant and armed conquest from the West. From the East, Arabian trade brought technology and culture across southern France to Moorish Spain. In the opposite direction, Europe's Crusades seized wealth forcibly by sacking Constantinople. The Crusades were blessed from their inception in 1096. Less than a quarter-century earlier, in 1078, Pope Gregory VII presided over a Roman council that condemned commerce as sinful. The pursuit of personal gain by tradesmen and money-lenders conflicted with Christian ethical principles in a way that even war did not.

Yet the customers of merchants and bankers seemed eager to buy and borrow, and hence must have felt there was something to be gained from money-lending. If a mutual benefit could be demonstrated by the contracting parties, mercantile gains would be deemed just. The final impetus for legitimization was borrowing by governments, even when they borrowed to wage war.

### *Scholastic views on trade accommodate gain-seeking*

Commerce seemed to be grounded in nature itself. Each region specialized in what God uniquely favored it to produce. Some realms established skilled trades such as glassmaking, others produced rare minerals, spices or wines. Marketing and distributing these goods required merchants, whose activities had to be legitimized. The first practical task of trade theory therefore was to demonstrate how commerce contributed to social welfare. The second task was for the Schoolmen to define the legitimate elements of mercantile income. They concluded that commercial income was not exploitative if it merely enabled tradesmen to cover their direct expenses plus the normal risks inherent in their activities.

The activities of merchants enhanced rather than impoverished society as long as they were honest. This moralistic theorizing was the earliest move toward laissez faire, and it has been largely on the foundation of this rationale that more modern interpretations of trade have been built up. By the nineteenth century this line of theorizing evolved into a distinction between intrinsic value and market price, that is, between the necessary costs of production and the prices for which commodities or services exchange—a gap that includes monopoly rents or other non-production charges.

Given its low-surplus economy whose population subsisted at or just above break-even levels, Europe could not afford undue profiteering by wealthy merchants, except for the Jews, the "King's serfs" whom the royal tax collector bled of their takings. Within the Christian economy the issue was whether trade was part of a mutually beneficial activity or exploitative. In a zero-sum economy that produced no surplus but merely subsisted in a steady state, the tendency was for one party's gain to find its counterpart in another's loss. The question therefore was whether the merchant or money-lender obtained *more* than the value of his direct outlays, labor and other efforts involved in supplying his wares and services or risking his money?

The doctrine of Just Price recognized three legitimate ways to sell something for more than it originally cost. In the first place, workmen labored to transform raw materials into finished products, and their labor had value. Second, merchants bought goods from afar to sell at local markets. This involved expenditures for transport, credit and direct labor, as well as the risk of sinkage at sea, piracy, robbery, spoilage or other damage. Lenders who put out money at interest took the risk of not being repaid, while giving up the opportunity to use the money directly for their own gainful use. All these merchants, tradesmen and lenders deserved compensation for their efforts and the reasonable risks entailed in pursuing their occupations.

The economic historian Max Beer paraphrases St. Augustine's fifth-century defense of trade along these lines:

> I am procuring and bringing goods from far-off countries. I am simply trying to get wages for my labour, and the labourer is worthy of his hire. From this it follows that I can rightly sell dearer than the price which I gave. ... I do not approve of covetous traders ... but those failings [lies, cheating, etc.] are in the man and not in his trade, which can be carried on honestly. ... The Philosopher says that since everybody needs many things which he cannot himself produce for his sustenance, such as food, garments, housing, etc., man must live in society, that is, with other men of various vocations, and they form a trading association, in which their members exchange to their mutual benefit their goods and services. ... Trade and commerce are thus not evil, but in accordance with the Law of Nature. And when Cassiodor says that trading is illicit because it means buying cheap and selling dear, this can only apply to traders who are buying up all the goods necessary for sustenance, such as corn, in order to make them scarce and then sell them at prices arbitrarily fixed. Such traders shall be ejected from the Church and all holy places.

Augustine held trade to be evil "if pursued by persons who are forbidden to engage in trading, such as clergymen. Trading is illicit if pursued for sinful purposes, such as forestalling [to corner the market so as to charge extortionate prices]. It is forbidden in times that ought to be devoted to divine service and prayer, such as Sundays and Festivals," and in churches. However, it was lawful "when pursued honestly for the purpose of supplying our fellow-man with the goods he needs." The merchant's "travels and stewardship are labour and the labourer is worthy of his hire."[1] Making a profit was permissible as long as its remuneration represented the wages of honest labor and industry.

As the Church became increasingly worldly in response to the growth of commerce during the twelfth and thirteenth centuries, it rationalized most forms of gain as legitimate, even money-lending, but not extortionate prof-iteering such as *turpe lucrum* resulting from monopolizing essentials in times of scarcity, engrossing, or misrepresenting. "Whenever dialectic failed to remove doubt and misgiving," summarizes Beer, "the schoolmen judged institutions from the point of their effect on the well-being and ordered life of society, as well as on the subordination of self-interest to the commonweal."[2]

By incorporating the theory of property into natural law (*jus naturale*), the new theorizing transformed the Church's moral philosophy and economic ethics. Augustine's contemporary John Chrysostom had viewed trade as being lawful according to Church rules only when it involved the physical transformation of commodities by workmen. But in the thirteenth century Alexander of Hales (Alensis) wrote that transporting a commodity was on a par with manufacturing it.

Exchanging one region's specialties for those of another offered an oppor-tunity for gain to all parties, although there was as yet no clear idea of some countries being able to produce certain commodities at a particularly low cost. After all, trade tended to be either in luxuries or in geographically localized raw materials. Profit-oriented thinking thus related mainly to the top of the social pyra-mid. Some kingdoms enjoyed climatic or other natural advantages, others acquired technical skills in producing particular commodities. Feudal practice was to grant royal patents to produce a surplus of these goods to sell abroad or exchange for raw materials, spices, tropical products and luxuries from other regions.

The era's most modern defense of trade was put forth by the Englishman Ricardus de Media Villa (Richard of Middleton). Born in the mid-thirteenth century, he viewed trade as being lawful for three reasons:

---

[1]   Max Beer, *Early British Economics: From the XVII^th Century* (London: 1938), pp. 30–31.
[2]   *Ibid.*, p. 53.

First, the different wants of men and their consequent demand for mutual services, that is, exchange; secondly, nature rightfully dictates that men in their intercourse should assist one another "inasmuch as they are all under one prince who is God"; thirdly … it is natural that men should mutually exchange their superfluities and supply the deficiencies.

Ricardus took issue with the view that gainers from trade must necessarily injure their fellow men. Acknowledging that the merchant's aim was personal gain, he held that it was neither unnatural nor exploitative. Yet several centuries after Ricardus's time, Francis Bacon echoed the view of Aristotle that "whatsoever is somewhere gotten is somewhere lost."[3] Where Ricardus did follow Aristotle was to view use value as forming the essence of exchange value, that is, price. In remarkably modern fashion, he depicted increased utility as the foundation for just gains:

> Let us envisage two countries, A and B, unequally endowed by nature. A produces corn in abundance, but little wine, while country B has an abundance of wine and a deficiency of corn. We know that the market price or the just price of a commodity varies when plentiful is less appreciated than when it is scarce. In this manner a sextarium of corn in country A will be cheaper than in country B, while conversely a dolium of wine in country A will be dearer than in country B. Now, it is natural for the business of trade and commerce to equalize supply. The merchant, then, buys corn cheap in country A and sells it at the higher market price that is ruling in country B, or he buys wine cheap in country B and sells it at the higher market price that is ruling in country A, so that in reality the consumer is not in the least overcharged, for he pays for each commodity the normal price, the just price, which is ruling in his respective country. The exchanges are equal, yet the merchant earns his profit, and he does so rightfully, for, far from having injured either country, he brought benefit to both. His profit is therefore neither usury nor turpe lucrum. The same rule of equality of exchanges which we find in international trade applies also to the business transactions of individuals in their own country. The commodity which the consumer receives is of more immediate utility to him than the money he gives for it, while to the merchant the money he receives for his commodity is of greater immediate utility than the commodity which he surrenders, so that both draw equal benefits from the exchange.[4]

As Beer summarizes this discussion: "The Free Traders attempted to show that in trade both the exporting and importing countries gain, and that therefore international trade is quite in accordance with the principle of

---

[3]  *Ibid.*, pp. 40–41, referring to Aristotle, *Politics*, 1.3.8–9 and to Francis Bacon, *Essays*, Number 15 ("Of Sedition and Troubles").

[4]  Beer, *ibid.*, pp. 40–41, citing Ricardus, *Quodlibeta*, II. questio 23, art. i, and Sententiae, III, distinctio 33, art. 3, questio 4.

commutative justice." In modern jargon, it maximized economic utility. It was not a zero-sum game such as occurred in the case of usury where the creditor's receipt of interest was a direct loss for the borrower.[5] Money-lending would take longer to win acceptance. It did so only as access to financing became urgent in the face of Europe's internecine wars and the rapid extension of commerce following discovery of the New World in 1492.

### Monetization of Europe's economic life

The medieval Christian world had the semblance of an international state under papal authority. Its regional kingdoms were dominated by the Church of Rome. Technology was fairly uniform, as were living standards and cultural values for any given class of society. There was little regional jealousy—and relatively little economic surplus to exploit. Kings chose to rule by the grace of a Roman representative of God, and for a long time this involved little material sacrifice. But this unity could last only as long as Europe's regions remained economically equal and commercial life reflected traditional social and religious values.

The pattern of European payments consisted largely of transmitting contributions and tithes to Rome and other major Church centers, along with earnings on Church-owned mines, estates and industrial ventures. The Church made little attempt to spend these revenues in the regions where they originated. Rather, it drew a growing flow of wealth to its repositories in Rome or Paris, invested it in commercial ventures or spent it where it was most needed for charity and other religious functions. With the spread of commerce, Crusades and banking, this flow of money became a major source of strain that destabilized Europe's hitherto localized equilibrium.

During the Crusades a militarized Church order, the Knights Templar, emerged as Europe's bankers while the Hospitallers and other orders operated the major industrial enterprises and agricultural estates. Their economic role was founded upon the enormous sums of Levantine wealth seized during the Crusades. To ensure that their profits would remain within the order, the Templars took vows of celibacy. By the thirteenth century their temple banks extended across Europe, from Ireland to Armenia, financing far-flung Church operations akin to those of modern conglomerates. Henry III and his retainers stored their wealth at the London Temple, as other sovereigns did in their own local temple banks. The Paris Temple became Europe's monetary center, serving as a depository for papal and royal revenues. The order loaned its resources

---

[5]   Beer, *ibid.*, pp. 41, 43–44, 51, 36ff., quoting Ricardus, *Sententiae*, IV, distinctio 15, questio 36, membrum 4.

to borrowers against collateral (usually land or jewels), using various stratagems to charge interest. Inevitably, these financial activities led to accusations that the Templars were materialistic and even atheistic.

The more European wealth flowered, the stronger the backlash of piety and anti-materialism became, headed by the doctrines of the Cathars, Waldenses and other groups seeking to return to the ascetic communalist practices of early Christianity. Southern France became the center of an anti-Roman Christianity that sought to restore the Church's altruistic origins—and incidentally to hold the area's wealth at home rather than turning it over to Rome.

The south of France became the bloodiest battlefield Europe had yet seen. The Roman Church waged the Albigensian Crusade to crush the local Catharist "heresy," and also to distribute local lands among the northern princes whom it favored. It was primarily to destroy the Cathars and their allies that the Spaniard St. Dominic founded the Inquisition, which sponsored the seizure first of southern French wealth and subsequently of Arab and Moorish property in Spain. Instead of promoting Europe's further commercial and technological flowering, the Church became adverse to wealth and its associated material progress outside of control by its own elites.

This did not deter European sovereigns from taxing Church property in an attempt to participate in the growing prosperity. Frederick II of Germany was excommunicated early in the thirteenth century for his attempts to block the Templars. His will retaliated by enjoining restoration of their estates. Later in the century Philip IV of France sought to curtail the banking order's wealth and power by seizing the properties most recently added to its rolls. Yet he himself was soon obliged to borrow from it, and in 1303 he took refuge from his rebellious subjects in the Paris Temple.

To oppose these secular drives by Europe's rulers, Boniface VIII issued a papal bull in 1296 forbidding civil authority from taxing Church property without papal consent. Philip IV countered by prohibiting the exportation of any coin from France. This forced the Pope to back down in the face of a cessation of revenues from Europe's most prosperous kingdom. The Pope himself was captured by Philip in 1302, splitting the Church into Roman (cosmopolitan) and French (nationalist) factions. The French king settled matters by buying the papacy for his agent, Clement V, who moved his seat to Avignon. This so-called "Babylonian captivity" opened the way for overt persecution of the Templars. Its French members were arrested in 1307, and Pope Clement finally suppressed the order in 1313—the first nationalization of ostensibly cosmopolitan finance capital.

The burgeoning of commerce, banking and credit did not yet elicit an analysis of the economy as a whole. This would have been premature in an epoch when payment in kind still characterized most economic life. Subsistence production remained the norm, and specialization proceeded only to a modest degree. Prior to the discovery of the New World, rents and taxes were paid in the form of crops and corvée labor days rather than money prices that would have provided a common denominator for valuation. Families living in towns were sustained by the products of their neighboring countryside, where cottage industry on the land produced most basic handicrafts. Women typically spun each household's thread, wove cloth and made its clothes, while men did most of the agricultural work and performed military or corvée labor service.

As a subordinate branch of moral philosophy, economic thought sought to demonstrate that trade was efficient at producing commercial gains for entire populations, not just for merchants alone. Economies were not yet integrated into national markets, so trade restrictions and market regulations were not yet nationalistic. No country was obliged to trade as a precondition for its ongoing survival. However, local institutions were unable to cope with the agricultural and industrial revolutions that followed Europe's revival of trade. Monetization of its economic life stemmed from the influx of monetary metals through trade and war, the growth of public debts (mainly war loans), and the taxes levied to pay them.

The shift from payments in kind to money rents and taxes helped free society from serfdom and its rigidities, but the emerging cash nexus dissolved local wage customs and local self-sufficiency, often brutally as attested by the peasant wars. Money came to be loaned more easily against land, and mortgages were foreclosed when the stipulated payments were not met.

The guild system and its associated medieval regulations sought to freeze economic life into a myriad of self-contained local units, but money provided a common denominator to co-measure commodities and labor. This facilitated uniform costs and incomes among different localities and types of work. Land rents no longer had to be paid in the form of work days or crops, but were commuted for money payment. This led to increasing mobility, which helped promote the growth of commercial towns. Along with the spread of coinage, commercialism—and debt—helped create more uniform market and price functions, dissolving the medieval mentality by breaking down local autonomy and self-sufficiency. Towns and countrysides were integrated into larger political units as nations, having a much more complex and interdependent economic organization. As this occurred, materialistic, nationalistic and ultimately pecuniary values came to replace altruistic and universalist spiritual doctrines.

*Cosmopolitan Christendom gives way to national economies*

The Renaissance remained centered in Italy as long as the main route to eastern riches lay along the Venetian path eastward, where Marco Polo had traveled in the thirteenth century. Italian banking families took the place of the Templars, and their loans became the key to warfare and power, to crowns and even the papacy as bankers lent the growing aggregations of money to rulers to wage wars or buy their crowns (*e.g.* as in the case of the Fuggers' loans to the Hapsburgs).

But the Church establishment could neither withstand nor adjust to the dynamics that followed the massive influx of silver and gold after 1492. Europe's explosive financial, economic and technological dynamics spurred the development of nation-states and their desire to retain their wealth at home rather than transfer it to Rome. Increasingly centralized national economies replaced the confederation of semi-autonomous localities that had characterized medieval Christendom.

A wave of price inflation transformed land tenure systems, catalyzing enclosure movements converting public commons into private property, while a rural exodus swamped Europe's cities with serfs driven off their lands from the sixteenth through the eighteenth century. The growth of commerce, the agricultural-urban revolution and the associated monetary revolution were associated with wars, national debts private-sector banking and credit, inflation and rising taxes. This was the essence of the Reformation in its economic aspect. In each kingdom the motive force of development became increasingly commercial, financial, materialistic, anti-papist and military—in a word, *nationalistic* as Christendom divided into rival states whose foreign trade and colonialism laid the foundation for a vast credit expansion.

The merging of kingdoms and localities into unified national states became a process of commercial consolidation which, in time, integrated all economic life within national jurisdictions. The ensuing fiscal and commercial integration of royal economies led Henry VIII to expropriate the Roman Catholic Church's estates and establish the Church of England. Protestant revolutions soon followed in the German-speaking countries, led by Martin Luther and John Calvin. Europe's commercial advantage shifted to the northwest, along the Atlantic coast via Spain and Portugal to France, the Netherlands and England. Impelled along the path of economic, political and religious independence, these nations gave birth to the modern world of national cultures.

Discovery of the Western Hemisphere and the wealth of the East Indies gave nations a bounty to contest. The leading nations sought to link their colonial systems and domestic economy into a unified market. Cultivators driven off the land—"freed" from agriculture—had to find urban employment. Under these conditions nations did not seek to save labor as much as to employ the rural exodus. Their strategy in this struggle has been called mercantilism, but its theoretical foundation was based primarily on national security and a doctrine of national power resting increasingly on principles of market efficiency.

### Mercantilism as an economic system to create a surplus

The medieval system achieved balance and stability to the extent that it could feed local populations and meet their basic needs. The ideal was simply to be self-supporting. Indeed, surpluses tended to be disturbing factors in economies where one party's gain tended to be another's loss. By the sixteenth century, however, governments had become dependent on growing tax revenues to finance their wars, colonialism and programs of internal improvements. Subsistence production did not provide a surplus to tax, invest or export. Failure to draw new money into the system threatened to bring about fiscal and financial crisis.

The first step of economic theorizing in these circumstances, after having legitimized the drive for commercial profit, was to map out how governments might best mobilize this surplus to increase national power. However, market forces were endorsed only when directed by the state to promote national development. In cases where foreign trade and colonization did not sufficiently serve national ends when left to market forces, governments provided subsidies and protective tariffs or import quotas to make desirable lines of national trade and development sufficiently profitable to attract investors. To help transplant desirable industries, they offered economic inducements to skilled foreign workers to immigrate. Conversely, governments imposed prohibitions and excise taxes on activities deemed detrimental to the national interest, such as importing and consuming luxuries. The aim was to promote the creation of a national surplus by mobilizing the passions for personal gain in the service of national wealth and glory.

Unlike today's international economists, the mercantilists did not seek to determine how to reach a state of balanced trade and international equality. Just the opposite: They aimed to monopolize the world's gold and silver, and even its skilled labor, by spurring their workers to produce a growing economic surplus. The basic debate concerned how best to allocate this surplus. What proportions should a nation invest at home, spend on colonial ventures, military subsidies or other state projects, or produce semi-luxuries to spur the population to work harder in order to consume more?

The Old World was being broken asunder by the political economy of nationhood. It henceforth might be reunited under the power of whatever nations could best achieve commercial dominion over all others. Mercantilist economic policy became the instrument of national aspiration, aiming ultimately at achieving world dominance. Each nation strove to conquer and absorb its rivals, with the final objective being to create a new cosmopolitanism in which all the world's population and resources would fall under the sway of a single imperial power. Yesterday England, today the British Empire, tomorrow the world. England's wars with France, the latter's dreams of empire under Napoleon, and subsequent German aggression all sought to reintegrate Europe and its far-flung colonial systems along nationalist lines.

Toward this end, attention focused more on productive powers than on comparative costs. The objective was not to create an "efficient" world interdependency but to achieve national self-sufficiency while becoming more powerful than other nations. Nations taxed the surplus to subsidize industry and colonization, and to spend on wars and related projects of empire. Part of the remaining surplus was consumed in the form of luxuries, but as much as possible was reinvested in industry, agriculture and commerce, and was exported to draw yet more money (bullion) into the system to finance continued economic expansion.

### Monetary preconditions for economic expansion

In seeking to gain control of the world's scarce money, capital and skilled labor, each nation sought to direct the economic activity of its citizens and corporations. Mercantilists sought to employ labor, money and capital productively, defining productive labor and investment as that which created an economic surplus. Nations sought to profit as national entities. Profit was conceived not only as a gain in monetary bullion, but increasingly as mobilizing the means of production to earn it by exporting or to replace imports with domestic output.

The prerequisite for domestic industry was credit, which rested on a monetary base of coinage and bullion. Governments accordingly steered national industry to accumulate silver and gold from the New World directly or, more simply at first, via Spain and Portugal as intermediaries. "While trade was carried on by the exchange of consumable commodities," balanced in a virtual barter process, observed James Steuart in 1767, "its operation … little interested the state: consumption then was equal on both sides; and no balance was found upon either. But so soon as the precious metals became an object of commerce, and when, by being rendered an universal equivalent for everything, it became also the measure of power between nations, then the acquisition, or at least the preservation of a proportional quantity of it became, to the more prudent, an object of the last importance."[6] Nations vied with one another to possess as much gold and silver as possible, prompting statesmen to ask how best to manage foreign trade and colonization to earn the money to make their nations powerful.

Gold and silver inflows, and hence the superstructure of domestic credit expansion, historically have been a function of international trade and payments surpluses.[7] "Those Nations that have no Mines of Gold and Silver," wrote Matthew Decker in 1750, "have no Means to get them but by Foreign Trade, and according to the Degree of those Metals they retain, the Prices of their Commodities, the Numbers of their People, and therewith the Value of their Lands rise and fall in proportion."[8]

Monetary inflows, it was observed, need not force up prices as long as they were used to increase output by employing more labor and capital productively, that is, in a manner productive of a net investable or exportable economic surplus. The objective was to achieve a positive-feedback process characterized by balance-of-payments surpluses, monetary expansion, immigration of skilled labor, and rising domestic employment and output. In pursuing these objectives, mercantilist thought moved toward becoming a social science, the foundation for subsequent classical political economy. Gradually it evolved into economic liberalism, although this initially was defended on nationalistic grounds as a policy to extend an imperial nation's power over other nations.

### Shaping markets to serve the national interest

The mercantilists realized that over time a nation's political character and economic legislation outweighed its original natural advantages or disadvantages. As Adam Smith observed, hothouses could be built in Scotland to grow tropical produce if need be—that is, if the government made it a paying proposition. Social and political institutions were the regulatory framework that determined whether labor would be employed or idle, productive or unproductive, and hence whether a nation would earn or lose gold and silver, skilled labor and industry.

---

[6] James Steuart, *Principles of Political Oeconomy: Being an Essay on the Science of Domestic Policy in Free Nations* (London: 1767), Vol. I, p. 327 (Bk. II, ch. xxii).

[7] Jacob Vanderlint observed in 1734 that "Money (by which understand always Gold and Silver) can be brought into a Nation that hath not Mines, by this Means only: viz., by such Nation's exporting more Goods in Value than they import." *Money Answers All Things* (London: 1734), pp. 2–3.

[8] Matthew Decker, *An Essay on the Causes of the Decline of the Foreign Trade. Consequently of the Value of the Lands of Great Britain, and On the Means to Restore Both*, 2nd ed. (London: 1750), p. 1.

Contemplating the relationship between national policy and natural endowments in 1606, the Frenchman Jean Bodin concluded: "The government of every Citie is of great force in the alteration of the peoples natures and dispositions." The wise statesman would examine "What may grow in the minds of men from the ayre, water, winds, hills and vallies, what from religion, lawes, and customes, discipline, and from the state of every commonweale," and should not stop at observing the climate alone. Bodin recommended that "he that would see what force education, lawes, and customes, have to chaunge nature, let him looke into the people of Germanie, who in the time of *Tacitus* the Proconsull, had neither laves, religion, knowledge, nor any form of a Commonweale; whereas now they seem to exceed other nations in goodly cities, and well peopled, in arms, varietie of artes, and civil discipline."[9] Political structures and associated population qualities were seen to differ among nations to a greater degree than did initial natural endowments, and to be more important in determining productivity and costs.

Mercantilism distinguished itself from the liberalism of later times not by its goals—achieving growth in national output, capital accumulation, payments inflows and full employment—but by the means it proposed to achieve these national objectives. While mercantilism was based as much on the motive power of private self-interest as was the subsequent economic liberalism, it viewed public corporations and private enterprise only as a means to an end, not an end in itself. The statesman's task was to shape the market environment in which personal economic and social incentives operated, steering them into nationally desirable courses.

This objective could not be ensured by the unguided workings of private enterprise. It required state direction of economic life and even of personal values. Along these lines Bishop George Berkeley asked in the 1730s "Whether there not be an art or skill in governing human pride, so as to render it subservient to the public aim" and

> Whether ... a legislator ... should not be a person of reflexion and thought, who hath made it his study to understand the true nature and interest of mankind, how to guide men's humours and passions, how to incite their active powers, how to make their several talents co-operate to the mutual benefit of each other, and the general good of the whole?[10]

[9]  Jean Bodin, *The Six Books of a Commonwealth* (London: 1606), translated by Richard Knolles (Cambridge, Mass.: 1962), pp. 565–68.
[10] George Berkeley, *The Querist, Containing Several Queries Proposed to the Consideration of the Public. First Published in Three Parts in 1735, 1736 and 1737, and reduced to its present form in 1750*, reprinted in *The Works of George Berkeley*, ed. Alexander Campbell Fraser (Oxford: 1901), Queries 328 and 346. See alto Queries 24, 28 and *passim*.

In 1753, Josiah Tucker similarly argued that "to turn the principles of self love into such a channel that it should always operate for the public good … ought to he the sole aim of every government, if either good morals or national prosperity are expected." Toward this end he advocated establishment of a Board of Trade "as *the guardians of the public welfare*" to ensure a harmony of interests between individuals and the state.[11]

The liberalism of a later age would presume this harmony to be natural and automatic once the requisite institutional structures had been put in place. "The ruling principle of the science" of political economy, wrote Steuart,

> in all ages, has been to proceed upon the supposition that every one will act, in what regards the public, from a motive of private interest; and that the only public spirited sentiment any statesman has a right to exact of his subjects, is their strict obedience to the laws.[12]

As an example of how wise statesmen might direct personal tastes via such laws, Berkeley asked whether nations should not improve their balance of trade by encouraging the purchase of domestic rather than foreign luxury products. The statesman should ask, for example,

> Whether it may not concern the wisdom of the legislature to interpose in the making of fashions; and not leave an affair of so great influence to the management of women and fops, tailors and vintners?

> Whether we are not undone by fashions made for other people? And whether it be not madness in a poor nation to imitate a rich one?

> How far the vanity of our ladies in dressing, and of our gentleman in drinking, contribute to the general misery of the people?

> Whether these who drink foreign liquors, and deck themselves and their families with foreign ornaments, are not so far forth to be reckoned absentees?

> Whether our ladies might not as well endow monasteries as wear Flanders lace? And whether it be not true that Popish nuns are maintained by Protestant contributions?[13]

---

[11] Josiah Tucker, *A Second Letter to a Friend Concerning Naturalisation* (1753), p. 37n, quoted in Robert Livingstone Schuyler, *Josiah Tucker: A Selection from His Economic and Political Writings* (New York: 1931), p. 13 (hereafter referred to as Tucker, *Economic and Political Writings*), and Tucker, *A Brief Essay on Britain with Regard to Trade* [1749] (1787 ed.), p. viii. On these points see Edgar S. Furniss, *The Position of the Laborer in a System of Nationalism: A Study in the Labor Theories of the Later English Mercantilists* (Boston: 1920), pp. 6–7 and *passim*; William D. Grammp, "The Liberal Elements its English Mercantilism," *Quarterly Journal of Economics*, LXVI (November 1952), p. 487, and Douglas Vickers, *Studies in the Theory of Money: 1690-1776* (Philadelphia 1959), pp. 241–42.

[12] Steuart, *Principles of Political Oeconomy*, Vol. I, pp. 237, 482.

[13] Berkeley, *The Querist*, queries 13, 102, 104, 140 and 453.

Berkeley urged that if a nation's producers were to be rewarded with luxuries as an incentive to work more intensively, their drives should be channeled into a demand for housing and furniture, whose manufacture employed mainly domestic artisans rather than foreigners. In sum, private self interest would remain the motive force in economic life, but its efficacy in promoting national interests should be maximized by whatever elements of patriotism and planning could be used to shape it in the national interest.

### Augmenting the nation's skilled labor and other vital economic inputs

Prior to the nineteenth-century Steam Revolution the major form of capital took the form of labor skills. Many immigrants were trained artisans, especially in the textile industry. Adam Smith observed that manufacturers

> of silks, velvets and brocades, which flourished in Lucca, during the thirteenth century … were banished from thence by the tyranny of one of Machiavel's heroes, Castruccio Castracani. In 1310, nine hundred families were driven out of Lucca, of whom thirty-one retired to Venice, and offered to introduce there the silk manufacture.[14]

The cultural and even religious dimension of technology transfer became apparent as the Protestant revolution dissolved Roman Catholic Europe into competing national states, transforming the composition of national populations. Huguenots emigrated from France, the Pilgrims and other persecuted groups left England, and Dutch Jews fled to Brazil and other lands from Spain's persecutions in the Low Countries. England sought to gain skilled craftsmen by a policy of political and religious toleration bolstered by wage incentives. In 1690, Nicholas Barbon argued for political and economic freedom on the ground that "the Oppressed People remove into the next Country they can find Shelter in, & become the Subjects of other Governments."[15]

England could encourage immigration specifically to achieve technological advance. Josiah Tucker's "Polity for the Admission of Wealthy and Industrious Foreigners," which formed the second chapter of his *Elements of Commerce* (1755), made a number of observations and policy proposals that stand in sharp contrast to the international immobility of labor assumed by post-classical economists:

> I. Many of the *best* and most *useful* Subjects in foreign Countries and arbitrary Governments, are often harassed and oppressed by the *Minions* in Power …

---

[14] Adam Smith, *An Inquiry into the Nature and Causes of the Wealth of Nations* (1776). Book III, ch. iii (Cannan ed., 6th ed., London: 1961), Vol. I, p. 429. All future page references refer to this edition.

[15] Nicholas Barbon, *A Discourse of Trade* (London: 1690), p. 29.

II. The *Romish* Religion never ceases to persecute the Protestants in every Country, where it can; and these Protestants, generally speaking, are Merchants and Mechanics, Persons the most useful in a State, and the most wanted in our own …

III. In some Countries Merchants and Tradesmen are treated with great *Contempt* merely on Account of their *Profession*, and dare not make that *display* of their Riches which their Fortunes could easily support, lest they should give umbrage to the Government to oppress them with Taxes, or for fear of exciting the Envy and Jealousy of the *Noblesse* by the superior Figure they could make in Society …

IV. It is the Interest of this Nation to *invite* those Foreigners who have Money in the Public Funds to reside in *Great Britain*, because the Savings of the Remittances of so much *Yearly Interest* (now constantly sent abroad) would be a very great Addition to the National Stock …

V. As the Introduction of Foreigners brings in Riches … it presents us likewise with the Inventions and Sagacity of other Nations … thus impoverishing our Rivals, at the same Time that it enriches ourselves.

VI. … though *Great Britain* is open to all the Beggars of the Universe (who cannot be *legally* driven away after they are *once arrived here*) yet perhaps there is not a single Instance of any Person coming into this Country with a View to exercise the Trade of Begging …

VII. As the Rent of Lands depends on the Numbers of People, (for Land is quite useless without a Market for its Produce) the Introduction of Foreigners is a sure means of creating a Demand for all the Produce of a Landed Estate,— and consequently of raising the Value and Price of Land …[16]

Many writers suggested that relatively modest semi-luxuries might serve as suitable incentives to spur labor to work harder and out-produce its foreign counterparts. England's trade surplus might continue to grow despite the fact that—and indeed, precisely because—its consumption standards were rising above those abroad.

## *The objectives and costs of colonialism*

Secure supplies of raw materials were critical. Many could not be economically produced at home because they required tropical climates or mineral-rich ores. The acquisition of colonies having these resources prompted an international rivalry among the European nations. (The detailed strategy of this colonial rivalry will be discussed in the next chapter.)

---

[16]  Josiah Tucker, *The Elements of Commerce and Theory of Taxes* (1755), in *Economic and Political Writings*, pp. 80ff.

Military spending was needed to protect the nation and its commerce, especially its colonial trade, against foreign threats. The problem was that these military costs threatened to more than offset the gains resulting from colonization and trade. Such projects of empire threatened to become a more burdensome luxury than profligate personal consumption.

Recognition of this fact led an anti-colonialist movement to develop within mercantilism by the second half of the eighteenth century (to be discussed in Chapter 4). Economic drives based on striving for commercial excellence thus came to supersede military conquest as the preferred strategy to achieve power. England had watched Spain squander its colonial wealth by building churches, while France exhausted its riches by building fortifications and defenses (and imposing a widespread domestic royal bureaucracy on itself). Conversely, during the first half of the seventeenth century the English watched the Dutch government transform Holland from a ravaged ex-colony of Spain into Europe's leading commercial power. Policy makers concluded that well regulated nations could dominate other countries via the world marketplace.

England set out to supplant the Netherlands by a careful direction of its own domestic and imperial economy based on commercial domination. "To what a degree of power and honor has not England arrived!" exclaimed the Enlightenment jurist Emmerich de Vattel. "In former times her warlike Kings and people made brilliant conquests, which they afterwards lost by the uncertain chance of war; to-day it is principally by her commerce that she holds in her hand the balance of power in Europe."[17]

In a similar vein Governor Keith of Pennsylvania argued in the 1730s that Britain must dominate its colonies by means of economic superiority rather than by a costly force of arms:

> It is easy to talk of Penal Laws, Prohibitions, and suchlike Severities, to be executed by the Force of Power; but the most effectual and profitable Way of restraining the Subjects in the Plantations from interfering with *Great Britain* in her Home-Trade and Manufactures, will be, to take due Care that the Colonies be always plentifully supply'd with *British* Cloths, and other *European* Commodities, at a much cheaper Rate than it is possible for them to raise and manufacture such Things within themselves: And likewise, that the Importation of all such Product and Manufacture from the Colonies, as are fit to supply the Wants of *Great Britain*, and to assist the Public in the Balance of National Trade with other Countries, be properly encouraged.[18]

---

[17] Emmerich de Vattel, *The Law of Nations, or the Principles of Natural Law* [1758], tr. G. Fenwick (Dobbs Ferry: 1916), p. 39 (Book 1, ch. 8, para. 85).

[18] William Keith, *The History of the British Plantations in America* (London: 1738), p. 13.

The means to achieve commercial leadership involved financial, demographic, technological and military dimensions that remained largely political in character. Trade strategy was dynamic in aiming to transform productive powers rather than accepting them as given. The productivity of land, labor and machinery was to be increased rather than left in some allegedly original state of nature. Portugal's failure to pursue a policy of enlightened political reform and protection of native handworkers showed how easily a passive commercial policy could lead a country to dissipate its colonial wealth. The nation watched its textile industry fall into ruin following its free-trade 1703 Methuen Treaty with England.

By the third quarter of the eighteenth century, however, the statist doctrines of early mercantilism began to yield to the liberal Deist views of Enlightenment individualism. Before turning to the latter transition, it is worth examining how the strategy of mercantile colonialism laid the groundwork for the division of world labor and production subsequently accepted as "naturally" endowing the New World with African slaves, carving up the continent's lands into large export-oriented plantations and turning colonies into raw-materials monocultures.

# 2

## Imperial Origins of the World Division of Labor

### *How national endowments and cost structures evolved*

History shows that nations are not endowed with capital by physical nature. They accumulate it by deliberate policies. Lead-nation governments—first Britain and then other industrial powers—acted early to shape the world's price structure and their own specialization patterns further their own metropolitan development rather than that of their colonies, ex-colonies or other peripheral regions. If acquired advantage stems from policy, then "natural" advantage results simply from a lack of policy, that is, the context of market forces is left to countries after more politically active nations have developed their own world position. "The superiority of one country over another in a branch of production," wrote John Stuart Mill, "often arises only from having begun it sooner. There may be no inherent advantage ... but only a present superiority of acquired skill and experience."[1] It therefore is appropriate to review how today's industrial nations came to acquire their capital and elevate the status of their labor during the formative period of the modern world economy. Their advantages and endowments were not natural, but carefully acquired.

Laissez faire writers have denied the relevance of this investigation. "Whether the advantages which one country has over another be natural or acquired," wrote Adam Smith, is

> of no consequence. As long as the one country has those advantages and the other wants them, it will always be more advantageous for the latter rather to buy of the former than to make. It is an acquired advantage only, which one artificer has over his neighbour, who exercises another, trade; and yet they both find it more advantageous to buy of one another, than to make what does not belong to their particular trade.[2]

This is true as far as it goes. Yet only a political theory can explain how England rose from a comparatively less developed country to surpass Spain, Holland and France by endowing itself with much of their skilled labor, Iberian gold and other international resources. The nation certainly did not start out with a high ratio of capital relative to the size of its labor force.

---

[1]  John Stuart Mill, *Principles of Political Economy*, Ashley ed., Book V, ch. x, p. 922.
[2]  Adam Smith, *The Wealth of Nations*, Book IV, ch. ii, Cannan ed., Vol. I, p. 280.

By the same token, today's food-deficit monocultures were constrained in their colonial periods not by nature but by imperial policy to specialize in plantation agriculture, non-renewable mineral extraction and, most recently, low-wage manufacturing. Behind their capital/labor ratios stands a legacy of inadequate or malformed infrastructure, colonial land-grant patterns and corrupt oligarchic control, not to speak of the tariffs and other trade barriers of the sort industrial nations still impose against Third World products.

Acknowledgement of this historical legacy suggests that cost functions may be substantially lowered by development policies focusing on social infrastructure too often invisible to quantitative economists, whose vocabulary calls it "exogenous" and therefore outside the boundary of study. Countries may learn from European and North American experience how to use tariffs, subsidies and tax policy to guide market prices and incomes to reflect long-term development potential rather than passively to submit to world forces and international investment patterns steered by lead-nation diplomacy.

Euphemizing countries as having "endowments" of capital, labor, land and minerals abstracts the existing division of world labor from this historical context, brushing aside how today's industrial nations came to acquire their own capital and productive powers. One looks in vain for recognition of the role played by social and political institutions in transforming comparative costs and creating resources. Whatever cost structures exist at a given moment in time are accepted as inherent and grounded in nature itself. Marx poked fun at this attitude a century ago when he asked whether "You believe perhaps, gentlemen, that the production of coffee and sugar is the natural destiny of the West Indies? Two centuries ago, Nature, which does not trouble herself about commerce, had planted neither sugar-cane nor coffee trees there."[3]

To build up their industrial capability, the major European nations founded colonies to supply necessary raw materials in exchange for metropolitan manufactures. Slaves were imported into the sugar colonies in the Caribbean and what are now the southern United States, along with guns and other accoutrements of capital to aid their production of raw materials, but not their industry. India at the outset of its contact with Europe had a far superior accumulation of labor skills and tools, gold and other capital. It outstripped all European countries in textile production, the major industry of the sixteenth and seventeenth centuries. All that the factor endowment theory can tell us is that capital/labor ratios have not evolved in Europe's former colonial regions to anywhere near the extent that has occurred in their mother countries. The political reality is that colonialism imposed quasi-feudal institutions of land tenure that

---

[3]   Karl Marx, "An Address: Free Trade," delivered in Brussels, January 9, 1848 (New York: 1966), p. 42.

impeded their subsequent agricultural and social development, establishing the specialization patterns that have steered world commerce for many centuries, persisting even after Latin America and Africa won their nominal political independence.

The institutional policy dimension is what explains the rise of France, Holland, England and more recently industrialized nations such as the United States, Germany, Japan and the Soviet Union—and why Italy, which had been the major center of industrial and finance capital in the Renaissance, fell behind northern Europe, as did Spain and Portugal. For one thing, the lead nations did not view foreign trade merely as a passive consequence of existing proportions between capital and labor. Historically the first endowment required for industrialization has been a policy of protectionism. England in particular framed its Navigation Acts to nurture the production of commodities which the mother country needed to gain autonomy from continental European sources of supply.

The maldistribution of property had a negative effect on the evolution of labor in countries that did not throw off their colonial yoke early. Their population was employed in occupations that did not require investment in working skills or educational infrastructure. The key factor thus was the political and social context in which capital and population were employed. The system of European land grants in the North and South American (and later African) colonies established local oligarchies that sponsored a centralized economic and political *dirigisme* in the context of latifundia/microfundia systems which still persist today. When the Native Americans refused to submit to the plantations system and its personal servitude, armed appropriation of their land drastically reduced their "factor proportions."

## The strategy of mercantile colonialism

Although natural advantages in raw-materials production were recognized as being intrinsic to certain regions, this did not mean that colonies only produced the staples for which nature had especially endowed them.[4] Colonies were established to supply mother countries with specific raw materials, but were expected to become self-supporting in basic needs, if only so as not to be a

---

[4]  Along these lines Nicholas Barbon (*Discourse on Trade*, pp. 3, 7) was one of many who enunciated what is now called the staples theory of international trade:
   There are Different Climates of the Heavens, some very hot, some very Cold, others Temperate; these Different climates produce Different Animals, Vegetables, & Minerals … The Native Staple of Each Country, is the Foundation of it's Forreign Trade: And no Nation have any Foreign Commodities, but what are first brought in by the Exchange of the Native, for at the first beginning of Forreign *Trade*, a Nation hath nothing else to Exchange.

drain requiring subsidies from the mother country. After all, this was an epoch when European towns and their surrounding countrysides were self-sufficient in most essentials. Given the cost of transporting food and other bulky prod-ucts—and the fact that trade frequently was interrupted by wars—resources allocated to export production could not be at the expense of basic self-sufficiency. Even the poorest colonies such as New England were obliged to produce their own food and basic household essentials, for imperial nations did not welcome the prospect of having to support indigent dependencies. Centuries would elapse before countries specialized in export production at the price of foregoing self-reliance in food and other basic necessities.

But as soon as the colony was established on a self-reliant basis, it was directed to employ its labor and capital (or was supplied with slaves, colonists and guns) to produce sugar, molasses, rare woods and barks, naval stores, tropical products, ores, metals and other commodities desired in Europe. Colonies were to export surpluses of local products such as spices, tin and other raw materials, dyes and textiles, and other manufacturers over and above their own needs. As Schumpeter has summarized:

> Armstrong and Hales in the sixteenth century based international trade on the fact that different nations, living under different conditions, produce different commodities, the superfluous parts of which may be exchanged with advantage to all parties concerned: Even North thought of international trade in quite the same spirit as the "exchange of superfluities," much as had Grotius (1625).[5]

Adam Smith described how trade "carries out that surplus part of the produce of their land and labour for which there is no demand among them [the exporting countries], and brings back in return something else for which there is a demand. It gives a value to their superfluities ..."[6] The richest and most "naturally" endowed colonies became export monocultures, increasingly dependent on their mother countries or fellow colonies for their necessities as well as their superfluities. Anticipating the "curse of oil" in today's world, *the richer the colony, the higher the extreme to which its specialization was pressed, and the greater its domestic income disparities would become over time* as client oligarchies monopolized its natural resources and gained control of its public domain—and its political system as well.

---

[5]   Joseph A. Schumpeter, *History of Economic Analysis* (New York 1954), p. 369.
[6]   Smith, *Wealth of Nations*, Book IV, ch. i, pp. 468–69. John Stuart Mill derided this view as the "surplus produce" theory of trade in his *Principles of Political Economy, with some of their Applications to Social Philosophy* [1848], Wm. Ashley ed. (London: 1909), Book III, ch. xvii, para. 4, p. 579.
    John H. Williams revived this approach as the "vent-for-surplus" explanation in "The Theory of International Trade Reconsidered," [1929, repr. in his *Postwar Monetary Plans and Other Essays*, 3rd ed. (New York: 1947).

Mother countries established colonies in the first instance to displace non-imperial sources of supply, not to serve as markets. In the words of the historian George Louis Beer, "the ideal colony was one which would have freed England from the necessity of importing anything from her competitors,"[7] who would have demanded payment in bullion rather than accepting English manufactures. "If England imported the raw materials from her colonies, she could pay for the same in manufactures, the precious metals would not be drained from England, but might even flow thither from the colonies."[8]

The British Empire established a self-sufficient trade and payments system, running a surplus with regions outside the Empire. Instead of emulating Spain's and Portugal's crude policy of grabbing foreign gold by force, England built up its domestic and colonial production so as to earn the gold and silver of foreign countries. It used this money to finance further growth in domestic credit and investment—and to establish or protect its colonies militarily.

Like the other imperial powers, England directed the economic life of their colonies to dovetail into that of the mother country. "As far as it was possible," writes Beer, "the colony was to differ from England in its economic pursuits, producing nothing that interfered with the fullest development of any English industry or trade. It was to be the economic complement of the mother country, both together constituting a self-sufficient commercial empire."[9]

The time had not yet arrived to view trade in terms of cost savings. National security and monetary considerations came first. Mother countries enacted tariffs and bounties to render desired commodity lines profitable to produce in cases where colonial costs exceeded prices from non-imperial sources. France bought sugar from its West Indian possessions, and Britain bought naval stores from New England, for more than these commodities would have cost from outside their respective empires. Consumers had to pay more, but their payment usually remained within the imperial system, generally in the mother country itself where most colonial merchants kept their savings.

---

[7] George Louis Beer, *The Old Colonial System: 1660-1754* (New York: 1912), Vol. I, pp. 37–38. Historians have understood this process more clearly than economists. Mill (*Principles of Political Economy*, p. 918) was not historically accurate in accusing the mercantile system (in the spirit of Adam Smith's *Wealth of Nations*, IV, i) of holding that "colonies were founded for the supposed advantage of compelling them to buy our commodities, or at all events not to buy those of any foreign country: in return for which restrictions we were generally willing to come under an equivalent obligation with respect to the staple productions of the colonists." Relations actually developed in just the reverse order.

[8] Beer, *The Commercial Policy of England toward the American Colonies* (New York: 1948), p. 43.

[9] Beer, *Old Colonial System,* Vol. I, p. 38. See also p. 340.

The strategy was for the imperial center to exchange manufactures for colonial raw materials. Colonial administrators suppressed production that threatened to displace imports from the mother country. (Not always successfully. In New England especially, smuggling seemed as rife as the erection of illegal iron mills and other manufactories.) Still, the idea was that colonial labor and capital would earn at least as much by producing raw materials as they would have from producing manufactures. After all, most colonies were founded as remunerative projects for investors in the colonizing corporations. The typical sanctimonious mother-country belief held that colonies were not ready for industrial production. Had not God ordained each country to produce what other countries want, so that all could be friends? Was it not natural for colonies to fulfill their natural destiny by producing the raw materials that consumers and producers in the mother country wanted?

The small economic size of many colonies prevented them from diversifying even if they had sought to do so. A one-way dependency developed, reinforced by a political and military infrastructure highlighted by the mother country's protective tariffs and navigation acts. Colonies became reliant on metropolitan sources of supply, beginning with textiles and extending to other industrial products typically associated with technological learning curves and industrial capital accumulation. Little reverse dependency occurred.

## Regional characteristics of imperial trade and payments

England's colonial trade fell into four major categories, each designed to displace a set of supplier nations outside the Empire. In the first place, she sought to become independent of her Baltic trade with Sweden, Russia, Poland and Germany for the naval stores necessary for her shipping and the potash used in woolen manufacturing, the leading industry in the seventeenth and eighteenth centuries. As G. L. Beer explains: "From the standpoint of national security and of economic growth, this trade was all-important. A stoppage of these supplies, either through war or through their control by a rival, would prevent England from putting a fleet to sea, and could also retard the development of her merchant marine."

Queen Christina of Sweden had established a tar and pitch corporation in 1648 that exploited its monopoly position to the utmost. Consequently, "the earliest and most strenuous efforts were devoted toward developing colonies that would be able to compete in these products with northern Europe," especially in the production of masts, pitch, tar, hemp and potash. For these products England looked to its North American colonies. "At the time of the settlement of New England, it was expected that this region would supplant the

Baltic countries as England's source of supply for naval stores and that an extensive fishery would be developed in this region."[10]

A more apt name for these colonies would have been New Baltia or New Scandia, for their function was to duplicate the economies of Northern Europe, not that of England. It was a failure of British colonial policy that they ultimately became a new England.

A second branch of England's trade was with southern Europe in agricultural products and luxuries such as wine, silk, salt, sugar and dried fruits. This trade was to be supplanted by the American colonies south of New England, where the climate was more temperate.

In the third position came more specialized and tropical Oriental products, hitherto "controlled by Portugal, and subsequently by the Dutch, who sold them to England at enhanced prices."[11] These products included "dyes, saltpetre, and ... the spices that alone rendered the winter's stock of food palatable." India, the West Indies and England's southern American colonies—Virginia, the Carolinas, Maryland and Georgia—were to provide such commodities. "Their climate to a varying extent differed from that of the mother country, and consequently their products did not compete with those of England." The latter attempted to foster the production of tropical goods in Carolina by exempting from English customs duties "all silks, wines, currants, raisins, capers, wax, almonds, oils, and olives" imported from that colony, so as to make it virtually a New Mediterranea. The list of exports exempted from British duties "contained no one of the commodities already afforded by the existing English colonies. The new settlements were expected to avoid such

[10]  Beer, *The Origins of the British Colonial System: 1578–1660* (New York: 1922), pp. 56. 76, and *Old Colonial System*, Vol. II, p. 231. Klaus Knorr points out (*British Colonial Theories: 1570–1850* [Toronto: 1944], p. 91) that

This clear-cut division of economic functions between colonies and parent state was not merely regarded as an automatic outcome of natural conditions. Its strict and rigid maintenance, enforced with the help of legal regulations, was deemed imperative because—according to the prevalent doctrine of the value of the plantations—the profits of Empire depended exactly on the perpetuation of this division of labor.

Knorr adds (pp. 50ff.) that

at the time in question, the problem of important raw materials frequently carried great political significance. Countries which possessed a quasi-monopoly of a particular produce or controlled the bulk of the world supply available to European nations, were often disposed to exploit that opportunity by boosting its price to foreign customers. Portugal, for example, after she acquired Brazil, controlled more than half of the world production of sugar and thus was in a position to manipulate its price.

On the kindred political aspects of Europe's salt trade see Henry Hauser, *Les Origins historiques des problems economiques actuels* (Paris: 1930), pp. 17ff., 53–69.

[11]  Beer, *Origins*, p. 56.

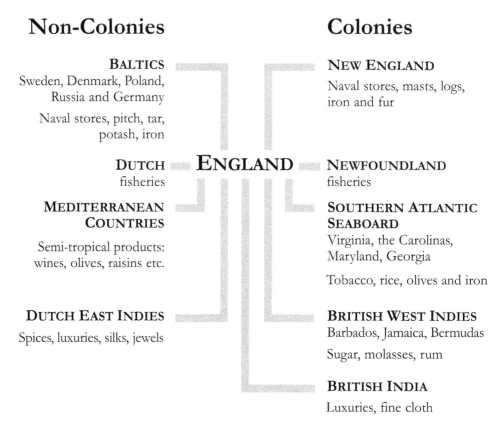

# Non-Colonies

**BALTICS**
Sweden, Denmark, Poland,
Russia and Germany

Naval stores, pitch, tar,
potash, iron

**DUTCH**
fisheries

**MEDITERRANEAN
COUNTRIES**

Semi-tropical products:
wines, olives, raisins etc.

**DUTCH EAST INDIES**
Spices, luxuries, silks, jewels

# ENGLAND

# Colonies

**NEW ENGLAND**
Naval stores, masts, logs,
iron and fur

**NEWFOUNDLAND**
fisheries

**SOUTHERN ATLANTIC
SEABOARD**
Virginia, the Carolinas,
Maryland, Georgia

Tobacco, rice, olives and iron

**BRITISH WEST INDIES**
Barbados, Jamaica, Bermudas

Sugar, molasses, rum

**BRITISH INDIA**
Luxuries, fine cloth

Figure 2.1 Britain's Imperial and Foreign-trade System

products as sugar and tobacco, in order not to further depress their price. This point was significantly emphasized in the statements of the proprietors."[12] In a similar vein William Penn attempted to introduce the cultivation of vineyards to Pennsylvania.

Newfoundland, the oldest colony in the Empire, represented a fourth element in England's colonial trade strategy. Its herring fisheries were established with the intention of making England and its colonies independent of the Dutch fisheries off the British isles. "Just as it had been recognized in the Elizabethan age that the mines of America constituted Spain's chief source of strength, so statesmen of the following era perceived that Dutch prosperity was founded on the herring fisheries." The Newfoundland fishing trade also served

---

[12]  Beer, *Origins*, pp. 265, 86 and *Old Colonial System*, Vol. II, pp. 178–79.

as a nursery to train English seamen, "and hence the crew of every English fishing vessel had to be composed in part of inexperienced and untrained men."

This latter consideration highlights the colonial system's military dimension. After 1605 "the men of the day argued in a circle of sea power, commerce, and colonies. Sea power enabled England to expand and to protect her foreign trade, while this increased commerce, in turn, augmented her naval strength."[13] Supporters of the East India Company argued that "The company's marine constitutes a sort of middle link between the Royal Navy and the Merchant service. Its officers joined the Company upon leaving the navy instead of entering the service of foreign countries. ... At the breaking out of war, the ten thousand seamen, composing the crews of the Company's ships, facilitate the manning of the Navy."[14]

A leading aim of England's gold accumulation was to sustain troop support payments in the event of war. Gunboats in turn reinforced political domination to ensure colonial subservience to the desired trade and development patterns throughout Europe's imperial systems. This system was idealized under the concept of reciprocity—or what today is called, with no less hypocrisy, interdependency.

Both the British and French empires established triangular trade patterns which C. R. Fay describes in his *Imperial Economy and its Place in the Formation of European Doctrine*:

> The seventeenth and eighteenth centuries exhibit the economics of the trade triangle, which in its simplest form was: fishing fleet from England to Newfoundland; fish to the Spanish Peninsula or the islands off Africa (Azores, Madeira, Canaries); wines and fruits to England. The emergence of the West Indies strengthened and complicated the triangle; fish to the West Indies, sugar to Europe, supplies to the fishery. And the triangle originating from England with the fishing fleet was met by a triangle in the reverse direction: Manchester cottons and Birmingham toys to the west coast of Africa; slaves to Barbados; sugar and cotton to England. ... Moreover the French had their own triangle, grounded on their own West Indies; and they sometimes enlarged the triangle by going out via Ireland, where they took on provisions. In this way Ireland escaped the worst consequences of exclusion from England's navigation code. Holland had no base for such triangular traffic, and she fell back into her original coastal role. Amsterdam was the emporium of the Baltic North and the Iberian South: here were granaries. Through Amsterdam timber and food (grain and fish) moved south; while salt and wines and fruits moved north. Into this coastal hegemony she injected the

---

[13] Beer, *Origins*, p. 62, and *Old Colonial System*, Vol. I, pp. 32, 16.
[14] "Cossim," *Considerations on the Danger and Impolicy of Laying Open the Trade with India and China* ... (2nd ed., London: 1813), pp. 124ff.

proceeds of her eastern preserves, spices, sugar, and the like. Right to the middle of the eighteenth century her mercantile marine was growing, but on the West Atlantic she hardly counted![15]

France's colonial system lacked the British Empire's self-sufficiency. Neither metropolitan France nor Canada could supply the food, lumber, livestock and other staples needed by the French West Indies. These goods therefore had to be obtained from England's North American colonies. France furthermore lacked the temperate-zone colonies possessed by England, and had little significant presence in Africa to take advantage of the profitable slave trade. Despite Colbert's best efforts in the eighteenth century, France was unable to spur trade between Canada and its West Indian colonies to anywhere near the extent that England's North American colonies traded with both the British and French West Indies.

Indeed, France's payments to its colonies for sugar, rum and molasses passed out of its empire as the West Indies spent them on the products of England's temperate-zone colonies in North America, which in turn spent these payments on British manufactures. Economically, the French West Indies became satellites of New England. While French consumers were taxed by the relatively high prices they had to pay for West Indian sugar, New England became a siphon by which England obtained the benefits and wealth of France's empire, an illegal trade that France was unable to prevent.[16]

The Spanish, Portuguese and Dutch empires were even less varied than that of France. Spain's looting of the New World thus was not an imperial exercise in the sophisticated mercantile sense, because it never created a self-sufficient and interdependent trading system. Its seizure of Incan and Aztec gold was not a mutual interchange of commodities but merely a reduction of local populations to servitude. This brutal tributary system only could run down once it had stripped away the native treasure. Spain paid the price for this economic barbarism by suffering the flow of bullion through its hands to other European countries. Early recipients of Spanish gold included the Netherlands, which had thrown off the Spanish yoke and were establishing colonies of their own in the East and West Indies and New Amsterdam (New York) during the early seventeenth century.

---

[15]  C. R. Fay, *Imperial Economy and its Place in the Formation of Economic Doctrine: 1600–1932* (Oxford: 1934), pp. 57–58.

[16]  Stewart L. Mims, *Colbert's West India Policy* (New Haven: 1912), pp. 334, 336. On this point see Beer, *British Colonial Policy: 1754–1765*, p. 292, and *The Commercial Policy of England Toward the American Colonies*, pp. 116ff. A similar development occurred in the twentieth century when the United States reaped the benefits of the British Empire's trade preference system. See Terence McCarthy, "British Empire Preference Aids U.S. Exports," *Barron's*, December 3, 1945.

However, the Dutch trading entrepots and plantations never formed a coordinated administrative system of the degree achieved by England.

To be sure, problems loomed on the horizon. England's landlords sought to produce the same goods in which the colonies were supposed to specialize. After the Restoration of Charles II in 1660 they won government protection for their relatively high-cost foodstuffs. The Corn Laws, established to block the importation of rye, barley, peas, beans, oats and wheat, and later of beef, pork, bacon, butter and other farm products, thwarted any hope for payments equilibrium within England's colonial system. Depriving New England of its markets in metropolitan England deprived the colonies of their means to purchase English manufactures, unless they could earn funds by exporting their produce to third countries. "Thus New England and later the Middle colonies, not being allowed to exchange their normal products for England's manufactures, were forced to begin manufacturing for themselves."[17]

Inward-looking English policy thus brought about the very thing it had been designed to prevent: the drive for commercial independence by its satellites. "In the beginning," observes Beer, "serious attempts were made to produce commodities desired in England, because those promised the greatest profits," thanks in part to England's bounty system. "Potent economic forces were, however, arrayed against this development. New England did not belie its name, and in resources was largely a counterpart of the mother country." It produced grain in competition with English farmers, exported fish in competition with English fishermen, shipped timber in competition with British importers of Scandinavian forest products, and sold food to the West Indies in competition with British producers and merchants. "Despite persistent efforts, it could not be moulded into the proper economic shape. It remained always a center of disharmony, out of accord with the spirit of British imperialism until ultimately,

---

[17] Beer, *The Commercial Policy of England Toward the American Colonies*, p. 75.
[18] Beer, *Origins*, p. 268, and *Old Colonial System*, Vol. II, p. 234. See also Vol. I, pp. 52–53, and Vol. II, p. 306: New England's "entire elimination from the globe would probably have been welcomed," Beer concludes. (How modern all this sounds even today.)
Yet, for many reasons, England could not afford to let the northern continental colonies renounce their allegiance. Under the prevailing conditions, political independence was for these colonies an impossibility; freedom from England inevitably implied subjection to some other European power, in this instance France. To England this would have meant an incalculable loss of prestige, and moreover, as a French colony, New England would have been an even more vexatious thorn in the side of the Empire, rendering insecure the invaluable possessions to the north and south—Newfoundland, the nursery of seamen, and the tobacco colonies, Maryland and Virginia. Thus England clung to this region, and even sanctioned its further settlement, not for any clearly defined economic advantages, but in order to obviate the greater negative political and military losses resulting from its domination by others.

when events were favorable, its secession and that of the other continental colonies disrupted the old commercial Empire."[18]

The Earl of Sandwich was quick to perceive New England's potential to rival the mother country, particularly in exporting manufactures to the British West Indies. He

> concluded that it was impossible "to prevent wholly their encrease and arrival at this power," and deemed it "advisable to hinder their growth as much as can be." He suggested that further emigration to the colonies be restricted, and that the northern colonies be removed to the southern plantations "where the produce of theire labours will not be commodities of the same nature with old England to out-trade us withall."[19]

This may help explain why it was New England that took the lead in breaking away from the mother country.

New England's ultimate economic advantage—which, from the standpoint of imperial Britain, turned out to be a distinct *dis*advantage—was precisely that it was *not* a producer of exotic products and raw materials. Indeed, from a "natural" standpoint it was poor rather than rich. Its inability to produce the tropical commodities needed by England left it with little option but to parallel the industrial economy of the mother country. This laid the foundation of its future economic as well as political independence.

England's objection to this independence stemmed from the fact that if its American colonies produced their own manufactures, they would have little need to recycle their export earnings (from their sales to Canada and the French West Indies) to Britain in payment for the latter's industrial products. Britain would earn less bullion. It therefore forbade its colonies to establish factories of their own, that is, to achieve industrial "factor endowments."

> The intention of Parliament was expressed in an Act passed in 1719 declaring it unlawful to set up in any colony furnaces for the production of cast-iron or for the manufacture of iron because "the establishment of manufactories in the colonies tends to make them more independent of Great Britain." ... [A]s new occasions arose, or as the enterprise of the colonists manifested itself in new directions, the laws became more strict, the limitations upon colonial activities

19   Quoted by Beer, *Old Colonial System*, Vol. II, p. 234.
20   Edward Stanwood, *American Tariff Controversies in the Nineteenth Century* (Boston: 1903), Vol. I, p. 13. "No idea of the economic conditions of former days could be more erroneous," warns Eli Heckscher, "than that which is conveyed by the content of such prohibitions and retractions. The regulations, as a matter of fact, constitute merely an expression of what the holders of power wished to see realized, and accordingly may be said to illustrate, primarily, nothing more than the economic views of the time." (*The Continental System: An Economic Interpretation* [Oxford: 1922], p. 15.)

became more numerous, and the execution of all restrictive regulations increased in severity.[20]

This increasing strictness actually was an indication of England's inability to enforce its restrictions. Its regulations may be interpreted more as statements of intent than reflections of actual behavior. Still, the protection of domestic English industry laid the groundwork for its future supremacy. "Parliamentary action against manufacturing [in the colonies] first found expression in the textile industries," writes Witt Bowden. This was particularly the case with woolens, which were

> carefully shielded from every adverse wind. As early as 1699 a law was therefore passed forbidding the making for the market of any articles whatsoever consisting in whole or in part of wool. Any ship or vessel, horse, cart, or other carriage laden with such goods for transportation to market was subject to confiscation, together with the manufactures; and in addition there was a fine of £500. The law was renewed in 1732. It was obviously impossible to prevent household spinning and weaving, and concerning homespun the law was discreetly silent. In 1732 a similar enactment forbade the making of hats for the market. ... An incidental method of discouraging manufacturing in the colonies was by passing laws to keep industrial skill at home. The exportation of specified kinds of tools and machines to the colonies or elsewhere was prohibited, and skilled artisans were forbidden to leave the country.[21]

These restrictions applied only to market output. Household manufactures of clothing and other essentials were not banned, could not be banned, and would not have been banned if they could have been. Only the sale of marketable production was regulated, for it was axiomatic that each region must produce its own common household necessities. The virtues of such self-sufficiency were demonstrated during the Napoleonic Wars when England withstood the French blockade.

The essence of this trade pattern was that exports represented truly surplus output. In keeping with the prevailing vent-for-surplus view of foreign trade, when Adam Smith and his mercantilist predecessors spoke of the international division of labor, they referred to surplus production. The American colonies exported surplus tobacco and cotton, Portugal its surplus wine, Sweden its surplus iron and naval stores, France its surplus silks and wines, and England its surplus manufactures. All these economies remained self-sufficient in basic essentials, so that their exchange of mutually surplus products remained a more or less voluntary exchange rather than a life-or-death necessity.

---

[21] Witt Bowden, *The Industrial History of the United States* (New York 1930), pp. 99ff. See also James E. Thorold Rogers, *The Industrial and Commercial History of England* (London: 1892), esp. Part II, ch. x ("Home trade and international competition").

The specialization of production was far from reaching the extreme degree found in the late twentieth century.

Taken as a unit, Europe's colonial systems favored England and its satellites more than any other empire. And yet as the costs of defending and/or subduing its colonies came to exceed their net economic value, the administrative and military support costs of England's Old Colonial System rendered it less efficient than its sequel, the free trade policy toward which England moved following the American Revolution. Many English people viewed the loss of their North American colonies as a blessing. In Josiah Tucker's famous phrase, they had become an albatross around England's neck.

The fear was that letting them go might leave them to branch into industries competing with those of England. But on closer examination it seemed that colonial ventures were not all that likely to pose a serious threat. Colonial "endowments" had been put in place and their raw-materials export patterns were well established. Even more important, by 1776 industrial England had gained nearly a two-century head start over its colonies, and indeed over the rest of the world as well.

England gave its colonies their independence without more of a fight for two reasons: the heavy cost to English taxpayers of defraying the expense of defending and subsidizing these colonies, and the fact that overt restrictions no longer seemed necessary to maintain the nation's economic supremacy. Mercantilist statecraft had accomplished its objectives. All that England needed to do was to keep its domestic taxes and other costs low, by avoiding colonialism and other costly projects of empire. Recognition of this fact, and of the political character of England's carefully acquired competitive advantages, become the foundation for the transition to free-trade imperialism.

Before turning to that strategy, however, it is necessary to review the often overlooked domestic economic effects of international trade and payments. The most important question concerned what would happen domestically to nations running trade surpluses. Would they gain permanently, or merely see their prices inflated? Chapter 3 reviews the domestic monetary, employment and investment effects of Britain's foreign trade in the eighteenth century, on the eve of its transition to laissez faire.

# 3

## The Monetary Impact

### *The subordinate but critical role of money*

The pejorative catch-all label "mercantilism" derives from Adam Smith. In his chapter entitled "Of the Principles of the Commercial of Mercantile System" (Book IV, ch. i of *The Wealth of Nations*) he accused its advocates of confusing the substance of wealth with its monetary counters and regulating foreign trade simply to accumulate silver and gold. His label stuck. The *Oxford Dictionary* (to choose just one example) defines mercantilism as "a term used by Adam Smith and later political economists for the system of economic doctrine and legislative policy based on the principle that money alone constituted wealth."[1] Most of Smith's predecessors except for the Physiocrats (who like Smith advocated laissez faire) are widely believed to have held this superficial view, seeming to justify their subsequent neglect.

The political problem, according to Smith, was the role played by vested interests. Their trade monopolies and restrictions, colonialism and the wars it brought about, turned the system into a burden maintained at the expense of the economy at large. Like his liberal successors, Smith held out the ideal of a well-run economy not warped by trade restrictions, special-interest favoritism and other state intervention. Such an economy would be free of the high taxes and hence high prices needed to support the policies that economic liberals opposed. The result promised to be lower costs of production, and hence fuller and more profitable employment.

Smith claimed that the mercantilist aim was to establish colonies merely to serve as markets. If the goal was to accumulate bullion, he argued, foreign markets could best be conquered through peaceful competition, not by an expensive military system. He granted that national security was an overriding concern, but asserted that "accumulation of gold and silver is not necessary for carrying on distant wars." What was needed was current output, and this was most efficiently produced by economies enjoying low taxes and freedom from government interference. Low taxes would result from avoiding foreign wars and the colonial rivalries that bred them.

---

[1]   Quoted in R. L. Schuyler, *The Fall of the Old Colonial System: A Study in British Free Trade, 1770-1870* (London: 1945), p. 4.

"The discovery of America has benefited Europe not by the cheapening of gold and silver," wrote Smith, "but by opening up of a market which improved the productive powers of labor," by offering greater economies of scale for the division of labor (as opposed to the economic autonomy at which protectionist policies aimed). Silver and gold were sterile in themselves. To the new economic liberals, the money supply really did not seem to matter. Once production achieved its maximum potential, however, Smith warned that the effect of running trade surpluses for fully employed economies would be to inflate their prices.

Smith's accusations were a caricature of the sophisticated doctrines of statecraft developed by the third quarter of the eighteenth century. The mercantilists understood clearly that money was productive only when transformed into tangible capital. It was precisely for this reason that they excluded hoarded funds from their definition of the money supply, on the ground that such savings were unavailable for spending or investing. The purpose of acquiring bullion was not to hoard it but to use it as the basis for expanding paper credit and tangible investment. This anti-hoarding ethic is what endeared the mercantilists to Keynes. It was not gold and silver that they sought to accumulate, but productive capital to employ the nation's labor and land. A trade surplus simply was a precondition for obtaining the money need to finance investment and employment, and to hold down interest rates.

Mercantilism thus was ultimately a doctrine of productive powers. Smith acknowledged this in his accusation that "The mercantile system absurdly considers production and not consumption to be the end of industry and commerce."[2] With the exception of the word "absurdly," many of his predecessors would have agreed. When they endorsed higher consumption standards, as in providing luxuries to the labor force, it was not because they sought to raise consumption as such, but because they thought the availability of such goods would spur people to work harder to earn the money to buy them. The guiding idea was for output to grow by more than consumption, increasing the economy's net surplus.

William Petty, John Law, George Berkeley, Jacob Vanderlint, Charles Davenant, Richard Cantillon, James Steuart, Josiah Tucker and their contemporaries cannot be accused of being preoccupied with the balance of trade in itself. Their trade and monetary theories formed only a part of their broad analysis of England's national economy. Their objective in obtaining an adequate supply of money, whether gold or paper, was to finance domestic

---

[2]   Adam Smith, *Wealth of Nations*, Book IV, ch. viii, marginal gloss.

investment and full employment, and to bring down interest rates so as to lower national debt-servicing charges. Typical of the view that money was a means to achieve higher production and employment was the admonishment of Governor Keith of Massachusetts in 1738:

> As the Value of every Thing we desire to possess must he compared from the Use and Conveniency of it, in comfortably preserving and prolonging human Life, there is no intrinsic Worth or Estimation can be put on Gold and Silver, further than that, by universal Consent, those solid and permanent Metals, are become the Medium of all Kinds of Exchange, and the only unalterable Measure, whereby we rate the present Value of any other Thing: They are not therefore to be considered in themselves as a Merchandise, but only as the Means of procuring in Trade whatsoever the Variety of our Wants and Inclinations may require. For although *Spain*, by possessing the Mines of *Mexico* and *Peru*, may be said to be richer in that respect than any other Nation; yet as those Riches consist only in holding a greater Share of that necessary medium for carrying on a profitable Exchange in Trade, it loses considerably of its Value for want of being employed in that way; and tho' it may furnish the *Spaniards* with all the Product of other Mens Labor, which the most exquisite Luxury can desire, in the main it destroys Industry, by encouraging Sloth and Indolence, which inevitably must introduce both a Neglect and Contempt of the Arts and Sciences; whereas an industrious Commonwealth, who keeps her subjects employed in Manufacturers, and Foreign Trade, by continually furnishing *Spain* with such Things as there is a constant Demand for, to supply that People's Conveniency, and feed their Pleasures, must needs in Return command as great a share of *Spanish* Bullion as they want; so that in fact the *Spanish* Riches consist in digging up Gold and Silver out of the Earth for other People, whose superior Skill and Industry, in applying it to its proper Use, absolutely determines the Value of that Kind of Wealth; which, if it be not kept in continual Motion and employed in Trade, never fails to enervate the Owners, and render them unfit for relishing the superior and most national Enjoyments of human Society.[3]

Berkeley, Cantillon and Steuart emphasized the mere nominalism of money. An "inflationist" school of writers led by John Law argued that if England would supplant gold with paper currency at home, it could insulate its economy from the vicissitudes of foreign trade. thereby reducing the need to run a positive balance of trade and payments.[4]

Schumpeter called the doctrine of the trade balance "the first step towards an analysis of the economic system." Haberler acknowledged that "It was on the initiative of the mercantilists, and particularly of [Thomas] Mun himself, that the most burdensome of the restrictions on foreign trade were removed. ... Many of the mercantilist writers referred explicitly to items in the balance of payments other than the trade balance."[5] However, a full re-examination of the extent to which the pre-1776 literature contained the seeds of

---

[3]  William Keith, *History of the British Plantations in America* (London: 1738), pp. 34–35.
[4]  This was acknowledged even by Jacob Viner, *Studies in the Theory of International Trade*, p. 4.

classical and modern economic thought occurred only after World War II, headed by the studies of R. L. Schuyler, William Grampp and Douglas Vickers.

In 1945, Schuyler elaborated how the caricature of mercantilism as being narrow rather than broad, particularly with regard to its alleged view of money as an end in itself, did not well describe the economic literature published between 1500 and 1750. In 1952, Grampp complained that although Viner (who had acknowledged that Smith had been harsh on the mercantilists but nonetheless endorsed his evaluation of them) "is charitable to the later writings for their traces of free trade theory," he selected from mercantilist literature only what he wanted to find: either its most childish errors such as bullionism and beggar-my-neighbor tariff restrictions, or its anticipations of modern orthodoxy such as the quantity theory of money and the price-specie flow adjustment mechanism. In 1959, Vickers defended E. A. J. Johnson's estimate that "not ten percent of English mercantilist literature is devoted to the ill-fated doctrine of the balance of trade."[6] Subsequent scholarship has demonstrated that nearly all the later "mercantilists" (or political arithmeticians as many called themselves) viewed the accumulation of bullion not as an end in itself but as a means to achieve national power via prosperity, investment and full employment.

---

[5]   Joseph Schumpeter, *Epochen der Dogmen- und Methodengeschichte* (2nd ed.: 1924), p. 38, quoted in Gottfried Haberler, *The Theory of International Trade*, p. 25. Schumpeter later expressed this view in his *History of Economic Analysis* (New York: 1954), pp. 352–53.

Mercantilist writers understood the international transactions that must be debited or credited to trade accounts as being functionally related to them. Cantillon recognized such non-trade items in the balance of payments as

> the sum of money which one State sends into another for its secret services and political aims, for subsidies to allies, for the upkeep of troops, Ambassadors, noblemen who travel, etc., Capital which the inhabitants of One State send to another to invest in public or private funds, the interest which these inhabitants receive annually from such investments, etc. The exchanges vary with all these accidental causes and follow the rule of the transport of silver required … They have very certainly an influence on the increase and decrease of circulating money in a State and on its comparative strength and power.

Because these were essentially "accidental causes," however, Cantillon confined his analysis "always to the simple views of commerce lest I should complicate my subject, which is too much encumbered by the multiplicity of the facts which relate to it." (*Essay on the Nature of Trade in General* [1755], ed. Henry Higgs [London: 1931], pp. 263ff.) For the broad mercantilist recognition of non-trade items in the balance of payments see Viner, *Studies in the Theory of International Trade*, pp. 13ff.

[6]   William D. Grampp, "The Liberal Elements in English Mercantilism," *Quarterly Journal of Economics*, LXVI (1952), p. 466, and Douglas Vickers, *Studies in the Theory Money. 1690-1776* (Philadelphia: 1959), pp. 33-34, 16, defending E. A. J. Johnson, *Predecessors of Adam Smith* (New York: 1937) pp. 251-52. against Viner, *Studies*, p. 56 and *passim*. Johnson was one of the first in modern times to decry "the unhappy word 'mercantilism'" and the difficulties of defining it meaningfully.

These aims did not differ from those of subsequent British liberalism. Even the means were becoming similar. By the late eighteenth century most "mercantilists" had come to oppose England's overseas ventures and associated projects of state as being drains on the nation's gold. They increasingly believed that trade policy should favor small-scale merchants rather than the large Crown corporations founded as trading monopolies. As Schumpeter recognized, "free-trade forces did not simply assemble outside the mercantilist citadel and storm it … but to a much greater extent formed up inside it."[7]

Much of the interpretive problem was caused by arbitrarily describing the mercantilist "school" as having ended around 1750. This is the closest round date to avoid Hume's *Political Discourses* (1752), which led to a lively debate as to the nature of adjustment mechanisms in foreign trade. To laissez faire eyes the battle is settled by selecting some of Hume's statements out of context. But the fact is that his essays only fanned the flames of debate. During the quarter century that remained before Adam Smith published his *Wealth of Nations*, mercantilist political arithmetic achieved its great syntheses in Richard Cantillon's *Essay on the Nature of Commerce* (1775), Tucker's *Elements of Commerce* (1775) and his *Four Tracts Together with Two Sermons* (1774), and James Steuart's *Principles of Political Oeconomy: Being an Essay on the Science of Domestic Policy in Free Nations* (1767). Yet free traders left their works in limbo, preferring to knock over straw men.

In view of the fact that money did not play much of a role in the new liberal models, the balance of this chapter will discuss the pre-1776 theories that relate the balance of trade and payments to domestic monetary development, investment and output. Chapter 4 will relate these domestic developments to the underlying evolution of international productive powers. (Physiocracy, the French counterpart to this late mercantilist literature, had only a glancing concern with foreign trade.)

### *The monetary dimension of foreign trade and payments*

Unlike their free-trade successors, mercantilist writers did not treat money as a mere veil, a *numeraire* devoid of impact on the course of economic development. As Chapter 1 emphasized, foreign trade represented the way for nations without mines of their own to increase their monetary base of gold and silver coinage. It was a precondition for credit expansion, which in turn was a precondition for setting in motion the wheels of employment and investment.

---

[7]  Schumpeter, *History of Economic Analysis*, pp. 369–70. He adds that "the advance of analysis … was not a matter of free trade and nascent liberalism at all."

Because they did not assume a fully employed economy as their starting point, early writers recognized leeway for monetary flows to operate in ways other than simply to push up prices. As for their alleged obsession with running a trade surplus, they refrained from making a blanket generalization about the impact of international payments and consequent growth in the money supply and prices. The result of a monetary inflow depended on the extent to which it was used to employ labor. There was general recognition (to quote Schumpeter again) that "any satisfactory theory of the money supply implies a theory of the economic process in its entirety."[8]

The result was a mid-eighteenth-century synthesis integrating the monetary and goods-producing sectors which, apart from that subsequently achieved by Marx's *Capital*, went unrivalled until Keynes reintegrated the theory of money and general economic activity in the 1930s. Indeed, the mercantilists laid the basis for the two-sector model distinguishing what Adam Smith called circulating capital—later called the wages fund—from fixed capital invested directly in plant and equipment. It is an approach that has all but disappeared since Marx, having been revived only briefly by Keynes in his 1930 *Treatise on Money* to distinguish between a profit inflation and wage inflation.

Mercantilists viewed money primarily as a constraint, a "scarce factor" in production. New investment and employment required financing, but the world's supply of silver and gold was limited. As long as paper money was convertible into these monetary metals on demand, its domestic issue would remain a function of the "money of the world" as Steuart called it. The use of paper money might increase relative to the bullion base as people became more accustomed to it, but the expansion of paper would have to retain some relationship to gold. "Credit that promises a Payment of Money," observed John Law in 1705, "cannot well be extended beyond a certain proportion it ought to have with the Money."[9] A drop in the ratio of silver or gold backing for bank credit would tend to inspire a run on the banks, leading to financial crises and consequent interruption of economic activity. This "internal drain" characterized the monetary systems of all countries prior to World War I, and was as important as the external drain to settle balance-of-payments deficits. These two types of monetary drain explain why foreign trade and its associated flow of bullion were vital factors in domestic economic development.

---

[8]   Schumpeter, *ibid.*, p. 286.
[9]   John Law, *Money and Trade Considered, with a Proposal for Supplying the Nation with Money* (Edinburgh: 1705), p. 60.

## Monetary expansion increases employment before prices

Numerous writers prior to Hume enunciated what Frank Fetter termed the "price-specie flow" mechanism relating the trade balance directly to changes in the money supply and prices.[10] This in turn rested on the quantity theory of money, which holds that changes in the money supply (either upward or downward) are directly and symmetrically reflected in price changes. What is not generally recognized today, after a half-century of modern monetarism, is that only a minority of free traders such as John Locke and Isaac Gervaise accepted this as a *general* theory. Most writers acknowledged that under normal eighteenth-century conditions of substantial unemployment, the first effect of more money was to enable more labor to be employed. Only under full employment would monetary inflows tend to increase prices. This "two-phase" view thus represented as a special case today's view of money as affecting prices but not output.

Many writers went so far as to deny outright that more money would raise prices. In 1650, William Potter asserted in *The Key of Wealth* that output was elastic, needing only money to put labor and capital in motion: "An encrease of money cannot possibly occasion an encrease in the price of commodities," because it would increase output proportionally.[11] Law and his fellow inflationists agreed. Their analysis often did tend to be too facile in assuming that more money would increase output *ad infinitum*, irrespective of any full-employment limit or other constraint. But by and large the mercantilists were responding to the circumstances of their day. The mainstream of writers, including Hume as well as Vanderlint and Law, recognized the price-specie flow mechanism as a special case, toward which the economy tended only under full employment— which was the exception, not the rule. As Law put matters, "the many Poor we have always had, [but ... ] we have never had Money enough."[12]

In 1734, Jacob Vanderlint emphasized money's role in increasing employment and output, but acknowledged the impact of money on prices in one major passage:

> no Inconvenience can arise by an unrestrained Trade, but very great Advantage;
> since if the Cash of the Nation be decreased by it, which Prohibitions are

[10]  Viner, *Studies in the Theory of International Trade*, pp. 74ff.
[11]  William Potter, *The Key to Wealth* (1650), p. 10, quoted in Vickers, *Studies in the Theory of Money*, p. 21.
[12]  Law, *Money and Trade Considered*, p. 117. See also pp. 13–14, 105–06, 59–60. Law observed (p. 13) that "Domestic Trade depends on the Money. A greater Quantity employes more people than a lesser Quantity. A limited Sum can only act a number of people so Work proportion'd to it, and 'tis with little success Laws are made, for Employing the Poor or Idle in Countries where Money is scarce." This certainly seemed to be the case in France, and indeed throughout most of Europe in the early 1700s.

designed to prevent, those Nations that get the Cash will certainly find every thing advance in Price, as the Cash increases amongst them.

This was essentially the price-specie flow mechanism. Nonetheless, Vanderlint went on to say:

> if we, who part with the Money, make our Plenty great enough to make Labour sufficiently cheap, which is always constituted of the Price of Victuals and Drink, our Manufactures, and every thing else, will soon become so moderate as to turn the balance of Trade in our Favour, and thereby fetch the Money back again. Thus Money, on which Trade floats, like a Tide, by ebbing and flowing, will bring vast Business to our People, and furnish them with Employment and Happiness.[13]

Vanderlint recognized (as would Hume) that a growing supply of bullion—and hence money and credit—could increase production as well as prices, while monetary outflows and consequent deflation tended to have adverse productivity effects. Without money to finance new investment, how could production costs be lowered? If England suffered a trade and payments deficit, "though this may be some small Encouragement to the Exportation of our Commodities, because they come so much cheaper to the markets abroad, yet if our Trade goes on so, we shall certainly have very little Cash left." The trade balance would not automatically stabilize if the monetary drain resulting from a trade and payments deficit impaired industry and employment, creating a financial crisis and increasing interest rates. Even

> those Nations that can work cheapest, must have the Money, as sure as they will have the Trade; to which, I will add, that the People will always flow into those Nations that get the Money (i.e. have the Ballance of Trade in their Favour) because Trade, which is the Means of getting the Money, is that which employs and subsists them.[14]

An inflow of bullion would lead to increased investment and employment, more exportable output, an influx of immigrants, and generally higher employment and living standards. The greater employment and productiveness of the country's labor and land resources would lead to lower rather than higher production costs under properly managed conditions. And there would be more output to absorb the increase in money and purchasing power. Conversely, explained Law, "Most People think scarcity of Money is only the Consequence of a Ballance due [that is, of running a trade deficit]; but 'tis the Cause as well as the Consequence, and the effectual way to bring the Ballance to our side, is to add to the Money."[15]

---

[13] Jacob Vanderlint, *Money Answers All Things* (London: 1734), pp. 43–44.

[14] Vanderlint, *ibid.*, pp. 29–30. Viner quotes Vanderlint's earlier statement to assert his acceptance of the price-specie flow mechanism, but ignores its later qualifications.

[15] Law, *Money and Trade Considered*, pp. 115–16.

## Monetary theory and moral philosophy

Such views concerning the positive effect of bullion inflows on employment and output set the stage for Hume's famous but extreme retort in his 1752 essay "Of the Balance of Trade":

> Suppose four-fifths of all the money in GREAT BRITAIN is to be annihilated in one night. ... Must not the price of all labour and commodities sink in proportion, and everything be sold as cheap as they were in those ages? What nation could then dispute with us in any foreign market, or pretend to navigate or sell manufactures at the same price, which to us would afford sufficient profit? In how little time, therefore, must this bring back the money which we had lost, and raise us to the level of all the neighboring nations? Where, after we have arrived, we immediately lose the advantage of the cheapness of labor and commodities; and the farther flowing in of money is stopped by our fullness and repletion.
>
> Again, suppose, that all the money of GREAT BRITAIN were multiplied fivefold in a night, must not the contrary effect follow? Must not all labour and commodities rise to such an exorbitant height, that no neighbouring nations could afford to buy from us: while their commodities, on the other hand, become comparatively so cheap, that, in spite of all the laws which could be formed, they would be run in upon us, and our money flow out; till we fall to a level with foreigners, and lose that great superiority of riches, which had laid us under such disadvantages?[16]

Hume's essay "Of Money" illustrated the range of implications following from this fact, elevated to a central philosophical principle:

> There seems to be a happy concurrence of causes in human affairs, which checks the growth of trade and riches, and hinders them from being confined entirely to one people; as might naturally at first be dreaded from the advantages of an established commerce. Where one nation has gotten the start of another in trade, it is very difficult for the latter to regain the ground it has lost; because of the superior industry and skill of the former, and the greater stocks, of which its merchants are possessed, and which enable them to trade on so much smaller profits. But these advantages are compensated, in some measure, by the low price of labour in every nation which has not an extensive commerce, and does not much abound in gold and silver. Manufacturers, therefore gradually shift their places, leaving those countries and provinces which they have already enriched, and flying to others, whither they are allured by the cheapness of provisions and labour; till they have enriched these also, and are again banished by the same causes. And, in general, we may observe, that the dearness of everything, from plenty of money, is a disadvantage, which attends an established commerce, and sets bounds to it in every country, by enabling the poorer states to undersell the richer in all foreign markets.[17]

---

[16] David Hume, "Of the Balance of Trade," *Political Discourses* (1752), reprinted in *David Hume: Writings on Economics*, ed. E. Rotwein (Madison, Wis.: 1970), p. 63. See also "Of Money," p. 33.

[17] Hume, "Of Money', in Rotwein, *David Hume: Writings on Economics*, pp. 34–35.

By representing prices and wages as being proportional to the money supply, this passage has endeared Hume to today's monetarists. But he also recognized that learning curves ("superior industry and skill"), inventory accumulation ("greater stocks") and economies of scale (affording "smaller profits") characterized the richest industrial economies. His mechanism thus did not deny that economic benefits would accrue to nations running payments surpluses.

While Hume's monetary and trade theory turned on the inflationary impact of money under full employment conditions, he acknowledged the two-phase character of the relationship between money, output and prices. He thus retained the mercantilist emphasis on money, although downplaying its ability to expand employment and output.

What he actually was warning against was the assumption that monetary inflows could increase output *ad infinitum*. A protectionist strategy ultimately would prove self-defeating once full employment was reached and further inflows of money merely pushed up prices, preventing "in some measure" a few nations from aggrandizing their economic power at the expense of others. At the point where the mercantilist objective was achieved, precisely when the economy was fully employed and running a trade surplus, prices would rise until international payments felt back into balance. But below full-employment conditions an expansion of trade and its consequent monetary inflows would produce definite economic benefits.

It was as a political philosopher that Hume placed central emphasis on the quantity theory of money and prices. It represented the buttress for his attack on bullionist mercantilism. Prolonged trade surpluses would be settled by monetary inflows that would generate inflationary pressures under full-employment conditions, pricing the nation's exports out of foreign and domestic markets. Money would flow out of the country, ending the commercial expansion.

Most free traders forget that this was not Hume's *general* theory, but only the culmination of a two-phase sequence. Although in a few famous passages he reasoned as if prices always were proportional to the money supply, he granted that where underemployment conditions existed, monetary inflows tended to be self-justifying to the extent that they spurred higher output and productivity. "We must consider," he acknowledged,

> that though the high price of commodities be a necessary consequence of the increase of gold and silver, yet it follows not immediately upon that increase; but some time is required before the money circulates through the whole state, and makes its effect be felt on all ranks of people … In every kingdom, into which money begins to flow in greater abundance than formerly, everything takes a new face; labour and industry gain life; the merchant becomes more enterprising, the manufacturer more diligent and skilful, and even the farmer follows his plough with greater alacrity and attention.

Increased money and income thus worked to increase employment and output before they increased prices. Manufacturers and merchants

> are thereby enabled to employ more workmen than formerly, who never dream of demanding higher wages, but are glad of employment from such good paymasters, If workmen become scarce, the manufacturer gives higher wages, but at first requires an increase of labour: and this is willingly submitted to by the artisan, who can now eat and drink better, to compensate his additional toil and fatigue. He carries his money to market, where he finds everything at the same price as formerly, but returns with greater quantity, and of better kinds, for the use of his family. The farmer and gardener, finding that all their commodities are taken off, apply themselves with alacrity to the raising more; and at the same time can afford to take better and more clothes from their tradesmen, whose price is the same as formerly, and their industry only whetted by so much new gain. It is easy to trace the money in its progress through the whole common-wealth; where we shall find that it must first quicken the diligence of every individual, before it increase the price of labour.[18]

Hume conceded elsewhere that paper money, like metallic currency, "gives encouragement to industry, during the intervals between the increase of money and the rise of prices." Monetary expansion was associated with growth in production, employment, productivity and exports. But subsequent free-trade historians of economic thought have ignored these acknowledgments of its positive employment and productivity effects. Vickers has summarized Hume's views more accurately: "What we should call an elasticity of supply is postulated … The inflation initially is a profit inflation, rather than a price inflation. Rises in turnovers and profits are realized, rather than rises in prices. Changes occur in the 'manners and customs of the people.'"[19]

Vickers recognized the importance of one of Hume's footnotes studiously overlooked by Viner, Haberler and other free-trade advocates—a footnote that emphasized some far-reaching qualifications to the crude quantity theory of money and prices: "It must carefully be marked, that … wherever I speak of the level of money, I mean always *its proportional level to the commodities, labour, industry and skill, which is in the several states*."[20] Today's monetarists recognize a "proportional" relationship, but limit it to that between money and commodity prices, ignoring "labour, industry, and skill."

[18] Rotwein, *ibid.* pp. 283f. It was for this reason that Keynes observed that Hume "was still enough of a mercantilist nor to overlook the fact that it is in the transition that we actually have our being." (*General Theory of Money, Prices and Employment* [London: 1936], p. 343n.).
[19] Vickers, *Studies in the Theory of Money*, p. 228.
[20] Hume, *Economic Writings*, p. 66n. Italics added.

*Tucker's and Steuart's criticisms of Hume's adjustment mechanism*

The most rigorous alternative to the money-price adjustment mechanism that Hume postulated was sketched by the Reverend Josiah Tucker, who relayed his thoughts to Hume in 1758 through a mutual friend, Lord Henry Kames. Sixteen years later, in 1774, Tucker published these views as the first of his *Four Tracts and Two Sermons*, widely reprinted over the next few years. In 1767, Sir James Steuart devoted Chapter 28 and some other passages of his *Principles of Political Oeconomy* to criticizing the limitations of the price-specie flow adjustment mechanism. There followed a pamphlet literature on the character of international adjustment mechanisms and their long-term developmental (at that time called "theological") implications.

Steuart pointed out that the ebb and flow of inflation and deflation, prices and commodity demand was not as simple as Hume's full-employment price adjustment model implied. A country suffering a serious trade deficit, monetary drain and falling prices was likely to suffer financial crisis throwing industry into bankruptcy when economic activity fell below the break-even point. Producers could not operate at a loss for long in the face of falling prices and still remain in business, nor could wages fall below subsistence levels and still maintain employment. "If a certain number of inhabitants be employed in a necessary branch of consumption, there must be a *certain* demand preserved for it; and whatever can render this precarious, will ruin the undertaking, and those employed in it."[21]

Although profits and wages might fall less drastically in response to a milder monetary deflation, the decline might not be enough to restore the trade balance as Hume and his followers anticipated. In modern terminology, demand for the country's exports might not be sufficiently price-elastic for a price decline to excite much of an increase in foreign demand.

Matters were complicated further by the fact that the flow of money influenced the migration of labor and related demographic responses. For countries running trade deficits, monetary outflows led to falling income and employment levels, spurring emigration. Although price-adjustment mechanisms ultimately might re-establish balance, international payments would tend to stabilize at a lower level of activity, employment and population. For this reason a deflationary monetary outflow was more likely to induce a collapse into poverty than to restore the pre-existing balance.[22]

Conversely, for nations running trade surpluses,

---

[21]  James Steuart, *Principles of Political Oeconomy* (1767), Vol. I, p. 424.
[22]  Steuart, *ibid.*, p. 417

no sooner will demand come from abroad, for a greater quantity of manufacturers than formerly, than such demand will have the effect of gradually multiplying the inhabitants up to the proportion of the surplus above mentioned, provided the statesman be all along careful to employ these additional numbers, which an useful multiplication must produce, in supplying the additional demand ...

An influx of foreign labor, especially skilled labor, would alleviate the full-employment constraint. As long as employment and productivity kept pace with rising wages and monetary stocks, there need be no increase in the general price level, and hence no falling off of exports. Foreign labor and capital were not invariably waiting in the wings to compete as soon as prices changed marginally, because "in all new undertakings there is mismanagement and considerable loss; and nothing discourages mankind from new undertakings more than difficult beginnings."[23]

Steuart pointed out that the distribution of wealth and monetary gains also affected the price effects of monetary inflows. The price of labor and provisions need not be bid up if increases in the money supply were hoarded by the rich or invested abroad rather than put into circulation to employ more workers. He cited Hume's own description of Alexander the Great and the Hellenistic successors, whose "treasures were then ... a real addition to the value of their kingdoms; but had not the smallest influence upon prices."[24] Even when money earned abroad was spent domestically, its price effects depended largely "upon the occupation and distribution of the classes of inhabitants." The price of subsistence goods would vary according to the demand by the wealthy (presumably the exporters or other beneficiaries of foreign monetary inflows) to hire labor. If the export sector rested on only a narrow employment base, the monetary influx probably would have little general effect.

Josiah Tucker agreed that matters depended on how the new money was used. This often depended partly on how it was obtained. Hume neglected to consider "How came *England* to acquire this surplus of Wealth?" It made a great difference, Tucker pointed out, whether England earned foreign bullion from broadly based industry employing a large proportion of the population, or whether the money came from commerce or piracy without industry, or by the brute robbing and looting of gold in which Spain and Portugal had engaged with such debilitating effects—"in short, by any other conceivable Method, wherein ... very few Hands were employed in getting this Mass of Wealth (and

---

[23]  Steuart, *ibid.*, pp. 268, 235.

[24]  Steuart, *ibid.*, p. 438 See also pp. 296, 402. For a similar favorable view of monetary sterilization, coupled with an explicit statement of the price-specie flow adjustment mechanism that would tend to occur in the absence of such sterilization, see Cantillon, *Essay on the Nature of Trade in General*, pp. 209–10.

they only by Fits and Starts, not constantly)—and fewer still are supposed to retain what is gotten."[25]

Such income tended to be spent unproductively rather than invested in domestic industry and employment. It was a seizure of money without securing a lasting foundation to continue earning and reproducing wealth over time—and also without increasing domestic prices, because its owners were likely to turn around and buy foreign luxuries, or perhaps invest their money in foreign bonds, much as Dutch merchants put their money into British stocks. This remarkable scenario would apply to many Third World and post-Soviet countries today, but to eighteenth-century observers it was a special case, applicable only to countries devoid of the guiding hands of a wise statesman.

In making these points, Steuart and Tucker objected to Hume's *caeteris paribus* mode of reasoning (already called that in their day) which assumed money to increase while holding "all other things equal." Hume's theories, observed Steuart, "are so pretty, and the theory they have laid down for determining the rise and fall of prices so simple, and so extensive, that it is no wonder to see it adopted by almost every one who has writ after them." However, he added, "I think I have discovered, that in this as in every other part of the science of political oeconomy, there is hardly such a thing as a general rule to be laid down."[26] Like Cantillon, Tucker and most of their contemporaries, Steuart believed that the price-specie flow principle would not threaten nations which wisely managed their foreign commerce and domestic political institutions. The trade balance, international payments and price relationships depended more on political and social structures than on monetary inflows and outflows.

This view became a fairly common. To pick just one example from the pamphlet literature of the time, an anonymous writer on population stated in 1782 that the effect of monetary inflows thus depended largely on "how that wealth [is] acquired, whether by force or labor, by foreign conquest or internal industry." If bullion flowed into a nation to pay for its industrial products, output was likely to increase and prices therefore would remain stable (assuming unemployment to exist). "Each addition to the quantity of productive stock will create new demands for labor, and add new spurs to industry and ingenuity. The annual produce of the nation and the course of its power will be thus rapidly increased." Only if this money were merely "acquired by foreign conquests, and paid in tribute to the public treasury," would its effect be similar to that suggested by Hume.

[25] Josiah Tucker, *Four Tracts on Political and Commercial Subjects* [1774] (2nd ed., Gloucester 1776), pp. 21–26.
[26] Steuart, *Principles of Political Oeconomy*, pp. 394f. See also pp. 416, 429ff., and Tucker's letter to Lord Kames, July 6, 1758, in *David Hume, Writings on Economics*, p. 203.

The quantity of universal merchandise [that is, monetary bullion] being violently and suddenly increased, the price of every commodity is raised. Productive labor is not increased with it, consequently its comparative quantity is lessened. Hence those nations, whose comparative quantity of industry is greater, are enabled to undersell them. Their own people become idle by habit, while those, who supply them, become inured to labor. Thus their internal produce gradually diminishes, until at length they become dependent upon other nations, even for the necessaries of life, and are obliged to submit to whatever exactions are imposed upon them.[27]

Without taking into account the public policy of nations, Steuart concluded, "the riches of a country [that is, its money supply] has no determined influence upon prices" that could be stated with certainty, "a fact which Mr. Hume has attended ... on one occasion, although he has lost sight of it on several others."[28]

Suppose the specie of Europe to continue increasing in quantity every year, until it amounts to ten times the present quantity, would prices rise in proportion?

I answer, that such an augmentation might happen, without the smallest alternation upon prices, or that it might occasion a very great one, according to circumstances. If industry increases to ten times what it is at present, that is to say, were the produce of it increased to ten times its present value, according to the actual standard of prices, the value of every manufacture and produce might remain without alteration. ...

While a favourable balance, therefore, is preserved upon foreign trade, a nation grows richer daily; and still prices remain regulated as before, by the complicated operations of demand and competition; and when one nation is grown richer, others must be growing poorer ...[29]

The above argument may be expressed in symbolic formulas to make it compatible with modern discussions of the relationship between money, prices and economic activity. In Irving Fisher's formulation of the quantity theory, $MV=PT$, the symbol $M$ stands for the money supply in circulation (excluding private hoards), $V$ for its velocity of turnover, $P$ for price, and $T$ for commodity (and service) transactions in any given period. The main analytic problem arises from holding this output $T$ constant, assuming a fixed employed labor force $N$, and assuming that higher wage rates (when they do occur) are not positively correlated with labor productivity $Z$.

---

[27] [Anonymous], *Political Observations on the Population of Countries* (London: 1782), pp. 19, 22–23.

[28] Steuart, *Principles of Political Oeconomy*, Vol. I, p. 405.

[29] Steuart, *ibid.*, pp. 413-14, 422. Friedrich von Hayek remarks that "The suggestive and interesting. but essentially wrongheaded chapters on money in James Steuart's *Political Oeconomy* had no very wide influence." (Introduction to the 1939 reprint of Henry Thornton's *Enquiry into the Nature and Effect of the Paper Credit of Great Britain* [London: 1802].) However, Hayek does not begin to explain where Steuart's ideas were wrong.

Viner has summarized what today is called a "cost-push" theory of inflation under full employment in the following manner:

$$\text{Stock of money / number of persons} = \text{rate of money wages}$$
$$= \text{prices} \times \text{average real income}$$

Substituting the term "circulating capital" for "money," this income version of the Quantity Theory underlies the classical Wages Fund Doctrine. As the supply of money increases, wages rise and commodity prices follow suit. But as Hume noted, prices may remain stable below full-employment conditions if the change in $M$ equals that of $N$ ($\Delta M = \Delta N$, letting N stand for employment) and hence of output $T$. Hume accepted neither an unqualified quantity theory of money and prices nor one of wage levels and prices. He believed that the money-wage-price parallelism occurred only when the limits of economic expansion were reached, a condition that rarely applied in the eighteenth century. This explains why most economic writers did not assume a full-employment or full-capacity constraint.

Hume's theory of money and economic growth depended on the relationship between money, commodities, labor, industry and skill (see fn 20 above). A nation's output was the result of two sets of forces. Financially it depended on the availability of money and credit to set labor and industry in motion. From a "real economy" vantage point, output was a function of the size of the labor force $N$ multiplied by its per capita productivity $Z$. The variables recognized by Hume and his contemporaries may thus be represented as $MV = PT = NZ$. Potential growth in output $T$ was limited by the size of the labor force $N$ and its productive power $Z$, as well as financially by the money supply $M$ and its efficiency in supporting a paper-credit superstructure $V$.

It was generally recognized that growth in the labor force was composed of changes in the natural growth of population or its participation rate in labor force ($D_n$, for "natural demographic growth), plus net immigration ($D_i$, with the prefix D standing for the Demographic variable). However, growth of output was limited by the availability of monetary resources, because changes in the money supply influenced employment and productivity as well as prices. Higher wages and prices would increase labor-force participation, immigration, population growth and, to some extent, labor productivity.

As Tucker observed, labor—especially skilled labor—tended to emigrate (along with money and investment capital) to high-wage nations, bolstering their technological lead:

The higher Wages of the rich Country, and the greater Scope and Encourage-ment given for the Exertion of Genius, Industry, and Ambition, will naturally determine a great many Men of Spirit and Enterprise to forsake their own poor Country, and settle in the richer; so that the one will always drain the other of the Flower of its Inhabitants … the richer Country being always endowed with the attractive Quality of the Loadstone, and the poor one with the repelling; And therefore, seeing that the poorer Country must necessarily be the least peopled (if there is a free Intercourse between them) the Consequence would be, that in several Districts, and in many Instances, it would be impossible for certain Trades even to subsist; because the Scarcity and Poverty of the Inhabitants would not afford a sufficient Number of Customers to frequent the Shop, or to take off the Goods of the Manufacturer.[30]

This acknowledgement of wage-responsive mobility of labor should have dispelled any thought of postulating an immobility of labor and capital across national boundaries, and hence of intrinsic "factor proportions." Economies were "open," gaining or losing money, labor and capital resources as a result of their national policies.

Hume's friend James Oswald wrote to him in 1749 that although a mone-tary inflow and its associated "quick demand, in the first instance, tends to raise the rate of wages, yet, as it is corrected by the attraction of new inhabitants, it only produces permanently that good effect, while the want of it in poor countries destroys the manufacture themselves, and sends out the manufactur-ers."[31] Hume's essay "Of the Balance of Trade" duly acknowledged that "a diminution of specie" is "in time commonly attended with the transport of people and industry."[32] Monetary deflation would spur emigration. By recogniz-ing this adverse employment and output effect of deflation, Vanderlint and Hume showed themselves to be more sophisticated than today's IMF practition-ers of austerity programs who neglect the degree to which deflationary policies aggravate the problems of poorer countries rather than stabilizing their balance of payments.

The conclusion was that if a 10 percent increase in England's money supply worked to increase wage rates by 10 per cent, this would induce immigration. It also would increase the participation of its domestic population in the labor force, raising the population's overall productivity. As long as these variables increased by 10 per cent or more, the exportable surplus would grow and prices might actu-ally fall *below* their original level. Assuming that all increases in national output were available for export, and as long as $D_i$, $D_n$, $\Delta Z$ and $\Delta T$ are positive—as they tend to be in a growing economy—then $\Delta P < \Delta M < \Delta B$ (letting B repre-

---

[30] Tucker, *Four Tracts*, pp. 32–33.
[31] Viner, *Studies*, p. 42 n.
[32] James Oswald to Hume, October 10, 1749, in Hume, *Economic Writings*, pp. 195, 77.

sent the balance of trade). Higher prices (at least initially) would enhance rather than impair the balance of trade in situations where international demand patterns tended to be "inelastic." England's terms of trade might even rise over time if these developments helped establish foreign dependency on its exports, enabling England (or other industrial lead nations) to exert monopoly power. However, eighteenth-century economists only hazily perceived the degree to which changes in the physical volume of exports might affect the terms of trade.

The system-wide dynamics discussed by these writers suggests why Adam Smith elected to attack only the less sophisticated mercantilists, not mentioning Tucker or Steuart despite the fact that he was familiar with both men's books. Although he had endorsed the price-specie flow mechanism in his 1763 *Lectures on Justice, Police, Revenue and Arms*, his *Wealth of Nations* abandoned all reference to it. Viner finds this to be "one of the great mysteries of the history of economic thought."[33] But the reason seems evident enough: Smith apparently judged the theory to have been controverted. He made much of labor mobility, but on liberal political grounds, not economic wage grounds. (See Chapter 1, notes 14–16.)

Tucker, Steuart and other leading advocates of active government policy made no attempt to deny that economic development tended to favor the lead nations rather than being egalitarian. Indeed, they emphasized this principle. Properly administered, these nations could consolidate their head start over less developed countries. In this vein Steuart derided the idealistic Rousseauian "principles of an imaginary law of nature, *which makes all mankind equal*: nature can never be in opposition to common reason."[34] The world was organized and integrated not on the basis of the brotherhood of man, but on the superstructure of national and personal self-interest.

The unstated corollary was that if less developed economies (as England once had been) were to achieve economic equality with more advanced nations, they required an active government policy to shape market forces. This is how England achieved international power, and how the United States would acquire it in the nineteenth and twentieth centuries. For both England and the United States, the objective of national policy was to secure an industrial head start to consolidate its long-term earning power. National power came to be identified less with crude military greatness or with populousness in itself (if the population had low economic productivity), much less with the possession of hoards of bullion to finance foreign wars. Spain had possessed these qualities in the sixteenth century only to end up the poorest country in Europe, dominated even by its ex-colony Holland.

---

[33]  Viner, *Studies*, pp. 99, 87, 1.
[34]  Steuart, *Principles of Political Oeconomy*, p. 240.

## Summary

To summarize the "mercantilist" argument, increases in the money supply tended to spur employment and output when substantial labor was available to be hired. Even when no more free labor remained to be put to work, the high wage levels incident to monetary inflows might have a silver lining: Rising wage levels tended to increase productivity. It did this by increasing the quality of labor and by spurring the substitution of capital for labor.

Some of the higher output was consumed at home, but some was available for export. Only as capacity strains developed did monetary expansion begin to inflate prices—and only after this inflation had continued for some time did it impair the nation's trade balance, because trade patterns were hard to shift once they were established, and development of foreign competition took time to mature. Higher prices might even increase the trade balance if sufficient foreign dependency existed that customers abroad had little choice but to pay the higher prices.

It was these dynamic principles, concluded Viner, whose "refutation was a necessary preliminary to successful formulation of free-trade doctrine. The formulation of the quantity theory of money and the criticisms and qualifications of the balance of trade doctrine prepared the way, therefore, for the emergence of a comprehensive free-trade doctrine."[35] But instead of refuting the demographic and financial variables cited above, free traders merely ignored them. Their strategy was to narrow the discussion by treating emigration and immigration, wages and productivity, credit and interest rates as variables "exogenous" to trade theory. The resulting free-trade logic became "comprehensive" only by closing its eyes to the problem of resources going unemployed for want of money. As Schumpeter summarized the new liberal view:

> The Englishmen who started writing on monetary policy around 1800 knew very little about the English work of the seventeenth and even eighteenth centuries and still less, almost nothing in fact, of the non-English work of those centuries— an interesting example of how the advance of economics has been and is being impaired by those recurrent losses of previous accumulations of knowledge. In particular, they knew nothing about Cantillon and Galiani and not much about Steuart.[36]

Nor about Tucker, Vanderlint and others, he might have added. According to the new view, money was a mere measuring device, a "counter," a mirror reflecting the "real" economy but with no direct impact *on* it. If monetary inflows from abroad had no positive effect, there was little need for state policy to try and manage the economy to generate trade surpluses. Just the

---

[35] Viner, *Studies*, p. 91.
[36] Schumpeter, *History of Economic Analysis*, p. 706.

opposite: *The only domestic impact of the mercantilist drive to attract money from abroad would be price inflation.* At least this would be the case under the full employment conditions that free traders assumed.

The reality, of course, was that economies with unemployed resources needed money to put their population to work. The effect of obtaining more "money of the world" (that is, the universally acceptable precious metals) was to increase the monetary and credit base, setting in motion more labor and capital, increasing output accordingly. This laid the foundation for running even larger trade surpluses. Nations running such surpluses would be able to pull ahead of others, attracting skilled labor and investment in a snowball effect from countries running payments deficits, polarizing the world economy. These conditions justified—indeed, called for—an active statecraft making use of subsidies and tariffs. Even if some price inflation resulted, it might be passed on to one's customers if suitably strong trade ties had been formed.

There was one condition on which even mercantilists might agree to dismantle statist restrictions. It was a factor that Smith did not acknowledge, but which Tucker and other writers described. The lead nation might refrain from exercising its statecraft on the condition that other countries would refrain from pursuing protectionist development programs of their own. Underlying this bargain, at least from England's vantage point, was the conviction (well-founded as matters turned out) that as the world's leading economic nation, it had acquired sufficient advantages in underselling foreign industrial labor and capital to more than make up for the relatively modest incursions that less developed countries might make into its own agricultural market.

This was a far cry from the medieval and modern utilitarian views that trade is justified because all parties gain. Like mercantilism, early British free-trade theorizing viewed the end result of commerce to be monopolization of world productive resources and economic power. England could run a perpetual trade surplus that would finance increasingly productive capital investment in a self-feeding process, drawing in foreign skilled labor as well as money. Poorer countries would not benefit from their low wage rates if the rich and industrious nations possessed more than compensating productivity advantages. This argument envisioned the world economy polarizing as wealthy nations drew to their shores the world's skilled labor, investment funds and other resources.

Out of this initially monetary debate the idea of what constituted competitive advantage came to include such diverse elements as nurturing an urban industrial population with superior work habits, economies of scale and consequent perfection of skills resulting from a growing division of labor. Higher domestic incomes also supported wider markets, and hence more opportunity for the division of labor and its associated productivity gains.

# 4

# How Mercantilism Evolved into Laissez Faire

*How wealthy nations consolidated their head start*

The preceding chapter has traced how a nation (England in particular) could run a favorable trade balance to draw in foreign silver and gold, yet not experience a price inflation as long as it still had underemployed labor and capital, or as long as it could continue to attract foreign labor and capital in proportion to foreign bullion. Under these conditions more money would find its counterpart in higher output. Before countervailing forces—rising prices at home making exports less competitive, or new sources of competition from abroad—reversed the surplus and restored payments equilibrium, a trade-surplus nation might absorb foreign monetary resources for a considerable period of time. The lead nation's trade surplus might even push rival economies into financial depression, depriving them of the money needed to fund the capital investments needed to employ their low-wage labor.

This chapter reviews the broader discussion of how the lead nations consolidated head start, foreclosing industrialization in less developed countries—unless the latter withdrew from the free-trade system to protect their own infant industries. Tucker posed the issue as follows. Given a rich industrial economy and a poor country, "Which of these two nations can afford to raise Provisions, and sell their Manufactures on the cheapest Terms?" His answer was that richer nations had acquired sufficient commercial advantages so that they need not fear competition from poorer countries. Although the latter generally had cheaper raw materials, their manufacturers tended to be more expensive. Tucker concluded "that *operose* or *complicated Manufactures* are cheapest in rich countries; and *raw Materials* in the poor ones."[1]

This threatened to leave poor countries with only their native endowment of climate and mineral resources as the basis for an export trade, providing a relatively narrow employment base. (And if their export sector was largely foreign owned, they would suffer a monetary drain of repatriated profits.) Wealthy and more experienced nations had acquired superior capital stocks of all kinds—financial, physical and institutional, including what today is called

---

[1] Josiah Tucker, *Four Tracts on Political and Commercial Subjects* [1774] (2nd ed., Gloucester: 1776), p. 36.

human capital in the form of labor skills and sophistication in applying the most advanced technology.[2] Wages in these industrial nations tended to rise as a result of growing prosperity, and this tended to support superior growth of labor productivity, by inducing higher investment in education and what today would be called research and development:

> The richer country is not only in Possession of the Things already made and settled, but also of superior skill and Knowledge (acquired by long Habit and Experience) for inventing and making of more ... Now, if so, the poorer Country, however willing to learn, cannot be supposed to be capable of making the same Progress in Learning with the Rich, for want of equal Means of Instruction, equally good Models and Examples:—and therefore, tho' both may be improving every Day, yet the *practical* Knowledge of the poorer in Agriculture and Manufacturers will always be found to keep at a respectful Distance behind that of the richer country.[3]

The basic perception was that relatively high wage levels reflected themselves in even higher productivity advantages over competitors, and hence lower unit costs. "Is it not much cheaper to give 2s. 6d. a Day in the rich Country to the nimble and adroit Artist," Tucker asked, "than it is to give only 6d. in the poor one, to the tedious, awkward Bunglar?" Productivity advantages thus would enable England's unit labor costs to undercut those of countries with ostensibly low-wage labor. In fact, *the process of technological innovation was largely a direct function of income levels*. For starters, Steuart pointed out, richer countries could risk more money in testing and introducing innovations.[4]

Over and above their economies of scale and experience, the richer nations had improved their lands and made more extensive roads, water transport and other internal improvements (now called social capital or infrastructure). Also, reasoned Tucker, the London money market mobilized savings to lend out rather than hoard, contributing to "the low Interest of Money, [which] will insure the vending of all Goods on the cheapest Terms."[5] Lower borrowing costs meant that lower profits were required to cover expenses and undertake new investment.

A related factor giving wealthy nations superior competitive power was the fact that, "As the richer Country has a greater Number of rival Tradesmen," and hence broader markets affording a higher degree of competition, it had fewer opportunities for monopoly. In poor countries lacking a broadly based industry it was "easy for one rich, over-grown Tradesman to monopolize the whole Trade to himself and consequently to set his own Price upon the Goods ..."[6]

---

[2]  Tucker, *ibid.*, pp. 30, 34.               [4]  Tucker, *ibid.*, p. 32.
[3]  Tucker, *ibid.*, p. 31.                     [5]  Tucker, *ibid.*, p. 34.
[6]  Tucker, *ibid.*, p. 34. On this point see also his *Elements of Commerce*, in Schuyler (ed.), *Josiah Tucker: Economic and Political Writings* (New York: 1931), p. 64.

Only a broad distribution of property and income could provide a sound foundation for economic development. Unequal distribution or monopolization of wealth and income would tend to be squandered on luxuries rather than invested productively.

> Hence the Number of Coaches, Post-Chaises, and all other Vehicles of Pleasure, would prodigiously increase; while the usual Sets of Farmer's Carts and Waggons proportionably decreased: The Sons of lower Tradesmen and Labourers would be converted into spruce, powdered Footmen; … So that from being a Nation of Bees producing Honey, they would become a Nation of Drones to eat it up.[7]

In one of his letters to Hume, James Oswald emphasized that raw materials producers suffered unstable demand for their output:

> Poor countreys are ever at a great loss in the article of cheap necessarys, by means of their little cultivation, which every now and then renders the price of them dearer than in rich countreys—a circumstance which the manufacturers of such poor countreys cannot long support; while rich countreys, on the other hand, by the variety of their cultivation, are rarely subject to such accidents, and are easily supplied at the level rate.[8]

Oswald concluded that a trade-surplus nation possessing rich financial resources "would, in some measure, be the capital of the world, while all neighbour countries would … be as its provinces." Steuart and others also made this point, especially with regard to the dynamics between gold producers and industrial nations. Countries that could live well by producing gold (or by logical extension, other raw materials) were not compelled to put in place the industrial, agricultural and commercial infrastructure that alone could earn nations ultimate possession of the world's money. They were cursed by the temptation to live in the short run, relying on their mineral endowment and natural climatic advantages rather than by industry.

The industrial nations, which had little alternative but to develop the talents of their populations, thus seemed destined to garner the fruits of the division of world labor, rendering other countries increasingly dependent on them. As Jacob Vanderlint wrote in 1734, non-industrialized countries, especially raw materials exporters seemingly blessed with gold and silver mines, would

> certainly drop their Cultivation and Manufactures; since Men will not easily be induced to labor and toil, for what they can get with much less Trouble, by exchanging some of the Excess of their Gold and Silver for what they want. And if they should be supposed, as is natural enough in this Case, to drop their Cultivation, and especially of Manufactures, which are much the slowest and most laborious Way of supplying themselves with what they could so easily and

---

[7] Tucker, *op. cit.*, pp. 21-22.

[8] Oswald to Hume, in *Hume, Writings on Economics*, p. 195.

readily procure by exchanging Gold and Silver, which they too much abound in, they would certainly, in a great Measure, by so doing lose the Arts of Cultivation, and especially of Manufactures; as it's thought Spain hath done, merely by the Accession of the Wealth which the West Indies have produced them; whence they are become a poor Nation, and the Conduit-Pipes to disperse the Gold and Silver over the World, which other Nations, by making Goods cheaper than they can do, are fetching from them, to such a Degree, as that the Mines are scarcely sufficient to answer their Occasions; and though they are sensible of this, yet they find by Experience they can't prevent it.[9]

Natural wealth thus turned out to be a burden. It distracted Spain and its colonies from laying a more lasting foundation for economic development by nurturing a skilled industrial labor force and entrepreneurial commercial class fit for higher tasks than mining and plantation work. Tucker concurred. Iberia's apparent wealth actually constituted "real Poverty, as the Spaniards and Portuguese are [experiencing] at present." If England were to resort to such non-industrious means of gaining gold as the Spaniards had done in vanquishing the Indians— and as Hume had assumed in postulating that England's gold supply might be multiplied overnight without requiring any productive investment—"our Fate and Punishment would have been by this time similar to theirs;—Pride elated with imaginary Wealth, and abject Poverty without Resource."[10] Hume's price-specie flow mechanism seemed to apply mainly to conditions where more money was obtained without any corresponding growth in output—by purely exploitative conquest without domestic industry.

### Would free trade lead to greater international equality or polarization?

Hume acknowledged that rising wage rates and employment were associated with favorable productivity effects, but maintained that low-wage countries *ultimately* would enjoy production-cost advantages. Writing to Lord Kames in response to Tucker's points, he granted that "All the advantages [to the rich nations] which the author insists are real," but refused to concede Tucker's conclusions. He granted that

> great capital, extensive correspondence, skilful expedients of facilitating labor, dexterity, industry, &c., these circumstances give them [the richer nations] an undisputed superiority over poor nations, who are ignorant and unexperienced. The question is, whether these advantages can go on, increasing trade *in infinitum*, or whether they do not at last come to a *ne plus ultra*, and check themselves, by begetting disadvantages, which at first retard, and at last finally stop their progress.[11]

---

9   Jacob Vanderlint, *Money Answers All Things* (1734), pp. 52ff.
10  Tucker, *Four Tracts*, pp. 21–26.
11  Hume to Lord Kames, March 4, 1758, in *Hume, Writings on Economics*, pp. 200–01.

Over the long run, he believed, the advantages of cheap labor would outweigh its disadvantages (to say nothing of the food and raw materials advantages enjoyed by poor, sparsely populated countries). High-income nations would suffer a number of economic burdens, among which

> we may reckon the dear price of provisions and labor, which enables the poorer country to rival them, first in the coarser manufactures, and then in those which are more elaborate. Were it otherwise, commerce, if not dissipated by violent conquests, would go on perpetually increasing, and one spot of the globe would engross the art and industry of the whole.

This was the very strategy of mercantilism, of course. One might say that Divine Providence to Tucker was English, or at least had created a global state of affairs that favored England uniquely. (This attitude hardly should be surprising. The Church of England was nationalistic from its inception under Henry VIII.) To Hume, God was more cosmopolitan in favoring the underdog. As Hume remarked of Tucker,

> The author, conformable to the character both of a divine and a philosopher, draws the argument from the goodness of Providence; but I think it may be turned against him. It was never surely the intention of Providence, that any one nation should be a monopolizer of wealth: and the growth of all bodies, artificial as well as natural, is stopped by internal causes, derived from their enormous size and greatness. Great empires, great cities, great commerce, all of them receive a check, not from accidental events, but necessary principles.

In Hume's Deist world view, the Lord had created a fair and equitable global economy that protected poor countries against the rich. In time, according to this reasoning, the comparative poverty suffered by England's colonies and those of other European nations would enable them, to undersell their mother countries—until the living standards of their own populations caught up with those of the metropolitan center. Economies that lost bullion and suffered unemployment would be able to undersell the more affluent nations, making poorer countries the major beneficiaries of free trade. This meant that their governments had no need to enact the kind of protectionist policies that had enabled England to overtake Holland. Just the opposite was implied: England's government should protect *its* economy.

If Hume's theory were correct, the richer nations would be wise to maintain their protective tariffs and colonial controls. Otherwise, Tucker and Steuart pointed out, their high living standards would tend to fall to a level with those of the poorer countries. In Steuart's words, rich nations would have cause to feel anxious, lest their incomes and prices "be brought to such an equality" with poorer countries as to dissipate the fruits of their head start:

If, therefore, it be the interest of a nation, poor in respect of its neighbours, to have trade laid open, that wealth may, like a fluid, come to an equilibrium; I am sure it is the interest of a rich nation, to cut off the communication of hurtful trade, by such impediments as restrictions, duties, and prohibitions, upon importation; that thereby, as by dykes, its wealth may be kept *above* the level of the surrounding element.[12]

This hardly endorsed the liberal policy that Hume desired. But as matters turned out, it was not his logic that convinced England to adopt free trade nearly a century after he wrote. Ironically, the logic was that of Tucker, Steuart and Vanderlint.

Tucker did not disagree with Hume over the latter's advocacy of free trade. On the contrary, he believed that England could readily dominate world markets under laissez faire. As its labor force grew more skilled, the nation's superior accumulation of capital and higher labor productivity would result in lower export prices despite higher money wages. Rich nations would tend to get richer while poorer countries got poorer and more dependent.

Phrasing matters starkly, Tucker pointed out that Hume's doctrine that wages and prices were proportional to the money supply (by which he meant specie drawn in by a positive balance of trade) implied that "every poor Country is the natural and unavoidable Enemy of a rich one." Hence, the latter could maintain prosperity only by enacting protective tariffs and even "to make War upon the poor one, and to endeavor to extirpate all its Inhabitants." This hardly seemed to be an order of things consistent with "the fundamental Principle of universal Benevolence" established by Divine Providence.[13]

The pattern of global development suggested by Tucker and Steuart was scarcely more benevolent. It implied that the richer nations posed a growing threat to poor countries. As wage and profit levels rose in nations that had gained an industrial head start, their productive powers would grow even more, widening the development gap. This would concentrate physical and finance capital (along with the fruits of experience and technology generally) in these nations. Only protective tariffs by the poorer countries could stem this process. "True it is," Tucker wrote to Lord Kames in 1758,

> that *caeteris paribus*, the rich industrious country would always undersell the poor one; and by that means attract the trade of all poorer countries to itself:—but it is equally true, that if either of these poor countries hath any peculiar produce of its own, it may prohibit its exportation till it be wrought up into a complete manufacture. It is true likewise, that all of them have it in their power to load the manufactures of the rich country from entering their territories, with such high

---

[12]   James Steuart, *Principles of Political Oeconomy* (1767), Vol. I, pp. 423-24.
[13]   Tucker, *Four Tracts*, p. 19.

duties as shall turn the scale in favour of their own manufactures. ... Thus it is, in my poor apprehension, that the rich may be prevented from swallowing up the poor ...[14]

It was for this reason that Viner called Tucker "a protectionist of a some-what extreme protectionist type."[15] But Tucker was not protectionist as far as his own nation was concerned! Just the opposite. He believed that free trade would give England the best of both worlds. It would free the economy from the burden of its overseas colonial defense, while opening world markets to English exporters. Why entail the cost of acquiring and holding foreign markets by force when they could be gained by the much less expensive bonds of market forces? All that England need do was to persuade its raw-materials suppliers to follow a policy of free trade. "We have at present," Tucker wrote

the Means in our Power of treating with the Northern Potentates of Europe on very advantageous Terms: That is, we may signify to each of them (as we did formerly to *Portugal*) that in what Proportion soever, they will favour the Intro-duction of the *English* Manufactures into their Territories by the Repeal or Diminution of Taxes; in the same Proportion will we admit their Bar Iron, Hemp, Pitch, Tar, Turpentine, &c. into *Great-Britain*.[16]

Rather than unilaterally dismantling its restrictions (which Tucker felt it should do in any event) England should strike a bargain with other countries, offering to open its markets only to nations that did the same. Such a bargain would bring about a free-trade world on conditions that would sharply reduce England's defense expenditures.

---

[14] Tucker to Lord Kames, July 6, 1758. in *Hume, Writings on Economics*, p. 203. Tucker was not particularly sympathetic to the plight of the poorer countries. He merely advised them to make use of whatever local endowments they might possess. "In the natural world," he wrote in a passage reminiscent of the medieval Schoolmen (*Four Tracts*, p. 75), "our boun-tiful Creator hath formed different Soils, and appointed different Climates; whereby the Inhabitants of different Countries may supply each other with their respective Fruits and Products; so that by exciting a reciprocal Industry, they may carry on an Intercourse mutually beneficial, and universally benevolent." But this beautiful era implicitly lay beyond an interregnum of tariff protection. Under conditions as they then stood, free trade would weaken the position of less developed countries, not help them.

[15] Viner, *Studies in the Theory of International Trade*, pp. 99, 87. Viner acknowledged the fre-quently voiced desire by mercantilists to see higher wages on humanitarian grounds, but neglected entirely the "economy of high wages" doctrine enunciated by the more sophisti-cated protectionists who viewed high wage rates and the provision of semi-luxuries as a means to consolidate England's industrial supremacy as its domestic workers labored harder to improve their station in life and buy petty luxuries such as ribbons.

[16] Tucker, *A Series of Answers to Certain Popular Objections against Separating From the Rebellious Colonies, and Discarding them Entirely* ... (Gloucester: 1776), p. 49, and *Four Tracts*, p. 50.

The indicated line of defense for poor countries against falling into economic bondage would be to decline England's offer, and to "adopt … several useful Regulations of its richer neighbouring state," for example, protective tariffs, or as Tucker phrased it, "judicious Taxes, to discourage the too great or excessive Consumption of alien Manufactures. …" Such protectionist policies might enable less developed countries to use their raw materials advantage to acquire an industrial advantage over time. Berkeley had explained England's own logic in nurturing infant industries so as to close the technology gap, and in time even to secure an economic lead. Berkeley suggested something akin to "learning by doing" when he asked the following questions:

> Whether the use and the fashion will not soon make a manufacture? Whether faculties are not enlarged and improved by exercise?
> Whether the sum of the faculties put into act, or, in other words, the united action of a whole people, doth not constitute the momentum of a state?
> Whether such momentum be not the real stock or wealth of a state; and whether its credit be not proportional thereunto?
> Whether the mind, like soil, doth not by disuse grow stiff; and whether reasoning and study be not like stirring and dividing the globe?
> Whether, if each of these towns were addicted to some particular manufacture, we should not find that the employing many hands together on the same work was the way to perfect our workmen? And whether all these things might not soon be provided by a domestic industry; if money were not wanting?[17]

Cantillon indicated that the solution lay in industrial protectionism:

> If the Proprietors of Land and the Nobility of Poland would consume only the Manufactures of their own State, bad as they might be at the outset, they would soon become better and would keep a great Number of their own People to work there, instead of giving this advantage to Foreigners: and if all States had the like care not to be the dupes of other States in matters of Commerce, each State would be considerable only in proportion to its Produce and the Industry of its People.[18]

Steuart gave a classic argument for protecting domestic manufactures to obtain a head start:

> Infant trade, taken in a general acceptation, may be understood to be that species, which has for its object the supplying the necessities of the inhabitants of a country; because it is commonly antecedent to the supplying the wants of strangers …
> A considerable time must of necessity be required to bring a people to a dexterity in manufactures. The branches of these are many; … People do not perceive this inconveniency, in countries where they are already introduced; and many a projector has been ruined for want of attention to it.[19]

[17]   George Berkeley, *The Querist*, Queries 537, 581, 582, 583, 196, 415.
[18]   Richard Cantillon, *Essay on the Nature of Trade in General* [1755], translated by Henry Higgs (London: 1931), p. 77.
[19]   Steuart, *Principles of Political Oeconomy* (1767), Vol. I, pp. 301, 303.

In the most simple manufacturing, Steuart observed, the apprentice system was not required. One man taught another, with the simple instruction

> *do as you see others do before you.* This is an advantage which an established industry has over another newly set on foot; and this I apprehend to be the reason why we see certain manufactures, after remaining long in a state of infancy, make in a few years a most astonishing progress.

### How rich nations might lose their economic lead

Although "a taste for industry in the advancement of agriculture and of manufactures" required protective tariffs in the beginning, Steuart warned that "the scaffolding must be taken away when the fabric is compleated." Statesmen must he prepared to move from an inward-looking protectionism to a more liberal export-oriented expansionism:

> [N]ow that he intends to supply foreign markets, he must multiply hands; set them in competition; bring down the price both of subsistence and work; and when the luxury of his people render this difficult, he must attack the manners of the rich, and give a check to the domestic consumption of superfluity, in order to have the more hands for the supply of strangers.[20]

Maintenance of an industrial head start required an ongoing direction of the economy to enhance labor productivity while minimizing luxury consumption. By following such policies, nations might

> amass great sums of wealth, far above the proportion of it among their neighbours. ... It is not by the importation of foreign commodities, and by the exportation of gold and silver, that a nation becomes poor; it is by consuming those commodities when imported. The moment the consumption begins, the balance turns ...[21]

The key was to invest the economic surplus productively rather than consuming it luxuriously—or as Tucker put it, to design a system "whereby the Drones of Society may be converted into Bees, and the Bees prevented from degenerating into Drones."[22] Tucker elaborated this view in his *Four Tracts*:

> In one Word, the only possible Means of preventing a Rival Nation from running away with your Trade, is to prevent your own People from being more idle and vicious than they are; ... So that the only War, which can be attended with Success in that Respect, is a War against Vice and Idleness; a War, whose Forces must consist of—not Fleets and Armies,—but such judicious Taxes and wise Regulations, as shall turn the Passion of private Self-Love into the Channel of public Good.[23]

---

[20]  Steuart, *ibid.*, p. 475.
[21]  Steuart, *ibid.*, p . 418.

[22]  Tucker, *Four Tracts*, p. 29. See also pp. 21–22.
[23]  Tucker, *ibid.*, pp. 44-45.

Among these "judicious Taxes and wise Regulations" were protective tariffs—a logic that England's own commercial interests hardly wished to broadcast to other countries. As they came to advocate universal free trade, they lost interest in theories suggesting that their potential customers might benefit from enacting tariffs and industrial subsidies of their own on productivity grounds. This explains the eagerness to popularize Hume's international adjustment mechanism, and why Adam Smith elected to attack only the less sophisticated mercantilists, not addressing the dynamics on which Tucker and Steuart focused. The focus of trade theory made a shift that has lasted ever since.

If world economic convergence ultimately were to be achieved instead of English domination, it would be either because less developed economies would practice protectionism to achieve for themselves what England and other leading nations had accomplished, or because the enervating effects of wealth and luxury undercut the position of leading nations from within (a "rise and fall" theory of progress and decay). According to Steuart, a wealthy nation's social and political decay was most likely to stem from its own domestic polarization, culminating in the monopolization of production. At first, the nation's seemingly impregnable profits

> will provide a fatal blow to the first undertakings of rival nations. But when once they are fairly so consolidated, that prices can no more come down of themselves, and that the statesman will not lend his helping hand, then the new beginners pluck up courage, and set out by making small profits.

The wealthy nation's economic supremacy and luxurious living standards threaten to become its undoing:

> … when a nation begins to lose ground, then the very columns which supported her grandeur, begin, by their weight, to precipitate her decline …
>
> Thus it happens, that so soon as matters begin to go backward in a trading nation, and that by the increase of their riches, luxury and extravagance take place of oeconomy and frugality among the industrious; when the inhabitants themselves foolishly enter into competition with strangers for their own commodities; and when a statesman look cooly on, with his arms across, or takes it into his head, that it is not his business to interpose, the prices of the dextrous workman will rise above the amount of the management, loss, and reasonable profits, of the new beginners; and when this comes to be the case, trade will decay where it flourished most, and take root in a new soil. This I call a competition between nations.[24]

---

[24] Steuart, *Principles of Political Oeconomy*, pp. 235–36.

## *Anti-colonialist tendencies within mercantilism*

English trade strategists worried that (in Steuart's words) the "most extravagant profits … [might] become consolidated" in the form of monopolies and luxurious habits, sapping the nation's economic strength. This led Steuart, Tucker and many of their contemporaries to oppose the East India Company and other national monopolies. This logic also had obvious implications for English colonial policy. Tucker argued that the world marketplace would naturally secure the colonial markets on which England was spending large sums of money to defend. To monopolize world markets and money, the nation need merely stay out of wars (both European and colonial) and minimize its government overhead generally. The fewer military and colonial expenditures it had to make, the less it would need to increase its war-related public debt and the taxes required to service it. Lower taxes and interest rates would provide its producers with a cost advantage.

England embraced free trade once it became convinced that this policy would serve its national interest. When Parliament finally dismantled the protectionist Corn Laws and Navigation Acts, its legislators had come to believe that free trade would favor their nation more than poorer, less industrialized countries. "Free market forces" promised to deter these countries from nurturing their own industrial independence. The rhetoric was that of Hume and Smith, but the logic was that of Tucker and Steuart.

Tucker presented as powerful an argument as any writer of his time as to why England should dismantle its colonial system, commercial monopolies and mercantile restrictions. Schuyler and Semmel rightly consider him to have enunciated what became the rationale for British strategists to endorse laissez faire. The nation might accomplish what Hume had believed to be impossible, namely, to obtain the lion's share of the world's bullion and other resources. But to do this, England would have to free itself from its costly colonial system, whose *raison d'être* had faded away. The nation no longer needed to exert armed force or overt political control to secure foreign markets and sources of supply. (Tucker questioned whether it had needed its colonial projects in the first place.) It certainly no longer needed to bear its colonies' defense costs, because the world was becoming more open to trade in any event.

> The *French*, *Dutch*, and *Spaniards* have ships, which carry Masts, and require Pitch and Tar, Hemp, Iron, and Cordage as well as *English* ships. And happily for them, they have no Northern Colonies. Yet these Nations are supplied with all these Articles at a moderate price, and without Bounties. What therefore should prevent the *English* from being supplied from the same source, and on as good Terms?

If England were to lose its West Indies, it still could purchase its tropical supplies "at the best and cheapest market." Better yet, it might build up supplementary sources of supply.

> We should teach the much injured Natives of Africa, which might easily be done, and at a small Expence, to cultivate their own luxuriant and spontaneous Sugar Canes, and to manufacture Sugars, and several other Commodities, and more especially Rice and Indigo, in their own native Country; you would then exchange such Produce for our *European* goods and Manufactures:—Instead of this, we make Slaves of these poor Wretches, contrary to every Principle, not only of Humanity and Justice, but also of national Profit and Advantage ...[25]

Even if England did not promote raw materials production in such areas, it could rest assured that its vital supplies would not be cut off, and that it could buy in the cheapest market without being obliged to sustain overseas military and related colonial spending. The North American colonies had little choice but to

> send their Pitch and Tar, their Masts and Naval Stores ... to the *English* ... it is a Fact, that were we to withdraw our Bounties, it would be an exceeding difficult Matter for the Colonies to find any vent at all for these Articles.

Europe's colonial systems had outlived their usefulness. The military expenses attendant on England's overseas ventures, especially the costs of holding and defending its American colonies, prompted Tucker to make his famous complaint in 1783 that America "was a Milstone hanging about the Neck of this country, to weigh it down: And as we ourselves had not the Wisdom to cut the Rope, and to let the Burthen fall off, the *Americans* have kindly done it for us."[26]

Once England freed itself from the tax burden of having to support these projects of state, its commercial strength would secure the nation's position as workshop of the world. The locus of industrial power and the international distribution of money was becoming less a function of state projects than of private-sector competition. Free trade would earn gold and silver without the expense of colonialism and its wars. Natural market forces would achieve what princely fiat earlier had sought.

As Steuart put matters, the spread of trade and industry "owed their establishment to the ambition of princes, who supported and favoured the plan in the beginning, principally with a view to enrich themselves, and thereby to become formidable to their neighbours." But the spirit of the industry they fostered took on a life of its own:

---

[25] Tucker, *A Series of Answers*, pp. 34, 32, 21. See also pp. 38–39.
[26] Tucker, *Four Letters to Shelbourne on Important National Subjects* (London: 1783), pp. 7–8.

[A]n opulent, bold, and spirited people, having the fund of the prince's wealth in their own hands, have it also in their own power, when it becomes strongly their inclination, to shake off his authority. The consequence of this change has been the introduction of a more mild, and a more regular plan of administration …

When once a state begins to subsist by the consequences of industry, there is less danger to be apprehended from the power of the sovereign. The mechanism of his administration becomes more complex, and … he finds himself so bound up by the laws of his political oeconomy, that every transgression of them runs him into new difficulties.

I say, therefore, that from the time states have begun to be supported by the consequences of industry, the plan of administration had become more moderate; has been changing and refining by degrees.[27]

The result was that although "so powerful an influence over the operations of a whole people, vests an authority in a modern statesman, which was unknown in former ages, under the most absolute governments," yet "the sovereign power is extremely limited, as to every *arbitrary* exercise of it, and where, at the same time, that very power is found to operate over the wealth of the inhabitants, in a manner far more efficacious than the most despotic and arbitrary authority can possibly do …" Steuart concluded optimistically that

the legislative power is only exerted in acquiring an influence over the actions of individuals, in order to promote a scheme of political oeconomy … absolutely inconsistent with every arbitrary measure … it will at length come to resemble the watch, which is good for no other purpose than to mark the progression of time, and which is immediately destroyed, if put to any other use, or touched by any but the gentlest hand.[28]

This was a remarkable form of mercantilism indeed! Its new task was to explain the marketplace and its evolution. More broadly than today's economics, this political economy delved beneath the surface of supply and demand to deal with the laws of global development, in an epoch quite comfortable in believing that inequality was a normal characteristic of economic nature.

It was their forthrightness in acknowledging inequality and polarization dynamics that made these early political economists of Tucker's and Steuart's generation so repellent to subsequent liberals, in contrast to the happier writings of Hume. But as to the substance of their theorizing, they were as convinced as subsequent liberals that commercial restrictions and monopoly privileges had outlived their original aims. Henceforth, rising employment and investment would require their dismantling, just as pressure was growing to dissolve the legacy of medieval economic justice represented by usury laws and labor guilds.

---

[27] Steuart, *Principles of Political Oeconomy*, pp. 247ff. See also footnote 19 above for a similar statement.

[28] Steuart, *ibid.*, pp. 321–22.

The aim was for individualistic drives to serve the national interest without having to be directed any longer.

Mercantile economists had long advised the wealthy classes to eschew luxuries that did not contribute on balance to the nation's surplus-producing powers. Among the luxuries ultimately to be opposed was colonial empire, along with its associated commercial monopolies and military overhead, as well as the drive to remain self-sufficient in food behind protective tariff walls. Food, tea and other colonial products could be secured more efficiently through freer trade and a dismantling of colonial monopolies. Such monopolies, and the colonial systems associated with them, were perceived to be costly, rigid, inefficient, overbearing and riddled with corruption at the hands of the aristocracy and court favorites empowered to manage them. Anti-colonialist sentiment increased, while resentment grew against the East India Company for extorting high prices and blocking smaller merchants from participating in foreign trade and investment. Among the trading monopolies that came under special attack were those dealing in African slaves, a trade originally organized by the British and French governments largely to help pay off their national war debts, headed by the notorious South Sea and Mississippi Companies.

Led by the East and West India Companies of Holland, England and France, trading monopolies had been given exclusive trading rights as part of a bargain in which they were to bear the costs of defending their colonial regions. Their monopoly position obliged consumers to bear these costs indirectly, by paying higher prices for colonial goods. The alternatives were to pay higher domestic taxes to finance colonial military spending directly, or to tax the colonies to cover the expense of defending them. But taxing the domestic economy would have spurred a protest against colonialism, while taxing the colonies spurred rebellion, most notably in the North American response to England's Stamp Acts. Neither the colonies nor the mother countries wanted to bear these military costs. Anti-war and anti-tax liberals therefore aimed at greater transparency in order to mobilize opposition to military expansion, empire-building and its associated colonialism.

The liberal ideal was a cosmopolitan world economy with no inherent conflict among national interests. "The whole World as to Trade," wrote Dudley North in 1690, "is but one Nation or People, and therein Nations are as persons."[29] Adam Smith had described the drive for monetary gain as a universal instinct. The question was whether nations were to maneuver like individuals, within an existing status quo in a world they hardly could expect to change, or whether nations should exert active policy to shape markets so as to obtain the best advantage. Should they passively accept the existing array of productive powers, or seek to enhance these powers by public subsidies and tariffs?

[29]  Dudley North, *Discourses upon Trade* (London: 1691), p. viii.

The free-trade movement based its analysis of foreign commerce on the fact that production costs differed among countries. But instead of these cost differentials reflecting the government policies on which mercantilist writers had placed such emphasis, free traders attributed them to "nature" or "national genius" in the form of differing productivity of soils, mines and labor. Some countries (like some lands) were naturally suited to produce certain products. This focus on natural rather than political factors implied that productivity differences — and hence a specialization of production conforming to these differences — were as intrinsic as, say, differences in soil fertility.

Steuart had reminded his audience that "industry and labor are not properties attached to place, any more than oeconomy and sobriety." But free traders were unwilling to grant that princes and their advisors could lead their country well. This would have opened the gates to interference with market mechanisms of the sort that might have offset England's acquired advantages. So economic structures were taken as givens, and the political dimension of political economy was repressed. In this respect the globalist free-trade view was fatalistic rather than transformative. In rationalizing the status quo, liberalism became panglossian in its view that all was for the best in this best of all possible worlds. Opponents of state regulation shied away from analyzing differences in national policies and political institutions because their ideal world was one in which differences in trade policy would cease to exist. If all nations embraced laissez faire, they would dismantle their national regulatory and tariff apparatus.

Liberal political tendencies in most countries were leading to greater religious toleration, personal self-interest and freedom in general for the growing urban mercantile and industrial classes. Appealing to the universal principle of economic efficiency, liberals set to work dismantling government intervention in both international and domestic commerce. Their victory became complete when Britain repealed the last of its Corn Laws in 1846, and two years later the United States adopted a free-trade policy based on the assumption that it could obtain its industrial manufactures with least effort from Britain in exchange for its surplus crops, mainly plantation crops produced in the Southern slave states. Protectionist critics did not miss the irony: Slave production was accepted as part of the liberal view of national productivity differences that underlay Ricardo's postulated gains from free trade.

The emerging liberal view ignored the tendency for countries with the richest natural endowments to be associated with the widest disparities in wealth and income. Conversely, what initially appeared to be a regime of "natural" hardship, such as characterized the New England colonies, turned out to be an inducement to industrialization. This led to a more egalitarian prosperity than characterized mining and plantation economies. Only protectionists discussed how adverse monoculture trade patterns might shrink or distort the home market and deplete the soil. Subsequent free traders ignored the correlation between trade patterns and political-economic structure. They also ignored the impact of foreign trade *on* the evolution of productivity, save for the single example of trade offering wider markets for the division of labor to proceed.

Having passed from the Church into the hands of national governments, moralistic views of trade and society had given way to more worldly approaches that paid increasing attention to individual material welfare. Mercantilism's evolution into classical liberalism followed this trend, but claimed that government regulations no longer were needed to steer personal gain-seeking to serve the national interest in industrial growth. The long period of mercantilist incubation had achieved this.

Medieval Church doctrine described trade as increasing the prosperity and abundance of all nations together. Hume's Deist view asserted that no economies could long monopolize the gains from this trade, because of automatic adjustment mechanisms embedded in the way the world economy worked. Tucker and Steuart were free of the prejudice that the global economy was characterized by inherently egalitarian dynamics. Subsequent free traders cannot be said to have become more realistic in   accepting the view that private self-interest must coincide with national   interest. Something vital was lost in the process of insisting that laissez faire   would serve traditional social objectives and private business interests   simultaneously. Schumpeter has wisely remarked that as the "liberals" supplanted the "mercantilists" (his quotation marks),

> there was not only scrapping of outmoded error but also needless waste comparable to the waste that would result if successive teams of workmen smashed the products of their predecessors whenever they disliked the latter's politics. If Smith and his followers had refined and developed the "mercantilist" propositions instead of throwing them away, a much truer and much richer theory of international economic relations could have been developed by 1848 ...[30]

But such realism was not the objective of free traders. Smith and his followers were not merely being naive in ignoring the mercantilist points. Their abandonment of the most sophisticated mercantilist analysis served politically to avoid discussion of assumptions that would produce protectionist rather than free-trade policy conclusions for poorer countries. For the past two centuries, free traders have shied away from introducing productivity analysis or realistic capital-transfer theorizing into their discussions, or acknowledging international

---

[30]  Joseph Schumpeter, *History of Economic Analysis* (New York: 1954), p. 376. This is reminiscent of Kuhn's observation that intellectual revolutions inevitably involve a suppression of pre-revolutionary theorizing. Schumpeter seems to have been unfamiliar with Tucker's work at first hand, mentioning him only in passing in three scattered sentences.

movements of skilled and unskilled labor or capital. Viner goes so far as to imply censorially that the debate between Hume and Tucker was unfortunate for having touched on these issues at all! In the course of attempting to refute Hume's argument, he accuses, Tucker

> shifts unconsciously from a discussion of the effects on trade of more money to the effects of more wealth, and proceeds to a discussion of whether a rich country can compete successfully with a poor one, and Hume, in an unsatisfactory reply, himself follows this shift of issues.[31]

But what was "unsatisfactory"? The growing inequality among nations became the crux of the debate. It suggested that if poor countries refrained from protecting and actively steering their economic development, they would suffer a growing dependency and consequent loss of economic options—exactly what has happened in practice. To avoid coming to this conclusion, free-trade theory ever since has narrowed its scope to become a caricature of global reality.

Haberler is likewise one-sided in stating that "Mercantilism received its death-blow in 1752 when Hume published his *Political Discourses.*" As for his assertion that Hume's "classical theory ... was later refined and extended by Adam Smith, Thornton, Ricardo, Senior, John Stuart Mill, Cairnes, Bastable, Taussig, &c.,"[32] it would be more accurate to say that this line of theorizing became oversimplified and more narrow, as subsequent chapters of this book will demonstrate. The preceding chapter has described how mercantilists in the quarter-century following Hume's *Discourses* treated his full-employment "classical theory" as representing only a special case, as Hume acknowledged it to be. But free-trade theorists writing after the Napoleonic Wars ignored underemployment conditions. They assumed a fully employed economy operating at its limits, with no ability to draw in foreign skilled labor or capital.

Although diverging productivity and wage levels have characterized international development for many centuries now, free-trade orthodoxy since Hume and Smith has described convergence. And although labor and capital were becoming more mobile across international boundaries, subsequent free-trade orthodoxy presumed them to be immobile. This negated the idea of a "brain drain" of skilled labor or capital flight such as actually has occurred.

## Free trade as a strategy of English nationalism

Given the state of productive powers as they stood in 1776, and even more by 1815, pursuit of the principle of commercial self-interest in each country helped consolidate English economic supremacy. The nation's trade strategists therefore welcomed Adam Smith for defining national wealth as the sum of

[31]  Viner, *Studies*, p. 87.
[32]  Gottfried Haberler, *Theory of International Trade*, p. 26.

individual riches, and for advocating that a policy of laissez faire would leave individuals to pursue their own self-interest. His *Wealth of Nations*, published just a few months before the American Revolution, systematized liberal doctrines that had been gaining momentum since the 1690s.

Smith recognized that workers displaced by import competition might not readily find alternative employment. He conceded that national defense was more important than opulence, acknowledging the traditional argument for protectionism on grounds of national security and self-sufficiency. He also acknowledged that vested interests should be protected, retaliatory tariffs might be justified, and it might be wise to impose tariffs on articles that were taxed at home so as to ensure their continued production, sale and hence tax payments. As John Shield Nicholson observed in 1918,

> the present-day Free Trader will find in his Adam Smith a series of shocks and surprises. Instead of being cosmopolitan, Adam Smith was intensely nationalist, or rather Imperialist. This part of his work, after being entirely neglected, is now bearing fruit. Adam Smith wrote on the eve of the disruption of the British Empire by the severance of the North American colonies. He propounded as an alternative a great federation with a truly Imperial Parliament.[33]

It was above all the American Revolution that catalyzed Britain's evolution into the laissez faire phase of its world expansionism. For Britain, the problem became one of how to make colonial independence merely nominal, ending the nation's colonial overhead costs but not its export revenues and economic domination. Free trade enabled it to shed its obligations under *le pacte colonial*. When the American colonies gained their freedom, they lost their military subsidies from Britain, which easily retained the new United States as a market for its industrial manufactures. Seemingly natural economic bonds took the place of overt political trammels.

Under freer market relations, trade was conducted along basically the same lines of specialization that the old colonial systems had brought into being. Market forces induced citizens in the liberated colonies to produce the foodstuffs and raw materials they had been led to produce under England's trade and navigation acts. The legacy of colonial regulations, in conjunction with the sparsely populated condition of Europe's white colonies and the squalid plantation organization of its colored colonies, had nurtured a specialization of world labor and dependency that henceforth was maintained by market incentives alone. The New World, Africa and Asia became thriving agricultural or mining regions rather than industrial rivals to Europe—until the United States adopted protectionist policies after its Civil War.

---

[33] John Shield Nicholson, *War Finance* (London: 1918), 2nd ed, p. 416. On these points see George Crompton, *The Tariff: An Interpretation of a Bewildering Problem* (New York: 1927), p. 45, citing Smith, *The Wealth of Nations*, Book IV, ch. ii.

What was novel was the political-economic strategy by which the specialization of world labor was to be maintained. Britain abandoned its costly assertions of armed force, protective tariffs and navigation acts in favor of permitting the free play of personal and commercial self-interest in world markets. (Not until the 1870s did a new European scramble for colonies erupt.) Bernard Semmel's phrase "free-trade imperialism" is apt. Britain's objective in dismantling its colonial and commercial regulations was identical to that of its Old Colonial System, namely to maintain its status as workshop of the world while inducing its ex-colonies and other less developed regions to remain "hewers of wood and drawers of water."

While England built up its domestic industry after defeating France in 1763, France did just the opposite. Its Physiocrats held that only agriculture could create a *net produit*, an economic surplus. Industrial labor was deemed unproductive of such a surplus, subsisting off the bounty of agriculture created by nature working through the land. This doctrine, the opposite of mercantilism, led the French to sign the Eden Treaty with Britain in 1787, exporting crops and opening their markets to the products of British industry. It was an auspicious beginning for British confidence that free trade would promote its national interests.

Warfare between Britain and France lasted from 1793 through the end of the Napoleonic Wars in 1815. When the return to peace normalized foreign trade and caused widespread industrial distress outside of Britain, free-trade economists turned to the task of convincing less developed countries to join with Britain to dismantle tariff barriers.

Free trade obviously could not be defended by the nationalistic arguments that earlier had been directed to the British public. An exploitative theory of free-trade imperialism hardly would inspire the rest of the world to adopt laissez faire. A new generation of economic writers emerged, led by David Ricardo, claiming that all countries would gain equitably from freer trade, at least collectively if not individually. They held that as far as the wealth of nations was concerned, it made no difference whether countries industrialized or produced raw materials. Britain had chosen to industrialize, but other countries could maximize their incomes by providing it with raw materials—and thereby avoid the urban squalor that Britain had to endure the process of becoming an industrial economy. All countries were supposed to enrich themselves and each other under a regime of free trade. It was assumed that the gains from trade would be shared equitably, although no real attempt was made to empirically verify or quantify this assumption.

Francis Horner, a liberal Whig member of Parliament sympathetic to Lauderdale's criticism of Smith's doctrine of the invisible hand equating public and private interests, thought it prudent to keep his qualms to himself: "I should be reluctant to expose Smith's errors," he wrote to a friend, before his work has operated its full effect. We owe much at present to the superstitious worship of Smith's name; and we must not impair that feeling, till the victory is more complete. There are few practical errors in the "Wealth of Nations," at least of any great consequence; and, until we can give a correct and precise theory of the nature and origin of wealth, his popular and plausible and loose hypothesis is as good for the vulgar as any other.[34]

What was wanted no longer was an argument showing how international free trade worked to England's advantage. The new aim was to show its advantage for the less developed trading partners. Soon these countries would vie with one another to supply England with raw materials, and also with their money. Britain emerged as the world's preeminent industrial producer, merchant and banker. The lineaments of world control became its army of manufacturers and traders, securing commercial supremacy by means of individual self-interest.

At any given moment, merchants throughout the world found their self-interest to lie in trading in accordance with the self-endowment and head start England had secured under its earlier colonial system. As the Ricardian popularizer John Ramsay McCulloch emphasized:

> Our establishments for spinning, weaving, printing, bleaching, &c., are infinitely more complete and perfect than that exist elsewhere; the division of labour in them is carried to an incomparably greater extent; the workmen are trained from infancy to industrious habits. … Why, then, having all these advantages on our side, should we not keep the start we have gained? Every other people that attempt to set up manufactures must obviously labour under the greatest difficulties, as compared with us. Their establishments can not, at first, be sufficiently large to enable the division of employments to be carried to any considerable extent; at the same time that expertness in manipulation, and in the details of the various processes, can only be attained by slow degrees. It appears, therefore, reasonable to conclude, that such new beginners, having to withstand the competition of those who have already arrived at a very high perfection in the art, must be immediately driven out of every market equally accessible to both parties; and that nothing but the aid derived from restrictive regulations and prohibitions, will be effectual to prevent the total destruction of their establishments.[35]

This statement by a free-trader is striking confirmation of the polarization mechanisms that Tucker and Steuart described. But its free-trade conclusion for Britain had protectionist implications for less developed countries. As Steuart had put matters:

---

[34]   Francis Horner, *Memoirs and Correspondence* (London: 1843). Vol. I, p. 229.
[35]   John Ramsay McCulloch, *Commercial Dictionary* (London: 1830), quoted in Calvin Colton, *Public Economy for the United States* (New York: 1848), pp. 93–94.

Mankind daily profit by experience, and acquire knowledge at their own cost. We have said that what lays the foundation of foreign trade, is the ease and conveniency which strangers find in having their wants supplied by those who have set industry on foot. The natural consequence of this foreign demand is to bring in wealth, and to promote augmentations of every kind. As long as these go on, it will be impossible for other nations to rival the traders, because their situation is every day growing better: dexterity increasing, diminishes the price of work; every circumstance, in short, becomes more favourable; the balance never vibrates, but by one of the scales growing positively heavier, and it is constantly coming even by an increase of weight on the other side.[36]

In other words, every economic imbalance set in motion countervailing forces.

Having endowed England with the world's preeminent manufacturing plant, the nation's protectionism had run its course. If England kept its own markets closed, how could it expect other countries to open their markets to its exports? As the parliamentary architect of English free trade, William Huskisson, summarized the issue in 1826:

If the system of discriminating Duties for the encouragement of Shipping, were a secret known to this country alone; if a similar system were not, or could not be, put in force in every other country, I should not be standing here to vindicate the measure to which I have just referred, and the present policy of his Majesty's Government … But is this the present state of the world? Did the United States of America, in the first instance, for the purpose of raising to themselves a great commercial Marine, and of counteracting our Navigation Laws, adopt, in their utmost rigour, the rules of those laws, and carry, even further than we had ever done, in respect to foreign Ships, this principle of discriminating duties against our Shipping? Can we shut our eyes to the fact that other nations have followed, or are following their example? Do we not see them, one after the other, taking a leaf out of our own book? Is not every Government in Europe, if possessed of sea-ports, now using its utmost endeavours to force a trade, and to raise up for itself a commercial Marine? Have we not boasted of our Navigation Laws, till we have taught other nations to believe (however erroneous that belief), that they are almost the only requisite, or, at least, the *sine qua non*, of commercial wealth and of maritime power? Did these vauntings excite no envy, no spirit of rivalry, no countervailing opposition in other countries? Did the success of the United States of America create no desire in those countries to follow her example?

Under what circumstances did England found her Navigation System? When her commercial Marine was, comparatively, insignificant, her wealth inconsiderable, before manufactures were established, and when she exported corn, wool, and other raw materials. When, on the other hand, Holland and the Netherlands were rich, possessed of great manufactures, and of the largest portion of the

[36] Steuart, *Principles of Political Oeconomy*, p. 232.

carrying trade of Europe and the world. What has followed? The commercial
Marine of the latter countries has dwindled away, and that of Great Britain is now
immense. But, in the progress of the change, England is become the great seat
of manufactures and trading wealth, frequently importing, and never exporting,
corn; drawing raw materials from, and sending out manufactured goods to, all
parts of the world. This was our state, though in a far less degree than at present,
when America became independent. She started by applying towards us the system, which we had applied towards Holland. She was then poor, with a very
small commercial Marine, without manufactures, having corn and raw materials
to export;—and we know what her shipping now is. Let Gentlemen reflect on
these circumstances, before they decide that it is necessarily wise to center upon
a similar contest with other poor and unmanufacturing countries. Let them seriously consider whether a system of discriminating duties,—now that the exclusive
*patent* by which we held that system is expired,—is not the expedient of such a
country as I have described, rather than the resource of one which already
possesses the largest commercial Marine in the world. They will then see, that it
may possibly be a wise policy to divert such countries from that system, rather
than to goad them on, or even leave them a pretext for going into it.[37]

This perception pressed the old mercantilism to a new phase. England
might augment its power by economic rather than military methods, appealing
to market forces rather than using overt political control. Its trade surplus and
the associated monetary inflows increased domestic employment, population,
immigration, investment, productivity and output. England absorbed a rising
portion of the world's gold, skilled labor and capital, and became the world's
major banker and foreign investor—and in the 1880s the leading neo-colonialist
power in Africa and Asia.

The nationalistic ideal of British free trade, like that of earlier mercantilism, held that strong economies would grow stronger while poor countries
would become more dependent. This view was epitomized during the Corn Law
debates in 1846, when (as Semmel quotes), "one Whig, speaking before the
House of Commons ... described free trade as the beneficent 'principle' by
which 'foreign nations would become valuable Colonies to us, without imposing
on us the responsibility of governing them.'" All that was necessary was for
England to repeal its Corn Laws "to create a vast English market for foreign
grain; in this way, the agricultural nations of the world might be given a stake in
England's Empire of Free Trade."[38]

[37] William Huskisson, "Exposition of the State of the Navigation of the United Kingdom"
(May 12. 1826), in *The Speeches of the Right Honourable William Huskisson* (London: 1831),
Vol. III, pp. 29–32.
[38] Bernard Semmel, *The Rise of Free Trade Imperialism*, pp. 8, 205. quoting *Parliamentary Debates*,
3rd Series, LXXXIII (February 23, 1846), pp. 1399–1400.

This is the kind of admission—almost a secret knowledge—that subsequent free traders have been eager to forget. The British economist Lionel Robbins, to be sure, acknowledged that free trade first emerged as a national rather than cosmopolitan economic strategy, and finds little evidence that the classical economists

> went beyond the test of national advantage as a criterion of policy, still less that they were prepared to contemplate the dissolution of national bonds. If you examine the ground on which they recommended free trade, you will find that it is always in terms of a more productive use of national resources. ... I find no trace anywhere in their writings of the vague cosmopolitanism with which they are often credited by continental writers. I do not claim this as a virtue—or as a deficiency; the question of the extent to which, at the stage of history, it was incumbent on political thinkers to transcend the ideas and the criteria of the nation-state is a matter of great difficulty. All that I contend is that we get our picture wrong if we suppose that the English Classical Economists would have recommended, because it was good for the world at large, a measure which they thought would be harmful to their own community.[39]

In other words, increasing the world's wealth as a whole does not necessarily increase that of each national part. The economics discipline thus has come a long way from Adam Smith's idea of personal gain as representing that of the economy as a whole—or one nation's wealth as increasing that of the whole world accordingly.

Most of the technical concepts and comparative-cost mechanisms discussed in Part II of this book tend to endorse passive free trade rather than protectionist policy. Ricardo and his followers constructed their logic in such a way as to imply a natural international tendency toward convergence. More realistic perceptions dating from mercantilist times easily convert these assumptions into polarization dynamics in the international economy.

---

[39]  Lionel Robbins, *The Theory of Economic Policy* (London: 1952), pp. 10ff.

# PART II

## The Creation and Division of World Product and Income

Cecily:     That certainly seems a satisfactory explanation, does it not?

Gwendolyn: Yes, dear, if you can believe him.

Cecily:     I don't. But that doesn't affect the wonderful beauty of his answer.

Oscar Wilde, *The Importance of Being Ernest*, Act III

# 5

## Comparative Costs and the Gains from Trade

As Chapter 1 has reviewed, Richard of Middleton in the thirteenth century described gains from trade based on the relative cheapness of importing specific products from abroad. Where these products were cheaper, he attributed their low price to their greater abundance in their country of origin. The causes of a country's superior cost efficiency hardly could be analyzed more deeply at a time when labor was not yet a homogeneous common denominator from town to town or between town and country. Production costs—and hence, a theory of value and price formation—could not be standardized as long as feudal society was divided into separate localities, each possessing its own distinct set of taxes, rents and prices. Economic life had to become more fluid and national in scope before common denominators such as labor time and productivity could be abstracted from the maze of local variations in wages and guild regulations, land tenure, living costs and profits.

### Cost value, political institutions and the specialization of labor

Gradually, economists developed a more refined theory of value reducible to commodities' labor content and other common costs. In 1662, William Petty illustrated his labor theory of value by describing the exchange of gold and silver for other commodities. In an example that referred explicitly to relative international costs, his *Treatise on Taxes and Contributions* explained that English grain

> is worth ... so much as the money which another single man can save, within the same time, over and above his expence, if he imployed himself wholly to produce and make it; *viz.* Let another man go travel to a Countrey where is Silver, there Dig it, Refine it, bring it to the same place where the other man planted his Corn; Coyn it, &c. the same person, all the while of his working for Silver, gathering also food for his necessary livelihood, and procuring himself covering, etc. I say, the Silver of the one, must be esteemed of equal value with the Corn of the other: the one being perhaps twenty ounces and the other twenty Bushels. From whence it follows, that the price of a Bushel of this Corn to be an Ounce of Silver ... If a man can bring to London an ounce of Silver out of the Earth in Peru, in the same time that he can produce a bushel of Corn, then one is the

natural price of the other; now if by reason of new and more easie Mines a man can get two ounces of Silver as easily as formerly he did one, then Corn will be as cheap at ten shillings the bushel, as it was before at five shillings *caeteris paribus*.[1]

This elaborated the medieval concept of Just Price by viewing the value of commodities as proportional to their labor content, assuming corn-growing labor to be on a par with silver-mining labor. In an epoch when food typically absorbed about half the average worker's income, the value of labor reflected the price of subsistence. Cantillon sought to integrate a land-productivity and labor-time concept of value based largely on agricultural productivity. From country to country, commodities had varying coefficients in the amounts of labor and land needed for their production.

> The Land is the Source or Matter from whence all Wealth is produced. The Labour of man is the Form which produces it …
>
> One Acre of Land produces more Corn or feeds more Sheep than another. The work of one man is dearer that that of another … according to the superior Skill and Occurrences of the Times.
>
> … the Price or intrinsic value of a thing is the measure of the quantity of Land and of Labour entering into its production, having regard to the fertility or produce of the Land and to the quality of the Labour.
>
> But it often happens that many things which have actually this intrinsic value are not sold in the Market according to that value: that will depend on the Humours and Fancies of men and on their consumption.
>
> There is never a variation in intrinsic values, but the impossibility of proportioning the production of merchandise and produce in a State to their consumption causes a daily variation, and a perpetual ebb and flow in Market Prices …
>
> Land is the matter and Labour the form of all produce and Merchandise, and as those who labour must subsist on the produce of the Land it seems that some relation might be found between the value of Labour and that of the produce of the Land …
>
> … the Labour of the meanest Peasant … is worth double the produce of the Land which serves to maintain him (but) this varies according to the mode of living in different countries. In some southern provinces of France the Peasant keeps himself on the produce of one acre and a half of Land and the value of his Labor may be reckoned equal to the product of Three Acres. But in the Country of Middlesex the Peasant usually spends the produce of 5 to 8 acres of Land and his Labor may be valued as twice as much as this.
>
> Sir Wm. Petty … considers this Par, or Equation between Land and Labour, as the most important consideration in Political Arithmetic …
>
> … the real value of everything used by man is proportionable to the quantity of Land used for its production and for the upkeep of those who have fashioned it …

---

[1] *The Economic Writings of Sir William Petty*, ed. C. H. Hull (Cambridge: 1899), Vol. I, p. 43.

It is clear that the quantity of Produce or of Merchandise offered for sale, in proportion to the demand or number of Buyers, is the basis on which is fixed or always supposed to be fixed the actual Market Prices; and that in general these prices do not vary much from the intrinsic value.[2]

Henry Higgs, Cantillon's modern translator, comments that the theory "reminds us at once of the phrase 'land and labour of the country' upon which Adam Smith is so frequently harping. Yet it holds the balance between the elements of production more evenly than almost any subsequent treatise."[3] The Physiocrat François Quesnay emphasized the land element of value, Smith the labor element, but Cantillon integrated both.

Long before Ricardo, economic writers recognized that nations with the most productive land or labor were able to exchange their products for those embodying relatively more land or labor of other countries. "When a state exchanges a small product of land for a larger in Foreign Trade, it seems to have the advantage,"[4] wrote Cantillon. This implied a productivity theory of pricing based on differing labor, land and mine productivity among countries.

Implicitly, the exporting country with the lowest costs would tend to establish a product's international price. Again, the monetary metals were taken as paradigmatic. "Money will be most plentiful," wrote Vanderlint, "where the Mines are: ... Gold and Silver will as certainly be less valuable where the Mines are, then at any other Place which is supplied with those Metals by them ..."[5] The mining countries would export their surplus bullion in exchange for foreign manufactures, just as agricultural countries exported the products of their land and rural labor. Also implicitly, international prices depended on supply and demand.

Innovations that reduced the cost of supporting workers or increased their productivity tended to lower the cost of producing exports, and hence of obtaining imports. These innovations included political institutions. Vanderlint in 1734, for instance, urged England to extend its agricultural enclosures so as to reduce land rents and hence food costs and wage levels:

> All Things, that are in the World, are the Produce of the Ground originally. ... The more Land therefore shall be improved and cultivated, &c. the greater will the Plenty of all Things be ... which will make the Price of the Labour of Working People much lower; for the Rates of labour are always settled and constituted of the Price of Victuals and Drink: And all Manufactures will be vastly cheaper;

---

[2] Cantillon, *Essay on the Nature of Trade in General* [1755], translated by Henry Higgs (London: 1931), pp. 3, 27, 29, 31, 39, 43, 115, 119; *viz.* Petty's famous passage in his 1662 *Treatise of Taxes* that "labour is the father and active principle of wealth, as lands are the mother" (cited in Higgs' essay in Cantillon, p. 343).

[3] Cantillon, *ibid.*, p. 343.              [4] Cantillon, *ibid.*, p. 227.

[5] Vanderlint, *Money Answers All Things*, p. 3.

for the Value of all Manufactures is chiefly constituted of the Price or Charge
of the Labour bestowed thereon. ... the Price of Labour is always constituted of
the Price of Necessaries, and the Price of all other Things chiefly of the Price
of Labour.[6]

Vanderlint concluded that labor's power to create profits for its employer
and for the national economy as a whole "will be greater, when the Necessities
of Life are so much cheaper, that a fourth Part less Wages will purchase near
half as many more Necessaries as the present Rates of Labour will do."[7] This
seemed to be near the maximum degree of improvement possible by extending
Britain's enclosures.

Recognition that political and social institutions affected prices and the
size of the net surplus led to early discussions of the virtues of the republican
relative to monarchical forms of government, of free relative to slave societies,
and of industrial states relative to more socially rigidified plantation economies
and raw-materials exporters.

There was general agreement that specialization would give countries an
opportunity to economize on resource allocation. Industrial England sought a
division of world labor that would provide opportunities for it to import raw
materials in exchange for its manufactures. As the preceding chapters have shown,
its mercantilists not only endorsed the international specialization of labor, *they
hoped to bring about an increasing dissimilarity of economic structure and specialization
patterns among nations* in a way that would increase England's opportunities to gain
from its foreign trade. The Industrial Revolution greatly intensified this idea.

### The return to peace after the Napoleonic Wars spurs a tariff debate

The more severe the war, the more serious will be the postwar adjustment.
Commercial isolation during periods of hostility nurtures domestic self-reliance,
creating vested interests which, upon the return to peace, seek to retain their
home market. But not since medieval times was economic isolation as pronounced as the twenty-one year struggle between England and France during
1793–1814.

In 1806, Napoleon imposed the Continental System to blockade Britain,
prohibit the importation of British goods into French-controlled ports, and to
exclude from these ports any neutral-country ships that had landed in Britain.
England retaliated with Orders of Council that rendered all vessels trading with
France liable to seizure, Napoleon responded with his Milan Decree forbadding
neutrals to trade in any articles imported from the British Empire.

---

[6]   Vanderlint, *ibid.*, pp. 6–9, 15.          [7]   Vanderlint, *ibid.*, p. 87.

This interruption of trade obliged England to increase agricultural production to meet domestic needs. The rise in food costs was aggravated by a number of crop failures that almost doubled grain prices between 1804 and 1813. After the Treaty of Ghent ended hostilities in December 1814, England's landed aristocracy used its control of Parliament to keep the domestic market for itself at the high wartime level of grain prices. New Corn Laws forbid grain imports if the price of home-grown wheat sank below a given target level. Riots broke out in London, and the industrial and commercial classes sponsored parliamentary reform to wrest political control from the aristocracy. The ensuing Corn Law debate pit free-trade industrialists against landowners.

A mirror-image struggle was waged abroad, where the positions of agriculture and industry were reversed. Overseas manufacturers became the protectionist counterpart to England's landlord class, demanding tariff barriers to enable them to charge prices high enough to protect their industries. Agricultural interests (in the majority in all countries) fought to block these tariffs, hoping to buy less costly English manufactures. The upshot was that high-cost producers— agriculturalists in England, industrialists abroad—argued for tariff protection of their home markets, while low-cost producers—industry in England, farmers abroad—urged free trade so as to buy products in the cheapest market.

Each country was obliged to choose whether its trade policy would support agriculture or industry, ushering in a new form of domestic conflict. Under mercantilism the agricultural and industrial classes had spoken of a harmony of interest inasmuch as they afforded reciprocal markets for each other's output. Only after 1815 did they become set against each other over trade policy and its implications for food costs, wage levels, industrial pricing and general industrial competitiveness.

English free traders pointed to how much more cheaply the nation could obtain its grain abroad and therefore feed its labor, enabling its manufacturers to underselling those of foreign countries. As a Member of Parliament, the stockbroker Ricardo took the lead in demonstrating the potential gains England could reap from free trade by exporting textiles in exchange for foreign lower-cost wheat. Other countries likewise could save by depending on England for manufactures rather than on their own high-cost factories. Both British and foreign free traders thus argued for England to become and remain the workshop of the world. Shipping and banking interests also endorsed free trade, especially along the seacoasts and border areas.

England's agricultural protectionists were led by Thomas Robert Malthus, who emphasized the importance of domestic demand by landlords in sustaining a market for industrial output. His argument anticipated that of John Maynard Keynes's 1936 *General Theory* by shifting the focus from inherent costs of production to market (*i.e.*, money) demand. In the United States, industrial advocates described how a thriving urban labor force might provide a home market for domestic farmers so that they need not depend on England for sale of their crops. However, British manufacturers set their sights on foreign rather than domestic sources of demand, as did farmers in the United States and other countries. But for a generation, foreign industrialists were not as successful as English landlords in protecting their markets from a flood of imports.

### International economics and domestic value theory

Analysis of how international prices and the terms of trade evolve over time rests on ideas of how domestic economies function. Trade theory is *logically* presented as a product of domestic relationships. What is ironic is the degree to which theories of how the domestic economy works have been inspired largely by their implications for tariff policy. This may seem to be a case of the tail wagging the dog, but the great debates over value, price and rent theory, as well as monetary theory, have stemmed from the application of these theories to international trade policy. The quantity theory of money was first popularized in its application to international trade, playing a key role in Hume's price-specie flow mechanism. Similarly, in the decades leading up to 1846 the tariff controversy was the major domestic economic and political issue.

The debate over England's protectionist Corn Laws spurred the controversy waged between Malthus and Ricardo over the theory of value and rent. The class conflict between agriculture and industry in almost every country became even more intense than the monetary struggle between creditors and debtors—and the latter conflict itself resulted largely from the financial convulsions following the return to peace as wartime inflations gave way to postwar deflations.

Ricardo elaborated his theory of comparative advantage in the seventh and final theoretical core chapter of his *Principles of Political Economy and Taxation*, published in 1817. His trade model was built on his theories of value and price, rent, wages and profits, which he presented first in the relative straightforwardness of a closed economy before applying them to foreign trade. But it was the tariff debate that inspired his basic concepts. Protectionists likewise presented their tariff policy conclusions as following from the concepts of productivity, social utility and rent that backed up their theory of national development.

Opposition between protectionist and free-trade theories ultimately reflected differing views of the domestic economy, and especially whether economies were characterized by increasing or diminishing returns. Free traders assumed diminishing returns, while protectionists (in good mercantilist tradition) assumed increasing returns to be the norm. The analysis also turned on rent and tax theory as the struggle over England's Corn Laws became an occasion to explain the theory of the excess of price over production costs ("value," including normal profit). This theory was formulated almost simultaneously in five pamphlets published in February 1815, two by Malthus, the others by Ricardo, Edward West and Robert Torrens.[8]

Agricultural and industrial parties both in England and abroad defended their tariff views by pointing to the implications for national development. Their arguments ranged afield to cover broad cultural issues. Opponents of industrial tariffs juxtaposed the idyllic character of rural life to what they considered to be the decadence of crowded urban industry. Aristocratic British writers reflected nostalgically on the ordered society of feudalism in a romanticism replete with traditions of a free yeomanry. In the United States, Jeffersonian democracy viewed agriculture as the bulwark of political freedom—with Jefferson himself spearheading the Louisiana Purchase to extend plantation cultivation westward. Industrial advocates saw an agricultural destiny as being synonymous with maintenance of slavery, provincialism and soil depletion resulting from plantation monocultures "mining the soil." Advocates of protective tariffs and free trade alike thus discussed the cultural, moral and social consequences of balanced industrial development as compared to that of an agricultural destiny.

### Arguments of the tariff debate, 1815–1848

Ricardo analyzed the price England would have to pay to maintain agricultural self-sufficiency if it did not open its markets to foreign grain. A growing population would require more food, necessitating recourse to poorer and less accessible soils, largely through further enclosure of wastes and common lands. The higher cost of production on these marginal lands would push up food prices, creating superprofits—economic rents in the technical sense of the term—for landlords on richer and more accessible soils. Assuming real wages to remain near subsistence levels, Ricardo's distribution model juxtaposed industrial profits to agricultural rents. Employers would have to increase wages

[8]  For a discussion of Ricardian economics in its political setting, see Wesley Clair Mitchell, *Types of Economic Theory* (New York: 1967), and Edwin Cannan, *History of Theories of Production and Distribution in English Political Economy, from 1776 to 1848* (London: 1917), as well as his subsequent *Review of Economic Theory* (London: 1929).
The literature on England's Corn Law debates is immense. Good general reviews are C. R. Fay, *The Corn Laws and Social England* (Cambridge: 1932) and Donald G. Barnes, *History of the English Corn Laws from 1660–1846* (London: 1930), as well as the comprehensive report issued by the Office of the Society for the Protection of Agriculture and British Industry, *The Battle for Native Industry: The Debate upon the Corn Law ... and other Financial Measures of the Government, in Session 1846. Reprinted from "Hansard's Parliamentary Debates* (London: 1848), 2 volumes.

to cover the rising price of subsistence, pricing the nation's manufacturers out of world markets as high domestic food prices transferred income to landlords. The economy would grind to a halt as countries with lower food prices undersold English producers. But under a regime of free commerce and low-priced grain imports, the world's industrial markets seemed to be England's for the taking.

Agricultural protectionists in Britain, like their industrial counterparts in America, concentrated on the conditions necessary to realize increasing returns. Malthus argued that the Corn Laws enabled landlords to increase their investment in agriculture, raising productivity and thereby bringing down food prices. This reflected the realities of Europe's agricultural revolution. In fact, the theory of economic rent was first put forth in 1777 by the Scottish agriculturalist James Anderson specifically in reference to increasing returns. In assuming diminishing returns, Ricardian free-trade doctrine was based on a more pessimistic analysis that degenerated into what Thomas Carlyle called the Dismal Science because it closed its eyes to the prospect of technological or institutional progress altering comparative-cost ratios. Free traders focus on prices and income distribution under existing conditions of production, not how to improve productivity ratios. This analytic framework is called comparative statics because it takes for granted the existing state of productive powers. The result is a model of how to distribute a fixed level of output and income, not how to produce a growing stream.

Assuming cost structures to be inherent and presumably permanent, the Ricardians asked what the benefits of free trade were for each country, as opposed to the costs of protective tariffs. The answer was to measure how much more labor England would have to use to produce its own grain, as compared to the labor needed to export industrial manufactures in exchange for foreign wheat. In America, agricultural interests inverted this question: How much more would they have to pay for products of domestic industry than for similar goods from England?

Protectionists urged a more long-term frame of reference. Like the mercantilists, they focused on increasing productive powers by tariffs and internal improvements. Also like the mercantilists, they presented their policy as benefiting all classes—industry and agriculture, labor and capital alike, whereas free-trade policies set these classes at odds. This harmony-of-interest approach explains why most socialists disdained the protectionists as spokesmen for industrial capital, despite their common advocacy of government intervention in economic life.

Although England's industrial and commercial classes were radical in challenging the control of politics by the landed aristocracy and its groundrent, they adopted static technological models while the more conservative landed aristocracy framed the tariff debate in a more dynamic setting. This striking contrast is explained by the fact that agricultural protectionists were eager to show that farm productivity was increasing as a result of investment in the land—and later in the 19th century, the application of the fertilizers and chemicals that were beginning to be marketed on a large scale. To undertake such investment, agriculturalists had to earn enough income to recoup their costs, and this required protective tariffs. By contrast, free traders assumed that the productivity of English land was fixed, and insisted that neither capital improvements nor artificial fertilizers could alter intrinsic soil fertility. Ricardo's facile assumption that soil fertility was inherent and permanent rather than requiring constant care and crop rotation gives an indication of the kind of farmer he would have made had he himself been obliged to relocate to the land. The Ricardians refused to acknowledge that tariff-supported incomes might finance investment in agricultural capital which, over time, might increase productivity and provide England with lower-cost food. They reasoned as if money paid for tariffs vanished into thin air rather than being invested or spent on public infrastructure—or used to cut other taxes. To have acknowledged that tariff-protected or public-financed investment could increase productivity would have opened the door to endorsing protectionism.

America's industrial protectionists hoped to use tariff proceeds to build roads and canals, schools and other internal improvements. Over time, they believed, tariffs and higher industrial incomes would reduce production costs for infant industries to those of England, and ultimately even to undersell its producers. Led by Mathew and Henry Carey, American protectionists developed a doctrine of class harmony to show that supporting urban industry would create a home market for farmers. By contrast, free trade and its consequent specialization of production was described as impairing farm productivity. By the 1840s and 1850s protectionists in the U.S. Patent Office were quantifying how export-oriented agriculture led to soil depletion and calculated its environmental costs. By focusing on the growth or impairment of productivity, and by emphasizing potential rather than present cost structures, protectionists stressed the opportunity to reduce costs, given sufficient investment in new technology behind the price umbrella of protective tariffs.

Assuming each country's productivity rates to be fixed, Ricardo's model demonstrates that when commodities can be produced less expensively in one country than others, each country's advantage lies in depending on others to produce whatever they can make with the greatest *relative* cost advantage. In contrast to mercantilist concerns with "favorable" and "unfavorable" trade and specialization patterns, free-trade *doctrine* implies that nations *should* live in the short run and follow the dictates of international cost differentials as they exist at any given moment in time rather than erecting trade barriers. Protectionists reply that this strands poor countries in low-productivity pursuits and leads to worsening terms of trade and deepening international dependency.

### The methodology of comparative-cost doctrine

Ricardo illustrated his model of comparative costs with a hypothetical example of English cloth exchanging for Portuguese wine. Emphasizing that comparative advantage was a function of *relative* rather than absolute costs, he patronizingly assumed for illustrative purposes that Portugal had an absolute cost advantage in producing both industrial and agricultural goods, making both cloth and wine with less labor per unit of output than England could. However, Portugal had a *relatively greater* advantage in producing wine. It therefore could improve its position by trading.

> Under a system of perfectly free commerce, each country naturally devotes its capital and labor to such employments as are most beneficial to each. This pursuit of individual advantage is admirably connected with the universal good of the whole. By stimulating industry, by rewarding ingenuity, and by using most efficaciously the peculiar powers bestowed by nature, it distributes labor most effectively and most economically. ... It is this principle which determines that wine shall be made in France and Portugal, that corn shall be grown in America and Poland, and that hardware and other goods shall be manufactured in England.[9]

Ricardo's example of the labor costs of producing cloth and wine in England and Portugal is as follows:

|  | Man-hours of work | | Domestic price ratios | |
|---|---|---|---|---|
|  | per gallon of wine | per yard of cloth | wine to cloth (gallon per yard) | cloth to wine (yard per gallon) |
| England | 120 | 100 | 1.20 | 0.83 |
| Portugal | 80 | 90 | 0.80 | 1.12 |

|  | Output per 100 man-hours | | |
|---|---|---|---|
|  | wine | cloth | difference |
| England | 0.83 | 1.00 | 0.17 cloth |
| Portugal | 1.25 | 1.11 | 014 wine |

[9]  Ricardo, *Principles of Political Economy and Taxation*, ch. vii (*Works*, Vol. I), pp. 133–34. For a review of the nature and origin of the doctrine of comparative advantage see Viner, *Studies in the Theory of International Trade*, chapter viii, and Schumpeter, *History of Economic Analysis*, pp. 373-74. Underlying Ricardo's theory of international exchange is his labor theory of value: Exports exchange in proportion to their (marginal) manhour costs of production, including the labor embodied in the capital consumed in their production.

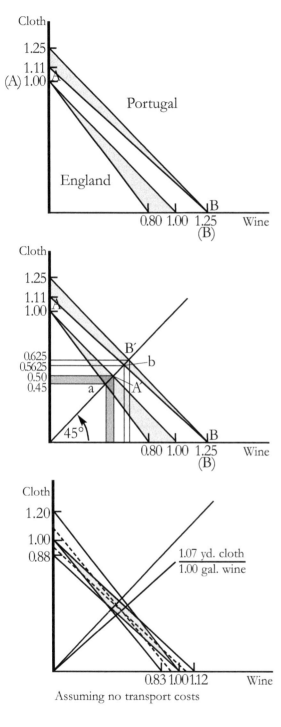

Fig. 5.1: Ricardo's Example of Comparative Costs

Ricardo assumed that England and Portugal were merely two nations in a world of many nations, so that shifts in their output and trade did not affect world prices. For illustrative purposes he assumed that a gallon of wine exchanged for a yard of cloth. Given England's and Portugal's linear cost functions (neither increasing nor diminishing returns), and assuming full domestic mobility of labor and capital between cloth-making and wine-making, it will pay England to specialize in producing cloth (position A on the cloth axis in Fig. 5.1) and Portugal to specialize in wine (position B on the wine axis).

To quantify the improvement in England's and Portugal's positions after specializing in production, the ratios at which wine is consumed relative to cloth must be specified. Assuming "wine" (representing agricultural products) and "cloth" (signifying industrial manufactures) to be consumed in equal proportions, England will improve its position by shifting its production patterns from *a* to *A* (that is, producing all cloth and no wine) and then trading for the wine it no longer produces (*A'*). It will use its 100 manhours to produce one yard of cloth and will trade half a yard for half a gallon of Portuguese wine, rather than producing the 0.45 yard of cloth and 0.45 gallons of wine that represents its domestic output in the absence of trade. England thus gains the equivalent of 12 manhours of labor that it would need to produce the additional 0.05 gallon of wine and 0.05 yard of cloth domestically.

Portugal will shift its production pattern to produce all wine and no cloth, and will trade its surplus wine to buy cloth (reaching position B'). In Ricardo's example it uses its 100 manhours to produce 1.25 gallons of wine. It could, of course, trade all this wine for cloth. But inasmuch as it consumes agricultural and industrial products in equal proportions, it will trade only half its wine (0.625, or ⅝ of a gallon) for ⅝ of a yard of cloth (vs. the 9⁄16, or 0.5625 gallon wine and 9⁄16 yard of cloth it could have produced of the absence in trade). Its net gain by moving from *b* to *B* to *B'* is thus 1⁄16 gallon of wine and 1⁄16 yard of cloth.

As long as England can buy a gallon of wine for less than 1.2 yards of cloth, it will do so. As long as Portugal can buy a yard of cloth for less than 1.12 gallons of wine, it will do so, up to the limit of its specified consumption ratio. The price at which wine will exchange for cloth must fall within the trade-off lines of $\frac{1.00 \text{ yard cloth}}{0.83 \text{ gallon wine}}$ for England, and $\frac{0.8 \text{ yard cloth}}{1.0 \text{ gallon wine}}$ for Portugal. Ricardo did not say just where the international price would settle. His example of a gallon of wine exchanging for a yard of cloth slightly favored England but was roughly equitable for the two trading countries. (Dividing 1.20 by 1.12 yields 1.07 yard of cloth for each gallon of wine as an equal gain-sharing price.)

Ricardo did not note that the 12 manhour equivalents Britain gained in his example were twice the amount gained by Portugal. All he tried to show was that each trading party could achieve *some* improvement by the price settling anywhere between the two countries' cost lines. The international counterpart to Ricardo's concept of rentless lands would be a country trading on its own comparative-cost line. In this case there would be no gain from trade. There also would be no gain if all countries had identical cost *ratios*, although not necessarily identical absolute costs. Only if Portugal or other countries exchange goods at exactly the same comparative-cost ratios as those of their own domestic production would their after-trade position show no net improvement. This means that the more widespread technology becomes, the lower the gains from trade will be. The greater the disparity in domestic production costs among countries, the larger will be their potential improvement in consumption levels through trade.

This implies what would seem to be an anomaly. The more unbalanced economies—those with the narrowest range of production possibilities and hence the highest short-term cost of diversifying—seem to obtain the largest gains from trade. This means that they would have to make the largest relative sacrifice to produce the full range of commodities at home—for example, to set up their own textile industries alongside their export-oriented vineyards and other plantations. Yet by *not* sacrificing these "gains from trade," they will suffer the "opportunity cost" of not developing their own industry or agriculture.

Ricardo ignored Hume's assertion that one party tended to "get command of the better commodity." England (the ostensibly high-cost country, contrary to economic reality at the time) was able to produce *something*. Had Ricardo used Portugal as his high-cost example, readers might have been quicker to recognize the prospect of countries suffering general unemployment or under-utilization of resources. After all, only a portion of Portugal's labor and capital could be devoted to wine-making, given the limited area of suitable soil and limited world demand for its port and Madeira. What was the rest of its labor to do?

As Gunnar Myrdal has observed, Ricardo revealed his genius in the precision with which he specified "the unrealistic assumptions which are required if this theory is to hold."[10] Controversies over the doctrine of comparative advantage have focused on the scope and nature of the eight most serious such assumptions:

1. *Constant returns to scale.* All countries are characterized by linear production functions, so that comparative-cost schedules remain unchanging over time. There are no increasing or diminishing returns (unlike Ricardo's domestic rent theory), no learning curves, technological obsolescence or resource depletion, nor does Ricardo distinguish between short-run (existing) and long-term (potential) cost curves.

2. *The traded goods are produced in both countries.* Without this assumption there are no relative cost functions to compare. In this case (as Malthus pointed out) international prices become a function of relative supply and demand.

3 *No trade in common inputs* (capital goods, raw materials, etc.). Otherwise, comparative-cost schedules among nations would be linked into an absolute-cost system, with common worldwide prices for basic inputs such as fuels and other raw materials, capital goods, etc. Some countries might be priced out of the world market and their own home market across the board.

4. *No underutilization of labor, capital or land, and no import-displacement of domestic labor and capital.* Workers are presumed to be fully mobile throughout the domestic economy so that there is always full employment, regardless of trade shifts. (Ricardo later made some caveats to this full-employment assumption in his analysis of the domestic economy.) Capital displaced from one sector readily finds employment in another.

5. *No emigration or capital outflow.* Each nation's resources remain constant, or at least are not affected by foreign trade patterns.

6. *No imbalance in international trade and payments.* This assumption makes money and prices neutral. Otherwise, growing indebtedness and capital transfers would impair the terms of trade (as John Stuart Mill pointed out), as when debtor countries are forced to dump their exports in order to raise the funds to pay debt service.

7. *No impact of monetary inflation or deflation, or of domestic and foreign debt on comparative costs.* Inflation or deflation of costs and prices are supposed to occur evenly across the board— for wages, profits and rents alike, and for agricultural and industrial prices. There are no leads and lags (such as the tendency for wages to lag behind the inflation rate, reducing "real" wage levels). Debt service and its associated taxes and duties are assumed to fall neutrally across the economic spectrum.

8. *No conflict between private interests and general long-term social utility.* Market prices are assumed to reflect social (use) values, so that the workings of the marketplace maximize output and general welfare as well as private fortunes.

These assumptions may now be discussed in detail.

---

[10] Gunnar Myrdal, *The Political Element in the Development of Economic Theory* (London: 1953), p. 62.

1. *Constant returns to scale*

Ricardo's trade theory assumed that production functions are constant and linear, with no economies or diseconomies of scale, increasing or diminishing returns. This assumption of stable cost functions reflected his underlying concept of "the peculiar powers bestowed by nature" and his equally static belief in "the original and indestructible powers of the soil." International cost differences seemed to be products of nature, not policy. Trade had no impact on productivity, so that no soil or mineral depletion resulted from exporting raw materials, and no industrial productivity increase resulted from wider markets.

In making these assumptions Ricardo failed to integrate his theory of foreign trade with his belief that, over time, productivity would increase in industry and decline in agriculture. Most Ricardian-type models acknowledge only the prospect of diminishing returns. Haberler notes that this assumption implies that the more a country produces of any given commodity, the higher its cost of its production will be. This means that countries must lose their cost advantage in one product line after another as they increase their specialization. A country specializing in agriculture will suffer diminishing returns until it reaches the point where its costs become as high as those of more densely populated economies. The implication is that all countries ultimately will reach similar comparative-cost ratios, presumably bringing the process of world specialization and trade to an end.[11]

Neither Ricardo nor other free traders analyzed what happens in the case of *increasing* returns as assumed by Tucker, Steuart and most nineteenth-century protectionists. The reality is that increasing returns have steadily widened the cost advantages enjoyed by wealthy industrial nations—in their agriculture as well as in manufacturing.

Agriculture and other primary production in the nineteenth century was characterized by moderately increasing returns, while industrial productivity increased by leaps and bounds. Even if agricultural productivity did not increase, England's production-possibilities curve in Ricardo's example would rise in cloth-making. By specializing in wine or other agricultural commodities under free trade, Portugal looses the opportunity to progress industrially—what today is called an opportunity cost. It could end up on the higher curve only by nurturing its textile industry to diversify into cloth-making, that is, by *not* following its short-term comparative advantage. This option would require a cost in the form of higher tariffs and at least temporarily higher prices to finance the requisite industrial investment.

[11]  Haberler, *The Theory of International Trade*, p. 142.

Assuming pure and equitable competition, Ricardo reasoned as if industrial economies would pass on the fruits of increased efficiency by reducing prices to reflect productivity gains. This meant that wages and living standards in economies that specialized in agriculture or other sectors where productivity was relatively low or subject to diminishing returns would not suffer, because the fruits of increasing returns would be shared equitably among nations. But as Raul Prebisch and other Latin American economists have pointed out, unit export prices for the industrial nations have risen, affording their citizens considerably higher living standards than those of raw-materials exporters.

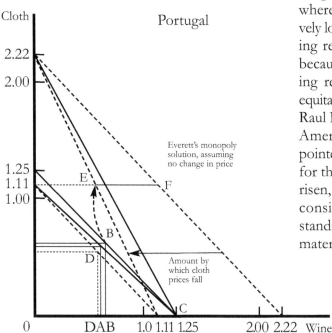

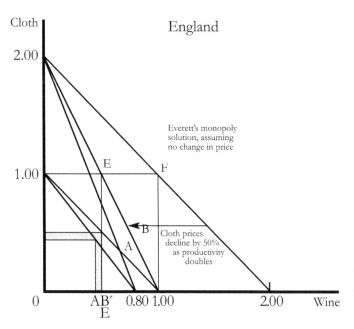

Note: Portugal's production-possibilities curve remains unchanged at either *B* or *C*.

Fig. 5.2: Assumption of Increasing Productivity in Industrial Manufactures

### 2. *The traded commodities are produced in both countries*

In Ricardo's example Portugal enjoys a 10 per cent productivity advantage *over* England in cloth-making, but a 33 per cent advantage in wine-making. It follows that even though it had more efficient industry than England, Portugal should give up industry and specialize in wine-making. Economies were more diversified than they subsequently have become, so industrial advantage was not as absolute as it is today. By focusing on *relative* rather than absolute cost advantages, Ricardo assumed countries to have roughly similar production capabilities. Each economy can produce the entire range of traded commodities if need be, so that countries choose to specialize merely as a matter of efficiency.

One reason why Ricardo believed the terms of trade would settle equitably may have been that no nation needed to trade as a life-or-death decision. England's economy would not grind to a halt for lack of wine, and Portugal could have made its own clothing if it lost its overseas wine markets. Today, more economies are seeking to diversify in order to regain the choice of whether or not to trade. They are beginning to produce more of their basic needs such as food, steel and energy, over whose international pricing and marketing they have little influence. Diversification reduces their foreign dependency, precisely to realize the Ricardian assumption that commerce is a matter of free choice under a system of fair rewards.

By contrast, trade dependency would hook countries on basic imports regardless of the prices being charged. This is how trade in fact has developed between industrial nations and raw-materials exporters, largely the result of countries following free-trade policies rather than maintaining their diversification. The irony of Ricardo's comparative-cost doctrine is that it has served as a rationale for bringing about a world that stands increasingly at odds with his underlying assumptions! No comparative-cost ratios could be constructed if England could not produce wine and Portugal could not produce cloth. Malthus focused on trade among countries possessing absolute cost advantages in natural-resource products that some countries could not produce at all. Such cases, he pointed out, could be dealt with only by a supply-and-demand approach to pricing:

> The great mass of our imports consists of articles as to which there can be no kind of question about their comparative cheapness, as raised abroad or at home. If we could not import from foreign countries our silk, cotton and indigo … with many other articles peculiar to foreign climates, it is quite certain that we should not have them at all. To estimate the advantage derived from their importation by their cheapness, compared with the quantity of labour and capital which they would have cost if we had attempted to raise them at home, would be perfectly preposterous.[12]

[12]   Malthus, *Principles of Political Economy* (London: 1820), pp. 461-62. On this point see Viner, *Studies*, pp. 527–34.

Where prices for specialized commodities could be determined only by market forces, the gains from trade were to be measured by their utility, that is, by "the increased [use] value which results from exchanging what is wanted less for what is wanted more."

### 3. *No trade in common production inputs*

Ricardo's gains-from-trade model applies only to consumer goods, not capital goods, raw materials or other production inputs. Exporting capital goods would violate his assumption of fixed factor productivity, because the purpose of importing machinery is to *improve* production functions. English economists discussed whether the nation should export its machinery or keep it at home as a technological monopoly. Protectionist writers feared that machinery exports might help lower-wage countries undersell its industrialists. But free traders convinced Parliament that exporting capital goods would help consolidate rather than threaten English leadership. The nation lifted its restrictions on machine exports in 1824, and those on textile machinery somewhat later. England's long experience and institutions, its commercial and banking infrastructure, engineering skills and superior access to immense sums of long-term investment capital and short-term trade financing provided it with real advantages that more than offset foreign cost advantages in producing food and raw materials, whose prices would be set by English demand under free trade.

Quite apart from altering productivity, trade in capital goods, raw materials and other common inputs links comparative-cost schedules into a common set of *absolute* costs. By linking international cost schedules along absolute-cost lines, *trade in common denominators opens up the path for high-cost producers to be uncompetitive across the board*, freezing them out of world markets. Today's world exports use energy, steel, grains and other production inputs that share a uniform price. This means that raw-materials producers have no advantage in producing industrial manufactures based on their own natural resources, for these are available to foreign buyers at the same price for which domestic can buy them.

The essence of Ricardo's theorizing about *comparative* rather than absolute cost levels is that every country has *something* to export, even if it is in a high-cost position across the board, no matter how high its food prices, taxes, debt servicing charges or interest rates. Despite absolute cost disadvantages, a country's exports will balance its imports automatically. For England, meanwhile, this same logic implied that with common world prices for gain and capital goods it could dominate world trade even with its higher wage levels. It would get the benefit of foreign natural resource efficiency, but would not need to share the fruits of its own industrial productivity. Ricardo's trade model thus neglected important factors that English policy makers well understood. One might almost say that his theory itself was designed exclusively for export.

What point is served by computing *comparative* costs when food and raw materials are commonly priced inputs at *absolute* prices throughout most of the world? The purely domestic cost variables are the prices and productivity of labor, real estate—and hence, housing and office space—and the mode of financing capital equipment. These are institutional in character, dependent more on policy decisions than on nature. They are what make national economies different from each other.

### 4. *Fully employed and domestically mobile labor and capital*

Ricardo's theory of comparative costs assumes fully employed resources used to their optimum potential. Labor and capital can readily be shifted from one sector to another, so there can be no unemployment resulting from import competition. There are no bankruptcies or scrapping of plant.

But suppose that Portugal decides to take the model's advice and move from a diversified economy to one specializing in wine-making. Its urban labor will migrate back to the land to produce wine, while England's rural labor moves to urban factories to produce cloth. Capital sunk in either of these sectors is assumed to be transferred readily to the other, being perfectly homogeneous. "A manufacturer never can, whatever may be the restriction on importation, get, for any length of time, more than the general and ordinary rate of profit on his capital, and therefore if he could easily remove his capital from one trade to another his loss would be inconsiderable, from the removal of restrictions," wrote Ricardo.[13] This is a big if. He did not explain how to transform cloth-making machinery into wine-making capital.

The reality is that labor and capital inflexibility imposes heavy retrenchment costs and write-offs. Throughout the world, rural labor has migrated to the cities to seek industrial employment. But few Portuguese cloth-making workers moved back to the land to become grape pickers and wine pressers. True, in newly settled countries such as the United States, the 1817 industrial depression (caused mainly by renewed commerce with England) led many urban workers to move west in search of new means of livelihood. They supported themselves on the land to secure a standard of life they could no longer earn in industry. But Europe's land already was fully appropriated, affording little opportunity for an American-type demographic shift to the backwoods, except

---

[13]   Ricardo, *Notes on Malthus*, in *Works*, Vol. II, p. 200. The more free-trade mercantilists also had denied that underemployment could result because of labor immobility. Thus Tucker, in his *Reflections on the Expedience of a law for the Naturalisation of Foreign Protestants* (p. 13) asks "Whether it is possible in the nature of things for all trades and professions to be overstocked?" His answer is that "If a particular trade is at any time overstocked, will not the disease cure itself? That is, will not some persons take to other trades, and fewer young people be bred up to that which is least profitable?" (However, he urged the maintenance of consumer demand to ensure full employment.)

for unemployed industrial workers willing to become low-paid seasonal laborers. Whatever industrial skills urban workers had acquired thus were rendered unmarketable when devoted to purely rural pursuits.

What actually happened was that Portuguese cloth-makers and other industrial labor emigrated to England, or to America to pursue their industrial livelihood rather than move back to the countryside which they or their fore-bears had abandoned in search of bettering their station in life. Unlike his predecessors, Ricardo's analysis of the gains and losses resulting from free trade did not acknowledge this emigration, or the degree to which the opening up of Portugal's domestic market following the Methuen Treaty of 1703 thus reduced its material and human capital resources. Its cloth-making machinery could not be converted into pitchforks, and its skilled labor could not apply its mechanical skills to wine-making.

American anti-Ricardians opposed the assumption of perpetually full employment and labor mobility. Quantification of the gains from trade, asserted E. Peshine Smith in 1853, "evidently depends upon the question, whether or not [domestic labor and capital] could obtain employment or not."

> If there be a single individual in Connecticut who sits idle—able to make shoes, but incapable of any other species of productive industry—it presents a case where the advantage of a system of domestic exchanges which shall secure him the opportunity is readily appreciable![14]

With regard to this linkage between trade patterns and market demand, Adam Smith had recognized that the sudden reliance on foreign sources of supply would divert spending away from the domestic economy. Writing from the vantage point of England buying goods from Portugal, it followed that the income that Portuguese wine-makers had spent to buy domestic cloth would be sent abroad to maintain foreign textile workers.

> The capital which is employed in purchasing in one part of the country in order to sell in another, the produce of the industry of that country, generally replaces by every such operation two distinct capitals ... and thereby enables them to continue that employment ...
>
> The capital employed in purchasing foreign goods for home consumption, when this purchase is made with the produce of domestic industry, replaces, too, by every such operation, two distinct capitals; but one of them only is employed in supporting domestic industry. The capital which sends British goods to Portugal, and brings back Portuguese goods to Great Britain, replaces by every such operation only one British capital. The other is a Portuguese one. Though the returns, therefore, of the foreign trade of consumption should be as quick as those of the home trade, it will give but one-half of the encouragement to the industry or productive labour of the country?[15]

---

[14] E. Peshine Smith, *Manual of Political Economy* (New York: 1853), pp. 189, 182.
[15] Adam Smith, *The Wealth of Nations*, Book II, ch. v.

Ricardo reasoned more simplistically than Smith. Portuguese consumers could enjoy the full cost saving that resulted from buying their manufacturers in England. The domestic employment effect of this shift to foreign suppliers was supposed to be fully offset by a shift of Portugal's cloth-making labor and capital into wine-making—assuming that (1) no diminishing returns would occur in wine-making and other agricultural pursuits (contrary to Ricardo's own rent theory) and (2) all the increased wine output could be sold abroad without impairing Portugal's terms of trade. But under conditions of labor and capital immobility, a shift of demand from domestic to foreign suppliers tends to reduce domestic employment and output. This extinguishes the supposed gains from trade by turning unemployed labor into a social-overhead expense.

Unemployed labor either must be fed by those who remain employed, or it must emigrate. Labor historically has shown itself to be more mobile among nations—but within the same profession—than it is among differing sectors within the same nation. Henry Sidgwick in 1883 described the laborer's real choice as being between working in a given industry or not working at all.[16] To quantify the labor-transfer effect requires an estimate of occupational shifts, unemployment and emigration.

Likewise for the Portuguese cloth-making capital that must be abandoned with the onset of import displacement. Loss of this capital reduces the country's capital-to-labor ratio, impairing even further its comparative-cost advantage in capital-intensive "high technology" manufactures.

### 5. *No emigration or capital outflows*

The Ricardian assumption of domestic labor mobility but international immobility flies in the face of the great emigrations of the nineteenth and twentieth centuries. It seems ironic that in the mercantilist era, when skilled artisans faced legal prohibitions against emigrating and England banned exports of machinery, Tucker and Adam Smith recognized migration as an important feature of the world economy. This recognition faded in Ricardo's time, when artisans were freely permitted to emigrate. To a growing extent nineteenth-century emigration was *from* countries that pursued free trade at the cost of foregoing their own industrialization. Most notable was the emigration within the British Empire, especially from India to British plantation enclaves (such as Africa and the Caribbean), and from Ireland to the United States. Indeed, a major aim of protective tariffs in the United States was to *attract* foreign artisans, as announced by Alexander Hamilton in his 1790 *Report on Manufactures*. Like English mercantilist policy in the eighteenth century, protectionist policy throughout the nineteenth century was formulated with specific reference to attracting skilled labor and investment capital.

---

[16]   Henry Sidgwick, *Principles of Political Economy* (London: 1883), pp. 497–98.

Dropping the assumption of international labor immobility transforms the gains-from-trade computation. A shift to free trade (following the terms of Ricardo's example in Figure 5.3) would induce producers of 50 manhours of Portuguese cloth-making labor to migrate to England rather than move to the local countryside. These manhours would be transferred from Portugal's production possibilities curve to that of England in a "brain drain" of its industrial labor. This is anything but a symmetrical sharing of the gains from trade between the two countries. The moral is that price alone is not the only thing to be considered in drawing up the balance sheet of protectionism versus free trade.

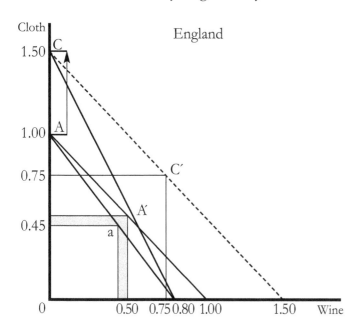

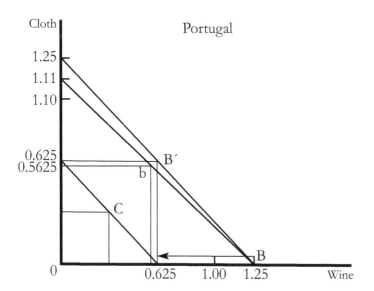

Fig. 5.3: Effect of Acknowledging the International Migration of Labor

6. *No imbalance in international trade and payments*

Haberler similarly recognizes that "Our first modification must be the introduction of money. ... The flow of international trade is determined directly by absolute differences in money-price and not by comparative differences in labor-cost. Our first task will be to explain the mechanism by which the latter are transformed into the former."[17] This is not something that can be done simplistically.

Ricardian theory ignored all complications involving the monetary impact of trade. (Part III will discuss this financial dimension.) Although Wesley Mitchell has described Ricardo as showing himself in many essays to be "acutely conscious of the complications which the use of money introduces into economic theory," he elaborated his theory strictly on the basis of barter. "His first essay, *The High Price of Bullion*, was an effort to prove that the currency and its purchasing power was variable, that it was not a constant factor in business." But he then set this problem aside, not only in his *Principles* but also in other works, this being "one of the few suppositions which he makes explicitly—that the price level will not vary; that is, he makes the purchasing power of money a constant." This over-simplification meant that "Ricardo missed the whole range of fascinating problems concerning the bearing of the money economy on economic behavior."[18] Mitchell notes that this was a chronic failing of classical British economists in the free-trade period.

What made this dismissal of financial considerations so striking was that Ricardo himself was a stockbroker. (In his day the term meant dealing more in bonds than in stocks, as England's public debt securities were called "stock.") At first glance it might be expected that he above all others should have taken the lead in explaining how debt affected foreign trade pricing. But for a sounder analysis of the impact of money and debt one must turn to Malthus, who observed that "we are much more likely to obscure our reasonings than to render them clearer, by throwing it [money] out of our consideration."[19] He believed that Ricardo's reluctance to deal with financial matters stemmed largely from his reaction against mercantilist concerns:

Theoretical writers in Political Economy, from the fear of appearing to attach too much importance to money, have been too apt to throw it out of their consideration in their reasonings. ... The circulating medium bears so important a part in the distribution of wealth, and the encouragement of

---

[17]  Haberler, *Theory of International Trade*, p. 131. Haberler is referring only to differing wage rates, not to monetary considerations in their financial or institutional context.
[18]  Wesley C. Mitchell, *Types of Economic Theory*, Vol. I, pp. 347–48.
[19]  Malthus, *Principles*, p. 324 n.

industry, that it is hardly ever safe to set it aside in our reasonings, and all attempts at illustration, by supposing advances of a certain quantity of corn and clothing, instead of a certain quantity of money ...cannot fail to lead us wrong.

7. *No impact of domestic or foreign debt or monetary inflation or deflation on comparative costs*

What is important in evaluating Ricardo's trade theory is not only what he said, but what he did not say. He theorized as if the national debt, its interest charges and taxes had no relevance to the trade issue. This enabled him to avoid advocating that the moneyed interest be taxed, that interest rates be lowered, or that England's debt be paid off. His reasoning diverted attention from the financial impact of domestic and foreign debt (at a time when about a third of England's public debt was held abroad, largely by the Dutch). This neglect was no mere oversight, nor can it be said that the times were not yet prepared for such theorizing. A debate had been raging for half a century over the economic consequences of England's massive war debts. During the Seven Years' War with France (1756-63), and especially after the Revolutionary War with America (which ended only in 1786), liberals such as Tucker and Adam Smith depicted the national debt as burdening English industry with taxes of over £1 million annually in interest to foreign bondholders.

Given near-subsistence wage levels, it hardly was possible to tax labor, so either agriculturalists or industrialists had to bear the burden. Malachy Postlethwait explained that debt service added to the economy's costs, threatening to price English manufactures out of world markets. The problem became more serious after the Napoleonic Wars.

The reality is that international debt service, military subsidies and other payments affect relative costs among the *types* of goods exported. Taxes and debt service fall asymmetrically on wages, rent, profits and interest. But implicit in Ricardo's analysis was the assumption that any shift in prices and cost schedules resulting from monetary deflation or inflation would equally affect all industries, commodity markets, wage and profit rates, so that *relative* production costs and incomes—the heart of Ricardian trade theory—would not be affected. As he put matters: "The value of money cannot alter, without affecting, in the same degree, the prices of all things."[20]

Milton Friedman and his monetarist followers are still repeating this idea today, along lines that Chapter 14 will review in detail. Ricardo endorsed a crude version of Say's Law in the international economy as in the domestic economy:

---

[20]   Ricardo, *Notes on Malthus*, p. 180.

Supply created its own demand, with no balance-of-payments deficits or surpluses to complicate matters. Relative money prices and production costs are supposed to remain unaffected by inflation or deflation, international finance, domestic debt and taxes.

Yet already at the time Ricardo wrote, the monetary debate in every country turned on the debt question. To ignore its impact was essentially a defensive strategy as far as the financial classes were concerned. In this respect Ricardo's approach was censorial rather than enlightening. Like members of any class or profession, those of the creditor class contended that they were helping the economy develop. If harm was visibly being caused, it was blamed on some other class—usually the government. The ensuing blind spot concerning finance and the adverse consequences of international debt service (and also the domestic debt overhead) has plagued above all the economists who came from the financial profession itself! Ricardo claimed that foreign economies would not be hurt by the trade deficits that resulted from their growing dependence on English manufactures.

Ricardo tread a dangerous political track in accusing the landlords of being *rentiers* who would benefit from rising prices in a merely passive and parasitic manner as marginal lands were brought into cultivation. As the Scottish statistician James Sinclair pointed out, accusing landlords of being *rentiers* laid the groundwork for including bondholders and bankers—Ricardo's class—in the same category.

The American protectionist Calvin Colton chided Ricardian doctrine for implying that it made no difference to the farmer whether he sold his crop or his ploughs—his output or his capital inputs—to pay for his consumer goods. Referring to money as the "tools of trade," Colton defended protectionism on balance-of-payments grounds. "We want," he concluded,

> a system of public economy, which shall not only tend to keep in the country what is commonly reckoned enough of money, to carry on its trade and commerce; but we want a system that shall tend to increase that amount, as far as may be, in a degree, commensurate with the development of the means for its profitable use.[21]

Crop failures caused financial convulsions in agricultural countries, which periodically found themselves without enough income to purchase foreign goods. Ricardo and his followers did not touch on the instability of agricultural and raw-materials prices and incomes in response to the weather and other

---

[21] Calvin Colton, *Public Economy for the United States*, pp. 211, 227. Colton earlier had asserted (*Life and Times of Henry Clay* [New York. 1946], Vol. II, p. 482) "that CURRENCY is a part of political economy necessarily connected with protection: that the very existence of a sound currency depends on an adequate protective system."

environmental causes, but protectionists noted it. They defended industrial balance as a way to even out income streams and thus avoid national bankruptcy and its consequent property transfer from rural debtors to urban creditors.

8. *No conflict between private-sector interests and social utility*

The *doctrine* of comparative advantage assumes that private-sector gains imply corresponding national gains. Exchange values are supposed to reflect use values. This assumption assigns national development policy over to the marketplace as it is structured at any given moment of time. To elevate the theory of comparative costs to the status of doctrine guiding national policy, it thus is necessary to assume that all imports and exports are in the economy's long-term interest.

Lauderdale's 1804 *Inquiry into the Nature and Origin of Public Wealth* demonstrated that the principles of exchange value often were opposed to those of use value, as when scarcity and consequent high prices enriched producers. Goods in private hands were deemed valuable not according to their use value, but according to their exchange value, which stemmed in large part from their scarcity. "Yet the common sense of mankind," Lauderdale pointed out, "would revolt at the proposal for augmenting the wealth of a nation, by creating a scarcity of any commodity generally useful and necessary to man."[22] The proper aim of a national economy was to increase the abundance of commodities, not pecuniary fortunes. Physical abundance often connoted low market prices, especially for price-inelastic commodities such as food and raw materials.

Adam Smith's doctrine of the invisible hand depicted the drive for private profit as working to maximize productive powers. The drive to build up private fortunes, he believed, would augment society's flow of use value. The American protectionist Daniel Raymond protested that industries often gained at society's expense, especially in the case of commercial monopolies, and went so far as to claim that "Individual riches are perpetually at variance with national interests."[23] Other protectionists satisfied themselves with distinguishing between the interests of the few and those of the many, as the German-American economist Friedrich List observed in 1828:

> In consequence of my researches, I found the component parts of political economy to be (1) individual economy; (2) national economy; (3) economy of mankind. Adam Smith … teaches how an individual creates, increases, and consumes wealth in society with other individuals, and how the industry and

---

[22] Lauderdale, *Inquiry into the Nature and Origin of Public Wealth* (London: 1804), p. 43.
[23] Daniel Raymond, *Elements of Political Economy* (Baltimore: 1823), Vol. I, p. 45. See also pp. 33–36.

wealth of mankind influence the industry and wealth of the individual. He has entirely forgotten what the title of his book, "Wealth of Nations," promised to treat.[24]

List later asserted that "this is evidently not a system of national economy, but a system of the private economy of the human race."[25]

Viewing trade in national terms rather than those of the private market economy made it possible to take into account implicit or "external" costs and benefits not reflected in the market pricing. This made it possible to give precedence to long-term production considerations as distinct from short-term commercial gains. "The protective system," asserted Willard Phillips in 1850,

> considers people, in their character of producers, as substantially all of ours are. They inquire, not merely how you may make a good bargain in the exchange of what you already have, which is a very proper inquiry; but also, which is immeasurably more important, what course of policy is best calculated to put you in the way of producing something more; that is to say, to give you a chance for industry.[26]

This doctrine is reiterated today by such writers as W. Arthur Lewis in his statement that "social costs and private costs will diverge significantly over large areas of the underdeveloped countries due to various market imperfections and structural rigidities, particularly those affecting the allocation of labor between rural and urban sectors."[27] Free trade may involve lost opportunities for development, causing international dependency and poverty.

By treating tariffs as a pure cost borne by the nation's consumers, the free-trade model of comparative costs has nothing to say about social utility as such, dismissing it as an "externality," that is, of little importance to private-sector balance sheets. Tariff revenues are treated as if the money simply was extin-

---

[24]  Friedrich List, *Outlines of American Political Economy* [1827] (New York: 1909), p. 152. See also John Rae, *Statement of Some New Principles on the Subject of Political Economy, Exposing the Fallacies of the System of Free Trade, and of Some other Doctrines Maintained in the "Wealth of Nations"* (1834), Book I: "Individual and National Interests are not Identical"; Colton, *Public Economy for the United States*, ch. xvii: "The Gain of individuals not always the Gain of the Community," esp. pp. 264f.; Willard Phillips, *Propositions Concerning Protection and Free Trade* (Boston: 1850), Prop. IX: "It is not true that the industry every individual, independently of any law, deems to be advantageous so himself, is so to the public. Free trade asserts that it is so"; and E. Peshine Smith, *Manual*, pp. 21, 140–43.

[25]  Friedrich List, *National System of Political Economy* [1841] (London: 1885), p. 170. See also pp. 356 and 137f., as well as Raymond, *Elements*, Vol. I, pp. 406, 139, 34 and 173, and Colton, *Public Economy*, pp. 33–34.

[26]  Willard Phillips, *Propositions*, p. 31. On this point see also List, *Outlines*, pp. 202, 212 and 214, and *National System*, pp. 259–60.

[27]  W. Arthur Lewis, "Economic Development with Unlimited Supplies of Labor," in Agarwala and Singh, *The Economics of Underdevelopment* (New York: 1963), p. 185.

guished, not to finance internal improvements and related economic infra-structure. Subsidies paid to domestic producers likewise are used to finance capital investment, not just wasted. Even Ricardo was careful to remind his popularizer, John Ramsay McCulloch:

> You say that the corn laws have the same effect as if a tax of 24 millions and a half were levied from the consumers of corn for the public expenditure. I should add, provided the 24 millions and a half received by the landlords be all expended as revenue, and no part added to capital.[28]

Protectionists pointed out that if tariffs played their proper role, the added revenue paid to purchase domestic products at higher prices would be invested to increase the nation's capital stock.

## *Recasting Ricardo's free-trade assumptions dynamically*

Just as free-trade theory took into account only the current costs of protectio-nism, not its long-term benefits, so the comparative-cost model acknowledged only the short-term gains from trade, not the long-term loss of opportunities by monocultures locked into trade dependency reinforced by financial austerity. As the following chapters describe, their trade has become increasingly compul-sory ("price-inelastic") at declining terms of trade that force them deeply into debt in order to feed their people, carry on their basic economic activity, and obtain the foreign exchange to service their debts.

Ricardo's theorizing overlooked too many real-world complications to accurately map reality. Yet his pedagogical model was taken as a policy guide for the real world. All but forgotten was the fact that it was largely for heuristic purposes that he assumed productivity disparities among nations to remain fixed over time. Rather than analyzing the ratios and productivity of capital and labor in commodity production, Ricardo examined the "comparative statics" of market exchange and income distribution at a given instant in time. As Mitchell's lecture notes spell out, Ricardo's logical method of exposition is

> better characterized by "imaginary experimentation" than by "deduction." Dangers lurking in this type of economic theory. At times Ricardo will recognize facts upon which he cannot theorize; at times he will theorize on assumptions that he knows distort the facts. (1) Misleads readers and even the writers themselves. (2) Temptation to adopt a double standard of truth: Observation for facts. Logical consistency for theories. Keep the two things separate. (3) This attitude impedes scientific progress, because it excuses theorists from reconstructing their work when conclusions are out of line with facts. Tends to make economics an "idle" science. (4) Investigator may be deceived regarding

---

[28] Ricardo to McCulloch, March 29, 1820, in *Works*, Vol. VIII, p. 172.

the representative character of his assumptions. (5) Two stages of economic investigation. First, theorizing on assumed premises; second, inquiry whether theories explain facts. Second stage seldom entered upon in practice.[29]

Approaching the economy with a specific policy conclusion in mind, Ricardo and other free-traders focused on certain aspects at the expense of others. It is normal for economists to begin by formulating intuitively what they believe to be a justifiable policy, and then to reason out the logic needed to defend it. A particular world view inspires the development of technical tools and methodology. This is how theoretical innovation historically has been made, in the natural sciences as well as in the social sciences.

The problem is that Ricardo's viewpoint had narrow blinkers that were highly ideological in character. It may have seemed logical enough for free traders to use a static rather than dynamic long-term analysis. But the perpetuation of this approach in modern times is much less forgivable, as it excludes and even censors discussion of productivity, financial and development issues. Its shortcomings and narrow scope have been pointed out again and again, these criticisms have been willfully ignored. The insistence by free traders on writing the history of trade theory as if these criticisms never had been made is intellectual dishonesty of the first order. It breeds a purposeful ignorance of the dynamic character of international trade and payments—problems whose solutions call for an economic methodology much broader in scope than free traders are willing to acknowledge.

Ricardo's comparative-cost doctrine deftly sidestepped the world economy's most dynamic changes and self-transformation, especially with regard to the monetary and financial dimension. It ignored the emigration of labor and capital (and particularly of skilled labor) to the richest nations—precisely the movement about which Tucker and Steuart had promised England would reap under free trade. In its triumphalist British form, free-trade doctrine excluded the nature and consequences of the technological changes resulting from the steam revolution, the chemical revolution and the general move toward more capital-intensive production based on increasingly skilled labor. Free-trade doctrine also neglected "external" benefits and economies of scale. The loss of such benefits represented an opportunity cost to countries not industrializing. These countries also suffered "external" costs in the form of depletion of their natural mineral endowments. Instead of such indirect long-term costs being balanced against the Ricardian gains from free trade, they were left out of the calculation.

---

[29] Mitchell, *Types of Economic Theory*, Vol. I, pp. 328-29.

In pursuit of its free-trade objectives, Ricardian analysis has indoctrinated students with static assumptions that neglect these dimensions of economic reality. Either deliberately or unconsciously, free-trade models have served the economic interests of the most efficient nations, and adversely affected the production functions of less efficient countries. The aim of importing goods to take advantage of their lower prices is not an unalloyed benefit if it stifles domestic investment and employment. Lord Brougham recognized this in 1816 when he exhorted the House of Commons that "it was well worth while to incur a loss upon the first exportation, in order, by the glut, to stifle in the cradle those rising manufactures in the United States which the war had forced into existence contrary to the natural course of things."[30]

Only by making Ricardo's rigid assumptions more dynamic can trade theory explain the brain drain from poor countries, the flight of what little investment capital they are able to generate, and the widening international lag in capital investment and the income gap between industrial nations and raw-materials monocultures. As John H. Williams has put matters,

> the English classical theory of international trade ... assumes for each trading country fixed quanta of productive factors, already existent and employed, and asks how, subject to the assumptions, these may be most effectively applied under conditions of free international trade ... The classical theory assumes as fixed, for purposes of the reasoning, the very things which, in my view, should be the chief objects of study ... the relation of international trade to the development of new resources and productive forces is a more significant part of the explanation of the present status of nations, of income, prices, well-being, than is the cross-section value analysis of the classical economists, with its assumptions of given quanta of productive factors, already existent and employed.[31]

Ricardo's mathematical example, depicting Portugal as enjoying an absolute cost advantage over England in both agriculture (wine) and industry (cloth), failed to predict that once Portugal relaxed its protective tariffs, it would suffer industrial poverty, emigration of skilled labor and loss of monetary resources. Nor did the Ricardians care to remember the historical policies by which England had increased its industrial productivity. But following the Methuen Treaty, Portugal became increasingly dependent on England's burgeoning textile industry rather than enjoying the across-the-board productivity advantages that Ricardo attributed to it.

---

[30] Lord Brougham, speech before the House of Commons, April 9, 1816, quoted in Crompton, *The Tariff*, p. 32. Crompton also discusses other aspects of England's dumping of manufactures in the United States after the Treaty of Ghent.

[31] John H. Williams. "The Theory of International Trade Reconsidered," *Economic Journal* (June 1929), repr. in American Economic Association, *Readings in the Theory of International Trade* (Philadelphia: 1949), pp. 253ff.

England's economies of scale resulted largely from its export markets, in particular the captive market of India. As with its other colonial possessions, this market was secured in the first instance by military force, not by superior English industrial efficiency. Nearly all histories of India have traced how the country enjoyed an absolute cost advantage over England in producing textiles as well as other manufactures. England prohibited India from rivaling the mother country in any commodity that its own producers desired to export. But gunboats do not appear in Ricardian trade theory.

Far from being intrinsic as implied by Ricardo, England acquired its competitive advantage in industrial manufactures by government policy—protectionism at home and colonial restrictions abroad. Comparative-cost models could quantify this acquired advantage once it was gained, but was silent as to the process by which it was secured. It failed to acknowledge the extent to which market forces are themselves the product of government strategy and diplomacy.

Like most other classical economists, Ricardo assumed that full domestic employment would be ensured by the free mobility of domestic labor and capital. It is now recognized that government action is required to prevent trade-induced unemployment. In the nineteenth century the United States led the way in prohibiting imports or subjecting them to quotas. Today, Europeans and North Americans are erecting barriers against Asian imports in order to prevent unemployment in their heavy industry.

Ricardo's model assumed that the terms of trade would settle at price levels providing each nation with an equitable share of the gains resulting from the international specialization of production. He also anticipated that raw materials would tend to be priced near their high-cost margin of production. But foreign investment—backed by U.S. and European foreign-aid diplomacy and international financial consortia—has created a sufficient abundance of raw materials and manual-labor products to depress their international prices near their low-cost margin of production, at substantially less than their replacement cost will be when these non-renewable endowments are exhausted. Raw-materials exporters can share equitably in the gains from trade only if they exert a countervailing coordination by means of producer-nation agreements such as OPEC.

In sum, the assumptions underlying Ricardo's model of comparative costs have not applied from 1815 to the present day. The underlying theory at best can serve as a foil against which to measure how far the conditions necessary for equitable world trade to occur are missing. The irony is that if reality is to conform to the Ricardian logic, it requires protectionist policies and an active economic diplomacy. Only through national development policies can the assumptions underlying laissez faire doctrine be realized in practice to achieve an equitable division of world production. If nations are to have comparative-cost ratios to compare, they must diversify their economies—and this can be done only by government subsidy. If national economies are to behave *as if* labor is flexible, they must protect employment, job retraining and public education. This calls for a strategy more akin to that of the mercantilist epoch. But laissez faire doctrine seeks to strip away the power of government to pursue these policies.

Classical economists assumed that free markets work automatically to maximize national wealth. The reality is that the lead nations have established a regulatory environment to steer enterprise to serve social ends. Headed by the United States, they increased their productive powers and stabilized employment to achieve self-sufficiency in essentials, improved their terms of trade, and guided the allocation of national resources toward the most development-oriented sectors by using tariff or quota protection to finance economic infrastructure. Any modern study of international trade therefore must include an analysis of government diplomacy, its objectives and its successes or failure.

# 6

## Terms-of-Trade Analysis in its Historical Context

### *Mill explains how supply and demand affect international prices*

Ricardo was interested mainly in intrinsic value reflecting costs and productivity, not changes in market demand or how shifts in the supply and demand for exports and imports influenced their prices. He assumed that a yard of English cloth would exchange for a gallon of Portuguese wine and left matters at that. These terms of trade provided an approximately equal gain for both England and Portugal. But was this necessarily the case in practice? John Stuart Mill tackled the problem of how international prices actually were determined.

> We know the limits, within which the variation [of international prices] is con-fined, are the ratio between their costs of production in the one country, and the ratio between their costs of production in the other … [but] what is it which, in the case supposed, causes a pipe of wine … to be exchanged in England for exactly that quantity of cloth? We must accordingly … fall back upon an ante-cedent law, that of supply and demand.[1]

Mill's appeal to market forces more in line with Malthusian price theory. His analysis of how shifting volumes of exports, imports and capital transfers affected the terms of trade was (in Viner's words) "in the main a pioneer achievement, and probably constitutes his chief claim to originality in the field of economics."[2]

Ricardo believed that over time English food prices would rise as population growth and urbanization forced recourse to less fertile, less well-situated and hence higher-cost land. This was why the nation needed to import its grain from countries that could produce it more cheaply. In discussing Malthus's protectionist views, Ricardo acknowledged that tariffs such as the Corn Laws would reduce England's demand for foreign commodities, causing an inflow of gold that would raise prices generally. It was for this monetary reason that he believed England could sell its exports "at a high money price

---

[1]  Mill, *Principles of Political Economy*, Ashley ed., pp. 587, 584, 592. He originally composed his analysis in 1829, and published it as the first of his *Essays on Some Unsettled Questions of Political Economy* (1844). He further elaborated it in Book III, ch. xviii ("Of international values") of his 1848 *Principles of Political Economy*.

[2]  Viner, *Studies in the Theory of International Trade*, p. 535.

and buy foreign ones at a low money price." However, he added, agricultural tariffs would deprive the economy of the potential gains from trade stemming from higher efficiency. It therefore "may well be doubted whether this [terms-of-trade] advantage will not be purchased at many times its value, for to obtain it we must be content with a diminished production of home commodities; with a high price of labor, and a low rate of profits."[3]

Emphasis on supply and demand was not original to Mill. What was original was his clarity of expression in analyzing the impact of tariffs and transport costs on quantitative import demand and the terms of trade. Within the constraints of his limiting assumptions, Mill applied this analysis of demand elasticity and shifts in supply curves to the problems of monopoly pricing, the incidence of transport costs and protective tariffs, and how the gains from international trade were shared. The resulting array of possibilities constitutes what Edgeworth has termed the pure theory of international trade.

In Mill's model, England and Portugal became the only two trading countries, so that shifts in their supply and demand were large enough to influence import and export prices. Cloth and wine were the only two commodities produced and traded—the two-commodity, two-country model taught in classrooms ever since. A rising English demand for imported grain would bid up its world price, unless foreign demand for English manufactures grew even more rapidly.

Mill's analysis may best be traced by means of F. Y. Edgeworth's graphic representation of his argument, on which Figure 6.1 is based.[4]

Emphasizing supply and demand purely in themselves, without explicit reference to shifting costs of production as between the cost ratios of England (OE) and Portugal (OP), Mill traced the market supply and demand curves of varying quantities of Portuguese wine exchanging for English cloth (line OW, Portugal's offer curve) and of English cloth exchanging for Portuguese wine (line OC, England's offer curve). Any price ratio of cloth to wine falling to the right of (below) line OE will be to England's advantage. Its residents may obtain more wine for their cloth than they could produce at home. Conversely, any price ratio to the left of (above) line OP will be to Portugal's advantage. Its residents may obtain more cloth per gallon of wine (and by implication, per manhour of their labor) than they could obtain in domestic production.

[3]   Ricardo, *Notes on Malthus*, in *Works*, Vol. II, p. 155.
[4]   F. Y. Edgeworth, "The Pure Theory of International Trade," *Economic Journal*, IV (1894), repr. in his *Papers Relating to Political Economy*, Vol. II (London: 1925).

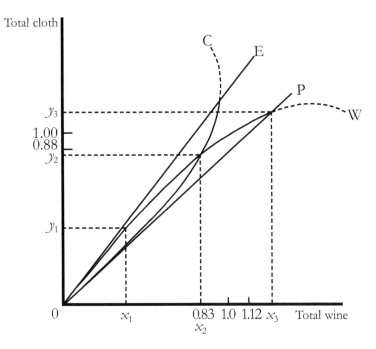

Fig. 6.1 Edgeworth's Graphic Treatment of Reciprocal Demand Applied to Ricardo's Example

Key:    Line OE: England's price ratio in the absence of foreign trade
        Line OP Portugal's price-ratio in the absence of foreign trade
        Line OC: England's offer curve of cloth
        Line OW: Portugal's offer curie of wine in exchange for English cloth

When Portugal or other countries have comparatively little wine to export $(OX_1$ amount) or a small demand for English cloth, they will enjoy favorable terms of trade—that is, a price ratio closer to the English production coefficient line (OE) than to their own. This means that Portugal may reap for itself most of the cost savings in exchanging wine for cloth.

However, as Portugal increases its wine exports (or as other countries increase their own exportable surplus of wine), or as its demand for cloth (or that of other countries) increases, it must give more wine per unit of English cloth in order to clear the market. The exchange ratio of wine for cloth will move in England's favor. The more cloth Portugal buys from England, the more wine it must give per yard. This is indicated in Figure 6.1 by moving from $OX_1$ to $OX_2$ (where the benefits of international specialization of labor are equally shared) and on to $OX_3$, where Portugal finds the terms of trade forced back onto its own cost-constraint line where it receives none of the gains from trade.

If, therefore, it be asked what country draws to itself the greatest share of the advantage of any trade it carries on, the answer is, the country for whose productions there is in other countries the greatest demand, and a demand the most susceptible of increase from additional cheapness ... It also gets its imports cheaper, the less the extent and intensity of its own demand for them. The market is cheapest to those whose demand is small. A country which desires few foreign productions, and only a limited quantity of them, while its own commodities are in great request in foreign countries, will obtain its limited imports at extremely small cost ... in exchange for the produce of a very small quantity of its labor and capital.[5]

Mill couched his initial discussion in terms of two countries, but its essential point of reference is trade in two commodities, or in general commodity groupings such as agricultural and industrial products. Countries find in practice that the products of other nations compete with their own exports, exerting downward price pressure. (The degree to which prices respond to shifts in supply and demand is called *price elasticity*.) Meanwhile, consumer demand in other countries supplements their own demand, bidding up the price of foreign supplies. This supply-and-demand analysis applies to the overall trade patterns of industrial nations vis-à-vis raw-materials exporters.

Mill's supply-and-demand approach retained a number of over-simplifying assumptions from Ricardian trade theory, such as linear production functions, full domestic mobility of labor and capital, but little international mobility, "because persons do not usually remove themselves or their capitals to a distant place without a very strong motive."[6] Mill did not analyze how foreign trade affected productivity, or its impact on long-term "external" economies or domestic economic transformation. He acknowledged the technological and institutional aspects of production to the extent that they influenced the relative supply of products, but not how trade might influence productivity.

Although Mill played a pioneering role in 1829–1844 in analyzing the impact of debt service and other capital transfers on the terms of trade (as Part III will review) his 1848 analysis retrogressed and treated money merely as a veil, so that all "real" variables in the economic system were determined independently of the financial system. He treated monetary gold as a normal commodity import. This meant that debt payments or military spending would influence the terms of trade simply by increasing a country's need to export goods for gold. Money (at least the gold by which trade balances were settled) appeared as neutral in its economic effects, part of a vast barter system rather than an institutional entity whose impact on general prices altered the relationships between wages, profits, rent and interest. "All trade is in reality barter," Mill claimed,

---

[5]   Mill, *Principles*, p. 591.                    [6]   *Ibid.*, p. 575.

"money being a mere instrument for exchanging things against one another." In fact, he went so far as to adopt an extreme

> law which … may be appropriately named, the Equation of International Demand. It may be concisely stated as follows. The produce of a country exchanges for the produce of other countries, at such values as are required in order that the whole of her exports may exactly pay for the whole of her imports.[7]

### *The political context of early terms-of-trade theorizing*

As industrial nations increased their productivity, could they exchange their manufactures for raw materials at the pre-existing price ratios (the monopoly case)? Or would competition force down the price of manufactures to reflect their lower production costs (the no-monopoly case)? Mill showed that supply and demand conditions would determine whether economies could monopolize the fruits of their technological progress rather than passing them on in the form of falling prices. As he put the problem, suppose "an improvement, for example, in the process of manufacture. Will the benefit of the improvement be fully participated in by other countries?"[8]

The Ricardians played down the issue of how productivity shifts affected the terms of trade. Assuming pure competition, they advocated that England industrialize simply to avoid the increasing costs of producing its food and other raw materials at home. Yet as noted earlier, until 1824, England prohibited the exportation of textile machinery so as to maintain its monopoly power in clothing manufacture and extort high prices from consumers abroad. Mill accordingly did not close his mind to the possibility that one nation or group of nations might monopolize the fruits of world technological progress. "It is even possible to conceive of an extreme case," he remarked,

> in which the whole of the advantage resulting from the interchange would be reaped by one party, the other gaining nothing at all. There is no absurdity in the hypothesis of that, of some given commodity, a certain quantity is all that is wanted at any price; and that, when that quantity is obtained, no fall in the exchange value would induce other consumers to come forward, or those who are already supplied to take more.[9]

Today's economic jargon calls this "price-inelastic trade." Its analysis along the lines suggested by Mill is an example of "elasticity pessimism." If world demand for English cloth is price-inelastic, then the added export volume thrown onto world markets as a result of increased English productivity will force prices down *more* than proportionally to the productivity gain. This leaves England worse off than before ($OC_1$ in Figure 6.2), until such time as it shifts its industrial labor to produce commodities more in demand.

---

[7] *Ibid.*, pp. 583, 592.     [8] *Ibid.*, p. 593.     [9] *Ibid.*, p. 587.

In the case of unitary demand elasticity, England's increased exportation of cloth would be just offset by its proportional decline in price, so that its overall export revenue would remain constant (OC$_2$). Only when the increased supply at a lower price substantially extends the realm of consumers would the "elastic demand" case be in effect, enabling England to gain somewhat *more* wine per unit of cloth-making labor (OC$_3$).

Price inelasticity occurs when only a given amount of output is wanted regardless of how low prices may fall—or how high they may rise. Populations need to eat, they need energy and often are willing to pay exorbitant prices for replacement parts. This leads many nations to strive for self-sufficiency in these types of commodities—and to make their customers dependent on them for their supply.

Fig. 6.2: Effect on England's Terms of Trade of Doubling its Industrial Productivity (Based on Edgeworth's diagram from "The Pure Theory of International Trade," p. 293).

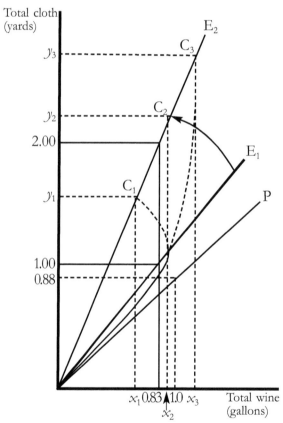

Key: C$_1$: inelastic demand for England's added cloth
        output
      C$_2$: unit elasticity of demand for English cloth
      C$_3$: elastic demand for English cloth (income terms-
        of-trade increase with added English produc-
        tivity and output)

Agricultural countries produced commodities in general world oversupply. Stated in the language of Mill and Edgeworth, their crop surpluses forced their offer curves back against their own domestic cost-constraint lines (as Portugal's terms of trade for its wine were forced toward OX$_3$ in Figure 6.1). They could avoid falling export prices by developing their own urban markets to consume their crops at home rather than leaving them to be sold on world markets. This would involve shifting labor out of agriculture into industry to produce manufactured goods to displace imports, thereby weakening industrial prices on world markets.

Mill applied an analysis along similar lines to determine which countries would bear the costs of transporting international commodities. Shipping costs were a kind of overhead to be paid for out of the overall gains from trade. The effect was like a tariff, narrowing the width of cost differentials among nations. "It may seem at first," Mill remarked,

> that every country will pay its own cost of carriage; that is, the carriage of the article it imports: ... This, however, cannot be affirmed with certainty. ... No absolute rule, therefore, can be laid down for the division of the cost [of transport], no more than for the division of the advantage.[10]

The incidence of transport charges depended on the laws of supply and demand. Countries exporting products in relatively abundant supply (for instance, food and other raw materials) tended to bear the incidence of transport costs, a point that Mill's protectionist contemporaries in the United States stressed in arguing how American farmers suffered from existing trade patterns.

Terms-of-trade analysis indicated that forward-looking economies should specialize in the production of industrial products whose long-term demand was rising relative to their supply. Tariff protection was required to render such investment and employment profitable. Initially lower industrial efficiency (and hence higher domestic prices) would be partially compensated by the positive impact on the terms of trade for the crop output that remained after satisfying domestic urban demand. This was the ground on which Henry Clay argued for protective tariffs to transform the United States from a raw materials exporter into a self-sufficient industrial power. "If we do not create some new market, if we persevere in the existing pursuits of agriculture," he argued in 1824, "the inevitable consequences must be, to augment greatly the quantity of our produce [to be exported], and to lessen its value in the foreign market."[11]

Matters were aggravated by the fact that population growth—and hence, the number of producers—in the "newer" countries that exported raw materials tended to outstrip demographic growth in Europe's more densely populated industrial nations. Producing a world surplus of primary commodities relative to that of manufactures would lead to chronic weakness in the price of primary commodities relative to industrial goods. And in 1820, Clay anticipated Mill's reasoning that the smaller the exportable surplus for any given commodity, the better its terms of trade would be.

The actual state of our population, and the ratio of its progressive increase, when compared with the ratio of the increase of the population of the countries that have hitherto consumed our raw produce, seem, to me, alone to demonstrate the necessity of diverting some portion of our industry from its accustomed channel. We double our population in about the term of twenty-

---

[10]  *Ibid.*, p. 589.
[11]  In Colton, *Life and Times of Henry Clay*, Vol. II (New York: 1846), p. 264.

five years. If there be no change in the mode of exerting our industry, we shall double, during the same term, the amount of our exportable produce. Europe, including such of her colonies as we have free access to, taken altogether, does not duplicate her population in a shorter term, probably, than one hundred years. The ratio of the increase of her capacity of consumption, therefore, is, to that of our capacity of production, as one is to four. And it is manifest, from the simple exhibition of the powers of the consuming countries, compared with those of the supplying country, that the former ate inadequate to the latter. It is certainly true, that a portion of the mass of our raw produce, which we transmit to her, reverts to us in a fabricated form, and that this return augments with our increasing population. This is, however, a very inconsiderable addition to her actual ability to afford a market for the produce of our country.[12]

Assuming no net change in factor productivity between Britain and the United States, Clay's model depicted the balance between world supply and demand as depending on the rate of population growth and output in the raw-materials exporters as compared with that in the industrial nations:

$$\Delta \left( \frac{\text{population}_{US}}{\text{population}_{Eng}} \right) = \Delta \left( \frac{\text{output}_{US}}{\text{exports}_{Eng}} \right) = \Delta \left( \frac{\text{export}_{US}}{\text{export}_{Eng}} \right) - \Delta \left( \frac{\text{export prices}_{US}{}^{food}}{\text{export prices}_{Eng}{}^{ind}} \right)$$

Productivity factors also had to be considered, of course. If agricultural countries were characterized by diminishing returns, their export surplus would not keep pace with their population growth. World food prices would indeed rise, as the Ricardians feared. Conversely, despite slower population growth in the industrial nations, their exportable surplus of manufactures might keep pace with the volume of world raw-materials exports, thanks to technological progress and its increasing returns in industry.

The question was, what would grow more rapidly: industrial relative to agricultural productivity, or the world's agricultural population and its output relative to the supply of industrial exports? Protectionists developed the "home market" argument urging America to nurture an urban population to consume the West's farm surpluses, thereby removing this output from world markets so that it would not force down the price of food relative to that of industrial manufactures. For the industrial terms of trade to decline, industrial pro-ductivity would have to grow as rapidly (or exceed) the rate of population growth and output in the agricultural countries, and the demand for industrial products would have to be elastic relative to that for food and raw materials.

Along these lines some protectionists in the United States—most promi-nently Alexander Everett, a Bostonian associate of John Quincy Adams and Daniel Webster—projected a strategy for exploitative U.S. trade. In a debate

---

[12]  Speech of April 20, 1820, quoted in Colton, *ibid.*, p. 147.

with Professor George Tucker of Virginia, an opponent of industrialization, Everett asserted that if industrial productivity in the United States increased (which he thought would occur automatically in proportion to the nation's rising population density), and even if domestic prices declined in keeping with these lower production costs, industrial export prices need not necessarily fall. Supply and demand conditions, he hoped, might enable industrialized America to avoid sharing the benefits of its productivity gains.

Everett's logic was that the relative command of industrial-nation labor over that in agricultural countries would increase in proportion to its productivity gains—assuming productivity in agricultural countries to remain unchanged while their growing rural populations increased food production to meet (and even surpass) the growth of food demand in the industrial nations. Under these assumptions America's manufacturing productivity would double with every doubling of its population, enabling the nation to import twice as much food or raw materials from other countries per industrial worker.

To this argument Prof. Tucker replied in typically Ricardian fashion:

> As soon as the improvement [in industrial productivity] has lost its temporary character of monopoly, and becomes diffused, the article produced falls in price according to the amount of that saving, and it will take a proportionately greater amount of it to purchase the same quantity of raw produce.[14]

Everett conceded the point, and the remainder of his argument was basically Ricardian. Because of diminishing returns in agriculture, the United States must become an industrial power simply in order to obtain cheap foodstuffs once its land came to be "fully occupied" to the point where diminishing returns threatened to characterize its agriculture. Whereas this prospect formed an argument for English free trade to minimize that nation's labor costs of production, it thus formed an argument for protective tariffs in the United States. The idea was to develop an industrial potential to export manufactures at a future date when the United States would become like England, a high-cost producer of raw materials.

Marx held that "most agricultural peoples are forced to sell their product *below* its value," that is, below the high-cost margin of production in the industrial nations, "whereas in countries with advanced capitalist production the

---

[13] Furthermore, elaborated Colton (*ibid.*, p. 316): "All who work at manufactures and trades established by a protective policy, are withdrawn from agricultural pursuits, and give to the residue employed in agriculture better chances for a ready market and high prices."

[14] "The Malthusian Theory—Discussed in a Correspondence between Alex H. Everett and Professor George Tucker, of the University of Virginia," *The United States Magazine and Democratic Review*, XVII (November 1845), p. 381. Everett's fellow Boston protectionist, Francis Bowen, reiterated his ideas in his *Principles of Political Economy, applied to the Condition, the Resources, and the Institutions of the American People* (Boston: 1856).

agricultural product rises to its value."[15] This meant that less developed countries had to expend more labor of low industrial productivity (or high raw-materials productivity) to produce a product that exchanged for one requiring less labor of higher industrial productivity (or using high-productivity capital) in the industrial lead nations. (To make matters worse, sugar produced by tropical countries is sold today below the price that U.S. sugar brings in the American market, much as American oil companies in the Middle East bought oil for many years at prices far below that which domestic U.S. oil was bringing in its own protected market.) As long as labor time was the measure of value, high-productivity industrial nations would receive more labor in any international exchange. Marx and the protectionists were in agreement in this conclusion. The solution was for agricultural peoples to develop their own urban markets.

With regard to the cost of tariff protection, the question was the extent to which its favorable impact on the terms of trade would compensate for its cost to consumers. In a 1903 memorandum to Parliament, Alfred Marshall applied a supply-and-demand analysis to the question of which foreign countries might be made to bear the incidence of English tariffs. For a country "to throw any considerable share of the burden of her tariff on other countries," Marshall analyzed, she (using the feminine pronoun for Mother England) must be

> in a position to dispense with a great part of the goods which she imports from them; while she is at the same time in the possession of such large and firmly established partial monopolies, that those countries cannot easily dispense with any considerable past of their imports from her. So far as the latter condition is concerned, England was in a strong position early in [the] last century.

The issue turned on the relative "urgencies of these reciprocal demands … The burden of these [import] taxes will be thrown mainly on B in the exceptional case in which B's demand for A's goods is very urgent (and inelastic) while A's demand for B's goods is not." England had approached such a favorable position when it sold wool to Flanders, and in the early nineteenth century when it exported "manufactures made by steam machinery, which was not in general use anywhere else." Meanwhile, England easily obtained tropical products from economies that faced the alternative cost of producing manufactures at prices increasingly beyond their means, so that it did not seem worthwhile to begin industrializing. Indeed, concluded Marshall, "it is possible that the rest of the world would have given twice as much of their own goods as it did give … rather than go wholly without" English manufactures.[16]

---

[15]  Marx, *Theories of Surplus Value*, Vol. II, p. 475.
[16]  Alfred Marshall, "Memorandum on Fiscal Policy of International Trade" (1903), in *Official Papers* (London: 1926), pp. 372–73, 376.

By putting industry further out of the reach of non-industrialized countries, wider cost disparities among nations increased the opportunity to exert monopoly power. The wider the cost divergences, the larger the Ricardian "gains from trade," but also the opportunity for exploitative trade. Conversely, England's ability to shift the burden of its tariffs onto the shoulders of foreigners would be eroded if industrial technology spread to other countries, while the growth of its own domestic population required higher imports of food and other raw materials. But Marshall concluded that the industrial nations seemed likely to secure most of the gains from trade. Lower transport costs also would work to the advantage of industrial nations (much as did their rising productivity), by leaving a wider range in which to extort an economic rent ("superprofit") on their exports. "In so far as the increasing economy of transport and manufacture enables Western goods to be disposed of in backward countries where before they could not compete with handmade products, the exporting country gets a great share of the benefit."[17]

Even if the commodity terms of trade were to decline in response to higher productivity, countries experiencing increasing returns would gain *as long as the decline in their export prices was less than their productivity gain*. They would produce a given export volume with less labor, capital and land, enabling these inputs to purchase a larger quantity of imports for each unit of input.

## *The factoral terms of trade*

Mill incorporated productivity shifts into his terms-of-trade analysis by emphasizing that

> a country gets a commodity cheaper when it obtains a greater quantity of the commodity with the same expenditure of labor and capital. In this sense of the term, cheapness in a great measure depends upon a cause of a different nature: a country gets its imports cheaper, in proportion to the general productiveness of its domestic industry; to the general efficiency of its labor.[18]

An exporting economy would gain if its industrial, agricultural or mining productivity were to double (wage rates remaining constant) while export prices for these sectors declined by less than 50 per cent. Although its commodity terms of trade would fall, the return to its factors of production would increase.

Classical economists did not leave capital investment out of account in calculating labor productivity. They recognized capital inputs as well as direct labor content. In 1937, Jacob Viner followed this approach in recognizing total factor costs—that is, the overall labor, capital and land costs of producing exports

---

[17]  Marshall, *Official Papers*, p. 403.          [18]  Mill, *Principles*, p. 604.

(but not "external" costs such as economic infrastructure or the replacement cost of depletable minerals)—in elaborating this distinction between the commodity terms of trade (sometimes called the barter terms of trade) and the *factoral* terms of trade, which trace the ratio at which the products of a country's "factor inputs" (labor and capital, and sometimes land) exchange for those of other countries.

Using modern symbols, let N represent the commodity terms of trade, $P_x$ the export price index, and $P_m$ the import price index, so that $N = P_x/P_m$. Viner defines the single factoral terms of trade (S) as representing the commodity terms of trade (N) adjusted for "the index of cost in terms of the quantity of factors of production used per unit of export," that is, $F_x$, (factor productivity in the export sector). Thus, $S = N(F_x)$. Even if N declines, a net improvement in S occurs as long as the increase in $F_x$ exceeds the decline in N—that is, as long as productivity gains in the export sector surpass the decline in export prices relative to the price of imports. And in fact, the factoral terms of trade have diverged steadily from the commodity terms of trade as productivity rates have diverged throughout the world.

Today's writers often use a simple labor-productivity concept in terms of output per manhour that relates productivity changes only to direct labor costs, not total factor costs. This leaves the cost of capital out of account, as well as social infrastructure and other inputs. If output per manhour is termed Z (after Gerald Meier's usage), and $Z_x$ represents output per manhour in the export sector, then the formula for the single factoral terms of trade $S_z = N(Z_x)$ treats capital as a cost-free production input. To trace shifts in the exchange of one country's labor *and other productive factors* for those of other countries, Viner pointed to what he termed the "double factoral terms of trade" (D), so that $D = N(F_x/F_m)$, or in Meier's more limited usage, $D_z = N(Z_x/Z_m)$, with $Z_m$ representing labor productivity in the supplier countries exporting to the country whose terms of trade are under analysis.

The older writers usually accepted the double factoral terms of trade as identical in their trend with the commodity terms of trade, which would be correct under their assumptions of production under conditions of constant costs and historically stable costs. But with cost variable, whether in respect to output or to time, the trends of the two indices could be substantially divergent. The double factoral terms of trade index would approach more closely to an index of the international *division* of gain than to an index of the absolute amount of gain for either country.[19]

---

[19]   Viner, *Studies*, pp. 561-62.

The double factoral terms of trade increase when a unit of domestic factors exchanges for more units of foreign factors embodied in imports. This is the ultimate measure of equity in export pricing, because rising output per manhour does not result from cost-free technology, after all. Capital costs money, and any measure of the "fair" terms of trade must reflect returns to the investment embodied in capital-intensive exports. To use modern terminology, only if labor were the sole input would the double factoral terms of trade remain constant among nations under an equitable exchange, that is, one in which the barter terms of trade deteriorate to reflect increases in output per manhour. Capital entering the production process requires compensation by depreciation (the return *of* capital) as well as profit (the return *to* capital). The higher the capital/labor ratio, the greater will be depreciation and profit as a proportion of total value. Even under the purest competition, the commodity terms of trade will decline more slowly than the increase in output per man-hour, because a higher capital investment is required per unit of output.

Meier contends that a country's position improves if it obtains a rising volume of imports per unit of labor embodied in its exports, regardless of whether workers in its trading partners obtain an even greater bargain. "What matters to the importing country is whether it receives more goods per unit of its 'exported factor input' (an improvement in S [the single factoral terms of trade])," [20] not whether these imports happen to contain more or less foreign factor input units than before. He therefore finds the single factoral terms of trade to be the most appropriate welfare measure.

Mill and his contemporaries would not have agreed. In discussing how productivity gains were shared, they adhered to the double factoral terms of trade as an indicator of exploitation of one labor force by another. Since then, less developed countries have suffered more from deteriorating double factoral terms of trade than from falling commodity terms of trade. This is because productivity gains in the industrial nations have outstripped those in Third World countries, in agriculture as well as industry, but the commodity terms of trade have not fallen to reflect these gains.

Raul Prebisch views this as an index of exploitation. While rising productivity in the industrial nations tends to support rising incomes, union labor in these nations secures the fruits of productivity gains, exploiting low-wage non-union labor in Third World countries where surplus agricultural labor and chronic inflation depresses real wages and impedes the development of labor unions.

---

[20]  Gerald Meier, *The International Economics of Development* (New York 1968), p. 44.

Furthermore, the United States and Europe support farm income with price supports to provide farmers with income parity vis-à-vis industrial labor. Third World countries enjoy no such supports, to the detriment of their agricultural investment. These "structural dynamics" depress Third World income, while their declining terms of trade cause trade deficits that spur currency depreciation and hence domestic inflation. Prebisch's United Nations report concludes that "the great industrial centers not only keep for themselves the benefit of the use of new techniques in their economy, but are in a favorable position to obtain a share of that deriving from the technical progress of the periphery."[21]

Prebisch does not explain why low-wage Third World labor cannot undersell the union labor of the industrial nations, or how high-wage labor drives low-wage labor out of the market. He points to the fact that industrial economies can produce many raw materials or industrial substitutes (such as oil and rubber) at considerably less expense than the cost to less developed countries of undertaking the investment and creating the infrastructure necessary to produce for themselves the food and manufactures they now import from the more sophisticated and evenly balanced economies.

Prebisch is reminiscent of Henry Clay in attributing the deterioration in the Third World's terms of trade to "the relatively slow rate at which world demand for primary commodities grows in comparison with that of industrial products."[22] Industrial economies tend to become more self-sufficient and broadly diversified over time, while raw-materials monocultures become more dependent on foreign trade. This renders them more prone to exploitation by their suppliers. But whereas Clay pointed to the different rates of population growth as between the periphery and industrial center, Prebisch cites Engel's Law, which states that as incomes rise, a diminishing proportion is spent on food and clothing, and a rising share on services and manufactures. The substitution of low-cost industrial synthetics for raw materials—for example, plastics for steel—suggests that Third World exports are relatively income-inelastic.

Hans Singer has observed that "Technical progress, while it operates unequivocally in favor of manufactures—since the rise in real incomes generates a more than proportionate increase in the demand for manufactures—has

---

[21] United Nations Economic Commission for Latin America, *The Economic Development of Latin America and its Political Problems* (Lake Success, New York: 1950), p. 14.
[22] United Nations, *Towards a Dynamic Development Policy for Latin America* (New York: 1963), p. 78.

not the same effect on the demand for food and raw materials."[23] (This represents Edgeworth's case OC$_3$ in Figure 6.2.) These technological and income-elasticity dynamics create a structural problem for raw-materials exporters, whose income cannot grow as fast as those in the industrial nations "without generating a chronic deficit in the balance of payments."[24] Less industrialized countries become more import oriented as their incomes rise and consumer spending shifts toward industrial products, while the industrial nations import fewer raw materials relative to their growth in income. Although their incomes rise more rapidly than those of less developed countries, their demand for raw materials lags behind world demand for manufactures. (Werner Sombart postulated this as a "law" of the falling importance of foreign trade as national income increases.)[25]

Haberler counters that although Engel's Law "is well established as a description of household behavior in homogeneous populations" as applied to food, "it is a long way from there" to generalize about price relationships between primary and manufactured comodities.[26] He argues that the declining share of world trade represented by primary commodities results mainly from (1) specific classes of raw materials being replaced by synthetics or experiencing substantial cost reductions for their production; (2) cyclical swings around trend lines whose slope depends largely on one's choice of where the trend should start; and (3) a decline in shipping costs and other overhead charges. It may be added that for many Third World countries, especially those exporting copper and oil, their food deficits have tended to outstrip their dependency on industrial products. This is just the opposite of what Engel's Law would suggest. The problem stems mainly from their agricultural backwardness.

Contrary to Ricardian expectations, the industrial nations have become major food exporters. Since the early 1960s the most rapid rise in U.S. exports (next to arms sales) has been in grain, while rural India has found the most active component of its export growth to be manufactured goods and, most recently, information services! In view of the chronic food deficits that tend to accompany monoculture export patterns, it is simplistic to view the specialization of world labor as representing an industrial center and a raw-materials exporting periphery.

---

[23] Hans Singer, "The Distribution of Gains between Investing and Borrowing Countries," *American Economic Revue, Papers and Proceedings*, Vol. II (May 1950), repr. in James Theberge ed., *Economics of Trade and Development* (New York: 1968), p. 242.

[24] M. June Flanders, "Prebisch on Protectionism: An Evaluation," *Economic Journal* (1964), repr. Theberge, *op. cit.*, p. 317.

[25] On this point see Haberler, "Terms of Trade and Economic Development" (1961), reprinted in Theberge, *op. cit.*, p. 333.

[26] Haberler, "Terms of Trade ...," in Theberge, *op. cit.*, pp. 331–32.

Although Prebisch points to the fact that wage levels and living standards have risen more rapidly in the industrial nations, not all of the terms-of-trade benefits enjoyed by them stem exclusively from wage differentials. They result increasingly from the returns to (and of) capital. Comparison of international trends in *total* factor productivity therefore mutes the Prebisch "wage divergence" measure of exploitation. Some of the failure of industrial export prices to reflect reductions in cost of output per manhour is "earned" by the capital responsible for this saving of labor. A similar over-simplification neglecting the need for investors to earn profits and depreciation on their capital characterizes the popular view that domestic wage rates should rise in proportion to increases in output per manhour. As noted above, this assumes capital to be a cost-free factor of production. It therefore is necessary to move away from Prebisch's factor-productivity $Z_m/Z_x$ measure to the more appropriate Mill-Viner factoral $F_m/F_x$ measure.

Over and above these capital costs of production are "external" costs in the form of social infrastructure spending. These should be recaptured largely out of export proceeds if the host country has to borrow from the World Bank or other international consortia to put in place an extractive infrastructure (power, roads, harbor facilities and so forth) to induce multinational corporations to engage in mineral depletion, these social costs should be recognized and treated as a subtrahend from what the firm or industry brings into the country. But today's pro-business laissez faire models avoid taking such costs into account.

Labor in the United States or Germany is highly productive partly because of expensive educational to obtain technological skills. Some portion of labor's higher wage levels in the industrial nations represents compensation for these costs educational and other costs needed to achieve superior productivity. Oligarchic Third World governments are as responsible for this state of affairs as are labor unions in the industrial nations. Higher education in repressive countries is associated with political instability stemming from student revolts and the spread of modern political values that stand at odds with the regressive social and political institutions imposed on these countries.

Properly used, the factoral terms of trade can focus attention on productivity rather than only on commodity prices. To the extent that falling terms of trade reflect technological progress, they enable countries to undersell their competitors in world markets. Rather than signifying a deterioration in the international position of innovative economies, cost-cutting becomes a policy aim.

Today's orthodox theorizing tends to pigeonhole technology as an "exogenous" topic lying outside the boundaries of economics proper. Neglect of its institutional aspect has led Prebisch and the United Nations Conference on

Trade and Development (UNCTAD) to urge terms-of-trade compensation as a subsidy to provide agricultural and other raw-materials exporters with a "retransfer [of] whatever income they may have lost through the operation of market forces whose action has been preventing the leveling-up of their income with that of the urban sectors."[27] The problem is that such income-transfer schemes leave in place existing production and dependency patterns. They would subsidize the lack of domestic self-sufficiency rather than reallocate resources away from the export sector to focus on domestic development as the United States did in the 19th century.

---

[27] Raul Prebisch, "Development Problems of the Peripheral Countries and the Terms of Trade," repr. in Theberge, *op. cit.*, p. 294.

# 7

## Technology and Trade Theory

By the early nineteenth century most observers recognized that capital was displacing labor and even land. Protectionists used this to argue that governments should subsidize capital accumulation by tariffs and subsidies. Marxists saw a class struggle between capital and labor. Free traders sought to avoid such conclusions simply by not talking about technology. One result was the factor-proportions model discussed in the next chapter. The present chapter reviews how broadly technology was perceived in the Industrial Revolution's early years, and how free-trade and protectionist models have differing concepts of capital and technology, and hence of what constitutes the productive services of labor, capital and the soil.

### *The substitution of capital for labor at declining cost*

As early as 1804, Lauderdale pointed out that Hume's wage-equalization and price-specie flow mechanism failed to take into account the industrial technology that was replacing labor with capital.

> When Mr HUME, in the middle of last century, supposed that the progress of human industry, in any country, was bounded and confined by the check it must receive from the augmentation of wages, and "that manufactures gradually shift their places, leaving those countries and provinces which they have already enriched, and flying to others, whither they are allured by the cheapness of provisions and labour, till they have enriched these also, and are again banished by the same causes"; he did not sufficiently attend to the unlimited resources that are to be found in the ingenuity of man in inventing means of supplanting labour by capital; for any possible augmentation of wages that increased opulence can occasion, is but a trifling drawback on the great advantages a country derives, not only from the ingenuity of man in supplanting labour by machinery, but from capital laid out in roads, canals, bridges, inclosures, shipping; and employed in the conduct of home and foreign trade, all of which is alike engaged in supplanting the necessity of paying the wages of labour.[1]

---

[1] Lauderdale, *Inquiry into the Nature and Origin of Public Wealth* (1804), pp. 298-99, quoting David Hume, *Discourse on Money* (Edinburgh: 1752), p. 43. On the evolution of the concept of capital, see Eugen von Böhm-Bawerk, *Capital and Interest: A Critical History of Economical Theory* (1890), Karl Marx, *Theories of Surplus Value*, and Edwin Cannan, *A History of Theories of Production and Distribution* (London: 1917), esp. Chapter 4.

If labor alone created products, and if it were equally productive through-out the world, then wages and profits in one country could not long surpass those in other countries under free trade. However, capital-intensive production complicates the analysis of how wage differentials and variations in output per manhour influence international costs. England's power looms produced textiles at a much lower price (and in far greater quantity) than even India's low-paid subsistence workers could match, emerging victorious over foreign and domestic cottage industry alike, including skilled workers operating spinning jennies in their homes. Industrial looms provided great profits for English manufacturers even in the face of rising subsistence wage costs. And in time, technology enabled well-equipped and protected high-wage American and German labor to undersell the products of English industry, despite the latter's stagnant wage levels.

The distinguishing feature of the Industrial Revolution was that machin-ery performed production services hitherto supplied by manual labor, at only a fraction of the cost. As early as 1691 (in a passage probably written in 1665), William Petty anticipated that labor-saving technology would become an alternative to increasing the population: "introducing the Compendium, and Facilitations of Art," he wrote, "is equivalent to what men vainly hoped for from *Polygamy*. For as much as he that can do the Work of five men by one, effects the same as the begetting of four adult Workmen."[2] By 1695, John Cary "considered the introduction of machinery as the means whereby the cost disadvantage of high wages could be avoided in foreign competition."[3] In 1757, Josiah Tucker forecast that the

> System of Machines, which so greatly reduces the Price of Labor, as to enable the Generality of a people to become Purchasers of Goods, will in the End, though not immediately, employ more Hands in the Manufacture, than could possibly have found Employment, had no such Machines been invented.[4]

Citing the occupations of machine tenders, makers and bookkeepers as being spurred by capital-intensive production, Tucker pointed out that an ex-panding economy would hire more workers as machine builders and tenders than were displaced by mechanized production.

James Steuart likewise found that mechanization posed no inherent threat to labor. "Machines," he wrote, "I consider as a method of augmenting (virtually) the number of the industrious, without the expence of feeding an additional

---

[2]  William Petty, *Verbum Sapienti* (1691), in *Economic Writings*, Hull ed., Vol. I, p. 118. See also Steuart, *Principles of Political Oeconomy*, Vol. I, p. 159 (quoted below in Ch. 10).

[3]  John Cary, *An Essay on the State of England in Relation to its Trade* (1695), cited in Edgar Furniss, *The Position of the Laborer in a System of Nationalism* (Boston: 1920), p. 176 n.

[4]  Tucker, *Instructions for Travellers* (1757), in *Writings*, Schuyler ed., pp. 241–42. (cited in Samuel Hollander, *The Economics of Adam Smith* [Toronto: 1973], p. 66).

number." Machines provided work effort at a lower cost than would be necessary to enable the human laborer to perform a similar amount, but "this by no
means obstructs natural and useful population. ... We have shewn how population must go on, in proportion to subsistence, and in proportion to industry."
Capital accumulation led to more output, and hence to greater opportunities to
export manufactures for the crops needed to feed the growing population.

Steuart emphasized that "the machine eats nothing, so does not diminish
subsistence," which formed the ultimate cost of wages. It followed that "industry
(in our age at least) is in no danger of being overstocked [with capital] in any
well governed state." Population would proportion itself to the growing capital
stock rather than being impaired by it. There was no solid ground for viewing
labor-abridging machines as a "scheme for starving the poor." What England
needed was a plan

> enabling the industrious to feed themselves at the expense of foreigners. The
> introduction of machines is found to reduce prices in a surprising manner. And
> if they have the effect of taking bread from hundreds, formerly employed in
> performing their simple operations, they have that also of giving bread to
> thousands, by extending numberless branches of ingenuity which, without the
> machines, would have remained circumscribed within very narrow limits. What
> progress has not building made within these hundred years? Who doubts that
> the conveniency of great iron works, and saw mills, prompts many to build? And
> this taste has greatly contributed to increase, not diminish, the number both of
> smiths and carpenters, as well as to extend navigation ... the first inventors gain
> thereby a superiority which nothing but adopting the same invention can
> counterbalance.[5]

Adam Smith likewise believed that more capital would increased employment. "The number of useful and productive labourers ... is every where in
proportion to the quantity of capital stock which is employed in setting them to
work." More machinery or other types of capital would require additional workers
to be hired.

Smith attributed productivity growth and hence industrial advantage to
the division of labor, which, "so far as it can be introduced, occasions, in every
art, a proportionable increase in the productive powers of labor." He further
viewed the division of labor as a function of market size, thereby endorsing the
extension of world markets through freer trade.[6] Smith defined the productive

---

[5]   Steuart, *Principles of Political Oeconomy* (1767), Vol. I, pp. 123, 295.
[6]   Smith, *Wealth of Nations*, Book I, Ch. i. On Smith's views see Hollander, *Adam Smith*, pp.
      217, 209. Marx was one of the first economists to criticize Smith for "the subordinate part
      which he assigns to machinery" and perceiving no factor in economic or technological
      progress save the division of labor. See *Capital*, Vol. I (New York: 1906), quoted in Hollan-
      der, *Adam Smith*, p. 215.

powers of capital in terms of its ability to save labor, but said little about the role played by capital in mechanizing the production process or whether this might displace or compete with labor. His view of technology thus was essentially pre-industrial. Instead of noting the steam-powered production just then getting underway, he focused on pin making, a process that used labor almost unaided by capital! The implication was that productivity gains derived from the efforts of labor alone, aided only by simple tool-like capital. As Samuel Hollander has observed, this assumed merely marginal technological break-throughs taking the form of *minor* changes generated by machine users.[7]

But was capital in the form of simple tools such as hammers the same as more complex, steam-powered machinery? Capital hitherto had not seriously threatened to compete with and displace human labor, but it was shifting from being a labor-supplementing to a labor-supplanting tool. Although Smith made specific reference to the steam engine (then called a fire-engine) and was a friend of his fellow Scot James Watt (who invented the principle of separate condensation in Glasgow in 1765), he did not perceive the radical transformation brought about by this invention ushering in an epoch of mechanized production.

Lauderdale posed the question of whether employment would necessarily keep pace with the rate of capital accumulation and output as employers installed machines to save and "abridge" labor:

> The idea, that capital puts labour into motion, that it adds to the productive powers of labour, gives rise to the opinion that labour … is every where proportioned to the quantity of existing capital; that the general industry of a country is always proportioned to the capital that employs it; and therefore authorises the inference, that the increase of capital is the sovereign and unbounded means of augmenting wealth.[8]

Far from this being the case, he warned, capital might well be a source of unemployment, as when machinery was introduced to save the cost of hiring labor.

> Some fire-engines draw more water from a coal-pit in one day, than could be conveyed on the shoulders of 300 men, even assisted by the machinery of buckets; and a fire-engine undoubtedly performs its labour at a much smaller

---

[7]  Hollander, *Adam Smith*, pp. 212ff., citing Smith's *Lectures* p. 385 (Cannan ed., pp. 167–68), and *Wealth of Nations*, p. 10. Hollander observes (p. 226) with reference to Book I, ch. viii of *The Wealth of Nations*) that Smith confused the size of individual funds with society's aggregate of capital stock in stating that the average production unit would expand as the national stock of capital increased. "The argument of Smith implies strongly that an increase in the wage rate, if unaccompanied by increased scale of plant (or by external economies), would *not* in itself lead to the generation of labour-saving inventions or the adoption of existing labour-saving processes."

[8]  Lauderdale, *Inquiry*, pp. 203–04. See also p. 161.

expense than the amount of wages of those whose labor it supplants. This is, in truth, the case with all machinery.[9]

Lauderdale concluded that

capital, whether fixed or circulating, whether embarked in the home or in foreign trade, far from being employed in putting labour into motion, or in adding to the productive powers of [unaided] labour, is, on the contrary, alone useful and profitable to mankind, from the circumstance of its either supplanting the necessity of a portion of labour, that would otherwise be performed by the hand of man,—or of its executing a portion of labour, beyond the reach of the power of man to accomplish …

Ricardo likewise acknowledged that mechanized production could result in unemployment. In 1817, during the industrial depression that followed the Napoleonic Wars, he wrote: "Thus then is the public benefited by machinery: these mute agents are always the produce of much less labour than that which they displace even when they are of the same money value." That is, a more productive machine cost less to operate than to buy an equivalent sum of work performed by manual labor.[10]

The result was that while England's rural exodus from the land supplied loom fodder for the Industrial Revolution, its population of steam engines and other machinery performed work tasks at a fraction of what it would have cost human labor to subsist while performing a similar production service. Employment increased, but wage rates did not rise to reflect the higher productivity, thanks to capital's labor-competing powers. Profits were invested in machinery and equipment rather than used to hire more labor, although some compensation existed in the fact that more labor was employed to produce capital goods and perform the new types of tasks associated with mechanized production.

In contrast to Smith's emphasis on labor productivity resulting from the extension of markets, Lauderdale was almost alone among the major British economists in retaining the mercantilist stress on capital's role in increasing the nation's productive powers. This approach was picked up primarily outside of England. American protectionists in particular pointed out that the labor-displacing powers of capital could create compensating employment opportunities among machine builders and operators only in a broadly industrialized economy. They further advocated industrial tariffs to finance the accumulation of such capital. Such tariffs, they promised, would protect domestic labor from having its wage rates reduced to the level at which England's machine power could perform a similar quantum of work effort.

---

[9] Lauderdale, *ibid.*, pp. 166–67.
[10] Ricardo, *Principles of Political Economy and Taxation*, p. 42.

American and continental European labor was threatened not as much by England's low-paid labor as by its growing population of steam engines, which provided production services at a far lower price than even the lowest paid Indian worker could match. "The employment of machinery," wrote Alexander Hamilton in 1790,

> forms an item of great importance in the general mass of national industry. It is an artificial force brought in aid of the natural force of man, and, to all the purposes of labor, is an increase of hands, an accession of strength, unencumbered, too, by the expense of maintaining the laborer …
>
>     To illustrate this last idea, let it be supposed that the difference in price in two countries of a given quantity of manual labor requisite to the fabrication of a given article is as ten, and that some MECHANIC power is introduced into both countries which, performing half the necessary labor, leaves only half to be done by hand, it is evident that the difference in the cost of fabrication of the article in question in the two countries, as far as it is connected with the price of labor, will be reduced from ten to five in consequence of the introduction of that POWER.[11]

Hamilton pointed out that Smith's argument as to the superior opportunities offered by industry for the division of labor was a good reason *not* to apply the principle of specialization of production internationally. If the United States depended on England to be the workshop of the world, it would have to become England's granary and cotton supplier, foregoing its own opportunities for industrial division of labor. Specializing in agricultural pursuits would oblige women and children to remain idle a large part of the time, and also would lose much male labor potential during the winter months when farming was slow. Manufacturing would afford employment to "persons who would otherwise be idle (and in many cases a burden on the community), either from the bias of temper, habit, infirmity of body, or some other cause, indisposing or disqualifying them from the toils of the country." Each nation should provide as wide a field as possible to exploit the diversity of character of its inhabitants. To realize the maximum range of personal specialization, tariffs and subsidies were required to establish industry on a national scale.[12]

England widened its industrial advantage over the United States by substituting steam engines for manual labor with increasing efficiency. "Mr. Clay had occasion to note, as long ago as 1824," wrote his biographer Calvin Colton in 1848:

---

[11]  Alexander Hamilton, *Report on the Subject of Manufactures* (1790), reprinted in Frank W. Taussig, ed., *State Papers and Speeches on the Tariff* (Cambridge, Mass.: 1893), pp. 17, 35.
[12]  Taussig, *State Papers*, pp. 8, 15, 19.

that some British authorities estimated the machine power of Great Britain as equal to two hundred millions of men. The number of operatives to apply this machinery has never amounted to one million. Here, then, is a nation, with a population of some twenty-five millions, with a producing power of two hund-red millions. Its capabilities of producing wealth by artificial means, is so great, that its natural power is scarcely worthy of being brought into the account. ... One man at home did the work of two hundred, less or more ... Science, which makes one man as powerful as two hundred, or a thousand, left to their natural powers, will and must prevail against numbers. That nation which cultivates the useful, mechanic, and manufacturing arts, all of which have their foundation in science, and which excels in them, other things being equal, will excel in strength, and maintain a superiority.[13]

This type of comparison between man and machine permeated U.S. economic doctrine throughout the nineteenth century, resulting in a view of inter-national trade in which capital, operated by increasingly skilled labor, emerged victorious in competition with the efforts of unskilled low-wage workers.

The English social observer Henry Mayhew computed that by 1850 his nation's machine power had risen to the equivalent labor power of 600 million human beings).[14] Citing his computation, American protectionists argued that their nation's relatively high wage levels had to be defended against English industrial technology which threatened to undersell, by a widening margin, the employment of the human body as a supplier of raw work effort. Just as rail-roads powered by steam locomotives were rendering the horse population obsolete, *so unskilled manual labor would become obsolete in world markets unless provided with an appropriate complement of industrial capital.* Nations that did not raise their labor with sufficient skills to operate machine-driven mass production faced the prospect of a widening economic gap separating them from the lead-ing industrial powers. No matter how little their labor might be paid, its price of sustenance would still exceed the machine costs of supplying a comparable volume of work effort. The result would be unemployment and poverty in countries that failed to introduce modern production techniques.

The American school of technologically oriented economists co-measured labor and capital in terms of their output of work effort—horsepower, man-power, or energy measures such as joules, ergs or kilowatt-hours. The key measure was work output relative to cost. Ricardian analysis evaluated capital simply in terms of its manhour costs of construction and operation, not so much for its technological role in production. To the extent that Ricardo presented his gains-

---

[13] Colton, *Life and Times of Henry Clay*, Vol. II (New York: 1846), pp. 159–60. By "natural power" Colton referred to manual labor effort.

[14] Henry Mayhew, *London Labor and the London Poor* (London: 1851), p. 439, quoted in E. Peshine Smith, *Manual of Political Economy* (New York 1853), p. 72.

from-trade analysis as a branch of distribution theory, he neglected to consider the productive potential resulting from technological transformation. Like Smith, the Ricardians treated the hammer and the steam engine, the hand-fed loom and the steam-powered loom as similar forms of capital. Rising capital productivity would generate more output, but it would not produce more exchange value once the innovation spread into general use—unless nations were able to charge monopoly prices. Protectionists pointed out that they could do this only if their customers refrained from industrializing.

Smith defined capital as that portion of a nation's assets used to generate a net profit (income). This capital consisted of "circulating capital"—money, inventories of raw materials and finished goods, plus the "wages fund" or provisions used to pay laborers, and "fixed capital"—machinery and the stock of tools used by workers, buildings generating net income and, in the case of agriculture, the farm tools and livestock used by the farmer as well as improvements of land. Also included in Smith's notion of capital was what today is called human capital in the form of labor skills, that is "the acquired and useful abilities of all the inhabitants or members of the society."[15]

Being opposed to mercantilism and protective tariffs, Smith did not include the internal improvements undertaken by the state such as those cited by Lauderdale in the form of "roads, canals, bridges, inclosures, shipping," unless they were profit-making investments by private businessmen. This led Friedrich List in 1841 to write that Smith

> has merely taken the word capital in that sense in which it is necessarily taken by matters or merchants in their bookkeeping and their balance sheets. ... He has forgotten that the ability of the whole nation to increase the sum of its material capital consists mainly in the possibility of converting unused natural powers into material capital, into valuable and income-producing instruments, and that in the case of the merely agricultural nation a mass of natural powers lies idle or dead which can be quickened into activity only by manufactures.[16]

In other words, some countries had more potential than they were using, which did not appear on private-sector balance sheets. The key to realizing this potential was national policy.

Failure by less developed countries to accumulate industrial capital represented a logical complement to England's remarkable industrial growth. Displaced English industrial labor might find new employment in building machines or entering service professions, but such a shift abroad would be foreclosed in the absence of protective tariffs. This helps explain why technological analysis

[15]   Smith, *Wealth of Nations*, Book II, Ch. i.
[16]   Friedrich List, *National System of Political Economy* [1841] (London: 1885), pp. 227–28.

tended to be concentrated in the United States and Germany, whose protectionists were more concerned with what the growth of productive powers implied for international wage and employment trends than with income distribution as it would occur under the constant or diminishing returns of Ricardian analysis. From their analysis of technology, they concluded that protective tariffs were a precondition for securing an Economy of High Wages feedback principle through investment in capital goods and skilled labor (discussed in Chapter 9).

Smith endorsed the Economy of High Wages doctrine in his observation that

> The same cause ... which raises the wages of labour, the increase of stock, tends to increase its productive powers, and to make a smaller quantity of labour produce a greater quantity of work. ... There are many commodities, therefore, which, in consequence of these improvements, come to be produced by so much less labour than before, that the increase of its price is more than compensated by the diminution of its quantity?[17]

High-productivity labor reduced unit labor costs even though it might earn higher per diem wages. In making this observation Smith implied that larger-scale and higher-wage production tended to be more capital-intensive (that is, following "the increase of stock"). But he did not follow up the implication of this for trade strategy, or note that the converse of this principle was an Economy of Low Wages syndrome suffered by countries that failed to industrialize. This was the problem that Josiah Tucker described when he observed in 1776 that

> The inhabitants of a poor country, who ... generally live from hand to mouth, dare not make such costly experiments or embark on such expensive or long-winded undertakings as the inhabitants of a rich country can attempt and execute with ease?[18]

Such countries could not afford to apply the capital-intensive modes of production used by industrial nations. Their workers would face difficulty finding employment unless they could achieve the skill levels needed to enable them to use the increasingly sophisticated capital required for high-productivity labor. Attainment of such skills required relatively high incomes, and also government spending on public education supported by protective tariffs. Without such tariffs, less developed countries would have to export increasing amounts of raw materials and low-wage manufactures to pay for their industrial imports. The world economy would experience an Economy of High Wages alongside a Low-Wage obsolescence syndrome.

---

[17]  Smith, *Wealth of Nations*, Book I, Ch, viii, p. 86.
[18]  Tucker, *Four Tracts*, p. 24.

*Technology and the terms of trade*

A debate ensued as to how capitalists and their employees (along with landlords) would divide the output and income provided by the new technology. Steam-powered capital and related technology greatly increased the power of industrialists, heralding an era of great combines and trusts. This had far-reaching international as well as domestic consequences with regard to how the gains from international trade were divided. In both cases supply and demand factors played a role, as did monopoly power. It was recognized that technological innovators would reap initial superprofits until market competition drove returns back down to normal levels. For instance, when Gutenberg invented movable type, he sought to sell his printed bibles at the same high price as hand-copied ones. Prices dropped only gradually until printing returned normal profits. But with the great international trusts that were emerging, instead of industries being brought from infancy to maturity and then lowering their prices once tariffs no longer were necessary, they tended to evolve into vested interests seeking to retain their monopoly profits. Often this was done by cooperating with other monopolies to control the world market across national boundaries.

It seems incredible that free-trade economists remained blind to the fact that instead of the products of English labor being thrown onto the world market in competition with those of foreign labor, manufactures produced increasingly by capital were competing with labor-intensive foreign products. This was clearest in textile production. Even if the innovating nations and their customers shared the gains from trade equally (with export prices reflecting about half the cost savings), English producers would enjoy a widening international lead under conditions of increasing returns.

A parallel phenomenon existed in the domestic market. "It is true that the capitalist and labourer share in the productiveness of capitalist undertaking," noted the Austrian economist Eugen von Böhm-Bawerk, "but they share in this way, that the worker usually receives little—indeed very little—while the undertaker receives much." By contrast, "In the old handicrafts, entrepreneur and wage-earner, master and apprentice, belonged not so much to different social classes as simply to different generations. What the one was the other might be, and would be." However,

> It is quite different in great capitalist industry. ... Capital had gradually become a power. Machinery had appeared on the scene and won its great triumphs; and machinery everywhere helped to extend business on a great scale, and to give production more and more of a capitalist character. But this very introduction of machinery had begun to reveal an opposition which was forced on economic life with the development of capital, and daily grew in importance—the opposition between capital and labour.

Capitalist and worker belonged to different classes with opposing interests. "Machinery had shown how sharp could be the collision of interest between
capital and labour. Those machines which bore golden fruit to the capitalist
entrepreneur had, on their introduction, deprived thousands of workers of their
bread."[19] Industrialists aggravated matters by failing to pass on their productivity gains to consumers.

A similar statement could have been made for the international economy
as industrial nations kept the fruits of their technology at home rather than
passing on their productivity gains to less developed countries through falling
export prices. By maintaining their monopoly position in world markets,
producers extracted the price which their customers would have had to expend
to produce similar products for themselves. England's industrial monopoly thus
threatened to put the rest of the world in the same unenviable position as its
own working class. And upward mobility was becoming more difficult. The
entry price for less developed countries to join the ranks of the industrial
nations was becoming too high, given the industrial technology's critical mass
and indivisibilities of scale.

### *The sociological dimension of industrial technology*

Capital-intensive investment has shaped the distribution of income, the concentration of savings, and public spending needs for education and infrastructure,
as well as foreign investment patterns. Each of these economic dimensions pit
protectionism and socialism against laissez faire doctrine.

William Nassau Senior attributed profits to the capitalist's "abstinence"
from spending on consumption. In his view capitalists earned more than workers
because they were thrifty and used their income for productive purposes rather
than for immediate gratification. By logical extension, this view attributed
wealth and technological differences among nations to social and cultural habits
of thriftiness, bringing the Protestant Ethic into play. Also on the cultural plane,
free-trade proponents of agricultural monocultures in the southern slave states
of America prior to 1860 opposed industry by decrying the brutalizing effects
of urbanization, its loss of family self-sufficiency and rejection of pre-industrial
values. While Marx lauded the new industrial epoch as freeing mankind from
"the idiocy of rural life" it was left to protectionists to describe how industrial
progress supplanted manual labor with increasingly skilled labor and power-
driven capital.

---

[19] Böhm-Bawerk, *Capital and Interest*, p. 175.

Such considerations were what made economic thought truly *political* economy prior to the 1870s. At issue were social and political attitudes, government spending patterns, tax and trade policy. Laissez faire theory downplayed the role of such policy, and avoided discussion of how the existing status quo came into being.

Senior's theory, for instance, failed to explain why capitalists had so much income to allocate between consumption and investment in the first place, while workers could barely make ends meet. Similarly, the theory of comparative costs failed to explain how some nations had come into the possession of more capital than others. Merely noting that England grew richer by saving and investing more of its income than did less industrialized economies begged the question of what provided it with the initial surplus income over and above its consumption needs. Why did other economies not possess equally large capital surpluses? To what extent was this a matter of national policy, as the mercantilists explained a century earlier?

Economies that operated near subsistence levels could not invest as much as England did. If corrupt colonial or former colonized regions did generate a economic surplus, their oligarchies tended to appropriate it and spend it on personal consumption (largely to emulate their counterparts in the mother countries in what sociologists have termed the "demonstration effect") rather than to invest it in new means of production at home. Industrial progress is difficult where aristocracies are entrenched, where land ownership patterns are polarized between latifundia and microfundia, and where political freedom and economic mobility is lacking.

A special problem with labor in less developed countries has been the tendency to improve one's status and income by going into public service, the church, law, medicine or other service professions rather than industry or commerce. Labor that seeks commercial or engineering training tends to emigrate as part of the "brain drain." Such industry as peripheral countries do establish is likely to be foreign financed or foreign owned, so that its profits, depreciation, depletion and other revenues are sent abroad. Domestic investment in any case tends to be export-oriented, contributing to the world oversupply of raw materials and low-wage manufactures whose profits are offset by external diseconomies such as mineral depletion and a malformed economic structure. There is less and less attempt for dependent economies to be more self-reliant. Taken together, these tendencies leave the gains from trade mainly for the industrial lead nations.

## Summary: International implications of the technological revolution

The Steam Revolution and its associated revolutions in chemistry, agriculture, transport and electricity transformed the world economy far beyond what Adam Smith had envisioned. Protectionists accused free trade and the specialization of world production of helping England's industrial and finance capital threatened to widen its industrial head start over raw-materials exporters that did not insulate their markets to modernize themselves. E. Peshine Smith, Jacob Schoenhof, Simon Patten and a handful of other economists cited in Chapter 9 recognized that instead of promoting world income equality, free trade split the world economy between technological leaders and laggards. As high-productivity lead-nation labor and capital competed with less productive peripheral labor and capital, the more efficient production methods rendered inefficient producers obsolete and unemployable. The counterpart to technological progress and rising incomes in the most advanced nations thus was an obsolescence of labor, capital and land tenure in countries failing to participate fully in this progress. This Obsolescence Syndrome concentrated industrial and agricultural development in the most technologically advanced nations, whose high-wage labor was able to undersell less skilled labor throughout the world, thanks largely to the machinery it operated.

The analysis of technology along these lines passed into the hands of protectionists mainly because their objective was to maximize productivity growth over time, not merely to maximize consumption at a given moment of time by purchasing goods in the cheapest market. They sought to concentrate resources in commodity lines characterized by increasing returns and/or improving terms of trade. In the United States and continental Europe, protectionists warned that unless employers provided their workers with power-driven capital, and unless their governments supplied appropriate educational facilities and related social infrastructure, their incomes would lag behind those of England and other lead nations. Wage differentials might widen, yet the world economy still be in "equilibrium" on a productivity-adjusted basis, because low-productivity labor simply was not worth as much as high-productivity labor. The affluence and technological innovation of England and other capital-rich nations thus found its counterpart in the backwardness, dependency and political instability of less developed "capital-scarce" countries.

The protectionist argument was that direct investment in industrial and agricultural capital required not only a government-financed infrastructure, it also needed prices high enough to enable investors to recoup their industrial investment until native industry achieved parity with the lead nations. Prices could be supported most readily by protective tariffs, whose proceeds should be invested in internal improvements and subsidies to compensate latecomers for the head start and economic infrastructure that the leading industrial nations already had put in place. Tariffs paid by consumers did not disappear into thin air. By subsidizing growth in public infrastructure and capital investment, tariffs financed a national learning curve.

Free traders refused to accept lines of reasoning that might lead to this conclusion—and this obliged them to ignore the implications of technology for inter-factoral competition between capital, labor and land. Although earlier liberals had used the "head start" argument to convince England's parliament to enact free trade without fear of losing the nation's leading industrial position (as described in Chapter 4), they narrowed their argument once they had won the battle. Henceforth their fight was to convince less industrialized countries to adopt free trade rather than to emulate England's protectionist mercantilist experience. To acknowledge cross-competition between capital and labor would suggest that efficient lead-nation capital might drive down Third World wage rates below subsistence levels, rendering manual labor as obsolete an economic input as horsepower. To avoid this conclusion, free traders put forth a more superficial view of market competition, described in the next two chapters.

Against warnings by free traders that protective tariffs would nurture monopolies, U.S. protectionists replied that to the extent that free trade con-solidated the gains from trade in the leading industrial nations, it would bolster their own global industrial cartels. This seemed especially the case in view of the foreign investment patterns by the leading nations, not to speak of Europe's renewed wave of colonial rivalries in the 1880s. Protectionists depicted free trade as non-progressive in the sense that it bolstered systems of economic dependency and pauper labor in less developed countries. Economic progress in the lead nations tended to exclude populations in poorer countries from employment in the education- and technology-intensive industries of the future where increasing returns were concentrated. In the popular biblical phrase of the time, free trade dictated that poorer countries should remain "hewers of wood and drawers of water."

In making these warnings, protectionists in the United States and Germany developed an increasingly sophisticated technological rationale that even achieved a note of social idealism. The new protectionism sought to transform the international status quo in favor of less developed economies, much as socialism sought to modernize economic and social structures. Internationally, protectionism was needed to protect the poor from the rich. Many socialists felt a kinship with the protectionism on this ground. Although they supported labor rather than capital and concentrated on domestic reforms rather than interna-tional inequality, socialists leveled many similar criticisms against laissez faire orthodoxy. Marx acknowledged that if an alternative to Ricardian economics was to be developed, it probably would come from Henry Carey's technology-oriented American School.[20]

Protectionists as well as socialists drew heavily on historical analysis, stressing the importance of social and cultural institutions in shaping development in the face of the technological revolution on which free-trade orthodoxy turned its back. But like the socialists, protectionists found trouble getting their views heard. In fact, the major reason why business schools were formed in the United States (headed by the Wharton School at the University of Pennsylvania) was to provide a broader body of teaching than free-trade academia offered. Free traders accused these business schools of being anti-intellectual for rejecting the English liberal doctrine, and deemed protectionist concerns with technology and social structures to lie outside the boundaries of economics proper. No longer called political economy, the discipline narrowed to become synonymous with free-trade orothodoxy.

Given the fact that it was apparent over a century ago (indeed, more than two centuries ago) that as the world economy already experiencing inter-factoral competition between capital, labor and land, skilled labor tended to undersell lower-paid manual labor thanks to its superior productivity, why did economic theory in the twentieth century not use this perception as its takeoff point? The explanation lies in the free-trade school's success in blocking consideration of these complexities. The complex long-term development problems they tackled required protectionists to elaborate a much more dynamic and comprehensive system of analysis than did the comparative statics of free-trade theorizing, forcing protectionist writers to make their points in new interdisciplinary fields such as sociology. This academic discipline was established largely by protectionists in America (the institutionalists, among whose leaders were Simon Patten and Thorstein Veblen) and in Germany, whose Historical School was likewise protectionist.

---

[20] Marx, *Grundrisse. Foundations of the Critique of Political Economy* (London: 1973), pp. 883–89.

# 8

## The Factor Proportions Theory of Comparative Costs

To protectionists, the Industrial Revolution called for tariffs to prevent international polarization resulting from England's emergence as the workshop of the world and major financial power. Socialists meanwhile urged government regulation to counteract domestic exploitation. Free traders replied that no government action was necessary, because inherent tendencies worked to promote international equality among nations and domestic harmony between labor and capital.

To less developed countries they explained that the gains from trade paid them not to "artificially" nurture their industry. The implication was that these countries should provide raw materials for European industry. Free traders did not acknowledge the extent to which subsidies, tariffs and public infrastructure spending influenced capital investment and productivity. Each country was supposed to have a distinctive ratio of capital to labor—its "factor endowment"—which provided a relative advantage in products that happened to be naturally characterized by the wage and profit rates resulting from this capital/labor ratio.

The underlying assumption was that capital competed only with other capital, and labor only with other labor. Instead of a doctrine of class warfare and international exploitation, competition was held to occur only *within* classes, not between capital and labor. More capital was depicted as increasing the demand for domestic labor and lowering the export prices of capital-intensive products. Capital accumulation was supposed to depress profits, not wage levels, and was not supposed to grow so large as to develop monopoly power.

### Nineteenth-century discussions of factor proportions

During England's Corn Law debates the Ricardians focused on the man/land and capital/population ratios as determining whether a nation would be more efficient at exporting industrial or primary products. Capital-rich countries were deemed to be industrial exporters primarily because they were densely populated, giving them a "national genius" for manufacturing. Their natural policy was to exchange manufactures for the food and other raw materials of less land-scarce countries. This trade would increase profits for England's relatively abundant resource—capital—while lowering rents on its relatively scarce land.

Land-rich countries were said to be natural food exporters. Income for their abundant land and mines would rise in response to the demand for their products by more densely settled countries, whose land was fully occupied and whose mines were largely depleted. Meanwhile, importing manufactures from the older European nations would lower profits for the comparatively scarce capital of sparsely settled countries. *An open world economy would bid up the price of each country's relatively abundant resource, while moderating incomes for its "scarce" resource and thereby making income proportions similar throughout the world.*

In this spirit U.S. free traders attributed labor's high wage rates to the low man/land ratio, pointing to the accessibility of the great American backwoods. The idea was that if factories did not offer high wages, workers could set out as pioneers on the continent's western lands and annex new territories (in practice, mainly for slave plantations). Sophisticated protectionists replied that free availability of land might have been an early precondition for high living standards, *high industrial wage rates could not be paid unless American factories were sufficiently productive to sustain them.* It followed that urban labor's interest lay in fostering high-productivity capital accumulation, not in annexing more Mexican and other western territories under the program of Manifest Destiny. Workers should support what Henry Clay called the American System of tariff protection, internal improvements and a national bank to provide credit to finance industry.

America's labor shortage (relative to land) and relatively high wage levels catalyzed investment in the labor-saving capital that ultimately provided the nation with its industrial advantage. The fact that high wage and profit levels went together rather than being mutually opposed became the basis for what Henry Carey called the harmony of interests among labor, capital and land. Portraying high income levels as increasing labor and capital productivity, he argued that this positive wage/productivity and profit/productivity feedback would widen U.S. industrial advantage over time. The resulting industrialization would nurture a home market for farmers, who would use their rising income to improve their lands and augment soil fertility.

In contrast to Carey's optimistic doctrine that rising income levels would raise productivity and enhance rather than undercut the competitive advantage of prosperous nations, Ricardians endorsed the class warfare that characterized England by praising the competitive power of low wages. The Ricardians also assumed diminishing returns in agriculture. Although Malthus, Richard Jones, Justus Liebig, Peshine Smith, Marx and other writers controverted the assumption that capital could have only a minor impact on soil fertility, the idea remained central to the Dismal Science. Soil and other inputs were supposed to become less productive as the man/land ratio increased and they were used more intensively.

The American anti-Ricardians added that agriculture as well as industry experienced increasing returns with the application of capital, fertilizers and mechanization (see Chapter 9). However, they warned, raw-materials monocultures such as the southern United States exporting tobacco and cotton suffered soil depletion. Fertility needed to be maintained by crop rotation and hence diversification. E. Peshine Smith's *Manual of Political Economy* (1853) explained that balanced growth between industry and the countryside, with an urban labor force growing up alongside the nation's farm communities and consuming meat, would support animal herds that would supply natural fertilizer for the soil, along with urban "nightsoil" refuse. The inference was that government policy should promote investment in high-productivity production.

Malthus and Marx agreed with the protectionist position that agricultural productivity tended to increase with industrialization and its associated rising population density. The implication was that industrial nations actually might improve their agricultural powers relative to those of the poorer countries. As income levels rose, their farm output would increase while their rate of population growth would taper off. Lower-income countries would suffer from industrial and agricultural stagnation and hence a deteriorating ability to compete in world markets.

Still, the general view was that industrial growth in the wealthiest nations would provide an agricultural advantage to poorer countries, whose populations were supposed to increase more slowly as a result of their lower incomes. Fewer people would put less pressure on marginal soil fertility than would the more rapidly growing populations of high-income nations. This doctrine was reminiscent of Hume's views of automatic mechanisms promoting the economic destiny of poorer countries. Few observers anticipated that less industrialized countries would face an over-population problem. The essence of Malthusian theory was that higher incomes would spur population growth, while low incomes would deter it. The impliction was that labor scarcity and overpopulation would be self-curing. Scarce labor would see its wages bid up, spurring higher fertility rates and hence reducing wage rates. But American anti-Malthusians such as Peshine Smith pointed out that high rates of population growth were a function of relative poverty, not prosperity. Population grows most rapidly in the poorest countries, while in any given country it is the lowest income groups that have the highest rates of reproduction.

Throughout the nineteenth century there was lively discussion over the relative productivity of high-wage versus low-wage labor, sophisticated power-driven capital versus simple tools, and scientific agriculture versus the exploitation of raw virgin land. Protectionists took the lead in investigating the nature of competitive advantage in the world economy, and how capital was competing with both labor and land domestically. A primary premise was that high-wage labor working with high-productivity capital was able to undersell low-wage labor.

And indeed, since the nineteenth century an increasing disparity in factor proportions has emerged between capital-rich and capital-poor countries. Nations with high investment per capita have become more self-sufficient in food as well as in manufactured products. Countries with little capital have become relatively poorer, with high population growth rates. This has shrunk their capital/labor ratio, but not increased their competitive advantage in labor-intensive products. Few such lines exist, as agriculture and mineral production have become more capital intensive, along with manufacturing.

A laissez faire reaction explained the return to capital in a way that avoided supporting protectionist policies. It depicted wage and profit levels as reflecting purely quantitative supplies of labor and capital unadjusted for productivity differentials. This attributed high profits simply to a scarcity of capital, not to its labor-displacing ability and to the fact noted by Adam Smith, that profits often were highest in countries going fastest to ruin, being largely in the character of monopoly rents. To free traders, the prescribed way to reduce high profits was to prevent labor unions, reduce wages and to lower tariffs, not raise the incomes of capital and labor.

Ricardo's theory of comparative costs at least credited countries as enjoying a comparative advantage because of productivity criteria. Portugal could produce a gallon of wine with a third fewer manhours than could England. Wage and profit differences among the two countries did not play a role, nor did the proportion of capital to labor matter. Ricardo believed that the profitability of English capital would fall over time, but not because of its abundance. In the absence of free trade in grain, the price of subsistence would rise, raising wage levels—assuming diminishing returns in agriculture. Ricardo feared that English capitalists could not pass on these costs in the face of competition from less densely populated countries whose soil fertility was higher and food-wages consequently lower. Profit rates in England therefore would fall because of a cost squeeze stemming from deteriorating soil fertility, not because of an increasing supply of capital relative to labor as such.

*The factor proportions theory depicted incomes as stemming merely from the relative scarcity or abundance of capital and labor, not from relative productivity, government policies to increase it or the labor-displacing trend resulting from technological progress.* Countries are supposed to be "endowed" with their proportions presumably by nature, not self-endowed by government policy. The theory thus avoids discussing protective tariffs, subsidies or other policies to shape market forces, or even the training and education of labor to use sophisticated capital.

### The "factor endowment" approach of Heckscher and Ohlin

Two Swedish economists developed an extreme formulation of the new theory. In 1919 Eli Heckscher published his essay on "The Effect of Foreign Trade on the Distribution of Income," and four years later his pupil, Bertil Ohlin, wrote his dissertation on Heckscher's theories. He then traveled to the United States to study under the free trader Frank Taussig at Harvard, and in 1933 elaborated the factor endowment theory in his *Interregional and International Trade*. Paul Samuelson of the Massachusetts Institute of Technology (MIT) mathematized the theory to give it pseudoscientific garb. In 1953 and 1956, Wassily Leontief tried to test it empirically, sticking to the unrealistic assumption that the productivity and factor proportions of labor and capital within any given industry throughout the world were identical. It hardly is surprising that he obtained nonsensical results—his famous "paradox."

Nonetheless, free-trade orthodoxy has retained the theory as a standard textbook paradigm. International cost and price variations are attributed to the *relative incomes* accruing to labor and capital, based solely on variations in their relative supply: "The prerequisites for initiating international trade," wrote Heckscher, "may thus be summarized as *different relative scarcity, i.e., different relative prices of the factors of production in the exchanging countries, as well as different proportions between the factors of production in different countries.*"[1] "*Each region,*" Ohlin reiterated, "*has an advantage in the production of commodities into which enter considerable amounts of factors abundant and cheap in that region,*" The basic function of trade is to place "the demand of one region in touch with the supply of productive factors in another."[2]

From this vantage point it would seem that Portugal has a comparative-cost advantage in making wine because that is a labor-and land-intensive product and Portugal is a labor-rich and land-rich (that is, capital-poor) country, so that its labor and land are cheaper relative to capital. Cloth is a capital-intensive good, and the profits earned by capital are relatively low in capital-rich England. It is as if England and Portugal can each produce wine and cloth with identical expenditures of manhours, acres of land and "units" of capital, at constant returns to scale. But profits are held to be lower, relative to wages, where capital is abundant, giving such countries a comparative advantage in capital-intensive exports. Likewise, agricultural countries possess more land relative to capital and labor—but not necessarily more fertile soil as the Ricardians had assumed.

[1]  Eli Heckscher, "The Effect of Foreign Trade on the Distribution of Income" (1919), translated in Ellis and Metzler eds., *Readings in the Theory of International Trade* (American Economic Association, Philadelphia: 1949), p. 274.
[2]  Bertil Ohlin, *Interregional and International Trade* (Cambridge: 1935), pp. 20, 22. See also pp. 24–29.

*Productivity is depicted neither as declining as postulated by the Ricardians, nor as increasing as held by protectionists.*

Under free trade, countries will tend to export commodities produced by industries that employ a mix of labor and capital whose optimum factor proportions just happen to be unique to that country. Each industrial sector is supposed to be characterized by a single most efficient labor/capital ratio. This suggests that each country may specialize in quite a narrow range of products. One recent factor-proportions theorist acknowledges that "there is every *a priori* reason to believe that specialization rather than diversification must result from their factor proportions. … Given the observed difference in factor endowments between developing countries and the industrialized world, it seems reasonable to develop a model of complete specialization rather than one of factor-price equalization."[3] Instead of recognizing that this conclusion invalidates the theory's practical meaning, it often is insisted that reality actually would tend towards this extreme position if not impeded by protectionist policies.

It may not be unrealistic to suspect that where labor is abundant, its wages will be relatively low. But this would give a cost advantage in labor-intensive products only if there were product lines that were inherently labor-intensive. A country with a given proportion of capital to labor is supposed to be ideally suited to produce the goods of industries calling for this particular capital/labor rate. The factor-endowment theory implies that each economy has its own capital/labor ratio, which is deemed appropriate for specializing in some particular industry characterized by a specific and unique ratio.

Calling labor and capital "endowments" suggests a natural source of each economy's factor proportions. Fixed proportions would be intrinsic only if there were no factor mobility across international boundaries and no variations in domestic investment and population growth rates. This assumption of immobile labor and capital across national boundaries (in contrast to their presumed full mobility *within* countries) has become the distinguishing contrast between international and domestic economics today. *Factor immobility is supposed to perpetuate existing factor proportions and to be responsible for production patterns and variations in relative wage and profit levels among countries.*

The factor proportions theory has tried to modernize itself not in terms of economic realism but in adopting a mathematical and pseudo-statistical treatment. It reaches free-trade conclusions by means of the general equilibrium supply-and-demand apparatus of Walras and Cassel—a vast system of simultaneous equations to determine relative factor incomes and prices at a given

---

[3]   Anne O. Krueger, *Growth, Distortions, and Patterns of Trade Among Many Countries* (Princeton: Studies in International Finance, No. 40, 1977), pp. 43, 1.

moment of time on the basis of quantitative relationships. The resulting analysis is complex in mathematical detail, but its assumptions are too simplistic to explain dynamically evolving economies. Thus, when Ohlin claimed that his trade theory was "in harmony with the mutual interdependence theory of pricing—the universally accepted price theory today and thus independent of the classical about theory of value,"[4] he accepted the shortcoming of price and income models that view the world's operative ratios as being technologically frozen.

### Leontief tests the factor-proportions theory and finds a statistical paradox

The factor-proportions theory assumes that a common set of production functions exist among nations, with each industry characterized worldwide by its own "optimum" capital/labor ratio. It assumes equal factor productivity among countries, no interfactoral competition, constant returns to scale, and presumably constant relative factor proportions over time. The unreality of this assumption became apparent in 1953, when Wassily Leontief used 1947 U.S. input-output data to test whether the theory could explain existing trade patterns. Largely because input-output statistics and capital/labor ratios were available at that time only for the U.S. economy, he assumed—in keeping with the factor proportions theory—that capital/labor ratios for America's trading partners in specifies industrial and agricultural sectors were identical to those of the United States. Without this assumption no link could be made between an economy's capital/labor ratio and its alleged advantage in producing and exporting certain types of products.

Inasmuch as the United States was the world's most capital-rich economy, Leontief anticipated that his data would show the nation to export capital-intensive products and import labor-intensive ones. But the statistics seemed to indicate just the opposite:

> an average million dollars' worth of our exports embodies considerably less capital and somewhat more labor than would be required to replace from domestic production an equivalent amount of our competitive imports. ... America's participation in the international division of labor is based on its specialization on labor intensive, rather than capital-intensive, lines of production. ... The widely held opinion that—as compared with the rest of the world—the United States economy is characterized by a relative surplus of capital and a relative shortage of labor proves to be wrong. As a matter of fact, the opposite is true.

---

[4]  Ohlin, *Interregional and International Trade*, p. vii. For Ohlin's critique of Ricardian value theory see pp. 34, 571–72, 30–33, 23n.

Despite the fact that a major factor in America's capital-intensive modes of production seemed to be an attempt to economize on scarce ("high wage") labor, Leontief concluded rather brashly that "in terms of the relative production possibilities here and abroad, the United States is rich in manpower and poor in capital. This country resorts to foreign trade to save its capital and dispose of its relative surplus labor."[5]

This finding was his "paradox"—or more accurately, a simplistic misuse of input-output tables. They can be helpful in tracing how input-output and capital/labor ratios evolve over time, or how they differ among countries. U.S. input-output ratios might be compared with those of foreign economies on an industry by industry basis to highlight differences in capital and labor productivity. But foreign input-output and capital/labor data was not yet available. Instead of using this "compare and contrast" method to analyze America's trade patterns, Leontief simply assumed that the entire world's input-output and capital/labor ratios were *identical* to those of the United States on an industry-by-industry basis. His "paradox" (that is, a seeming contradiction to reality) thus stemmed from an absence of sufficient realistic data.

Common sense told Leontief that the United States actually used capital-intensive production methods. How then could it be viewed as having a labor surplus relative to other economies? He saved appearances by arbitrarily adjusting the data to fit the theory: "Let us ... make the plausible ... assumption that in any combination with a given quantity of capital, one man year of American labor is equivalent to, say, three man years of foreign labor."[6] This number, virtually plucked out of the air, tripled the labor content of U.S. imports by deeming American labor to be three times as intensive as foreign labor. But if one is going to pluck a figure out of the air with no statistical attempt to defend this factoral increase on the basis of either productivity or wage differentials, why be so careful about the underlying empirical or "objective" statistical foundation to begin with?

The way in which Leontief saved appearances actually undercut the essence of the theory he was trying to defend. His solution implied that production functions (and hence factor productivity) *did* differ among nations. If American labor were three times more productive than that of its trading partners, the whole point of the factor-proportions model went out the window, because productivity relations overshadowed factor proportions.

---

[5]  Wassily Leontief, "Domestic Production and Foreign Trade: The American Capital Position Re-examined," *Proceedings of the American Philosophical Society*, September 1953, reprinted in Caves and Johnson, eds., *Readings in International Economics* (Homewood, Ill.: 1968), pp. 522–23.

[6]  Leontief, "Domestic Production." He updated his views in "Factor Proportions and the Structure of American Trade: Further Theoretical and Empirical Analysis," *Review of Economics and Statistics*, XXXVIII (November 1956), pp. 386–407.

Some balance might retained by assuming that American labor was *paid* three times as much, but there was little way to incorporate this kind of correction factor into the system. Leontief did not define his "average" unit of capital or labor input in reference to productivity or to any other measure. One may readily acknowledge that U.S. labor historically has been more productive, being more highly educated and skilled, better fed and housed than foreign labor. But modern economic orthodoxy does not explain *why* it is more productive.

Two causes suggest themselves: higher wages and more capital equipment per capita than its foreign counterparts. But to acknowledge these causes would open the floodgates of reality, which would be fatal for the factor-proportions theory. If U.S. labor productivity can be expressed in terms of global-average labor equivalents, why not make a similar adjustment for capital or land productivity? This would raise the question of whether to emphasize labor-time equivalents or a labor- and capital-productivity approach such as E. Peshine Smith proposed—a common energy measure of value such as horsepower per production worker, or the kilowatt-hours or ergs per unit of output suggested by the Technocrats in the 1920s and 1930s. But this line of analysis would endorse policies to upgrade labor and capital productivity, which the factor-proportions model set out to reject in the first place!

### Erroneous assumptions underlying the factor-proportions theory

Six major fallacies underlying the Leontief "paradox" indicate what is wrong with the factor-proportions theory and the lengths to which its defenders were willing to go to retain it.

1. *The entire world is supposed to share the same set of production functions for each industry.* Leontief's methodology took U.S. output per manhour and capital/output ratios (and hence labor productivity) on a sector-by-sector basis as proxies for the entire world economy. Agriculture was the largest single trade category in his study, comprising one-quarter of U.S. exports and one-tenth of its imports in 1947. Although U.S. farmers did not produce coffee, rubber or other tropical crops, their capital/output ratios for producing grain and other farm crops were held to coincide with those of foreign countries producing U.S. imports of coffee, sugar and other plantation crops, which tend to be more labor-intensive.

It is a caricature of reality to assume that commodities are produced in all countries with identical capital/labor ratios. P. T. Ellsworth pointed out that those for foreign economies were considerably lower than those of the United States in any given sector.[7] Boris Swerling singled out agriculture in observing

---

[7]   P. T. Ellsworth, "The Structure of American Trade: A New View Re-Examined," *Review of Economics and Statistics*, XXV1 (August 1954).

that U.S. input-output data for 1947 were unduly weighted by the capital/labor positions of a few industries with high export or import positions,[8] making it unlikely that foreign agriculture was (or is) as capital intensive as that of the United States. Recomputing Leontief's statistics on the basis of 1958 input-output ratios and 1962 trade patterns, Robert Baldwin reversed Leontief's findings for U.S. trade with western Europe and Japan, finding exports based on U.S. natural resources to be *less* capital intensive than import-competing commodities.[9]

For the factor-proportions model underlying Leontief's approach to be valid, other countries would have had to increase their capital investment per agricultural worker and per acre as rapidly as U.S. farmers have done. This is known not to be the case, just as foreign industry countries was not as capital-intensive as U.S. industry until fairly recently (and even then, primarily in host countries to U.S., European or Japanese investment). Anne Krueger, one of factor proportions theory's erstwhile defenders, has acknowledged that "If production functions are significantly different in any meaningful sense, it is by no means obvious that comparative advantage will bear any systematic relationship to factor endowments ..."[10] This awareness of differing international input/output and capital/labor ratios is enough in itself to render the factor proportions theory obsolete.

2. *Inadequate recognition of the number of factors of production.* The model recognizes only two factors of production, labor and capital. But the international economy is characterized by a widening range of labor qualities and categories. Employment may be divided into white-and blue-collar categories at various skill levels, as well as into distribution and other non-production tasks. Similarly with regard to capital, a labor-complementing tool such as a hammer is different from labor-displacing machinery such as a power loom or word processor.

Baldwin observed that "the straightforward application of the two-factor (capital and labor) factor-proportions model along Heckscher-Ohlin lines is inadequate for understanding the pattern of U.S. trade."[11] Numerous other fac-

---

[8]   Boris C. Swerling, "Capital Shortage and Labor Surplus in the United States," *Review of Economics and Statistics*, XXVI (August 1954).

[9]   Robert E. Baldwin, "Determinants of the Commodity Structure of U.S. Trade," *American Economic Review*, LXI (March 1971), p. 141.

[10]  Krueger, *Growth ... and Patterns of Trade*, p. 43. She adds (p. 3) that the model's policy conclusion that "all industries would employ more labor-intensive techniques at a lower wage-rental ratio under any efficient allocation" is not empirically useful in view of "the impossibility of identifying homogeneous factors across countries."

[11]  Baldwin, "Determinants of the Commodity Structure of U.S. Trade."

tors must be taken into account to explain trade, such as mineral endowments. Many U.S. imports in any case are raw materials that cannot be produced in the United States in sufficient quantities to meet domestic demand, or are purchased from abroad to conserve U.S. resources over time, such as oil.

Another type of input that differs widely from country to country consists of public infrastructure such as roads, power and educational systems. This tends to be capital intensive, although it may be provided as a free service and thus not show up on input/output tables at cost. Recently built infrastructure is more expensive than that installed long ago, giving a statistical illusion of more infrastructure per unit of output for economies that have financed it most recently, *e.g.,* OPEC economies since the 1970s.

Like the factor-price model, Leontief's statistics leave out of account the role played by finance capital, debt/equity ratios, interest rates and the way in which capital costs are reported for tax purposes. Ecological cleanup costs also are not recognized, while other external economies are dismissed by treating them as "exogenous."

3. *Failure to perceive the gamut of economic proportions for any given nation.* The factor-proportions theory confuses each country's *average* capital/labor ratio with the ratios for specific sectors. But it is misleading to imply that each country's economic activity is concentrated around an average number, or that factor proportions are not changing steadily. Nations possess industries covering a broad range of capital/labor ratios. A wide range of ratios may exist within a given industry, as well as a wide range of wage and profit levels, as in the U.S. auto and textile industries.

4. *Failure to acknowledge the tendency for production to become more capital intensive.* Industrial, agricultural and mining production throughout the world has become increasingly capital intensive in order to reduce production costs. In some cases labor-saving investment is made to reduce labor costs with no plans to increase output at all. But the assumption of constant factor proportions— that is, fixed capital investment per worker—implies that new investment will increase output proportionately, not displace labor. By neglecting the tendency for productivity to increase by substituting capital for labor and land, the factor proportions theory leaves no basis for acknowledging widening productivity gaps among nations. Heckscher and Ohlin failed to acknowledge this long-term rise in capital/labor or capital/land ratios. They were unwilling to grant the seemingly obvious fact that capital, labor and land provided competing production services, as described in the preceding chapter. In the third (1821) edition of his *Principles of Political Economy and Taxation*, Ricardo acknowledged that capital occasionally competed directly with labor. By denying this, the factor proportions theory blocks itself from explaining the world economy.

Krueger recognizes that capital per worker is increasing throughout the world, but draws the simplistic conclusion that this creates an oversupply of capital that will bid up wages. She points out that factor-proportions theorists imply "decreasing food output throughout the capital-accumulation process (and, perhaps, a shift from food exports to food imports)."[12] The implication is that countries progress from specializing in agriculture to industry. It seems that the model is stuck back in the early nineteenth-century world when agriculture was still thought of as carried on with hoes rather than combines and other sophisticated forms of capital that agribusiness has introduced. But Malthus has been proved correct in his claim against Ricardo that given sufficiently high income incentives, farmers invest their earnings in productivity-increasing capital, not to mention pesticides, herbicides and improved seeds. In recent decades the most rapidly growing U.S. trade surplus has been in agriculture, not industry—while growth in American agricultural productivity has surpassed that of industry, thanks to the rate at which capital has been substituted for land and farm labor.

It is most realistic to view wages as increasing as a result of rising productivity enabling workers to share in the fruits of economic progress. It certainly is necessary to recognize that reported profits may fall with rising levels of investment and debt because of depreciation and interest charges, so that a rising proportion of revenue takes a tax-exempt form.

5. *Implication of dual economies for the factor proportions theory.* It is naïve to assume that factor proportions in the export sector reflect those in the domestic sector. Third World "dual economies" have modern foreign-owned export sectors insulated from labor-intensive subsistence economies in their hinterland. Mineral enclaves in particular are capital intensive in earth-moving and extraction, refining and shipping copper, iron ore and nitrates (from Chile), petroleum and iron ore (from Venezuela), tin (from Bolivia), and copper (from Zambia and Zaire). Although the domestic economies of these mineral exporters are capital-poor, the seemingly obvious fact that they do not possess a single uniform (or "homogeneous") capital/labor ratio contradicts the thrust of the factor proportions theory and invalidates much of Leontief's "empirical" evidence. It seems absurd to say that Chile engages in foreign trade to conserve its "scarce" labor and use up its "abundant" capital.

Ohlin might reply that Chile's truly abundant factor is mineral ore, but this cannot be depicted by an input-output table of capital/labor coefficients. Factor-proportions models count mineral endowments as "free." To take ore-bodies into account as a factor of production would imply a depletion function

---

[12]   Krueger, *Growth … and Patterns of Trade*, p. 15.

associated with international trade—and thus, the possibility of trade being conducted at an economic loss in failing to replace the value of mineral exhaustion, so that countries end up looking like West Virginia. (Extractive companies keep depletion allowances to invest elsewhere in the world rather than paying them to host countries for leaving holes in the ground.)

6. *Neglect of foreign investment's role in dual economies.* By the 1970s a number of academics had made reputations by explaining why the factor-proportions model had little relevance to how the real world works. Krueger conceded that the theory did not apply to Third World or other economies across the full spectrum (including trade in agricultural or mineral products), but only to manufacturing.[13]

One reason is that all U.S. petroleum imports prior to 1973 came from foreign affiliates of U.S. firms, as well as most of the nation's mineral imports and nearly 25 percent of its manufactured imports. Inasmuch as the production of these primary commodities requires heavy capital investments in drilling and mining machinery sunk into foreign countries' soil, *these investments reflect U.S. technology rather than the factor proportions of host countries.* Had Leontief adjusted his data to represent these foreign affiliates (and indeed, entire foreign export enclaves) as being functionally part of the U.S. economy, he would have found that domestically-owned sectors of host countries produce relatively labor-intensive products in keeping with the subsistence economy's factor proportions, while the foreign-owned sectors export capital-intensive products. Once this is recognized, Leontief's paradox turns out to be less paradoxical, and simply a case of semantic confusion as to what constitutes a "domestic" or "foreign" sector.

To take advantage of the domestic U.S. depletion allowance on their foreign operations, U.S. mining and oil companies consolidate the balance sheets of their foreign branches into the reported figures for the *parent* companies. This is realistic if one views foreign raw-materials enclaves as functionally part of the U.S. economy rather than that of their host countries. John Stuart Mill made a good agument for this in 1848:

> There is a class of trading and exporting communities, on which a few words of explanation seem to be required. These are hardly to be looked upon as countries, carrying on an exchange of commodities with other countries, but more properly as outlying agricultural or manufacturing establishments

---

[13]  Krueger, *Growth..*, and *Patterns of Trade*, pp. 1, 24, 43, 20. Seeking to explain why sparsely populated land-rich countries such as the United States and Argentina in the nineteenth century had high capital-labor ratios and became capital-intensive industrial producers, Krueger states (p. 20) that "Judgment of a country's factor proportions should be based on its manufacturing capital-labor ratio and not on its overall endowment."

belonging to a larger community. Our West India colonies, for example, cannot be regarded as countries, with a productive capital of their own. If Manchester, instead of being where it is, were on a rock in the North Sea, (its present industry nevertheless continuing), it would still be but a town of England, not a country trading with England; it would be merely, as now, a place where England finds it convenient to carry on her cotton manufacture. The West Indies, in like manner, are the place where England finds it convenient to carry on the production of sugar, coffee, and a few other tropical commodities. All the capital employed is English capital; almost all the industry is carried on for English uses; there is little production of anything except the staple commodities, and these are sent to England, not to be exchanged for things exported to the colony and consumed by its inhabitants, but to be sold in England for the benefit of the proprietors there. The trade with the West Indies is therefore hardly to be considered as external trade, but more resembles the traffic between town and country, and is amenable to the principles of the home trade. The rate of profit in the colonies will be regulated by English profits ... with the addition of compensation for the disadvantages attending the more distant and hazardous employment; ...[14]

Large international corporations whose head offices are domiciled in the industrial creditor nations have provided most of the capital for today's Third World export sectors. This investment has gone hand in hand with a growing agricultural and industrial dependency. The problem is not simply one of economic proportions. It involves a complex of government policies, lending and U.S. foreign food aid and diplomacy that has worked to retard modernization of land tenure and property taxation.

7. *Failure to consider government policy and institutional blockages or catalysts.* A major reason not to expect the factor-proportions model to apply to U.S. agriculture is that it is one of the most highly protected sectors in the world. Quotas limit crop imports to whatever marginal amounts U.S. farms cannot produce. While U.S. price supports may seem absurd at times (as when potatoes were dyed blue and dumped in the ocean), the program has resulted in the most rapid productivity gains for any industry in history. High farm incomes have enabled U.S. agriculture to become more highly capitalized than that of any other country. By the time the Nixon administration began to phase out price supports after 1970, the family farm was on its way to becoming a vested agribusiness interest.

---

[14] Mill, *Principles of Political Economy*, Book III, ch. xxv, para 5 (Ashley ed., pp. 685–86). Jonathan Levin (*The Export Economies* [Cambridge. Mass.; 1960], repr. in James T. Theberge, ed. *The Economics of Trade and Development*, pp. 11ff.) has analyzed dual economies and noted the fact that factor proportions "clearly could not have determined the location of the overseas raw material export industries. ... The location of these expert industries followed the same general principles as did the location of domestic industry, being determined by the location of the least mobile factors of production—such as climate, soil conditions, or mineral deposits—and accessibility to market."

Not acknowledging the role played by programs to upgrade capital/labor ratios, the factor-proportions theory depicts countries as "endowed" with capital as if by nature. The basis for competitive advantage thus does not appear to be policy. In this politically quiescent spirit, Heckscher granted that "no attention is paid to the advantages one particular country may achieve by means of protection, in altering the relation between the supply and demand of a certain commodity" and in the factors responsible for its production.[15] Yet as the preceding chapters have traced, today's leading industrial nations, whatever their initial factor proportions, attained their head starts by interfering with "free" trade.

How else can one explain why the world's first two great industrial powers, England and the United States, evolved from among the most densely populated and the most sparsely populated countries respectively? The factor-proportions theory attributes England's early accumulation of industrial capital not to its mercantilist policies but to the fact that its labor force was in sufficient oversupply to depress wage rates, contributing to relatively high profit opportunities and hence capital investment. But U.S. industry had relatively high wages behind protectionist tariff barriers whose revenue was used to finance public infrastructure investment. The common denominator was a policy of commercial, industrial and monetary nationalism, with tariffs playing a major role in endowing England, the United States, Germany and Japan with capital. Yet orthodox trade theory has dropped consideration of long-term demographic and technological change, capital accumulation, increasing returns and wage-productivity feedback, along with the role played by government policies to shape these dynamics.

Without recognizing the extent to which production patterns depend ultimately on government policy and social institutions, no *a priori* conclusions can be drawn as to how economies will evolve. Chile has the world's most abundant deposits of natural nitrates as fertilizer, and also substantial unemployed rural labor. These endowments would suggest that it should be a food exporter. But its land tenure was long polarized between latifundia and microfundia, and Chile's food imports have exceeded the foreign exchange derived from its copper exports. Factor-proportions statistics do not reflect this kind of institutional malformation.

Ohlin's reference to "varying natural aptitudes"[16] recalls Ricardo's unfortunate concept of "the peculiar powers bestowed by nature." Ignoring the political causes of differing international rates of capital accumulation, it fails to explain the international divergence in labor and capital productivity. It almost

---

[15]  Heckscher, "Effect of Foreign Trade," p. 274.
[16]  Ohlin, *Interregional and International Trade*, p. 10.

seems that industrial and finance capital were deposited by nature in machine mines or money mines, like copper or coal. The fact that capital has grown at a more prolific rate in the most politically active nations, while population has increased most rapidly in poorer and more labor-intensive countries, is more a result of policy and social institutions than of nature. Theories that ignore government's policy role will fail to explain how differing "endowments" were first brought into being along the lines described in Chapter 2. Capital "originally" was scarce in all countries. Some began with little and remained in that state; others advanced.

There is more at work in misleadingly narrow economic models than innocent "learned ignorance." By not applying to economies whose governments intervene to shape market forces, the model's limited scope is designed to *avoid* discussing the social, political and financial dynamics required to achieve technological competitiveness in the modern world along the lines undertaken by England, the United States, Germany and Japan in their rise to industrial and financial leadership. The result is stupidity with a political purpose. *Any* array of capital-per-worker proportions is supposed to give each country a competitive advantage in *some* industry. Each economy's technological profile is depicted in terms of an abstract proportion (capital per worker) without questioning how it came into being or what educational systems, public infrastructure, tax laws, environmental regulations and associated policy preconditions are required to keep labor and capital (and even the land) internationally competitive.

### *Policy shortcomings of factor-proportions ideology*

Despite criticisms that the factor-proportions model is irrelevant because it neglects government policies to spur investment and train skilled labor or attract it from abroad, free traders have used it as a normative guide to how countries *should* behave. Krueger argues that its thesis still

> could be correct, while observed production patterns ran counter to them owing to inefficient production patterns. … When factor market distortions are significant, all sorts of possibilities arise. … A variety of devices can provide the needed protection: credit allocations or tax exemptions to the favored industries, public enterprizes operating at losses financed through tax revenues, tariffs, quotas, and so on. … Subsidies can make any industry an export industry, even one that would not produce at all in an efficient allocation. Similarly, taxes can be levied on an industry that has comparative advantage which will penalize it enough to render domestic production entirely unprofitable.[17]

---

[17]  Krueger, *Growth* …, and *Patterns of Trade*, pp. 2, 42, 27. See also W. P. Travis, *The Theory of Trade and Protection* (Cambridge: 1964).

According to Krueger these taxes, tariffs and subsidies, along with currency overvaluation, import licensing or differential exchange rates may lead countries to produce and export the "wrong" commodities. Treating protectionism as an economic "distortion," the argument says in effect, "Alas, governments interfere with existing factor proportions and market forces to steer resources into 'uneconomic' sectors for which the factor-proportions model says they are not naturally favored."

Just what *is* an economic distortion? To define the norm as an unimpeded working of "market forces" means then any subsidy, trade barrier or political decision to influence the economy in *any* way is a distortion. This semantic twist makes the term "distortion" a synonym for any policy planning! It is an ideological label with a negative value judgment regarding what governments are supposed to do.

The model's implicit factor-price equalization theorem (discussed in the next chapter) defines "normal" international development as a pattern of converging incomes. For this to occur, economies must have similar productivity levels. The factor-proportions model assumes this at the outset, but in today's world—not unlike that of the 19th and 20th centuries—it requires active government tariff or subsidy policies for less developed countries to *avoid* the "distortion" of international economic polarization. If "normal" behavior is convergence, then free trade and laissez faire distort by impairing capital accumulation in capital-poor countries and promoting the transfer of resources *from* these countries to the wealthier nations.

Ideology is much like a factor of production in its effect on economic development, because it is the logic that guides public policy. Governments that refrain from shaping market forces in the national interest let their economies become malformed by nations pursuing a more active economic diplomacy. If the world is steered by what Krueger calls distortions, then *for any given country to drop these government policies is to allow its economy and domestic resources to be steered by those of nations with more nationalistic and protectionist trade regulations*, foreign aid strategy and diplomacy via the IMF and World Bank.

It is for ideological reasons that factor-proportions theorists dismiss government regulation as a distortion rather than asking what the world's pattern of regulation is and what its effects are. Krueger gives the game away when she criticizes the policy of favorable exchange rates for capital-goods imports, saying that it is wrong—or in economic jargon, "inefficient"—for countries to industrialize prematurely (as if every sector, even agriculture, were not being industrialized by higher capital intensiveness today). She is especially hard on countries seeking to upgrade the quality of their labor. Minimum wage laws, company housing, union agreements "and even the 'guilty' consciences of multinational corporations may all result in the payment of higher effective wages to workers than would obtain in a competitive market."[18] So unions should be broken, industrial wage rates ground down to a properly low ratio to profits, and the consciences of the multinationals assuaged into believing that they are only pursuing what is natural and, by reducing wage levels, helping poor countries achieve their optimum economic position.

The real issue is not whether governments should shape market forces—obviously they do, because that is the proper role of governments. The key is what they seek and how to best intervene to shape these forces. Successful governments have promoted self-sufficiency in essentials such as energy, grains and other basic needs, raised living standards, and often supported farm incomes to finance agricultural modernization, as the United States has done since 1933 and the European Community since 1957. Governments also may promote domestic food production to bolster their trade balance and prevent their terms of trade from deteriorating. Yet they are told to avoid all such policies by economists trained in nations whose own governments historically have pursued them.

## Diverging factor productivity

The factor-proportions model represents a retreat from more than two centuries of recognizing interfactoral competition between labor and capital, and specifically the tendency for capital to displace labor (and land) in production. A 1951 study by G. D. A. MacDougall showed that the U.S. export structure relative to that of England was a function of relative labor productivity in the two countries, not differences in factor incomes under conditions of similar technological production functions. U.S. exports in each industrial category reflected higher ratios of output per manhour than characterized England. Countries with productivity advantages in given industries export goods from these high-productivity sectors, subject to appropriate qualifications for wage differences, tax patterns and financing costs, and the availability of public infrastructure.[19]

---

[18] Krueger, *ibid.*, p. 31.
[19] G. D. A. MacDougall, "British and American Exports: A Study Suggested by the Theory of Comparative Costs," *Economic Journal*, LXI (December 1951), repr. in Caves and Johnson, *Readings in International Economics.* Similar findings were reported by Robert Stern, "British and American Productivity and Comparative Costs in International Trade," *Oxford Economic Papers*, October 1962, and Bela Balassa, "An Empirical Demonstration of Classical Comparative Cost Theory," *Review of Economics and Statistics*, August 1963. Jagdish Bhagwati questions the value of this evidence in "The Pure Theory of International Trade: A Survey," *Economic Journal*, March 1964.

Another key consideation should be the rate at which savings are transformed into new direct investment, and the role played by the "information revolution." Communications technology, which remains concentrated in the industrial nations, promises to revolutionize world cost structures as much as did the Industrial Revolution in steam power two centuries ago. But the measuring rod of factor proportions does not deal with this economic dimension.

The "product-cycle" theory of international trade patterns is not much more helpful. It depicts technological advantage as resulting not from favorable factor proportions or generally high productivity, but in novel innovations that afford monopoly profits. Innovators enjoy a transitory monopoly for new products, but are superseded by foreign emulators (exemplified by Japan). The fact that Japan and West Germany have displaced U.S. and British automotive, shipbuilding, consumer electronics, capital goods and steel producers but have few Nobel Prize-winning scientists is cited as evidence for the product-cycle approach. This observation does not address what specific policies produce an innovative investment climate and high capital/labor ratios.

Where do these lines of theorizing leave us? Current "factor endowment" trends threaten to congest population in less developed countries while the industrial nations substitute capital with growing efficiency for Third World labor, land and mines. Foreign investment by the industrial nations reinforces rather than offsets this polarization by aggravating the deteriorating terms of trade for Third World raw materials. As Chapter 11 will elaborate, the factor-proportions model does not acknowledge the international movement of capital, nor does it recognize the migration of skilled and low-wage labor to the wealthier economies.

One may wonder why Heckscher, Ohlin and their followers were so unwilling to note the existence of productivity differences. Why not simply propose that different relative factor incomes might result either from relative scarcity *or* productivity? To recognize productivity as well as income differentials would open up such interesting questions as whether high incomes offset or support productivity advantages. This would suggest an investigation of whether there is a limit to the ability of high wage levels to lead to more-than-increasing productivity advantages and thus "pay for" the higher wage rates. This line of analysis was formerly pursued. But from the 1970s onward, all we really find are reworkings of post-classical theorizing—which is why I see little reason to devote further chapters of this book to international economic theorizing since the 1960s.

A narrow scope of theorizing leads to short-sighted policy conclusions. The assumption that a country's "endowment" of factor proportions will persist over time—a major premise underlying laissez faire doctrine—suggests that sparsely populated, land-rich countries *should* export raw materials in exchange for foreign manufactures and grains. Trade is supposed to raise the incomes of these countries' most abundant resources (land and mines) and that is that. What is lacking is a calculation of how such trade may impair income-earning abilities over time, for instance, by the monoculture syndrome.

By attributing relative income levels uniquely to factor proportions, the theory diverts attention from how investment incentives may increase productivity. Even if the United States might be expected to import labor-intensive commodities under conditions of free trade, its tariff policy has counteracted this tendency, as demonstrated since 1970 by its protectionist textile quotas and agricultural price supports. The Leontief paradox is explained largely by the fact that the United States has erected the world's higheset agricultural trade barriers since the 1940s—quotas and tariffs still in effect. But the factor-proportions model both presumes a free-market economy and is an argument for it. Like Ricardo's comparative-cost model, the factor-endowment theory assumes that labor and capital are flexible enough to be fully employed with no need for rising investment per capita to save them from becoming obsolete.

Attributing income levels to labor's scarcity rather than to its productivity implies that national economies as well as individual employers find their advantage in having low-paid labor rather than raising productivity by paying higher wages. The theory also suggests that austerity programs can improve an economy's international position. Yet in terms of foregone productivity, such economizing impairs rather than aids modernization, while discouraging investment incentives and spending on infrastructure, research and development.

In sum, implying a tendency for international incomes to equalize under free trade, the factor-proportions model assumes no correlation between wage levels and labor productivity. Low wages are supposed to favor employment, not aggravate the technological obsolescence of labor. Low wages also are supposed to imply high profits, without taking into account their depressing effect on market demand. Contrary to the rosy picture the model suggests, the world economy is not settling at an equitable equilibrium as foreign trade evens out wage and profit disparities among countries. Free trade promotes international polarization dynamics, as the next chapter discusses in more detail.

# 9

## Polarization vs. Convergence Tendencies

Concluding the discussion that began in Chapter 7, this chapter describes how high-technology capital tends to replace manual labor and unimproved virgin soil, leading to polarization rather than convergence. Theories of how international incomes are supposed to become more similar as a result of free trade ignore international divergence in productivity, rendering their doctrine misleading when applied to the real world. In fact, such theorizing represents a great step back from the 18th-century theorizing of Steuart, Tucker and their contemporaries.

### The factor-price equalization theorem

The factor-price equalization theorem is a logical extension of the factor-proportions theory. Under free trade, and assuming minimal frictional transport and marketing costs or local preferences, international incomes are supposed to become more uniform as the products of highly paid "scarce" labor in one country are undersold by those made by relatively more abundant labor elsewhere. As Heckscher explained the theorem:

> If the conditions of production are the same in all countries … each difference in the relative prices of the factors of production [that is, their incomes] will make it profitable to get, by trading, any commodity that requires relatively more of a relatively scarce factor of production, for another commodity in which the relatively more abundant factor is predominant. Thus trade must continue to expand until an equalization of the relative scarcity of the factors of production among countries has occurred.

The fatal assumption here is that "the conditions of production are the same in all countries." The implication is that if wages rise, it is because of labor's diminishing supply relative to the availability of capital, not because of its higher productivity. But of course, productivity differs among countries. That is a distinguishing characteristic of the international economy. Ignoring this seemingly obvious fact, academic professors have spent over half a century explaining to students that a factor's relative scarcity is equalized via trade in the products it makes. Trade in these hypothetical models is supposed to produce a *similarity* in income structures (that is, the same average *ratios* of wages to profits), although not necessarily absolute income equality, unless there is trade in common denominators such as raw materials and capital goods at a uniform world price. But there *is* such trade, of course. As Chapter 5 has established, comparative costs or income proportions between labor and capital would become actual costs and income levels wuld be equalized throughout the world under this condition. Yet incomes are not equalizing, and have not for hundreds of years, despite common prices for world raw materials and capital goods, and despite large-scale international investment. Evidently some key determining considerations need to be brought into play to explain matters.

"*Free trade*," continues Heckscher, "only guarantees, under certain conditions, the same relative prices of the factors of production in different countries; *the mobility of the factors of production* guarantees the same [absolute] prices of the factors in different countries, not proportionality among the amounts of these factors."[1] And just as the free emigration of labor across national boundaries helps equalize wage levels, so foreign direct investment is supposed to equalize profit rates (adjusted for local variations in risk, liquidity and related investment considerations).

The main neglected factor here is the productivity of capital and labor. Paul Samuelson seemed to acknowledge productivity differentials when he observed that "Europeans plead 'Protect us from the "unfair competition" of high-paid, efficient American workers who have skill and machinery far better than out own.'" But he used this only to argue against the pauper-labor rationale for protectionism, pointing out that American labor needed no tariff protection against foreign "pauper labor," thanks to the high productivity of well-paid labor. Yet this very point controverts the factor-price equilibrium theorem which Samuelson has promoted so vigorously.

Samuelson also asserts that an emigration of labor—including presumably skilled labor—works to *raise* wages for countries losing it, while lowering wages in nations gaining it. If this were true, Third World countries would have little reason to complain when their best students remain abroad in a "brain drain."

If surplus population could have all migrated from Belgium to the United States, the law of diminishing returns implies that real wages here [in the United States] would fall toward equality with rising wage rates there [in Belgium]; and high land rents there would fall toward equality with rising wage rates here.[2]

[1]   Heckscher, "Effect of Foreign Trade ..." pp. 286, 296. Sec also Bertil Ohlin's nearly identical statement in *Interregional and International Trade*, p. 15, as well as Jacob Viner's discussion in *Studies in the Theory of International Trade*, pp. 501ff.
[2]   Paul Samuelson, *Economics. An Introductory Analysis*, 7th ed. (New York: 1967), pp. 672, 648.

On the other hand, if economic life is characterized by increasing returns to scale, it follows that when countries suffer a flight of labor—especially skilled labor—they are *less* able to increase their income, while countries receiving it are better able to build up their employment and high technology functions. And although it may seem counter-intuitive, high wage levels may be self-financing if highly paid labor is even more highly productive. For instance, the high wage levels of U.S. workers in the nineteenth century enabled them to invest substantial portions of their income in themselves and in educating their children. This set a positive feedback process in motion, enabling labor, land and capital in lead nations to become increasingly well remunerated relative to less productive factors in other countries. Factor proportions in such cases become irrelevant.

The factor-price equalization theorem is turned into a doctrine by advising Third World countries not to protect and upgrade their agriculture or industry. They are to accept their lot and specialize in low-wage labor-intensive pursuits, on the logic that this optimizes their economic potential by "doing what they're best at." Their low wage rates are supposed to favor employment, not thwart it by low productivity. Austerity programs are supposed to help by keeping wage levels down.

The reality is that Third World poverty curtails domestic investment, maintaining food dependency on the industrial nations. To acknowledge a correlation between high income levels and high productivity would mean that the austerity programs that the IMF and World Bank imposes on Third World countries retard their development rather than helping them.

### False analogies between the international economy and thermodynamic entropy

Much of the attraction felt by economists toward the factor-price equalization theorem stems from its parallelism with what must be the most misleading analogies ever foisted on the economics profession: a superficial analogy with the second law of thermodynamics, the law of entropy. The hope of free-trade economics is to make itself appear scientific by borrowing a paradigm from the physical sciences. It then dresses up the thermodynamic analogy of economic entropy in suitably abstruse mathematical symbols where no statistical evidence can be cited for the theories of international income and price equalization developed by Heckscher, Ohlin, Samuelson and their followers.

Entropic analogies might be valid if economic theory had as much relevance to the real world as thermodynamic theories have to physical nature. But the assumptions underlying economic convergence theories are not empirical but purely hypothetical. In the natural sciences, a theory must be empirically verified as well as internally consistent. Psychopathic mental patients are internally consistent, but not realistic. In economics, internal consistency is all important, as it is in any good science fiction.

The second law of thermodynamics states that heat flows from hotter to colder bodies. "Admitting heat to be a form of energy," writes Clerk Maxwell, "the second law asserts that it is impossible, by the unaided action of natural processes, to transform any part of the heat of a body into mechanical work, except by allowing heat to pass from that body into another at a lower temperature."[3] By analogy, exports are supposed to flow from "hot" high-income economies to "cold" low-income and hence presumably low-cost regions, unless blocked by trade barriers such as tariffs or quotas.

In a price-competitive world, economic activity may be converted into export trade when a nation's productive factors are less expensive—or, what would seem to be the same thing, more efficient than those of other countries. But inasmuch as the factor-proportions model ignores different productivity rates, the only recognized variable is income. This constraining assumption only permits the conclusion that free trade will even out international disparities in wage and profit rates.

The reason why perception of the wage-productivity feedback has fallen out of favor for over a century is that it opens the Pandora's Box of international economic polarization. If the appropriate analogy for the international economy is an expanding system characterized by widening inequality in income and productivity (bolstered by monopoly power and financial leverage), then less developed economies should renounce free trade and austerity in favor of protectionist development programs. It certainly would be more realistic to explain why high incomes in the most advanced nations have enhanced rather than undercut their export competitiveness. Recognition of positive wage-productivity feedback would counter the doctrine that if only governments do nothing to interfere with "free markets," an unseen benevolent hand will guide nations toward increasing equality.

Why not start off in the right direction? If a realistic analogy is to be drawn between international economics and the laws of physics, some new law of cosmology would have to be hypothesized on the basis of an expanding (negentropic) rather than an entropic universe. The amount of economic heat is growing steadily, and is flowing from colder so hotter bodies in seeming violation of the first and second thermodynamic laws as the rich nations grow richer with much greater ease and success than poorer countries. These "colder" low-income economies suffer their resources to flow to the "hotter," more highly industrialized high-income nations in the form of trade deficits, flight capital and the brain drain. This tendency of trade to concentrate the world's productive resources in

---

[3]   Clerk Maxwell, *Heat* (New York: n.d.) p. 152, The first law of thermodynamics states that work is transformed into heat and vice versa, abstracting all loss from friction.

the richest nations is just the opposite of the diffusionist inertia principle implicit in the second law of thermodynamics. An optimizing activity is indeed at
work, but it is not the one depicted by the economics of entropy.

### *Early refutations of income equalization tendencies*

Chapters 3 and 4 described the major eighteenth-century debates between
convergence and polarization theories. Hume's 1753 essay "Of the Balance of
Trade" epitomized the convergence analogy: "All water, wherever it communi-
cates, remain always at a level."[4] Tucker paraphrased this idea in 1774: "It has
been a Notion universally received, that Trade and Manufactures, if left at *full
Liberty*, will always descend from a richer to a poorer State; somewhat in the
same Manner as a Stream of Water falls form higher to lower Grounds." But
water seems to flow uphill in the world economy. Already in 1758, Tucker claimed
that it was merely a "vulgar error" to hold the view "that rival nations cannot all
flourish at the same time; that poorer nations will draw trade from the rich; that
low wages create cheap manufacture."[5]

In 1848 the American protectionist Calvin Colton reformulated Hume's
views to argue that free trade would impair the nation's high wage levels:

> It is manifest, that when the products of American labor … are brought into the
> free and open market with the products of European and other foreign labor of
> the same kind, the labor itself is in the same market; and that the tendency is to
> reduce the price of American labor to that of foreign labor. We say the tendency
> … We have before indicated the reason why American labor, in such a case, will
> not come entirely down to the old level of European labor. The water of one
> cistern which is higher than that of another, will raise the other, by being let off
> into it, before both come to a common level. If the capacity of the two cisterns
> were equal, the common level would be found midway of the difference. But the
> American cistern is a very small one compared with all the rest of the world, and
> being let off, would fall immensely, while the other would scarcely seem to rise.[6]

This came to be known as the "pauper labor" argument, and remained in
the repertory of protectionist politicians for over eighty years. (The Republican
Party Platform was still repeating it as late as the 1932 elections.) "The avowed
object of protective tariffs," criticized Francis Amasa Walker in 1876,

---

[4]  Hume, "Of the Balance of Trade" in *Economic Writings*, p. 63.
[5]  Tucker, *Four Tracts*, p. 17. and marginal note to part V. of his *Elements of Commerce* (1755),
     quoted in Edgar S. Furniss, *The Position of the Labourer in a System of Nationalism* (Boston.
     1920), p. 173.
[6]  Colton, *Public Economy for the United States* (New York: 1848), pp. 429-30. See also pp. 65,
     178–79. For a modern restatement of this theory see Samuelson, *Economics*, p. 667.

has been to keep wages from sinking to the level of Europe and Asia. The allusions to "pauper labor" which crowd the speeches of [Henry] Clay, [Rep. Andrew] Stewart and [Rep. William] Kelley have significance only as it is assumed that a day's labor in one place is the economic equivalent of a day's labor anywhere, and that one man's labor is effective in the same degree as that of any other man.[7]

Walker controverted this premise by citing the example of an English wood-sawyer able to perform as much work in a given day as thirty-two East Indians. He concluded that American workers had little to fear from foreign low-wage competition inasmuch as pauper labor turned out to be more expensive on a unit-cost basis. "In the contests of industry the civilized, organized, disciplined and highly-equipped nations may safely entertain much the same contempt for barbarous antagonists as in the contests of war."

This was no new idea. The title page of Vanderlint's *Money Answers All Things* (1734) quoted from Proverbs x: 15: "The destruction of the poor is their poverty." The opposite, a buildup of human and material capital via policies of high wage levels and high-technology investment, had brought about cost advantages for the most sophisticated industrial nations The advanced economies did not need protective tariffs.

This was a more sophisticated free-trade argument than the subsequent factor-price equalization theorem. But it was designed to appeal to the wealthy nations as an argument for *their* free trade, not holding out free-trade promises to poorer countries.

### The Economy of High Wages doctrine

The sixteenth-century economist John Hales observed in his *Discourse of the Common Weal of this Realm of England* that "the workman never travails but as the master provokes him with good wages."[8] Under normal conditions higher wages would motivate workers more, thereby increasing labor productivity. This would prove disadvantageous only if workers labored less intensively or for fewer days per week, or when their quality of labor deteriorated through luxurious living. "It has been observed," remarked Tucker in 1748, "that one of our laboring men who eats beef and pudding will do twice the work of one of these finical gentlemen who live upon herbs and roots, and if one of the natives can do as much work as two foreigners, he may afford to live better than a foreigner and sell his work cheaper."[9] The only redeeming feature of low wages was that

[7]    Francis Amasa Walker, *The Wages Question* (New York: 1876), p. 41.
[8]    John Hales, *Discourse of the Common Weal of this Realm of England* (repr. 1893), p. 59, quoted in William D. Grampp, "The Liberal Elements in English Mercantilism," *Quarterly Journal of Economics*, LXVI (November 1952), p. 487.
[9]    Tucker, *Considerations of the Bill for General Naturalization* (1748), p. 3, quoted in Furniss, *Position of the Laborer ...*, p. 184.

in some cases they might tend "to enforce industry and sobriety." But later observers noted that a more frequent result was the profligacy of hopelessness.

By the late nineteenth century the United States adopted this line of analysis as government policy. In Grover Cleveland's two Democratic administrations the State Department employed Jacob Schoenhof, a free-trade Democrat who had immigrated from Germany in 1861, to travel around the world comparing wage rates and labor productivity. His statistics confirmed that favorable productivity advantages more than offset America's high wage levels. This, the Democrats contended, obviated the need for protective tariffs to support wage levels. "It is not by reducing wages that America is making her conquests," wrote Schoenhof in 1884,

> but by her superior organization, greater efficiency of labor consequent upon the higher standard of living ruling in the country. High-priced labor means better food and better living, and these supply the American workman with the energy and nerve-power for which he is so justly celebrated. High-priced labor countries are everywhere beating "pauper labor" countries.[10]

America's industrial strategy should ride the crest of its high-wage and productivity levels, a feedback system that increased the nation's competitive advantage in world markets. "The survival of the fittest," Schoenhof concluded, "is, therefore ... the result of a high wage rate; and a high standard of living in industrial countries, becomes a prerequisite to a low cost of production."[11]

Instead of conjuring up the image of competition from foreign pauper labor, the Economy of High Wages model focuses on the need to raise living standards and accumulate sophisticated high-productivity capital. As production becomes more capital intensive, profits are reinvested under conditions of increasing returns. This enables firms in high-productivity economies to keep on underselling their rivals, whose relatively low profits deprive them of the funds necessary to keep pace with world-class capital productivity.

If labor in low-wage countries is less productive than in high-wage nations, then wage disparities do not necessarily indicate economic disequilibrium. Foreign trade equalizes unit costs of production, not wage levels. Trade may be in equilibrium on a unit-cost basis even as wages and profit rates diverged among nations. Under conditions of unequal productivity the ideal of stabilizing the factoral terms of trade is illusory. If labor exchanges for its manhour equivalent throughout the world, this would entail paying as much for inefficient labor as for high-productivity labor.

---

[10] Jacob Schoenhof, *Wages and Trade in Manufacturing Industries in America and Europe* (New York: 1884), p. 19. See also Schoenhof's *The Economy of High Wages* (New York: 1892), p. 385.
[11] Schoenhof, *Economy of High Wages*, p. 39.

Limits obviously existed as to just how far living standards in the United States or other leading nations could pull ahead of those in poorer economies and still generate a surplus out of which to pay higher wages and profits. Beyond some point higher wage levels would cease to be reflected in higher labor productivity. Luxury would become overgrown, as the early mercantilists had warned. But as long as the overall surplus grew, wages and profits could rise in tandem rather than being at odds with each other as in Ricardian and factor-proportions models. This perception underlay Henry Carey's postulated harmony between capital and labor: Enlightened employers would raise wage levels to reduce unit-labor costs. However, Carey emphasized, in order for rising wages in be associated with even greater productivity gains, employers might need protection of their capital investment in new technology. It thus was capital above all that needed to be protected to maintain a high-wage economy.

### *Obsolescence for low-productivity factors of production*

A productivity approach to international trade and income analysis suggests that modern capital-intensive production may render some types of labor obsolete. The world's horse population affords an instance of absolute uncompetitiveness since the invention of steam transport (especially in agriculture) and the internal combustion engine. Horses traditionally earned more than manual laborers, because their subsistence costs were higher. But by the turn of the twentieth century they were losing their economic functions. Their survival as economic inputs would require that the value of their services exceed their basic upkeep costs. The spread of steam-driven tractors, the automobile and other mechanized forms of transport left fewer tasks for horses to provide at rates that could cover these maintenance costs.

If resources always are fully employed, why were horses not simply shifted to tasks other than pulling carriages, milk wagons or tractors, or carrying cavalry officers? The answer (as Lauderdale pointed out; see Chapter 7, pp. 140f.) is that they could not perform these tasks as inexpensively or as competently as autos, tanks and other machines. In due course land that had grown hay and oats to feed the nation's horse population was used to grow more remunerative crops, enabling farmers to use the proceeds to purchase mechanized capital to sustain the horse-displacement dynamic. Producers that enjoyed a comparative advantage in "horse-intensive" products lost this advantage in the face of shifts to mechanized modes of production.

There may be a parallel here with unskilled labor. Like horses, manual labor in factories and farms was supplanted by steam engines, electric generators and internal combustion engines. Machines have driven manual labor from many fields as the cost of mechanically supplying work effort has fallen below the wages that must be paid to perform these tasks. In the race between machine and human, labor as a raw supply of manual work effort or performance of repetitive mechanical tasks is becoming as uneconomic as the horse. Unskilled workers are withdrawn from production as their minimum wage—their price of subsistence—exceeds the cost of machinery able to provide similar work effort. Indeed, the ability of machines to supplant human labor (not to mention draft animals) in the drudgery of production not only has freed men and women for higher tasks, it compels them either to elevate their status in production or become obsolete, remaining unemployed until they acquire working skills to elevate their skill status.

Fig. 9.1: Relative costs of producing industrial work effort

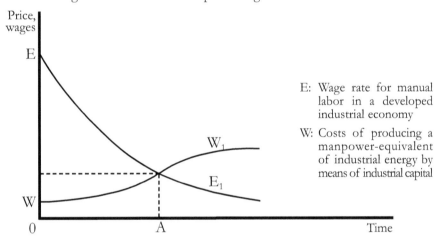

E: Wage rate for manual labor in a developed industrial economy

W: Costs of producing a manpower-equivalent of industrial energy by means of industrial capital

In Figure 9.1, line $WW_1$ represents the rising real wage rate for manual labor as it evolves in an industrial economy. Wages rise in response to the scarcity of labor during industrialization, and subsequently because of social welfare considerations. Line $EE_1$ represents the declining costs over time of producing a manpower-equivalent of industrial energy or servomechanism tasks by means of capital equipment. Already in the nineteenth century these costs felt below the cost of using the human body to convert the worker's fuel"—food, clothing and related necessities—into a given flow of caloric work effort.

In Ricardo's day, all that was required of rural migrants newly arrived in the city was the ability to exert manual effort with a modicum of intelligence. Children worked as servo-mechanisms at their looms. But today the willingness and ability to perform such simple tasks no longer qualifies one for employment. The exodus of farm boys and their sisters that contributed so strongly to Britain's industrial power two centuries ago represents a demographic burden for today's poorer economies.

The obsolescence of specific types of production factors—horses, unskilled labor, etc.—makes today's international economy more problematic than liberal economists recognized. While free-trade doctrine claims that what little advantage less developed countries may enjoy derives from their low wage levels, this conclusion follows only on the assumption that labor productivity is uniform internationally. The possibility exists that lead-nation capital may drive down Third World wage rates below subsistence reproduction levels, rendering more primitive forms of labor uneconomic as the increasing energy use per production worker raises labor productivity.[12]

A corollary to the Obsolescence Function may be termed the Complementarity Function with human and material capital. To be employable, workers require an appropriate complement of training and education, as well as high-productivity capital to operate. Failure to acquire skills or the requisite complementary capital results in an obsolete work force. In 1853 the American protectionist E. Peshine Smith observed that "as we rise to labor in connection with more complicated machinery the value of general intelligence becomes distinctly apparent."[13] Forty years later Schoenhof observed that

> In almost every employment of an industrial nature a very great amount of training is requisite to make it effective or to make it serviceable at all. Only in times of a very great demand and scarcity of labor would anyone employ crude labor in factories where skill is required.[14]

*This minimum necessary educational rises over time as labor requires more intensive training and education as a precondition for employment.* Wages must increase accordingly. Improved educational, dietary and other social standards thus are not mere consumer luxuries adding to costs without benefiting productivity and output. Investment in the quality of labor is a precondition for increasing the capital intensive character of production. The further the lead nations elevate their social standards, the further low-wage austerity-plagued economies will fall behind in their self-endowment of capital and competitiveness of their labor. The problem occurs when *low-paid workers cannot afford to acquire the training and/or education needed to raise their status in production at the rate required by modern technology.* This occurs when governments do not provide the basic education and other infrastructure necessary to make their economies competitive. Much labor finds itself unemployed as trade throws it into competition with more efficient production abroad. Rather than representing productive potential, such labor becomes a welfare charge on society.

---

[12]  See for instance Seymour Melman, *Dynamic Factors in Industrial Productivity* (New York: 1956), pp. 40–44.

[13]  E. Peshine Smith, *Manual of Political Economy* (New York: 1853), p. 107.

[14]  Schoenhof, *Economy of High Wages*, p. 27.

## *Obsolescence in agriculture and mining*

A similar example of economic obsolescence occurs in agriculture. The productive powers of "original" or "natural" soil fertility throughout the world have been undersold by the far less costly powers of U.S. and European farm machinery and related improvements, aided by fertilizers and pesticides. Natural or virgin soil fertility has become as obsolete an input as raw unskilled labor. This is why the industrial nations have emerged as major grain exporters.

Fig. 9.2:   Cultivation Costs: Land-intensive vs. Capital-intensive Production

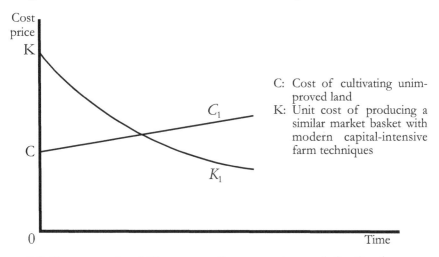

C: Cost of cultivating unimproved land
K: Unit cost of producing a
similar market basket with
modern capital-intensive
farm techniques

Figure 9.2 illustrates the falling cost of augmenting soil fertility by means of chemical additives, improved seed varieties, pesticides and herbicides as compared to production costs on virgin land where land-extensive modes of cultivation deplete the soil. In the nineteenth century it was common in sparsely cultivated countries such as the United States for transient cultivators to "mine the soil," exhausting it in one district and then moving on to new areas. This was a major impetus for America's westward expansion.

Fortunately the process is reversible by applying nutrients. For the industrial economies, line $KK_1$ represents the unit cost of producing a similar market basket of crops with modern capital-intensive farm techniques, and line $CC_1$ the cost of producing a similar volume of crops on virgin land (aggravated by the upward trend in land prices generally). Technology supplants soil much as it has supplanted manual labor, transforming the land into a capital instrument.

A similar development has occurred in mining. Naturally rich African copper mines where 4 to 5 per cent copper ore is the norm have become relatively high-cost as North American mines have substituted heavy earth-moving equipment for declining ore purity (and labor). Mining operations in the United States now handle ores whose copper content may average as little as 0.4 and

0.6 per cent, at a lower expense per ton of finished copper than the more labor-intensive operations in Zambia and Zaire. A similar cost reduction has occurred in iron mining as pelletizing has made it possible to exploit lower-grade ores with greater cost effectiveness. In recent decades one can say that the *lower* the mineral content (generally that of the more recently opened mines), the lower the unit costs of production tend to be, given sufficient commercial motivation for research and development. Likewise in the rubber industry, synthetics under-sell natural products with increasing ease. These examples recall Henry Carey's anti-Ricardian law of cultivation: Society progresses from the worst to the best soils and mines. These technological innovations have been developed precisely because the quality of copper and iron ore has declined throughout the world.

Rather than being anomalous, increasing returns are the rule in both mining and agriculture. The corollary is that the opportunity cost of *not* capitalizing industry, agriculture and mining is to lapse into a position of economic obsolescence. Thanks to capital investment and labor upgrading, the nations least endowed with natural resources have economically conquered the most naturally endowed economies. This is the lesson of the past three hundred years. Under these conditions free trade undercuts the ability of less productive economies to develop their own industrial and agricultural capital. Yet the income effects of trade are supposed to have no income-productivity linkage. Heckscher admits that "changes induced by foreign trade in the nature of the factors of production ("dynamic changes") [are] completely disregarded."[15] Only by ignoring nearly two hundred years of more traditional economic theorizing could so narrow a set of intellectual blinders be proposed and taken seriously.

### The dilemma of international ghettos

The preceding pages have established that economic obsolescence in less developed countries is a function of more rapid rates of capital formation, research and technological development in the lead nations. Resources that are not modernized will not be employed under free trade. Substantial subsidies and trade barriers are needed to modernize obsolete labor, land and capital. IMF austerity programs block such investment in the future, yet not to undertake such public spending is to doom the least developed countries to a fate of mendicancy.

The experience of England's weaving towns during the first half-century of its industrial revolution illustrates this principle. Ironically, the most highly skilled labor was the first to be displaced by machines. Power-looms supplanted the male hand-weavers, whose jobs were taken over by less highly skilled machine-tending women. Many observers concluded that the spread of machine production would degrade rather than elevate the quality of life. Yet England's

---

[15]   Heckscher, "Effect of Foreign Trade …," p. 274.

industrial economy ultimately entered a more advanced phase of mechanization. As its capital became increasingly skill-intensive it called for a new white-collar complement as well as for better trained blue-collar operatives. Contrary to forecasts by underconsumptionists, no vast displacement of labor ensued. Instead there developed a chronic tendency towards full employment of skilled labor. The Luddites and their machine-wrecker contemporaries were wrong. Technological progress ended up elevating the social and economic horizons of the working class by increasing output and hence making possible higher living standards.

However, this has been the case only in the advanced nations, whose social programs were designed to economically upgrade the population. Technology evolved evenly enough so that no great gap developed between modernity and obsolescence. By contrast, today's less developed countries have experienced a rural exodus that represents a social overhead of low-productivity labor. This places a growing burden on their economies. A burgeoning mass of consumers who are not producers must be fed and otherwise supported out of domestic output as they are displaced from their traditional living areas to flood the industrial and commercial cities. This population also imposes indirect costs by its impact on crime rates, ill health and general quality of life. Rising welfare taxes and spending on social amelioration increase private-sector production costs, eating into the surplus otherwise available to finance the educational system and other infrastructure needed to help prepare labor find employment in the modern world.

Although some effort is being made to modernize minority populations in the United States and other industrial nations, the situation in much of Latin America and Africa threatens a prolonged state of poverty as the international economy throws their labor and land into uneven competition with more modern producers abroad. The advanced nations enjoy economies of scale in marketing as well as production, creating a feedback effect of increasing sales and capital accumulation while less developed countries lose even their own home markets.

The debates over England's and Ireland's Poor Laws a century ago give an indication of the cruelty this situation inflicts. Upon inspecting the living habits of Manchester workers, Dr. James Phillips Kay, a physician, wrote that

> the introduction of an uncivilized race does not tend even primarily to increase the power of producing wealth, in a ratio by any means commensurate with the cheapness of its labour, and may ultimately retard the increase of the fund for the maintenance of that labour. Such a race is useful only as a mass of animal organization, which consumes the smallest amount of wages. The low price of the labour of such people depends, however, on the paucity of their wants, and their savage habits. When they assist the production of wealth, therefore, their

barbarous habits and consequent moral depression must form a part of the equation. They are only necessary to a state of commerce *inconsistent* with such a reward for labor, as is calculated to maintain the standard of civilization. A few years pass, and they become burdens to a community whose morals and physical power they have depressed; and dissipate wealth which they did not accumulate.[16]

The alternative would have been to transform the society that put them in this state. But only the radical socialists advocated this. Outdoing today's most reactionary attacks on welfare spending, Dr. Kay quoted from William Nassau Senior's *Letter to Lord Hewick on a Legal Provision for the Irish Poor*. To maintain and extend the Poor Laws, Senior asserted, would

> divide Ireland into as many distinct countries as there are parishes, each peopled by a population *ascripta gleboe* multiplying without forethought; impelled to labor principally by the fear of punishment; drawing allowance for their children, and throwing their parents on the parish; considering wages not a matter of contract but of right; attributing every evil to the injustice of their superiors, and, when their own idleness or improvidence has occasioned a fall of wages, avenging it by firing the dwellings, maiming the cattle, or murdering the persons of the land-lords and overseers; combining, in short, the insubordination of the freeman with the sloth and recklessness of the slave.[17]

The logical culmination of this polarization process was described in 1864 by the Rev. W. Winwood Reade with regard to the African population:

> This vast continent ... will finally be divided almost equally between France and England.
>
>       In Northern Africa, France already possesses the germ of a great military empire. She will ally herself with the Mohammedan powers. With a Mohammedan army she will overrun Africa ... while England, pursuing a more peaceful course, will colonize Angola by means of black emigrants, run a railway across Mozambique, and grow on the tablelands of Southern Central Africa the finest wool and cotton in the world.
>
>       Africa shall be redeemed. Her children shall perform this mighty work. Her morasses shall be drained; her deserts shall be watered by canals; her forests shall be reduced to firewood. Her children shall do all this. They shall pour an *elixir vitae* into the vein of their mother, now withered and diseased. They shall restore her to youth and to immortal beauty.

---

[16]  James Phillips Kay, *The Moral and Physical Condition of the Working Classes, Employed in the Cotton Manufacture in Manchester* (London: 1832), p. 52.
[17]  William Nassau Senior, *Letter to Lord Hewick on a Legal Provision for the Irish Poor,* quoted by Kay, *Moral and Physical Conditions ...*, pp. 53–54.

In this amiable task they may possibly be exterminated. We must learn to look on this result with composure. It illustrates the beneficent law of Nature, that the weak must be devoured by the strong.

But a grateful Posterity will cherish their memories. When the Cockneys of Timbuctoo have their tea-gardens in the Oases of the Sahara; when hotels and guide-books are established at the sources of the Nile; when it becomes fashionable to go yachting on the lakes of the Great Plateau; when noblemen, building seats in Central Africa, will have their elephant parks and their hippopotami waters, young ladies on camp-stools under palm-trees will read with tears *The Last of the Negroes*, and the Niger will become as romantic a river as the Rhine.[18]

These quotations are not merely antiquarian documents of the past, they are scenarios for the future. Market forces may be cited as reason to starve out populations that fail to join the course of economic progress. Droughts and famine will be blamed on nature rather than on deforestation, inadequate irrigation and related shortfalls in infrastructure spending. The ultimate question is not whether Third World labor is cheap enough, but whether it is so low-priced as to deprive it of earning the income necessary to invest in education and related human capital skills at a rate sufficient to make itself competitive in today's high-technology world.

---

[18] W. Winwood Reade, *Savage Africa: Being the Narrative of a Tour in Equatorial, Southwestern, and Northeastern Africa* (New York: 1864), pp. 451–52.

# 10

## The Changing Role of Foreign Trade in Economic Development

Theories of how foreign trade evolves depend on the assumptions one makes about trends in population; in the productivity of agriculture and industry; in wages, rents and profits; and, most important, in government policy. Export surpluses and import needs are, by definition, residual functions of domestic supply and demand balances. But these trade patterns in turn affect the course of domestic industry and primary production, as well as the type of economic infrastructure put in place. The preceding chapters have focused on the short-run microanalysis of foreign trade—the principles of comparative costs and the distribution of the gains from trade. This summary chapter makes a transition to a view of trade's role in long-term economic development.

"Stages of development" theories purport to describe how foreign trade and domestic development interact with each other in the industrial center vis-à-vis the less densely populated periphery producing raw materials. Being strategic in design, these theories are as politically motivated as is trade theory. James Steuart in 1767, Adam Smith in 1776, David Ricardo in 1817, Friedrich List in 1841, and Karl Marx in 1848 and 1864 supported their political programs with long-term views of how economies evolved, generally through three stages beginning with agriculture and then passing through the domestic "infant" industrial stage to culminate in an international commercial stage. Each body of theory focused either on an imminent or a "final" stage for which it recommended either protectionism or free trade, high wages or austerity, statist controls or market allocation of resources.

For Steuart the key was government policy. Once other countries learned how to develop by enacting protective tariffs, industrial England would have to fall back on autarky to maintain its living standards. Free trade should be prolonged as long as it benefited England, but ultimately would be thwarted by foreign protectionism, to which England would have to respond in like fashion. So free trade was only a transitional intermediate stage.

Smith held that free trade and laissez faire could sustain prosperity indefinitely, thanks to the productivity gains resulting from a greater division of labor as a result of specialization of world production. Unlike Steuart, he viewed state management as wasteful and inherently corrupt, at least as it was when politics was dominated by the vested interests of his day.

The Ricardians also urged free trade, but unlike Smith and Steuart they did so in a technologically pessimistic context of diminishing returns (at least in agriculture). Free trade could put off the day of reckoning by enabling England to buy low-cost food abroad. But ultimately diminishing returns would plague less developed countries as they became as densely populated as England.

Protectionists outside of England argued that free trade thwarted the development of their infant industries while the specialization of labor endorsed by Smith, Ricardo and their followers would lead to depletion of their soil and mines. Friedrich List viewed protectionism as an intermediate stage to nurture infant industries. Only after protective tariffs had done their work and all nations were on an equal technological footing would the world be ready for a cosmopolitan free-trade stage.

Marx agreed with the protectionists that free trade served England, but nonetheless endorsed it on the ground that trade was more than a mere exchange of commodities. It established a relationship between people and their social systems. What were being similarized were not merely prices and incomes, but entire systems of production and distribution. The victory of English industrial exports implied an exportation of England's industrial capitalism as a mode of production. Market forces under free trade compelled less developed countries to conform to its dictates, and thus promised to move the colonial periphery from a state of backwardness to one of mature capitalism—from which it presumably would evolve into socialism.

Despite their different policy projections, the above economists shared certain underlying premises. Each recognized agriculture to be the starting point for economic evolution. An economy's ability to support a non-agricultural population was a function of the productive powers of its land. Industry developed within the bosom of agriculture, and drew its urban employment from the rural exodus. But each writer differed as to the consequences of industrial development for lead nations and less developed economies, and the ability of the industrial nations to monopolize the gains from trade under conditions of increasing returns.

### James Steuart's view of ultimate autarky

Steuart's *Principles of Political Oeconomy* represents the last great mercantilist work advocating a managed economy culminating in a protected high-wage domestic market. As described above in Chapters 3 and 4, Steuart agreed with Josiah Tucker that under a regime of free trade, England would be an economic magnet for the world's money, skilled labor and capital. But he did not imagine that foreign countries would tolerate this state of affairs for long. They would adopt protectionism to embark on the same path that England herself had pioneered in overtaking Holland and France. This would force England (and other industrial nations at a similar stage of maturity) to fall back on autarky, whose policy objective would be to maintain demand for the products of domestic labor and land. There was no limit to how high demand might be increased, assuming an underlying momentum of technological progress to continue.

> Trade, considered in this view, divides itself into … three stages of life, as it were, *infancy, manhood,* and *old age.*
>
> During the infancy of trade, the statesman should lay the foundation of industry [and] must exclude all importation of foreign work. While luxury tends only to banish idleness, to give bread to those who are in want, and to advance dexterity, it is productive of the best effects.
>
> When a people have fairly taken a laborious turn … the scaffolding must be taken away when the fabric is completed. These incumbrances are high prices, at which he has been obliged to wink, while he was inspiring a taste for industry in the advancement of agriculture and of manufactures; but now that he intends to supply foreign markets, he must multiply hands; set them in competition; bring down the price both of subsistence and work; and when the luxury of his people render this difficult, he must attack the manners of the rich, and give a check to domestic consumption of superfluity, in order to have the more hands for the supply of strangers.
>
> The last stage of trade is by far the most brilliant; when, upon the extinction of foreign trade, the wealth acquired comes to circulate at home.[1]

Each of these three stages of development required the statesman's guiding hand, If the population were instilled with a desire to possess semi-luxuries, they would work harder to earn the requisite funds to purchase them. "Wants promote industry, industry gives food, food increases numbers: the next question is, how numbers are to be well employed?" Statesmen should

> encourage the manufacturing of every branch of natural productions, by extending the home-consumption of them; by excluding all competition with strangers, by permitting the rise of profits, so far as to promote dexterity and emulation in invention and improvement … To spare no expense in procuring the ablest masters in every branch of industry, nor any cost in making the first establishment; providing machines, and every other thing necessary or useful to make the undertaking succeed. To keep constantly an eye upon the profits made in every branch of industry; and so soon as he finds, that the real value [that is, cost] of the manufacture comes so low as to render it exportable, to employ the hands … and to put an end to these profits he had permitted only as a means of bringing the manufacture to its perfection.[2]

---

[1]  Steuart, *Principles of Political Oeconomy*, Vol. I, pp. 499f.
[2]  Steuart, *ibid.*, pp. 59, 85, 304.

If the first impulse to foreign trade was to dispose of the industrial surplus in exchange for money to fuel the expanding domestic circular flow, the second aim was to obtain food to feed the growing population and raw materials to work up into more industrial output. Regarding the pressure of population growth on the means of subsistence, Steuart leaned on the views of Robert Wallace, from whom Malthus also drew (although from an anti-labor vantage point). As it became necessary to import food from abroad, industrial nations might have to roll back their unit-labor costs and profit rates. However, the domestic market need not be depressed if rising labor productivity enabled wages to rise without increasing unit production costs. But population growth might have to come to a halt once agricultural productivity had reached its lower limit and the nation no longer could export manufactures in exchange for food.[3]

An economy would evolve from the stage of infant industry (Steuart's own term, calling for rising wage and profit levels to upgrade labor and capital) to that of foreign trade (which required either lower incomes of rising productivity to ensure competitive production), and then to autarky ("inland trade") as its labor and goods were priced out of world markets. Steuart's forecast for this isolationist stage was not as pessimistic as what John Stuart Mill called the stationary state of zero population growth, because Steuart (in the spirit of Petty) depicted the growing productive powers of machinery rather than population as being a mainspring of economic development:

> When they cannot augment their numbers, they will introduce machines into many manufactures; and these will supply the want, without adding to the consumption of their food. Foreigners, astonished at a novelty which lowers prices, and checks their growing industry, will copy the inventions; but being no more than scholars, who go awkwardly to work, this improvement will throw many of their hands into idleness: the machines will be cried down ...[4]

Still, the consequence of this process would be that less developed countries ultimately could undersell prosperous nations by emulating their innovations and national policies. To participate in this process, countries throughout the world would adopt government direction of economic life. Even the intervening stage of foreign trade was not conceived by Steuart as one of true laissez faire, because the economy was to be managed throughout.

---

[3] Steuart, *ibid.*, pp. 491, 118, 116. Malthus was inspired by Steuart's suggestion that the growth of industry would spur agricultural productivity as a result of rising "effectual demand" by the non-agricultural classes.

[4] Steuart, *ibid.*, p. 159. See also pp. 305, 119, as well as William Petty's observation cited in Chapter 7.

## Adam Smith's laissez faire view of economic progress

To Smith, commerce and its associated specialization of production represented the mainspring for each phase of European development. He believed that productive powers in agriculture and industry grew in keeping with population and the development of towns. The latter drew much of their prosperity from trade, and also "benefited the country because they afforded (1) a ready market for its produce, (2) because merchants bought land in the country and improved it, and (3) because order and good government were introduced" as towns became the bastion of freedom at a time when rural institutions were still characterized by serfdom and slavery.[5] People were free in the towns, and their spirit of freedom spread throughout the country. To be sure, Smith granted:

> According to the natural course of things … the greater part of the capital of every growing society is, first, directed to agriculture, afterwards to manufactures, and last of all to foreign commerce …
>
> But though this natural order of things must have taken place in some degree in every such society, it has, in all the modern states of Europe, been, in many respects, entirely inverted. The foreign commerce of some of their cities has introduced all their finer manufactures, or such as were fit for distant sale; and manufactures and foreign commerce together, have given birth to the principal improvements of agriculture …[6]

Like Steuart and Malthus, Smith held that rising income levels would spur population growth. This growth, along with a widening of foreign markets, would increase productivity by offering greater economies of scale. In this respect Smith (like Steuart and most of his predecessors) was a technological optimist. Not only did higher-wage labor lend to be more efficient than low-wage production but the associated increase in population density would facilitate the division of labor:

> The poor, in order to obtain food, exert themselves to gratify those fancies of the rich; and to obtain it more certainty, they vie with one another in the cheapness and perfection of their work. The number of workmen increases with the increasing quantity of food, or with the growing improvement and cultivation of the lands; and as the nature of their business admits of the utmost subdivisions of labours, the quantity of materials which they can work up increases in a much greater proportion than their numbers.[7]

Like Malthus (and unlike Ricardo), Smith believed that agricultural improvements would be made even after the lands were filled up. Thus, whereas Steuart held that higher income levels required economic isolationism beyond a

---

[5]   Smith, *Wealth of Nations*, Book III: "Of the different Progress of Opulence in different Nations" (Cannan ed., pp. 402, 428f., 432).

[6]   Smith, *ibid.*, pp. 405f. See also p. 428.

[7]   Smith, *ibid.*, Bk. I, ch. xi, pt. ii (Vol. I, p. 165).

point, Smith believed that foreign trade would remain the lead sector from the beginning to the end of the economic development process.

Widening the scope for commerce called for dismantling protectionism for it diverted income into the hands of vested interests, depriving the rest of the economy of the gains from trade. If foreign countries erected protective tariffs (the prospect that haunted Steuart), this would only slow their development, not help them catch up. Economic development throughout the world would therefore tend increasingly to become export-oriented and liberal in order to take advantage of the specialization of labor.

Smith neglected the monetary developments associated with trade and commerce. His three-stage schema said little about money putting industry in motion, in contrast to the mercantilists who perceived that the availability of financing was critical to extending commence and industry. Praise for money's role in economic expansion and facilitating the division of labor was left exclusively to the mercantilism and to subsequent protectionists outside of England.[8]

Smith acknowledged that protective tariffs served as a catalyst to domestic industry in its early stages, but feared (for sound historical reasons) that over time the guiding hand of state regulation would tend to discourage industry. Governments were prone to corrupt management and favoritism, so economic development was best served by leaving private self-interest to its own devices, subject to a modicum of social-welfare oversight.

### David Ricardo's pessimistic modification of Smith's principles

Ricardo viewed economic development in terms of a static technology subject to diminishing returns, especially in agriculture. Refusing to acknowledge any positive effect of industry on agricultural investment and productivity, he was more doctrinaire than either Steuart or Smith in insisting that population growth would push up food prices as recourse was made to lower-grade soils. The land had fixed and static "original and indestructible" powers, and that was that. If densely populated nations did not abolish their agricultural tariffs, the domestic landlord class would monopolize their incomes. Conversely, they could obtain relatively low-priced supplies of food and raw materials in exchange for industrial exports, which less developed countries should be glad to receive inasmuch as they could use their labor and capital to produce what they were relatively best at producing: food grain on land not as fully and densely occupied as that of England.

Unlike Smith, Ricardo refused to recognize even a temporary benefit to result from protective tariffs. They involved a loss of the potential gains from

---

[8]   For Smith's neglect of the role played by money, see *ibid.*, Vol. I, pp. 176f.

trade, and had no compensating long-term advantages. However, Ricardo's follower John Stuart Mill (followed by Alfred Marshall) acknowledged that protectionism might have positive effects: 'where industry has not come up to the limit imposed by capital, governments may in various ways, for example, by importing additional laborers, bring it nearer to that limit.'[9] (Here Mill clearly recognized the international mobility of labor that subsequent free-trade theorists have denied that he perceived.) Capital also could be imported, subsidized, nurtured or protected where land and labor were available. But Mill did not really pursue the idea of government aid for industrialization, fearing that tariffs might remain entrenched long after they had outlived their usefulness. Toward the close of the nineteenth century, tariffs indeed threatened to consolidate the power of monopolies and trusts.

The Ricardians expected the comparative advantage of nations to evolve from agriculture to industry not because of protective tariffs but simply from the growth of population and its concentration in cities. As the industrial center increased its demand for food and raw materials, less developed countries would find their interest to lie in not industrializing. By importing manufactured goods in exchange for their raw materials (whose international prices might he dictated by production costs on the highest-cost soils or ore bodies) they would gain an economic rent or super-profit as the world price was set *above local marginal costs of production in most of these countries*. They thus should remain raw-materials monocultures rather than emulate England's industrial (and protectionist) experience.

The specialization of world labor would increase as long as comparative-cost ratios continued to diverge between industrial and agricultural economies. However, as the latter became fully populated, they themselves would begin to experience diminishing returns, and hence, rising food costs. Comparative-cost differentials would shrink, until there was little remaining reason for commerce to occur. Less developed countries would find that as their populations grew, agricultural (and mining) cost differentials would widen within their domestic economies, creating their own *rentier* class much as had occurred in England. Unable to export food as readily as before, they would be driven to industrialize to produce their own manufactures as their populations congested in urban centers. Ricardian free traders in the United States accordingly warned that industrialization was hardly a destiny to be welcomed, much less hastened by protective tariffs.[10]

---

[9]   Mill, *Principles of Political Economy*, Book I, ch. v.
[10]  This point was made in particular by the Jeffersonian Democrat, George Tucker of the University of Virginia, in a 1844–45 debate with the American protectionist Alexander Everett. I have summarized the arguments in *Economics and Technology in 19th-Century American Thought* (New York: 1975), pp. 160–65. See also pp. 48-51.

As for England, its industrial exports would suffer deteriorating terms of trade as the worldwide cost of producing food and other raw materials climbed. More rapid industrial investment and new technology would not help matters. According to Thomas Chalmers, Robert Torrens and other Ricardians, capital accumulation and productivity gains in excess of the rate of population growth would tend to displace labor and thus bring about its unemployment. John Stuart Mill depicted this process as culminating in his "stationary state" in which capital accumulation had run down and the population no longer was able to expand, merely to reproduce itself. Free trade was only a temporary means to postpone this day of reckoning.

According to Malthus, higher farm incomes or industrial wages resulting from favorable natural situation or technology would spur population growth, which would absorb the higher income. *To the extent that economic convergence occurred among nations, it would result mainly from the leading industrial economies running down* (as a result of diminishing returns in agriculture, first at home and then in the less populous countries), *not by the industrial nations or less developed countries upgrading the productivity of their factors of production.*

This view underestimated the progress of industrial and agricultural productivity. Apart from Andrew Ure and Charles Babbage, it was the protectionist and socialist writers who developed the most realistic analysis of the economic impact of the industrial, agricultural, transport and commercial revolutions then underway.

### Friedrich List's historical approach

The main concern of economists in less industrialized countries, in particular the United States, Germany and Ireland, was with how free trade impaired their industrial development by throwing them into competition with more advanced industrial nations. Holland, Europe's first industrial leader, had not been obliged to face this problem because there was no first-comer ahead of it. But beginning with England, all subsequent powers industrialized largely by means of protectionism.

Drawing on Adam Smith's observation that urban industry provided a home market for local farmers, List warned that premature free trade, by stifling infant industries in their cradle, would impair the emergence of a thriving urban population. This in turn would hold down farm incomes. For example,

> Ireland is merely an outlying farm of England, cultivated merely to suit the trade with England, and not with a view to the best interests of the population; that is, such articles are cultivated as will bear transportation to, and sell in England. The industry of the country is narrowed down to agriculture, and that is narrowed to the consumption of Great Britain. The increasing population being

confined to husbandry, agricultural labor increased and cheapened, until it could scarcely live on land producing abundance; that is, although the land produced sufficient to feed the inhabitants, they could not earn enough at agricultural wages to purchase food …[11]

In the absence of industry, countries would lose the normal benefit of a home market. This would warp their agricultural development by preventing the diversification of crops. Fruits and vegetables could not be grown in commercial quantities because their perishable or bulky nature prevented their exportation. Meat had to be dried and salted or tinned to be shipped over long distances, reducing its appeal. This prevented the use of fields for fallow and grazing or using animals as a source of natural fertilizer. If a growing population was obliged to pursue agriculture exclusively, the result would be "a subdivision of farms and a small culture, both as prejudicial to the power and the civilization of a country as to its wealth."

Based on this disparity of development patterns between lead nations and latecomers, List summarized the phases through which less developed economies would have to evolve:

At first … by free trade with nations of higher culture, [countries] emerge from barbarism, and improve their agriculture; then, by means of restrictions, they give an impulse to manufactures, fisheries, navigation, and foreign commerce; then, finally, after having reached the highest degree of skill, wealth, and power, by a gradual return to the principle of free trade and free competition in their own and foreign markets, they keep their agriculturalists from inaction, their manufacturers and their merchants from indolence, and stimulate them to wholesome activity, that they may maintain the supremacy which they have acquired. In the first of these stages we see Spain, Portugal, and Naples, in the second, Germany and North America; France appears to be on the limits of the latter; but England alone has not only reached, but maintains an industrial and commercial supremacy.[12]

List did not claim that the protective system would be permanent. Nations would reach maturity to join England in an ultimately cosmopolitan free-trade world. But for the time being only England had reached this mature stage of free trade.

Whereas the Ricardians (like subsequent "factor proportions" theorists) viewed less developed countries as enjoying a competitive advantage in the form of low food prices and hence subsistence costs, List and other protectionists viewed physical capital (especially steam-powered machinery) as being the key to increasing national wealth, in agriculture as well as industry. Countries lacking such capital (along with its requisite social institutions) would become increasingly dependent:

[11]   Friedrich List, *National System of Political Economy* (New York: 1856), p. 195.
[12]   List, *ibid.*, pp. 81, 188. See also pp. 72, 77,

A universal association, proceeding from the overbearing influence and wealth of a single nation, based, consequently, upon the subjection and dependence of all others, would result in the annihilation of separate nationalities … such an association would only be a repetition of what has already occurred in the attempt to subjugate the world, made by the Romans; an attempt that would be more successful in our days, by means of manufactures and commerce, instead of, as formerly, by the sword: though either mode would restore the world to barbarism.[13]

Free trade was a declaration of economic war by England on the rest of the world, promoting class warfare in country after country. Ricardian theory had focused on the tendency for the landlord class to monopolize society's growth in income. But protectionists warned that this monopolization would occur only under conditions of technological stagnation of the sort caused by free trade for less developed countries. Ricardian economics, postulating a stagnant level of real income, implied that one class's gain would have to be another's loss. List and subsequent protectionists recalled the mercantilists in maintaining the harmony of interests between farmers, workers and industrialists. Under conditions of balanced economic development, rising incomes for each class would spur demand for the products of other classes,. But free trade would lead to specialization patterns that would block this mutual demand. It would foster industrial monopolies in the lead nations (primarily England), preventing other nations from enjoying normal growth in industrial productivity and markets, and hence rising agricultural productivity.

## Karl Marx's views on foreign trade

Numerous parallels existed between Marxian socialism and protectionism. Both doctrines emphasized the importance of money, technology, historical institutions and structural transformation in the context of economic progress rather than stagnation. Both also depicted glowing visions of the future if guided by appropriate state policies. And thanks to their repudiation of laissez faire and its rationalization of the status quo, socialism and protectionism had many points of contact. French protectionists merged easily with the Saint-Simonians to advocate a state-directed industrialization. Charles Fourier, an early follower of Saint-Simon, integrated his own brand of utopian socialism with industrial protectionism. Marx himself worked for many years as foreign correspondent for Horace Greeley's protectionist *New York Tribune*, edited by the quasi-socialist Charles Dana. In Germany the "socialists of the chair" represented the emerging protectionist Historical School of economics.

---

[13]  List, *ibid.*, p. 71.

But in contrast to the protectionists, Marx emphasized the rivalry rather than harmony of interests between labor and capital. His warnings were borne out after protectionism's success in the United States nurtured trusts and their union-busting activities. While protectionists were advocates of less developed countries in the international arena, Marxists defended the lower classes in each country. Protectionism came from above, and often became a means to block rising living standards (if industrialists controlled the state), whereas socialist statism "from below" focused on uplifting the working class. This prompted Friedrich Engels to warn against the simplistic identification of statism with socialism.

> To describe every interference of the State into free competition—protective tariffs. guilds, tobacco monopoly, nationalization of branches of industry, the Prussian State Bank, the royal porcelain factory—as "Socialism" is a sheer falsi-fication by the Manchester bourgeoisie in their own interests ... this alleged Socialism is nothing but, on the one hand, feudal reaction and, on the other, a pretext for squeezing out money, with the subordinate intention of converting as many proletarians as possible into officials and pensioners dependent upon the State, of organizing alongside of the disciplined army of soldiers and civil officials a similar army of workers. Pressure on voters exercized by superiors in the state apparatus instead of by factory overseers—a fine sort of Socialism! But that's where you get if you believe the bourgeoisie [saying] what they don't believe themselves but only pretend to believe: that the State means Socialism.

Engels shared Mill's misgivings concerning protectionism: "the worst of protection is that when you once have got it you cannot easily get rid of it."[14] At some point protective tariffs tended to entrench privilege rather than to promote progress.

Like his predecessors, Marx based his theory of stages on his prior analysis of domestic industry and agriculture. "With the advent of industrial produc-tion," he emphasized, "agriculture itself is revolutionized" by the application of agricultural capital and fertilizer. His 1857 *Grundrisse* notes and his drafts of *Theories of Surplus Value* (originally conceived as the introductory volume of *Capital*) contained numerous quotations from Justus Liebig, James Finley W. Johnston and other agriculturalists, in addition to Richard Jones who was quite explicit as to how agricultural productivity increased rather than diminished over time. Unlike the Ricardians he held that comparative-cost differentials among countries would naturally tend to be greater in industry than in agri-culture, and that agricultural investment might even give land in industrial nations a growing productivity advantage over the unimproved soils of less developed countries. However, Marx confined these departures from Ricardo

---

[14] Engels to Edward Bernstein, March 12, 1881, in *Marx and Engels on Britain*, 2nd ed. (Moscow: 1962), p. 557.

largely to his notebooks rather than elaborate them into a central tenet of his doctrine. Although he granted that the principle of diminishing returns was a source of economic rents during a transitional stage, he suggested a technologically optimistic grand sequence in the evolution of agricultural productivity relative to that of industry. "On the whole," he wrote,

> it can be assumed that under the cruder, pre-capitalist mode of production, agriculture is *more productive* than industry, because nature assists here as a machine and an organism, whereas in industry the powers of nature are still almost entirely replaced by human action (as in the craft type of industry etc.). In the period of the stormy growth of capitalist production, productivity in industry develops rapidly as compared with agriculture, although its development *presupposes* that a significant change between constant and variable capital has already taken place in agriculture, that is, a large number of people have been driven off the land. Later, productivity advances in both, although at an uneven pace. But when industry reaches a certain level the disproportion must diminish, in other words, productivity in agriculture must increase relatively more rapidly than in industry. This requires: 1. The replacement of the easy-going center by the businessman, the farming capitalist; i.e., with concentrated capitals. 2. In particular however: Mechanics, the really scientific basis of large-scale industry, had reached a certain degree of perfection during the eighteenth century. The development of chemistry, geology and physiology the sciences that *directly* form the specific basis of agriculture rather than industry, does not take place till the nineteenth century and especially the later decades.[15]

Marx also added a new dimension to the population discussion, upon which much trade theory ultimately rested. Wage levels were influenced not as much by rates of population growth as by the more rapid increase in machinery. If machines were labor substitutes pure and simple, then their rapid introduction would depress wages as Ricardo and the Luddite machine wreckers held. But Marx recalled Steuart in rejecting the view that more rapid capital accumulation would aggravate unemployment. Machinery required labor for its production and operation, and opened up entire new industries. Although capital investment might render labor in oversupply in specific industries, on balance, capital accumulation was a precondition for sustaining employment growth. This primary focus on the productive powers and positive employment effect of capital overthrew

> the whole of the absurd theory of population, that the workers must strive to keep their multiplication below the standard of the accumulation of capital. The opposite follows from Barton's and Ricardo's presentation, namely that to keep down the laboring population, thus diminishing the supply of labor, and, consequently, raising its price, would only accelerate the application of machinery, the conversion of circulating into fixed capital [that is, of wage payments into expenditures on machinery], and, hence, make the population artificially "redundant."[16]

[15] Marx, *Theories of Surplus Value*, Part II (Moscow: 1968), pp. 109f.
[16] Marx, *ibid.*, p. 578. On this point see Steuart, *Principles of Political Oeconomy*, Vol. I, p. 295 (quoted in Chapter 7, p. 173).

This reasoning had important implications for subsequent trade theories based on factor proportions. The fact that high wage levels spurred capital accumulation all the more rapidly in high-wage countries such as the United States suggested to Marx a new grand economic dynamics:

> During the second half of the eighteenth century ... wages fell continuously, population grew amazingly—and (so did) machinery. But it was precisely the machinery which on the one hand made the existing population superfluous, thus reducing wages, and on the other hand, as a result of the rapid development of the world market, absorbed the population again, made it redundant once more and then absorbed it again; while at the same time, it speeded up the accumulation of capital to an extraordinary extent, and increased the *amount* of variable capital [that is, wage payments], although variable capital fell relatively, both compared with the total value of the product and also compared with the number of workers it employed, to the first half of the eighteenth century, however, large-scale industry did not as yet exist, but only *manufacture based on the division of labor*. The principal component part of capital was still variable capital laid out in wages. The productivity of labor developed slowly, compared with the second half of the century. The demand for labor, and therefore also wages, rose almost proportionately to the accumulation of capital. England was as yet essentially an agricultural nation and a very extensive cottage industry— spinning and weaving—which was carried on by the agricultural population, continued to exist, and even to expand ... In the first half of the eighteenth century, variable capital was relatively dominant; in the second, fixed capital; but the latter requires a large mass of human material. Its introduction on a large scale must be preceded by an increase of population.[17]

Above all, the progress of capital and technological innovation altered the types of labor in demand:

> There are two tendencies which constantly cut across one another; (firstly,) to employ as little labor as possible, in order to produce the same or a greater quantity of commodities, in order to produce the same or a greater net produce, surplus-value, net revenue; secondly, to employ the largest possible number of workers (although as few as possible in proportion to the quantity of commodities produced by them), because at a given level of productivity—the mass of surplus-value and of surplus product grows with the amount of labor employed. The one tendency throws the laborers on to the streets and makes a part of the population redundant, the other absorbs them again and extends wage slavery absolutely, so that the lot of the worker is always fluctuating but he never escapes from it. The worker, therefore, justifiably regards the development of the productive power of his own labor as hostile to himself; the capitalist, on the other hand, always treats him as an element to be eliminated from production.[18]

---

[17]  Marx, *ibid.*, p. 583.          [18]  Marx, *ibid.*, p. 573.

Ricardo had pointed out that some of the displaced labor was transferred into machine-making industries. Another large portion, Marx added (in agreement with Malthus), became service-industry workers, whose incomes were paid out of society's net surplus. In any case, "the demand for labor will continue to increase with an increase of capital, but not in proportion to its increase: the ratio will necessarily be a diminishing ratio as the labor/capital ratio rises." This did not necessarily mean growth in unemployment, but merely that physical capital investment (and its associated growth in productive powers) would outstrip the rate of population growth as a rising proportion of corporate revenue was spent on accumulating more machinery and investing abroad. This was a far cry from Ricardo's anticipation that profits would dry up under conditions of agricultural protectionism at home and industrial protectionism in foreign countries.

In his critique of Ricardo in Part II of *Theories of Surplus Value*, Marx described how production tended to expand continually under capitalism, "firstly because the capital invested in production is continually growing: secondly because the capital is constantly used more productively; in the course of reproduction and accumulation small improvements are continually building up, which eventually alter the whole level of production." What stopped the investment process was not technologically diminishing returns but monetary and purchasing-power constraints. Marx's theory of the falling rate of profit was more accurately one of the rising capital intensiveness of production, or as he put it, the evolving organic composition of capital. Profits might fall as a proportion of total price (although the rate of return would not necessarily decline), but surplus value would grow steadily as investors increasingly derived their funds from the depreciation (or capital recapture) component of what accountants now call internal cash flow, "a fund for the continuous introduction of improvements, expansion, etc. ... This accumulation fund does not exist at levels of production and in nations where there is not much fixed capital." Capital-intensive economics thus tended to accumulate more and more capital relative to less industrialized countries. "The higher the development of production, the greater will be that part of surplus-value [profits plus depreciation and amortization] which is transformed into constant capital," that is, investment in plant and equipment.[19]

Revenue from domestic and export sales sought new investment outlets, prompting John Hobson, Rudolf Hilferding and V. I. Lenin to develop theories of financial imperialism. "Not a single responsible economist of the post-Ricardian period denies the plethora of capital," Marx observed. "It is ... in the nature of capitalist production to produce without regard to the limits of the market." Indeed,

[19]  Marx, *ibid.*, pp. 480, 497. See also p. 492.

In the crises of the world market, the contradictions and antagonisms of bourgeois production are strikingly revealed. Instead of investigating the nature of the conflicting elements which erupt in the catastrophe, the apologists content themselves with denying the catastrophe itself and insisting, in the face of their regular and periodic recurrence, that if production were carried on according to the textbooks, crises would never occur."[20]

Marx granted the protectionist argument that England and other industrial nations would widen their productivity advantages over less developed countries under a regime of free trade, at least in its initial phases. But the United States, Ireland and continental Europe could counteract this trend and catch up by enacting protectionist policies. "What the Irish need," he wrote to Engels, was

(1) Self-government and independence from England.

(2) An agrarian revolution. With the best intentions in the world the English cannot accomplish this for them, but they can give them the legal means of accomplishing it for themselves.

(3) *Protective tariffs against England.* Between 1783 and 1801 every branch of industry began to flourish. The Union, which overthrew the protective tariffs established by the Irish parliament, destroyed all industrial life in Ireland. The bit of linen industry is no compensation whatever. The Union of 1801 had just the same effect on Irish industry as the measures for the suppression of the Irish woolen industry, etc., taken by the English Parliament under Anne, George II, and others. Once the Irish are independent, necessity will turn them into protectionists, as it did Canada, Australia, etc.[21]

Engels agreed that for England free trade was nationalistic, self-serving, and retarded the industrial development of Europe and North America.[22] The policy sought to consolidate English industrial hegemony, just as protectionism reflected Irish and American nationalism. Engels believed that the United States was destined to outstrip England as the world's leading industrial power. The question was whether the nation should

carry on, for, let us say, fifty years, under free trade an extremely competitive war against the English manufacturers that have got nearly a hundred years' start; or else to shut out, by protective duties, English manufacturers for, say, twenty-five years, with the almost absolute certainty that at the end of the twenty-five years she will he able to hold her own in the open market of the world.[23]

[20] Marx, *ibid.*, pp. 497, 522, 500. On this point see Ricardo, *Principles of Political Economy*, p. 294, quoting Smith, *Wealth of Nations*, Book II, ch. v (Cannan ed., Vol. I, p. 395) that "when the capital stock of any country is increased to such a degree, that it cannot be all employed in supplying the consumption, and supporting the productive labor of that particular country, the surplus part of it naturally disgorges itself into the carrying trade, and is employed in performing the same offices to other countries."

[21] Marx to Engels, November 30, 1867, in *Marx and Engels on Britain*, p. 544.

[22] Engels, *The Condition of the Working Class in England*, quoted in *Marx and Engels on Britain*, pp. 29f.

[23] Engels, introduction written in 1888 to "Karl Marx, An Address: Free Trade," delivered in Brussels. January 9,1848 (Brooklyn: Socialist Labor Party. 1966), p. 20.

To take an express train, one had to pay a higher fare in the form of protective tariffs. But by the end of a protectionist interlude the United States might adopt free trade in its turn, probably outstripping England withina generation—a remarkable forecast!

Marx emphasized that just as England's Navigation Acts and associated mercantilist regulations had fostered its foreign trade, so in general "The system of protection was an artificial means of manufacturing manufactures, of expropriating independent laborers, of capitalizing the national means of production and subsistence, and of forcibly abbreviating the transition from the medieval to the modern mode of production." Protectionism remained progressive in England and other countries as long as it accelerated the development of national capitalism. By contrast, free trade could be progressive in peripheral areas of the world if it dissolved backward modes of production.

As noted earlier, whereas the bourgeois economists (as Marx called them) viewed international competition merely as equalizing market prices, Marx viewed it as similarizing modes of production: "Price is a relationship between people disguised as a relationship between things." The key to analyzing the impact of foreign trade on development lay in the political dimension of bringing different peoples and their social systems in competition with each other. In many countries foreign trade and colonial investment *created* a market to put their stagnant societies in motion, especially those plagued by Asiatic despotism. For these regions the greatest threat blocking capital accumulation was their protectionism. (In the lead nations the main threat was a perpetuation of capitalist forms that had become overgrown.)

Thus, even though Marx recognized that free-trade doctrine served as a form of British apologetics seeking to pry open foreign markets, he held that the struggle by English free traders "is resuméd in the watchword: Produce as cheap as you can, and do away with all the *faux frais* of production, with all superfluous, unnecessary expenses of production."[24] As he wrote in Volume III of *Capital*:

> The sudden expansion of the world market, the multiplication of the circulating commodities, the zeal displayed among the European nations in the race after the products of Asia and the treasures of America, the colonial system, materially contributed toward the destruction of the feudal barriers of production. ... The obstacles presented by the internal solidity and articulation of pre-capitalistic, national, modes of production to the corrosive influence of commerce is strikingly shown in the intercourse of the English with India and China ... In

[24] Marx, *Capital: A Critical Analysis of Capitalist Production* [1867] (London: 1987), p. 782, and Marx, "The Chartists" (August 10, 1852), in *Marx and Engels on Britain*, pp. 358f. On this point see Bernard Semmel, *The Rise of Free Trade Imperialism*, p. 210.

India, the English exerted simultaneously their direct political and economic power as rulers and landlords, for the purpose of disrupting these small economic organizations. The English commerce exerts a revolutionary influence on these organizations and tears them apart only to the extent that it destroys by the low prices of its goods the spinning and weaving industries, which are an archaic and integral part of this unity. And even so this work of dissolution is proceeding very slowly.[25]

In choosing his position in the tariff controversy Marx asked which policy would most rapidly promote economic evolution under existing local conditions throughout the world. Would the transmutation of world capitalism into socialism be promoted more by concentrating international productive powers in a single country (England), or by the broader but often slower growth of competing bourgeoisies abroad, typically in the context of vested interests reflecting precapitalist forms and centralist, quasi-feudal oligarchic power as in Prussia and much of Asia? Whereas nations relatively free of domestic oligarchies, such as the United States and Ireland, were ready for protective tariffs, India and Africa were not. What would be "protected" was their backward, quasi-feudal economic social institutions and that Marx hoped to see dissolved,

> The protectionist system conserves, while the free trade system destroys. It dissolves nationalism and forces the struggle between bourgeoisie and proletariat to its limits. In a word, the system of free trade hastens the social revolution. It is only because of this revolutionary impetus, gentlemen, that I vote in favour of free trade?[26]

Marx thus perceived the hypocrisy of free-trade doctrine and sympathized with Britain's exploited trading partners. But inasmuch as he believed that socialism would establish itself first in the most highly industrialized nations, not in the hinterland, at some point England's commercial victory would become that of socialism. To be sure, the process of integrating the world economy through trade often would be as painful as was the earlier breakup of feudal Europe's traditional harmony between towns and their neighboring countryside. Marx observed that England was the first country to experience this split.

> Now, externally, as the commanding power of the world market England distorts the harmony of economic relations in all the countries of the world. ... The harmony of economic relations rests, according to [Henry C.] Carey, on the

---

[25] Marx, *Capital*, Vol. III (Chicago: 1909), pp. 391ff.

[26] Marx, "An Address: Free Trade," p. 41. See also his *Grundrisse: Foundations of the Critique of Political Economy* (London: 1973), p. 858: "Trade will naturally react back to varying degrees upon the communities between which it is carried on. It will subjugate production more and more to exchange value; push direct use value more and more into the background; in that it makes subsistence more dependent on the sale than on the immediate use of the product. Dissolves the old relations. Thereby increases money circulation. First seizes hold of the overflow of production; little by little lays hands on the latter itself."

harmonious cooperation of town and countryside, industry and agriculture. Having dissolved this fundamental harmony in its own interior, England, by its competition, proceeds an destroy it throughout the world market, and is thus the destructive element of the general harmony.[27]

### The demise of "stages of development" theorizing

After the 1870s, just as Europe initiated a new colonialist expansion that culminated in World War I, orthodox economics stopped theorizing about the stages of development and its foreign-policy aspects. So inextricably had Marx identified the evolution of capitalism with the emergence of socialist institutions that the minds of orthodox economists snapped shut. A kind of fatalism, epitomized by the factor endowment view of comparative advantage, supplanted doctrines of active government development strategy. In advocating the avoidance of active government policy, economists dropped their concerns with technology and productivity. Henceforth their theories were marginal in a pejorative sense.

The term "marginalism" indicates its short time frame, precluding the analysis of structural (that is, more than marginal) change. Marginalist models lead to a stable equilibrium only by assuming diminishing returns, the very antithesis of trade's *developmental* implications. The trade theories of Alfred Marshall, F. Y. Edgeworth and their followers, down through Paul Samuelson and James Meade in modern times, have deemed technological and social innovation "exogenous" considerations. Like the classical "dismal economics" of Ricardo and Malthus, modern equilibrium analysis is based on theories of economic entropy. The essence of factor-price equilibrium is the assumption that all countries are at a similar stage of industrial and agricultural technology, which presumably has diffused throughout the entire world. This assumption precludes the analysis of trade among countries at different stages of development, or how trade may impair or upgrade the productivity of a nation's resources.

At best we have business-cycle models: if one country happens to pull ahead and earn more than others by entering a boom phase, then employment will expand and push up wages while putting upward price pressure on raw materials. Imports will increase as domestic capacity constraints are approached. The balance of trade will fall into deficit, interest rates will rise to stabilize international payments, direct investment will decline and the business cycle will enter its recession phase in which incomes decline, imports fall back and equilibrium is restored. This marginalist behavior is supposed to follow a more or less "steady state" ebb and flow, subject to certain empirical trend projections in exports and imports relative to income growth. But there is no longer an analysis of structural transformation of these trade and production patterns.

[27]  Marx, *Grundrisse*, p. 886

Notwithstanding this doctrinal preference, England and other leading industrial nations undertook a great colonialist expansion after the 1870s, marked by foreign lending and direct investment that did much more than commodity trade to transform world production patterns. Attempts were made to incorporate the description of this investment behavior into economic theory, as Chapter 12 will describe. But such writers were accused of leaving the international economics discipline. Before dealing with theories of international investment and finance it thus is appropriate to review how far the definition of international economics has narrowed to rule out this type of consideration at the outset—in contrast to the breadth of mercantilist theorizing.

# 11

## The Narrowing Scope of Trade Theory

Not all historians of economic doctrine find virtue in analyzing its scope and methodology. "It is indeed arguable," claims Jacob Viner, "that energy spent in trying to define the proper limits of disciplines is often worse than energy wasted."[1] But methodology is important because it determines content. Defining a discipline's scope determines the kind of questions it asks, and hence its subject matter.

For the past two hundred years or so, free traders have promoted an economic methodology designed to limit the content and conclusions of international economics. Liberal conclusions are pre-cooked by recognizing fewer and fewer variables as affecting competitive advantage, and focusing only on a short time frame. The history of international economics has been re-written to exclude broader approaches and theories of how the global economy has evolved.

### How methodology determines content

To define the scope and methodology of international economics is a political act. It implies at the outset whether the subject's conclusions will be laissez faire or protectionist, pro-creditor or pro-debtor. By taking for granted rather than questioning social institutions, productivity and other characteristics that rightly should be viewed as variables, *a narrow scope and methodology restricts content to an analysis of the status quo*, endorsing it as an implicit "given." Similarly, to assume negative-feedback (entropic) rather than positive-feedback (negentropic) mechanisms is to pre-determine that the conclusions will oppose rather than endorse active government policies. By assuming that the world economy tends automatically to readjust to the mythical concept of normal balance after any disturbance, equilibrium economics discourages government policies from counteracting market forces even as the world economy polarizes between rich and poor countries.

Chapters 8 and 9 have reviewed how the scope and methodology of trade theory has narrowed so drastically as to define itself today merely as *location theory*. Countries and regions are depicted as differing from each other simply in having different quantities of labor relative to capital. Dropped from analysis is the differing productivity from one economy to the next, the effect of trade on the overall economy and its demographic patterns (especially emigration or immigration), and the differing financial characteristics that Part III will discuss.

This modern line of theorizing views trade as barter, in which the commodities being exchanged are superfluities, that is, in excess of domestic requirements for the trading parties. There consequently is no absolute need to trade—dependency. One finds little inquiry into *how* national endowments have come to be supplied in their existing amounts. There is no acknowledgement of cartel power backed up by diplomacy, no gunboats, no invisible hand of foreign-inspired *coups d'etat* against regimes seeking to change their economic policies. The image conjured up is that of a world not troubled by major debt obligations or coercion. The financing of business throughout the globe is assumed to be homogeneous, as if all producers enjoy similar interest rates and debt/equity ratios. These assumptions are what economists call pure, meaning that global reality has been distilled out of them.

The result is a model that early economists hardly would have considered international at all. It fails to deal with what were the major concerns of their time: diverging productive powers among nations, capital-transfer problems, and how governments can best shape the economic environment in which labor and capital operate. Modern factor-endowment and general equilibrium theorizing leaves little room to deal with such questions.

Twentieth-century trade theorists have defined the scope of their subject in ever more limited terms. The residue of this narrowing methodology is a phenomenological approach based on surface appearances without inquiring into their underlying causes. The most serious consequence is to exclude policy from consideration as something "exogenous" to the relevant analytic variables. Any given status quo is assumed to be beyond the pale of policy to influence. The supply of capital is taken for granted, without examining how an economy may pursue policies to build it up. Also taken for granted are the supply and quality of labor. Government steps to encourage education, investment, research and development are neglected. This gives the resulting theory a partisan slant in favor of free trade and policy passivity.

### Rewriting the history of international economics

Just as international economic theorizing is political by its nature, so histories of the subject tend to be partisan—much more so, in fact, than histories of economic thought in general. This hardly is surprising, for each epoch writes history in accordance with its own prejudices, depicting earlier ideas as little

---

[1] Jacob Viner, *Studies in the Theory of International Trade* (New York: 1937), p. 594.

more than prelude to existing orthodoxy. As Thomas Kuhn has observed in reference to the history of scientific thought in general: "The temptation to write history backward is both omnipresent and perennial. … Why dignify what science's best and most persistent efforts have made it possible to discard?" References to the great minds of earlier ages are designed primarily to make

> both students and professionals come to feel like participants in a long-standing historical tradition … The result is a persistent tendency to make the history of science look linear or cumulative … [as if] science has reached its present state by a series of individual discoveries and inventions that, when gathered together, constitute the modern body of technical knowledge. From the beginning of the scientific enterprise, a textbook presentation implies, scientists have striven for the particular objectives that are embodied in today's paradigms.[2]

Reviews of international trade and financial theory are no exception. The best known studies remain those written in the 1930s by men committed to laissez faire, and hence to a narrow view of what international economies is all about. In what amounts to a doctrinaire expurgation of their subject, they ignored the history of differing views. Schumpeter aptly attributed their misrepresentation of Adam Smith's predecessors: Any contribution made by someone not a free trader was deemed a non-event by "interpreters of the history of economic analysis who were interested in nothing but free trade and knew no canon of criticism except the distance that separates an author from free trade."[3] Mercantilism has been misrepresented as mere bullionism and a beggar-my-neighbor, zero-sum activity, not as a theory of productive powers. A similar intellectual blackout is imposed on subsequent protectionist thought and the structuralist school of capital transfers that developed in the 1920s.

This censorial tendency is apparent in the two major existing reviews of trade theory, Gottfried Haberler's *Theory of International Trade* (1933), and Viner's *Studies in the Theory of International Trade* (1937). "The only really systematic theory of international trade we possess," wrote Haberler,

> is the so-called classical theory, of which practically all the component parts were worked out by such early writers as Hume, Adam Smith and Ricardo. It is characterized, on the one hand, by the doctrine of comparative costs and, on the other hand, by the principle that prices, exchange rates and money flows provide a mechanism which links together the money systems of different countries and ensures the automatic adjustment of the balance of payments.

Criticisms of these theories have been frequent, he granted, "but the critics have not succeeded in substituting for it anything that deserves to be called a

---

[2]   Thomas S. Kuhn, *The Structure of Scientific Revolutions* (1962), 2nd ed. (Chicago: 1970), pp. 137–40.

[3]   Schumpeter, *History of Economic Analysis*, p. 369.

new theory of international trade."[4] Like his fellow free traders, Haberler fatally oversimplifies the views of Hume, Smith and their contemporaries by using only their full-employment models with no international emigration and investment. No reference was made to the American protectionists, or the analysis of positive-feedback (polarization) tendencies developing within English theory itself, or to Marxian analysis or to the structural analysis of international debt problems.

Some writers acknowledge their limitations. Viner, like Haberler, limited his survey to theories of automatic balance-of-payments adjustment mechanisms (an exercise in strictly monetary and income analysis) and to the theory of comparative costs and its corollary gains-from-trade doctrine. At the outset of his work he stated its purpose as being simply

> to trace, in a series of studies of the contemporary source-material, the evolution of the modern "orthodox" theory of international trade ... to its present-day form ... My objectives have been ... to resurrect forgotten or overlooked material worthy of resurrection, to trace the origin and development of the doctrines which were later to become familiar, and to examine the claims to acceptance of familiar doctrine.[5]

In this attempt he provided an exhaustive work, but not one that seeks to be comprehensive in areas lying beyond the narrow pale of free-trade orthodoxy.

Most histories of international economics give a false impression of comprehensiveness. James W. Angel's *Theory of International Prices* (1925) and Chi-Yuen Wu's *Outline of International Price Theories* (1939) review demand-oriented theories of equilibrium pricing in keeping with the so-called mutual interdependency theory, which also characterizes Carl Iversen's *Aspects of the Theory of International Capital Movements* (1935). These books combed the history of international economic thought to examine simply how price formation under a system of fixed exchange rates tied to gold differs from a regime of flexible exchange rates under an inconvertible paper standard.

Given their pressing monetary concerns in a period of financial breakdown and national bankruptcy, one can understand why economists in the interwar period approached the theory of balance-of-payments and monetary equilibrium with certain simplifying productivity assumptions so as to concentrate on the seemingly major problem at hand. What is curious is that more pressure has not been felt in recent decades to re-examine the history of theories analyzing the interaction between trade and development. Economists in today's debtor countries have not yet adopted an economic theory capable of tackling their most pressing problems.

---

[4]   Haberler, *Theory of International Trade* (London: 1936), p.4.
[5]   Viner, *Studies in the Theory of International Trade*, p. xiii.

A major reason for this omission is the odd conceit that the interaction between trade and development was neither perceived nor discussed prior to World War II. This belief stands as testimony to how thoroughly laissez faire advocates have succeeded in expurgating the content of mercantilist and protectionist literature from the curriculum. Raymond Vernon, for instance, observed that the 1949 *Readings in the Theory of International Trade*, sponsored by the American Economic Association, "contained not so much as a single article on the subject of economic development." This was not even remarked upon at the time, inasmuch as "there simply was no body of systematic ideas ... sufficiently developed two decades ago to merit a place in the book." Not until the 1960s, he asserts, did interest awaken to the developmental aspects of trade theory. To defend this remarkable statement Vernon goes so far as to suggest that "development theory" was not enunciated by Marshall and his contemporaries because they lived in "an environment in which the assumption of swift technological and physical change was not yet taken for granted."[6]

This view may appear plausible only to those unfamiliar with the great technological changes taking place during the sixteenth, seventeenth, eighteenth, nineteenth and early twentieth centuries, or to those unaware of the dynamic role historically played by foreign trade in transforming national economies during these five centuries. It is quite true, as Professor Vernon states, that economic theory issues from the problems of its time. But I hope that Chapters 3, 4 and 7 have shown that it is wrong to believe that the phenomena of technological change and development are only of post–1945 origin, and have just been perceived by economists writing during the past three decades. What has happened is that the earlier theorizing has been forgotten or ignored—deliberately, not by accidental oversight. "If the eye offends thee, pluck it out."

## Breadth of early international economics

At the outset of economic theorizing in the seventeenth and eighteenth centuries, the world's dynamic political, imperial, technological and monetary factors hardly could have been ignored. Colonialism, foreign trade and investment were radically transforming the world economy. Markets were shaped by active government policy, and trade was anything but barter. It was the source of monetary metals for nations without mines of their own. In an epoch when money and credit remained based on silver and gold bullion, international commerce distinguished itself from domestic exchange primarily by its settlement of payments balances in monetary specie, thereby serving as the

---

[6]   Raymond Vernon, forward to James D. Theberge, *Economics of Trade and Development* (New York: 1968), p. v.

unique foundation for domestic credit expansion. Steuart's *Principles of Political Oeconomy*, the great synthesis of advanced mercantilist thought, drew the distinction "between the principles of *foreign* and *domestic* commerce" in the fact that "foreign trade, well conducted, has the necessary effect of drawing wealth from all other nations."[7]

To the nation as a whole, exports were viewed as more advantageous than domestic sales, for the gold and silver they earned was "the money of the world," in contrast to domestic transactions settled by mere transfers of existing purchasing power. To be sure, mercantilists recognized that national wealth depended ultimately on the productive powers capable of earning gold and silver. But they stressed that these productive powers could not be put in motion without an adequate supply of money and credit, which rested ultimately on a metallic base.

Emigration of Protestants and other persecuted workers skilled in dyeing and textiles, glass-making and other industrial arts represented the major form of technology transfer. Chapter 1 has illustrated how mercantilism recognized this emigration as being more a function of political considerations than of wage differentials. Simultaneously, the slave trade between Africa and the New World created a racial underclass throughout Europe's colonial systems. Chapter 2 has shown that this colonial settlement and investment was not simply a search for high profit. It was the result of government designs to achieve a self-sufficient imperial division of labor. Prices reflected the impact of subsidies, tariffs and other state policies, while international competition also was affected by wars and the debts they brought into being. In short, the world's economic and political structures were not simply a response to existing costs and prices. They transformed competitive relationships by directing (or at least trying to direct) the path of international monetary flows, colonization and emigration.

What has awkwardly been termed "mercantilist theory" (I prefer Petty's term "political arithmetic") dealt with these transformation processes. Its theoreticians addressed themselves more to governments than to merchants, although they saw commerce and colonization as major levers of national power. They analyzed the strategy and preconditions necessary to secure balance-of-payments inflows and acquire technological leadership by designing an international diplomacy and what might be called social engineering, treating private enterprise and commerce as means to achieve national ends.

Discussing how nations could draw the world's gold, silver and skilled labor to their own shores, economists prior to Adam Smith asked how government policy might steer personal incentives s to best shape the development of productive powers. The theory of international trade viewed nations as political

---

[7]  James Steuart, *Inquiry into the Principles of Political Oeconomy* (London: 1767), Vol. I, pp. 494, 327.

entities above all. In 1755 Josiah Tucker defined international economics as a distinct area of analysis as follows:

> When a set of Families, be they many or few in Number, are under the same Legislature, and constitute one People or political Society, the Commerce carried on between the Members of this State among themselves, is called internal or domestic: But when they traffic with the subjects of different States or Legislatures, such Intercourse with other Nations, and exchange of Commodities, is termed Foreign Commerce. Hence therefore it is very apparent, that the Ideas of Foreign and Domestic Commerce do not arise from the Distance or Nearness of Situation of one Place to another, but from the different Legislatures which there Places may be respectively under.[8]

Defined as a policy-making entity, the nation was the basic unit of international economics. Although the distance from Dover to Calais was only one-fiftieth of that which separated London from Newcastle, *the differing economic institutions and regulations between England and France distinguished the Dover-Calais trade from domestic commerce.*

Chapter 4 has traced how the early concerns with state policy, widening technological disparities among nations, immigration and international investment were dropped as mercantilism evolved into a doctrine of laissez faire. Largely to deter less industrialized countries from pursuing protectionist policies of their own, economic liberalism depicted world advantage—and inequality— as being the result of nature rather than of man-made social and economic policies. International economics ever since has excluded discussion of these policies—along with labor and capital mobility and inter-factoral competition— from its scope of analysis, on the ground that they are exogenous, non-economic factors. The mercantilists recognized them as belonging at the center of international economic analysis. National economies were expected to improve existing production structures, not merely to trade within their confines. The mercantilists' purpose accordingly was to determine which government policies were the best to follow by nations intent on building up their productive powers.

To be sure, free-trade doctrine originally dealt with the evolution of productive powers and national development. Indeed, it did so under conditions of increasing returns. Chapters 3 and 4 have described how, from 1750 to 1775, Hume, Tucker and Steuart (joined by Cantillon and other contemporaries) debated how long a nation could go on drawing in foreign wealth without suffering inflationary pressures and a dissipation of its early advantage. Both the English mercantilists and their free-trade successors saw that a favorable trade balance would provide money to finance additional investment and employ-

---

[8]  Josiah Tucker, *The Elements of Commerce and Theory of Taxes* [1755], repr. in R. L. Schuyler, ed.: *Josiah Tucker: A Selection from his Economic and Political Writings* (New York: 1931), p. 127. See also p. 140.

ment. Members of Parliament followed economic writers in defending free trade as a more effective policy to achieve a sustained trade surplus and hence to support domestic credit and investment functions by providing economies of scale and extending the division of labor in a positive-feedback process which presumably could continue indefinitely, to the benefit of all countries. Free-traders acknowledged that their policy would make industrial nations more industrial while inducing raw-materials exporters to specialize further in their existing production and trade patterns. Chapter 5 has shown how, as this specialization increased and international production costs diverged, Ricardian tautology depicted the apparent gains from trade as rising steadily for all parties.

The resolution of England's tariff debate ultimately was pragmatic: Which policy—free trade or protectionism—would contribute most to English economic power? Eighteenth century free-traders focused attention on how a wider international commerce would influence the division of labor and provide economies of scale. Liberals argued that England need not fear free trade, because its protectionist policies of the sixteenth, seventeenth and eighteenth centuries had succeeded in consolidating a technological lead that now could maintain itself under its own momentum.

Free-trade anti-colonialists such as Tucker foresaw that England's head start destined it to take the lead in a world transition to laissez faire. Its international payments surplus would increase rather than diminish as aristocratic privileges, state-sponsored monopolies, the Old Colonial System and its vested interests were phased out. A sizeable portion of English leadership favored giving America its independence even before the Revolutionary War forced the issue and became the watershed ending Britain's Old Colonial System. From 1776 through 1846, England dismantled its navigation acts, Corn Laws and other impediments to free commerce, inducing other countries to refrain from protecting nascent industry of their own.

### Ricardo's distinction between domestic value and international prices

Chapter 5 has traced how Ricardo tried to reconcile the labor theory of intrinsic value with the fact that trade was characterized by variations in the labor time necessary to produce given types of commodities. Where domestic costs varied widely, as in agriculture, the price would be set by the marginal cost of production on the highest-cost, least fertile land. A rising price of food gave better situated low-cost producers an economic rent or "super profit," defined as the excess of sales price over production costs including normal profit.

These economic rents were more pronounced in international trade than within the domestic economy. This restricted the labor-time theory of value (and related cost theories) to a merely national scope, and became for Ricardo the distinction between international and domestic economics, because it entailed abandoning the claim to find a *universal* labor theory of value. As Ricardo acknowledged to Malthus:

> The same rule which regulates the relative value of commodities in one country does not regulate the relative value of the commodities exchanged between two or more countries. ... The quantity of wine which [Portugal] shall give in exchange for the cloth of England, is not determined by the respective quantities of labour devoted to the production of each, as it would be, if both commodities were manufactured in England, or both in Portugal.[9]

Whereas domestic prices were determined by the marginal labor time needed to produce a given commodity, international prices were established largely by supply and demand. This was clearest in the case of goods produced only in some countries. In such cases, as Malthus had pointed out, there were no cost ratios to compare, unless some kind of import substitutes could be produced at home.

Just as Ricardo attributed agricultural rent differentials to the allegedly "original and indestructible" powers of the soil, so he attributed international comparative-cost differences to "the peculiar powers bestowed by nature." This view of "nature" was central to his doctrine of comparative adventage, but it had a serious problem. He viewed the evolution of international productivity differentials as being subject to diminishing rather than to increasing returns, above all in agriculture. This assumption had erroneous implications concerning how the terms of trade would evolve over time. The Ricardians and their successors seemed to be describing a different world from the dynamic and self-transforming one in which they actually lived. Malthus was more realistic in arguing that in a well-run world, costs would fall as increasing returns resulted from the application of capital in agriculture and industry. Ricardo argued that cost and productivity differentials either would remain fixed or (at least in agriculture) or would succumb to diminishing returns. Both men agreed that for internationally traded commodities, supply and demand factors determined whether their prices would be set near the high- or low-cost margin of production.

In arguing that cost differentials enabled countries to maximize their consumption by buying in the cheapest market, Ricardo tacitly assumed that trade had neither an adverse nor a positive effect on the development of productive powers. In making this assumption he and most economists of his time showed little concern with the transformation of productive powers underway since the industrial revolution and its parallel agricultural revolution.

---

[9]  Ricardo, *Principles of Political Economy and Taxation*, [1817], (repr. Cambridge: 1957), pp. 133ff. See also Mill, *Principles of Political Economy*, pp. 574f.

It was as if these revolutions in productivity occurred without being influenced by government policies. But if countries outside of England were to catch up, they needed public infrastructure spending, subsidies, and, protective tariffs. Alexander Hamilton drove home this point in his 1791 *Report on Manufactures* delivered to the U.S. Congress. But neither Ricardo nor other free traders paid much attention to the impact of state policy on immigration, internal improvements or other factors promoting the accumulation of capital or increasing labor's productivity and educational attainments. They glossed over the analysis of evolving political and social distinctions among nations that had been central to mercantilist thought as underlying international cost differences.

### The marginalists redefine international economics in terms of factor immobility

John Stuart Mill was the transition figure from classical to marginalist trade theory. Following Malthus and Ricardo he distinguished international from domestic economic analysis on the ground that international prices would settle somewhere within the range of relative comparative costs, at a point determined by supply and demand, in contrast to domestic prices reflecting labor-based value.

Ricardo's concept of cost referred to labor time, not hourly wage remuneration. To have used money cost would have deviated from his objective of finding an intrinsic labor-time basis of value. In any event, he tacitly assumed a tendency for wage rates to settle at subsistence levels (the so-called Iron Law of Wages). Mill brought supply and demand factors into play to determine not only the price of internationally exchanged goods but also to explain variations in the wages and profits. He described these disparities as being maintained by the reluctance of labor and capital to move across national boundaries. Within the domestic economy, by contrast, labor and capital mobility worked to equalize income levels. True, he observed, capital was "becoming more and more cosmopolitan," and "among the civilized countries ... both population and capital now move from one of these countries to another on much less temptation than heretofore. But there are still extraordinary differences, both of wages and of profits, between parts of the world."[10]

Mill's successors attributed international differences in wage and profit levels not to skill or productivity differences, but to variation in the relative supplies (or as they came to put it, "endowments") of labor and capital within each country. Nations with abundant labor (relative to capital) were characterized by low wages and high profits, supposedly giving them a comparative-cost advantage in producing and exporting labor-intensive goods. Wages would be relatively high where labor was scarce, so that the comparative advantage for

[10]   Mill, *Principles of Political Economy*, p. 575.

such countries would lie in producing capital-intensive goods—unless capital happened to be even scarcer than the scarce labor. High-wage countries tended to have relatively abundant land and other natural resources, for not every factor of production could be scarce simultaneously. "Young" countries such as the United States had land and mines in quantity, but were viewed as being both labor- and capital-scarce by European standards. This suggested that they should depend mainly on England for capital-intensive industrial manufactures, exchanging the food and minerals produced by their abundant lands and mines.

Factor immobility was held to be the underlying cause of (rather than merely a *precondition* for) wage and income disparities within the world economy, in contrast to the equally unrealistic assumption of *full factor mobility within domestic economies*. In 1874, to be sure, J. E. Cairnes developed his theory of non-competing groups to acknowledge that labor and capital often faced structural barriers and rigidities within their own economies. He also acknowledged, with Mill, that labor was becoming "less national and more cosmopolitan." Nonetheless, he held that labor's *relative* immobility across national boundaries was sufficient to distinguish international from domestic economics. C. F. Bastable, F. Y. Edgeworth and subsequent writers endorsed this view.[11]

What occurred was a revolution against cost-of-production principles. The use to which Marx put Ricardo's labor theory of value rendered it anathema, while the protectionists took over capital-productivity theories. An alternative body of economics was developed, a theory of marginal psychological utility rather than focusing on production functions and active government policy. The major figures were Stanley Jevons in England, Anton Menger and Friedrich von Wieser in Austria, and Leon Walras in Switzerland in the 1870s and '80s, followed by Alfred Marshall in the 1890s. Harking back to the ideas of Jeremy Bentham, their liberal utilitarian theorizing took individuals out of the social context that shaped and motivated personal drives.

According to laissez faire ideology a country's first objective should be to maximize consumer utility at any given moment of time, as evaluated by current (rather than potential) market prices. There was no concept of losses suffered through trade, such as mineral depletion or forgone opportunities to develop. Looking at the status quo in static Ricardian gains-from-trade fashion, Marshall, Walras and their followers down to the present day ignored the widening of international productivity differentials. For over a century, "labor," "capital" and "land" of presumably equal quality in every country have been held to be mixed together to produce commodities under conditions of diminishing returns—

[11]   J. E. Cairnes, *Some Leading Principles of Political Economy Newly Expounded* (London: 1874), p. 362, and C. F. Bastable, *The Theory of International Trade, with Some of its Applications to Economic Policy* (Dublin: 1887), pp. 9f.

during an epoch in which industry, agriculture and mining have achieved unprecedented breakthroughs in increasing returns.

The reason for assuming diminishing returns was not because this characterized economic reality. Rather, it was logically necessary to "close" heuristic economic models so as to mathematically determine a single optimum mix of labor, capital and land for each commodity and an optimum specialization of production for each country. The new academic vogue of scientific economics was to translate arguments into mathematical terms, in ways that suggested neat equilibrium solutions to each hypothetical problem.

The real world was in no such equilibrium. Part I has shown how Tucker, Steuart and other economic writers as early as the 1770s foresaw an explosive dynamic of increasing returns and positive-feedback relationships that would enable rich nations to increase their advantage over less developed latecomers. Nineteenth-century protectionists outside of England greatly elaborated the prospect of international polarization of productive powers and income. They perceived that as England gained a world monopoly position by virtue of its self-reinforcing head start, economies of scale and financial efficiency, less active government diplomacy was needed—as long as other countries refrained from subsidizing their own industrial development. (A few gunboats often were all that was needed, not formal imperialism.)

The industrial and agricultural revolutions implied government policies to coordinate the training and education of labor and other infrastructure spending. But free traders excluded the analysis and consequences of increasing returns from the realm of international economics, and from that of domestic economics as well. Its dynamics were beyond the ability of simple arithmetic formulas to handle, at a time when mathematical treatment of subject matter had become the very symbol of scientific method. Increasing returns implied a plethora of choices in an explosive world, not a single stable solution in an entropic world. It implied a focus on change, not preservation of the status quo. It suggested inherent tendencies toward monopolization of production, both for nations enjoying a head start and within each country. (By contrast, small-scale competitive production was supposed to be ensured by assuming *diseconomies of scale*, as if the twentieth century still were operating in Adam Smith's epoch of cottage industry.) Finally, the prospect of increasing returns implied the corollary concept of opportunity cost for countries *failing* to participate in economic and technological progress.

Despite these realities, free traders claimed an unwarranted generality for their conclusions by limiting the number of factors considered in describing economic development. Stripping economics of its classical political, social and technological concerns, they narrowed economic methodology even further than the Ricardians had done in their debate with Malthus and his fellow protectionists. The assertion that free trade results in an optimum development policy for all countries, irrespective of their level of development and productivity differences, can be defended only by dropping the technological, historical and institutional aspects of trade theory.

## *The factor-endowment theory of comparative advantage*

The factor-endowment approach to international economics inverted classical analysis based on productivity differences in the context of similar absolute (subsistence) wage levels in most "older" nations. Labor was able to emigrate, international investment was occurring, capital was being accumulated at differing rates among nations, and technological change was being induced by both political and economic motivations. Yet the factor-endowment theory postulated *uniform productivity but differing relative incomes* resulting solely from differing factor proportions (and hence, wage and profit relations) within a uniform technological, political and social environment.

Differing factor endowments—to which wage and profit variations among countries henceforth were attributed—were accepted as *a priori* phenomena, to be taken as the starting point for international economic analysis to the exclusion of national differences in productivity or government policies. No attempt was made to attribute the world's accelerating technological revolution to programs of government support or even to infrastructure spending on internal improvements and transport, education, research subsidies, or to the social and political environment.

Eli Heckscher in 1914, followed by his student Bertil Ohlin in 1935, pressed the postclassical line of theorizing to its logical conclusion. They redefined the concept of nationhood so that countries seemed to differ from one another *mainly in the sense of having different factor proportions*. These proportions were supposed to persist as long as labor and capital remained relatively immobile among countries. Productivity disparities were ignored, as were the political and social differences that influenced their evolution. Nations were defined as aggregations of labor, capital and land within a common worldwide production function. The characteristic feature of the international economy remained differing cost functions among nations, but instead of attributing these cost variations to differences in labor and capital productivity as in Ricardian and pre-Ricardian tradition, *the marginalists attributed cost differences to differing market wage rates and profit levels resulting from variations in the quantity of workers and other resources relative to that of capital.* Absolute cost functions and differentials, government policy and diplomatic leverage were given no role to play). The new trade theorists denied any structural problems underlying divergences in international incomes.

As early as 1887 Bastable suggested the term "interregional trade" to take the place of international trade.[12] This attitude was reflected in the title of Ohlin's 1935 *Interregional and International Trade*. According to Ohlin, "the theory of international trade is only part of a general localization theory," that is, "a branch of *Standortslehre*."[13] Cart Iversen followed Ohlin in reasoning that as long as the assumption of factor immobility remained the characteristic feature of international trade theory, "it becomes evident that international trade *is merely one form of interlocal trade*."[14] This denied the essential phenomena of nationhood: policy-making power such as taxation, infrastructure spending and financial policy, along with the productivity of labor and land, social climate and so forth.

Viner acknowledged that "the theory of international trade has not dealt nor pretended to deal … with the myriad long-term economic effects of the international migration of capital, or of labor."[15] These broader issues were left to specialists whose writing remained segregated from the body of orthodox international economics. Chi-Yuen Wu summed up the new theory, insisting that

> The classical economists never claimed that their definition of "nation" coincided with the political or the generally accepted definition of "nation." They only claimed that their theory was applicable to trade between "non-competing groups," *i.e.* groups between which labour and capital did not flow freely. Whether the immobility of labour and capital applies to nations or to regions is unimportant if we remember that the classical theory is a theory of trade between non-competing groups.[16]

This definition, at odds with the actual views of Adam Smith, Ricardo and Mill, ignored divergences in rates of technological change and the consequent development of international competition and dependency relationships. Although the new theory represented itself as being the intellectual heir to the classical theories of Smith and Ricardo, it actually was an abandonment of their

---

[12]  Bastable, *Theory of International Trade*, p. 12n.
[13]  Ohlin, *Interregional and International Trade* (Cambridge. Mass.: 1935), pp. viii, 589.
[14]  Carl Iversen, *Aspects of the Theory of International Capital Movements* (New York: 1935), p. 3. Theodore Otis Yntema (*A Reformulation of the General Theory of International Trade* [Chicago: 1932], p. 3), also defined international trade as being essentially interregional trade and expounded how it "is in the pure case distinguished from international or intra-regional trade by immobility of the productive agents between the countries or regions. Only the exchange of *products* takes place between countries." Although he granted (as had Iversen) that this idealization did not find its counterpart in economic reality, he confined his allegedly "general" theory of international trade to this "simplified, ideal case. We shall hereafter see the term 'country' as indicative of a region within which the productive factors are in competition, but beyond the limits of which they cannot move."
[15]  Viner, *Studies*, p. 600.
[16]  Chi-Yuen Wu, *An Outline of International Price Theories* (London: 1939), p. 155.

emphasis on differing productive powers among nations. As Edgeworth wryly observed the new approach in 1894:

> International trade meaning in plain English trade between nations, it is not surprising that the term should mean something else in Political Economy. In technical usage international trade is distinguished from home trade by the existence of barriers which prevent owners of the means of production in one region—or, more generally, sphere of industry—from employing those means in another sphere.[17]

Although Smith and Ricardo indeed discussed the relative hesitancy of labor and capital to move abroad, it was an incidental observation rather than a central pivot of their theorizing. When Smith observed that "a man is of all sorts of luggage the most difficult to be transported,"[18] he was referring to domestic labor mobility, contrasting it rigidly with the easier movement of goods from one market to another in response to price differentials. Ricardo's remark about "the natural disinclination which every man has to quit the country of his birth and connexions, and in trust himself with all his habits fixed, to a strange government and new laws,"[19] acknowledged that these differences in national habits, culture and laws were critical, just as when Tucker designated them as representing the distinguishing feature of international economics in 1755. To be sure, Ricardo said little about what *kind* of laws might be most appealing to the many emigrants who were leaving Europe for the United States, precisely because its laws were different—and better.

It cannot be overemphasized that writers prior to and including Mill placed central emphasis on productivity differentials. The classic comparison of the labor costs of producing wine and cloth in England and Portugal was based on differential manhour inputs, not differing wage rates or on profit levels. As for the post-classical attempt to distinguish between international and domestic economics in terms of differing degrees of "factor mobility" (and subsequently of factor endowments), Smith no more believed that labor was fully mobile domestically than Ricardo or Mill believed it to be immobile internationally.

---

[17]  F. Y. Edgeworth, "The Pure Theory of International Trade" (1894) repr. in *Papers Relating to Political Economy* (London: 1925), Vol. II, p. 5. Haberler, in *The Theory of International Trade* (p. 4), helped spread this misleading pedigree for the new theory, attributing to Smith and Ricardo an extreme view to which not even J.S. Mill would have subscribed fully:

> The classical school believed … that there was a fundamental difference between home trade and foreign trade. They pointed out that labor and capital moved freely from one branch of production and from one district to another within a single country. Between different countries, on the other hand, mobility was totally, or at any rate to a great extent, lacking. In the latter case, complete adjustment (*i.e.* the establishment of the same rate of wages and the same rate of interest everywhere) did not take place. Immobility was accepted quite naively by the classical school as the criterion of international trade.

[18]  Smith, *Wealth of Nations*, Book I, ch. viii, p. 14.

[19]  Ricardo, *Principles of Political Economy*, p. 136.

Inasmuch as this was an epoch of great international emigration and investment, Smith, Ricardo and Mill would have been derided had they clung to the extreme assertions attributed to them by Viner, Haberler and their post-classical followers.

One corollary of the unrealistic assumption of full factor mobility within domestic economies was its implication that unemployment could not exceed merely frictional levels. If imports or other causes displaced labor, it was supposed to be sufficiently flexible to find new work. At least Ricardo was realistic enough to acknowledge the prospect of serious unemployment, in the third edition of his *Principles of Political Economy and Taxation*, published in 1821 in the face of the dislocations resulting from the resumption of trade following the end of the Napoleonic Wars six years earlier. Labor clearly was being thrown out of work as a result of import competition. Skilled workers in particular were moving to countries where they could find work in their own professions rather than having to shift into new lines of employment at home.

All this was forgotten by the 1930s. Ricardo's and Mill's shift in emphasis from *absolute* costs to merely *relative* costs implied that each country, even if it had absolute high-cost positions across the board, could export something, and indeed enough to keep its international payments in balance perpetually! High-cost producers were held to be able to exchange their relatively "least high-cost" output for relatively higher-cost products. This approach recognized no common denominators such as capital goods or raw materials, or even a common interest rate determining capital costs linking the world economy to a single cost system. To have acknowledged such linkages would have meant opening the possibility of analysing how high-cost countries might suffer chronic unemployment culminating at some point in economic and technological obsolescence, and consequent structural unemployment.

In assuming the factor-endowment theory in the first place, and totally flexible domestic mobility of labor and capital in the second place, the new approach to trade theory ruled out the analysis of what now are called dual economies—raw-materials monocultures whose export sectors may be highly capital intensive despite a massive "overpopulation" of underemployed labor in the local subsistence economy. These dual economies have become a characteristic feature of today's world. The capital invested in their export sectors is not domestic but foreign-owned, mainly by multinational firms in the lead nations. Furthermore, much domestic capital is held abroad (seemingly anomalous from a purely economic point of view). This generalization holds for Canada as well as for Latin America and Africa. The phenomenon of capital flight on the part of wealthy Third World and post-Soviet citizens (especially those in the uppermost government positions) has become as well known as that of dual economies. To view labor as a resource that invariably can be employed at something remunerative flies in the face of today's structural unemployment.

The root of these errors is the assumption (discussed in Chapters 7, 8 and 9) that some types of products are inherently labor-intensive while others are capital intensive. The reality is that capital has been displacing labor in production in all sectors since the beginning of the Industrial Revolution. This is especially the case in agriculture, not to mention the industrial synthetics that have displaced Third World land and other natural resources (rubber and indigo, as well as copper and other metals whose place is now being taken by plastics). The factor-endowment theory collapses once we recognize capital as substituting its productive powers for those of labor and land. It is a non-technological theory constructed by minds eager to find some way in which given patterns of economic activity can be construed as working out for the best in this best of all possible worlds.

Taking technology into account suggests that low productivity levels in economies that fail to modernize prevent them from balancing their trade and payments. Ironically, to the extent that an international balance-of-payments problem was anticipated at all, deficits were forecast for the industrial nations rather than for Third World countries exporting raw materials!

### Income disparities resulting from underdevelopment

As discussed in Chapter 10, Ricardo's rent theory gave less developed countries little reason to interfere in the trade process. *Ricardo expected them to benefit from economic rent in raw-materials production by more than they would suffer from industrial cost disadvantages.* As the world's population grew and became more industrialized, it would force resort to ever poorer soils and mines, shifting international prices in favor of raw materials exporters. It seemed that they need do nothing actively to reap this natural consequence of the world's growing demand for food and raw materials, *assuming diminishing returns to characterize the agricultural and mining sectors of the industrial nations.* As England's growing population forced less fertile, higher-cost soils to be brought into cultivation, food prices would rise, unless the nation could obtain lower-cost food from more sparsely populated, rural countries. Mill's analysis implied that such imports would improve the terms of trade for these countries' food and other raw materials.

No one expected the raw-materials exporters to become food-deficit regions. As comparative-cost ratios widened over time, countries exporting raw materials were supposed to increase their export incomes more rapidly than could industrial exporters. Competition among English capitalists would pass on the benefits of cost-cutting innovations to their customers, while food prices would be pushed up toward the world's high-cost margin. Even though—indeed, precisely because—less developed countries would suffer diminishing returns in their agricultural and raw-materials production in time, price trends would favor them more than industrial exporters.

Ricardian analysis failed to appreciate the degree to which the industrial nations might increase their productivity in agriculture and mining as well as in industrial pursuits. For this failure he was chastised by Malthus and other protectionist spokesmen for England's landlord class. But no classical economist anticipated a chronic oversupply of world raw materials and a one-sided monopolization of industrial and farm technology by the lead nations.

Yet the supply-and-demand elaboration of trade theory did provide grounds for doubting that the terms of trade would favor less industrialized countries. England and other industrial nations tended to specialize in the production of commodities *for which demand tended to rise more rapidly than world income.* This was in accord with what subsequently was called Engel's law. As incomes rose, a rising proportion was spent on industrial goods and luxuries, while spending on food, rent and other essentials remained relatively fixed (that is, income inelastic). As long as England could remain the workshop of the world, it would be in a position to monopolize the supply of products for which demand was growing most rapidly. It might sell its manufactures at the high cost that its customer countries would have to pay to produce similar goods by their own infant industries. This meant that agricultural countries would buy an ever expanding range of industrial manufactures, while England's growth in food imports would be limited by the size of the human stomach, and the relatively slow rate of population increase in industrial (implicitly low-wage) economies.

Finance always has sought to be unseen, in order to be left alone and unregulated. It is significant that the bond broker and financial lobbyist Ricardo was most guilty of diverting attention away from money and finance. He acknowledged *rentier* income only in the form of groundrent, not interest and other financial charges. His monetarist shortcomings have plagued theories of international finance and the balance of payments down to the present day. It therefore is necessary to explain how the scope of international finance came to be so limited.

Mill re-introduced the financial dimension to Ricardian "barter" theory by tracing how capital movements—international lending and investment, and the return flow of earnings, interest and principal—turned the terms of trade against debtor countries. While exchanging their exports for those of creditor nations, *they had to run an additional export surplus to finance their capital payments.* This debt service required extra transfers of raw materials as a terms-of-trade penalty. If investors in the industrial nations purchased direct ownership of colonial mines, plantations and other natural resources, then *even if the price of these raw materials increased, the profits on their production* (or more technically accurate, their economic rents or "super profits") *would be remitted to investors in the industrial creditor nations!* This would create a balance-of-payments dependency on lead nation investment, enabling them to monopolize the gains for themselves, as investors if not as exporters.

Mill acknowledged that the leading industrial nations had achieved their favored economic position largely by virtue of their head start. This followed from the protectionist policies adopted at the outset of their industrialization. It seemed that they would increase their industrial cost advantage by what today are called learning curves—experience. (Mill might have added that plantation and mining monocultures were characterized by social institutions not amenable to industrialization, or for that matter to food production for the home market.) But less industrialized countries were discouraged from emulating the policy of England, by discounting its effectiveness. Tariffs were thought of aspure costs, a burdensome deadweight.

Although policy considerations were recognized as having provided an original advantage for Europe's leading industrial nations, these powers hardly were eager to broadcast a line of analysis highlighting the active role played (at least initially) by government policy. They preferred to drop the subject, along with any idea of a trade-off between long- and short-term interests. The short run was, for all intents and purposes, interpreted as indicating the long run.

Matters have turned out even worse for raw-materials exporters than Mill's analysis and Engel's Law suggested. Instead of raw-materials exporters receiving an increasing margin of economic rent for their primary commodities and foodstuffs as these became increasingly costly for industrial Europe to produce at home, just the opposite has occurred. Less developed countries have become increasingly dependent on the industrial nations, not only for their manufactured goods, which have turned out to be increasingly essential, but also for their grain. U.S. agricultural tariffs and price supports, emulated by Europe's Common Agricultural Policy (CAP), have fostered productivity gains that have surpassed even those of industry since World War II. Perversely, however, industrial food-surplus nations have kept prices for their crops from falling by subsidizing supply-management programs such as the U.S. "Soil Bank" and crop-purchase schemes. Meanwhile mineral exports from Third World countries have suffered price pressure from falling costs and competitive oversupply. Even the 1973 OPEC price jump for oil was wiped out by rising prices for U.S. and European grain, arms and manufactured goods.

A reverse kind of dependency has developed as trade has became a matter of vital necessity rather than a discretionary matter of choice for less industrialized countries. Adam Smith wrote that "The first object of political economy is to provide subsistence for the people,"[20] but specialization outside Europe and North America was been pushed to so high a degree as to neglect domestic food needs. Since achieving nominal political independence in the years following World War II, Latin America and Africa have depended increasingly on industrial

[20] Smith, *Wealth of Nations*, Book IV, ch, i, p. 449.

nations for their means of subsistence. Foreign trade no longer is merely an exchange of superfluities among self-sufficient regions. Today's Third World countries are absolutely dependent on imported food, fuels and a widening range of industrial essentials, not to speak of foreign credit.

This "need to buy" is the converse of Adam Smith's "vent for surplus" concept. Less developed countries unable to feed and otherwise supply their populations must import their necessities in exchange for whatever the industrial nations will take—mainly non-renewable raw materials or ownership of local resources. Meanwhile, the rich nations have maintained and even intensified protection of their own industries! Thus, neither the political promises nor the economic forecasts made by free-traders to less developed countries a century ago have been fulfilled. The Third World's trade balance has fallen into deficit financed by foreign borrowings whose carrying charges push their overall balance of payments even further into deficit.

Institutional and political factors have further complicated matters. Large-scale mineral and plantation production in less developed countries generally bolsters the conservative political power of their landed oligarchies and export-oriented cosmopolitan families. This political alliance has rendered land reform and other agriculture modernization all the more difficult. It also has discouraged development of the democratic political structures on which English eighteenth-century theorists placed such emphasis. Without personal freedom, education and opportunity, the climate for industrialization is thwarted. The approach of neoclassical marginalist analysis ignores the fact that client oligarchies act more as cosmopolitan aliens than as nationalists.

The capstone of dependency is a chronic balance-of-payments deficit that imposes domestic monetary austerity. Today's orthodoxy is prevented from recognizing this problem by treating the international economy as if it operated on a barter basis, devoid of monetary and debt problems. Free-trade theory since Ricardo's day has gone to the opposite extreme of the alleged mercantilist obsession with bullion by stripping away all discussion of the problem! As Part III will show, the laissez faire view depicts international debt problems as being self-curing under conditions of monetary and fiscal austerity. As matters have turned out, international polarization has become as pronounced in the financial sphere as it has in the technological area. Debtor countries are stripped of the resources needed to modernize their economies.

### *The need for a theory of international economic polarization*

Disparities in international incomes and terms of trade have widened between industrial creditor nations and indebted raw-materials exporters. Yet no body of theory now extant has explained why. There has been a *description* of various measures (the factoral and other terms of trade, net payments imbalances, debt service and so forth), but this is not the same thing as an explanatory model. To help rectify this situation, Part III of this book argues that the Third World's commodity terms of trade have worsened in part by having to raise an increasing volume of foreign exchange to service their foreign debts, whose repayment has obliged them to export a chronic surplus of raw materials in the face of limited world demand.

Although these economies borrowed enough new money to cover their debt service through the 1980s, this credit was made available on highly political conditions. Its recipients have been obliged to stifle domestic investment and consumption functions by imposing domestic austerity. Third World countries have been obliged to service their $1.3 trillion in foreign debt (as of yearend 1989) and to finance growing structural trade deficits by borrowing more, obliging themselves to transfer yet more interest and principal in future years. With the hearty approval of the international economics profession, they have climbed onto a treadmill of austerity and dependency. Investment outflows from the industrial creditor nations to purchase raw-materials resources in Third World economies have been recouped by their effect on holding down the terms of trade for host-country economies. The result has been a free ride for the investor nations.

The doctrine of productive powers voiced prior to World War I has all but disappeared from the history of economic thought, as protectionism has been abandoned in theory even as it has been adopted in practice. This is the great irony today. The United States and other industrial creditor nations adopted protectionism in the 1930s and continue to apply it, but defense of this policy has come mainly from politicians, lawyers and journalists not programmed to think "economically." As in the eighteenth century, protectionism's pragmatic basis emphasizes self-sufficiency in food, minerals and other essentials on national security grounds. Such measures are adopted largely as the result of lobbying by entrenched vested interests.

The result is that today's international economic orthodoxy seems mainly for export to less developed countries. It hardly can be said to describe today's world. The academic models underlying trade or capital-transfer exercises may call their trading parties Nation A and Nation B, or even "England" and "Portugal," but the behavior of these parties does not reflect that of actual nations. The real world is evolving in dynamic technological and institutional ways at odds with the static assumptions made by today's international price theory. As John Williams observed in 1929, orthodox theory "assumes as fixed, for the purposes of the reasoning, the very things which … should be the chief objects of study if what we wish to know is the effects and causes of international trade." As he subsequently quipped (after having benefited from the experience of serving as chief international consultant to the New York Federal Reserve

Bank): "About the practical usefulness of theory, I have often felt like the man who stammered and finally learned to say, 'Peter Piper picked a peck of pickled peppers,' but found it hard to work into conversation."[21]

The alternative is for international economics to address the problem of how to develop in an evolving world. One of its first tasks should be to define the consequences of debt service, military spending and other capital transfers. It also should spell out the costs required to achieve self-sufficiency in vital sectors such as agriculture, and to compare these costs with those of retaining existing dependency patterns. This would show how pursuing the short-term Ricardian gains from trade has led to deteriorating terms of trade, dependency, deepening foreign debt, economic obsolescence, and the loss of economic autonomy. For less developed countries, a rational choice as to whether the gains from protectionism outweigh the gains from free trade cannot be made until free traders and protectionists agree to talk about the same thing rather than at cross-purposes using different measures of economic well-being.

Those who are concerned with analyzing international economics from this broad vantage point must feel a kinship with the founders of political economy, whose central concern was nothing less than the wealth of nations. I have spent so much time reviewing the history of mercantilist thought because it was the matrix out of which both free-trade and protectionist theory evolved. In Adam Smith's day a lively debate sought to explain how foreign debts, military spending, colonialism and its associated growth in the domestic national debt would influence the course of economic development, monetary relations, investment functions and productive powers. This breadth of scope made the debate between English mercantilists and their free-trade successors not an effete academic exercise but vitally important. It centered on the prospects of running a sustained trade surplus providing lead nations with money to finance additional investment and employment, at a time when they were just beginning to pull ahead of the rest of the world.

To explain the resulting polarization I have tried to put the process in its broad historical perspective. Part II traces the protectionist and free-trade responses to the technological transformation of agriculture, industry and commerce in the nineteenth and twentieth centuries. Part III discusses the impact of capital transfers and the broad financial setting of world development. Chapter 12 forms a bridge by tracing how the classical economists recognized international investment, although today's historians of thought deny that they did. Investment in the world's less developed areas was in fact a precondition for the division of international labor and production they sought to shape.

---

[21] John H. Williams, "The Theory of International Trade Reconsidered," (1929), reprinted in *Postwar Monetary Plans and Other Essays*, 3rd ed. (New York: 1947), pp. 134f.

# PART III

## The Impact of Foreign Debt on Trade and Development

And when he reaches early adolescence he must become possessed with an ardent love for truth, like one inspired, neither day or night may be cease to urge and strain himself in order to learn thoroughly all that has been said by the most illustrious of the Ancients. And when he has learnt this, then for a prolonged period he must test and prove it, and observe what part is in agreement, and what in disagreement with obvious facts; thus he will choose this and turn away from that. To such a person my hope has been that my treatise would prove of the very greatest assistance. Still, such people may be expected to be quite few in number, while as for the others, this book will be as superfluous to them as a tale told to an ass.

Galen, *On the Natural Faculties*, Book iii, ch. 10.
(The Loeb Classical Library, pp. 279ff.)

We know, of course that history incessantly repeats itself. But it is amazing and perhaps a little sad to observe that economists, swayed by the prevailing humors of the hour, also repeat themselves and that, blissfully ignorant of their predecessors, they believe in each case that they are making unheard-of discoveries and building up a brand-new monetary science.

Joseph Schumpeter, *History of Economic Analysis*, p. 712.

# 12

## How International Investment and Lending Follow Trade

### *The practical need for foreign investment by industrial economies*

Europe's Industrial Revolution involved a parallel revolution in the mass production of food, minerals and plantation products throughout the world. Adam Smith explained how the division of labor required an extraordinary growth in stocks of raw materials and other inputs on hand:

> ... when the division of labour has once been thoroughly introduced, the produce of a man's own labour can supply but a very small part of his occasional wants. The far greater part of them are supplied by the produce of other men's labour. ... A stock of goods of different kinds, therefore, most be stored up somewhere sufficient to maintain him, and to supply him with the materials and tools of his work. ... As the accumulation of stock must, in the nature of things, be previous to the division of labour, so labour can be more and more subdivided in proportion only as stock is previously more and more accumulated. The quantity of materials which the same number of people can work up, increases in a great proportion as labour comes to be more and more subdivided; and as the operations of each workman are gradually reduced to a greater degree of simplicity, a variety of new machines come to be invented for facilitating and abridging those operations. As the division of labour advances, therefore, in order to give constant employment to an equal number of workmen a equal stock of provisions, and a greater stock of materials and tools than would have been necessary in a ruder state of things, must be accumulated beforehand.[1]

Increased industrial productivity and employment thus presupposed a growing availability of raw materials. Iron and steel factories, for instance, require large stocks of ore and coal as well as finished output for sale to distributors throughout the world. Marx made this point in his 1858 *Grundrisse* notebooks:

> The increased productivity of labour requires a greater outlay for raw material and instrument[s] ...
>
> Since the growing productivity of labour would lead capital to encounter a barrier in the not-growing mass of raw material and machinery, industrial development takes the following course: the introduction of labour on a large scale, as well as the employment of machinery, begins in the branches which are closest to being production of raw materials for industry ... Thus, in spinning

---

[1]   Smith, *The Wealth of Nations*, Book II, introduction (Cannan ed), pp. 291f.

before in weaving, in weaving before printing etc. First of all in the production of metals, which are the chief raw material for the instruments of labor themselves. If the actual raw product which makes up the raw material for industry at the lowest stage cannot itself be rapidly increased, then refuge is sought in more rapidly increasable substitutes. (Cotton for linen, wool and silk.) The same happens for the necessaries of life in the substitution of potatoes for grain.[2]

This explains why steam engines were employed in mining before industry. Bottlenecks in the primary raw materials production had to be solved before industrial specialization could proceed smoothly. In an attempt to alleviate this constraint as much as possible, the industrial nations took the lead in developing raw-materials supplies throughout the world to sustain their industrial expansion without running into the steep cost pressures that otherwise would have kept their business upswings on a tight leash.

The question was, which nations would get the main benefit of the rent-like gains from trade resulting from the natural resources of primary-producing countries? Adam Smith noted that economic expansion in the industrial nations would tend to bid up the price of food, fuels and other raw materials, first at home (to the benefit of domestic landlords and other resource owners, as Ricardo emphasized) and then abroad. As Samuel Hollander has summarized Smith's views, "the operative restriction upon increased labor productivity due to technical progress is not the previous availability of wages goods [*e.g.*, the wages fund] but that of raw materials (and simple tools)."[3]

Prices for raw materials vary much more sharply than for food, whose demand remains fairly stable relative to the size of the population as a whole. This prompted the industrial economies to do what they could to avoid chronic raw-materials shortages leading to scarcity-rents accruing to countries possessing key commodities.

The short run problem was the tendency for price increases for primary commodities to exceed the decline in "real" production costs stemming from rising labor and capital productivity. As Smith put it:

> There are … a few manufactures, in which the necessary rise in the real price of the rude materials will more than compensate [that is, cancel out] all the advantages which improvement can introduce into the execution of the work. In carpenters and joiners work, and in the coarser sort of cabinet work, the necessary rise in the real price of barren timber, in consequence of the improvement of land, will more than compensate all the advantages which can

2   Marx, *Grundrisse* [1858] (London: 1973), pp. 773, 775. Marx pointed out that inventories were more in the character of overhead than productive capital, and hence tended to lower the rate of profit.
3   Hollander, *The Economics of Adam Smith* (Toronto: 1973), p. 153.

be derived from the best machinery, the greatest dexterity, and the most proper division and distribution of work.[4]

Industrialization thus threatened to provide an economic rent for resource owners (landlords, mine owners and plantation operators), turning the terms of the trade in favor of raw materials exporters. On balance, Smith concluded:

> every improvement in the circumstances of the society tends either directly or indirectly to raise the real rent of land, to increase the real wealth of the landlord, his power of purchasing his labour, or the produce of the labour of other people ... That produce, after the rise in its real price, requires no more labour to collect it than before. A smaller proportion of it will, therefore, be sufficient to replace, with the ordinary profit, the stock which employs that labour. A greater proportion of it must, consequently, belong to the landlord.[5]

A key strategy of industrial capitalism therefore was to maintain prices for food, raw materials and other primary commodities at their low-cost margin of production rather than at a high monopoly price. And indeed, over time the agricultural landlord's share of national income has declined, thanks to rising soil productivity (and hence falling production costs) reinforced by growing competition among world suppliers. The tendency for raw-materials supply to outrun demand likewise has led to market prices falling in keeping with production and transport costs in mining as well as in agriculture. Largely responsible has been the widespread development and exploitation of minerals and plantation crops in less developed economies.

Many raw materials had to be supplied by regions with only limited capital to develop their own resources. The industrial nations therefore had to take the lead in financing international mining and plantation production, and this required a combination of colonialism and foreign investment—colonialism to carve out spheres of influence under mother-country control, and investment to provide resources to extract or produce and transport them—all in a way that remunerated investors in the companies engaged in these activities.

The colonial economy itself was of less interest than its exports to the mother country or at least under mother-country control. As Chapter 2 has described, the colonies were not intended to replicate the economic structures of their mother countries. They were to develop raw-materials resources and their associated commercial and transport infrastructure, not an industrial capability beyond basic local needs. This biased their economic development in an export-oriented manner, laying the seeds for today's monoculture syndrome.

Fearing diminishing returns in the production of food and other raw materials over time, Ricardo and his followers were concerned that price trends

---

[4]　Smith, *Wealth of Nations*, Book I, ch, xi. part III, p. 269.
[5]　Smith, p. 275.

would favor of the world's under-populated countries rather the more densely populated industrial nations. Furthermore, it seemed plausible that the latter, less developed regions might transform their raw materials advantages into industrial cost advantages. Wage levels would reflect their still relatively low food costs, while their industrial prices would reflect an equally low cost of domestic primary materials—assuming these to be kept at home by export embargoes or taxes.

The problem for industrial lead nations such as England was threefold: first, how to monopolize the fruits of their industrial technology in the form of higher national profits and, in some instances, higher wage levels; second, how to secure a secure on-going supply of raw materials; and third, how to benefit from the raw-materials productivity gains occurring in less developed countries by purchasing these materials at their low-cost margin of production.

The first task of industrial-nation diplomacy was to induce the world's less populated countries to supply (indeed, to oversupply) them with raw materials. By the 19th century, Europe's former colonial powers no longer could use overt force or political fiat and legal restraints to prohibit factory production in their dependencies. Instead, they simply channeled their investment mainly into the purchase of farmland, plantations and mineral resources throughout the less developed regions, increasing world output of food, minerals, cotton, tobacco, dyestuffs and other primary products—and their transportation to ports and via the great international canals of Panama and Suez.

The result was to supply Europe's factories with an abundance of relatively low-priced food and raw materials to work up into finished manufactures. Some of the latter could be resold to less developed countries at favorable terms of trade, enabling the industrial nations to finance yet further investment in foreign mines and plantations, as well as in their own domestic factories.

Over the past two centuries, international investment has been associated with government lending and foreign aid to install a transport infrastructure to facilitate raw-materials production, not to develop domestic industrial strength or otherwise achieve economic autonomy. The basic thrust has been to encourage raw-materials producers to become more industrially dependent, not self-sufficient.

The second objective of industrial-nation economic diplomacy was to create a single world market and common world price system for raw materials and manufactures. *A common world price for raw materials denied less developed countries the ability to utilize the special advantages resulting from their favorable raw-materials endowments.* Without the ability to make use of this advantage (and without high industrial prices behind protective tariff barriers), less industrialized regions could not overcome the productivity advantages of Europe's lead nations and work up their own primary materials into finished manufactures.

"Market forces" shaped in this free-trade manner helped ensure that former colonies would provide the industrial center with raw materials at the same relatively low price that local industrialists had to pay for these commodities.

International investment thus became a major factor guiding the development of less developed areas along different lines than those followed by the industrial nations. Only the latter were characterized by relatively balanced growth and modernization of their food-producing powers to support their domestic populations. Resources in less developed countries were diverted away from creating a complementary investment in industry and social infrastructure, and from the institutional modernization that occurred in Europe and North America (and subsequently in Japan and the Soviet Union). Growth in the productive powers of former colonies was limited to those sectors that complemented production needs in the industrial nations, not sectors that threatened to compete with them.

### The theory that falling profits in the industrial nations spur foreign investment

Whereas international trade theory deals with world prices for primary commodities vis-à-vis prices for manufactures, theories of international investment deal with how world trade patterns create profit opportunities for investors and creditors. The standard classical view was that a falling rate of profit in the industrial nations would lead their investors to seek higher returns in "younger" countries.

The concept of a mounting surplus of finance-capital was not radical. Semmel cites how Henry Brougham observed in 1803 that "the ancient world had seen many colonies established from 'overflowing populations ... the modern world alone had reached such a pitch of wealth, as to give rise to an overflowing capital' as well."[6]

By the end of the nineteenth century this view had become commonplace in the writings of Walter Bagehot and other economic journalists. Capital was supposed to flow from the industrial nations to less developed countries where profits had not yet fallen and where the margin of cultivation and whose mineral wealth permitted a high level of economic rent to be extract by exploiting natural resources.

Economists envisioned nations as growing more capital-intensive over time. As investors recaptured their original capital out of sales proceeds, they would reinvest it at home or abroad. If living standards (and hence the market

---

[6]  Harry Brougham, *Inquiry into Colonial Policy* (Edinburgh: 1803), Vol. I, pp. 217f., 222, cited in Bernard Semmel, *The Rise of Free Trade Imperialism: Classical Political Economy and the Empire of Free Trade and Imperialism, 1750–1850* (Cambridge: 1970), p. 222.

for consumer goods) were kept down, profit-seekers would be induced to invest in less developed countries, where rates of return were higher and consumer-goods markets were newly opening up or being won from native producers.

Mercantilist theorizing had been limited largely to trade relationships. When Semmel referred to the economics of Josiah Tucker and his successors as "free-trade imperialism," he had in mind monopolization of the gains from trade by increasingly efficient, high-wage, high-productivity economies (first England and subsequently other nations). Less densely-populated countries would produce a chronic world oversupply of raw materials, exporting them in exchange for manufactures priced relatively high by the industrial nations.

This trade pattern presupposed a large flow of international investment to bring it into being. In addition to assuming free trade in commodities it assumed an open door to international investors appropriating the land and subsoil resources of less developed countries, as well as their emerging manufacturing. This became the essence of John Hobson's theory of imperialism in 1902: "It is not too much to say that the modern foreign policy of Great Britain has been primarily a struggle for profitable markets of investment." He elaborated that

> as one nation after another enters the machine economy and adopts advanced industrial methods, it becomes more difficult for its manufacturers, merchants and financiers to dispose profitably of their economic resources, and they are tempted more and more to use their Governments in order to secure for their particular use some distant undeveloped country by annexation and protection.[7]

He called this competition for international investments the New Imperialism, and found it supported by government diplomacy. Lenin summarized Hobson's view in 1916: "Typical of the old capitalism, when free competition held undivided sway, was the export of goods. Typical of the latest stage of capitalism, when monopolies rule, is the export of *capital*."[8]

New investment was financed largely out of earnings on the growing mass of existing capital investment. The international investment process was aided by governments providing military and diplomatic support, and even helping to finance the export infrastructure and import dependency of less developed countries. Lenin simply was reflecting orthodox views when he wrote:

> In the backward countries profits are usually high, for capital is scarce, the price of land is relatively low, wages are low, raw materials are cheap … The need to export capital [from the industrial nations] arises from the fact that in a few countries capitalism has become "overripe" and (owing to the backward state of

---

[7]    John A. Hobson, *Imperialism: A Study* (3rd ed., London: 1938), pp. 53, 80f.
[8]    Vladimir Ilych Lenin, *Imperialism: The Highest Stage of Capitalism*, in *Collected Works*, XXII (Moscow: 1964), p. 240.

agriculture and the poverty of the masses) capital cannot find a field for "profitable" investment ... The more capitalism is developed, the more strongly the shortage of raw materials is felt, the more intense the competition and the hunt for sources of raw materials throughout the whole world, the more desperate the struggle for the acquisition of colonies.[9]

The theory of imperialism thus followed from that of international investment as developed by market economists themselves.

### The theory that investment helps less developed countries catch up

Like orthodox economic theory, the theory of imperialism assumed that international investment would accelerate the development of countries receiving it. This would increase their ability to compete with the more "mature" nations (assuming most economies to follow a similar development pattern). Although a calculated self-interest for the industrial nations might lie in keeping less developed countries retarded, wrote Rosa Luxemburg in 1913, "the imperialistic phase of capitalist accumulation which implies universal competition [to invest] comprises the industrialization and capitalist emancipation of the hinterland where capital formerly realized its surplus value."[10] Thus, to the extent that critics reject neoclassical theory as praising free trade as if it were in the interest of raw-materials exporters as well as the industrial nations, they also must rebel against the Lenin-Luxemburg paradigm of imperialism. Neoclassical and Leninist formulations both viewed international investment as working to maximize profit potential and aggregate world output, to the benefit of investing and capital-recipient countries alike.

Lenin viewed governments in the industrial nations as representing the "board of directors" of their national business communities. As evidence for this view, his followers have pointed out that monopolies—often granted to government insiders—have dominated Europe's foreign trade and investment since the beginning of the modern epoch with its "colonial patents." The tendency has been for colonial monopolies to be run by the same elite families that held the reins of government.

One reason why governments spurred private investment in the colonies was that the cost of providing naval and military protection was initially so high that governments were unable to finance it from their own modest tax revenues. The task was "farmed out" to large trading companies given monopoly privileges. England's Moscovy Company bore the cost of Russia's embassy to England, as well as financing the latter's embassy to Russia. "The large profits required to meet these extraordinary charges," remarks George Beer, "could not

---

[9]  Lenin, *Imperialism*, pp. 241, 260.
[10]  Rosa Luxemburg, *The Accumulation of Capital* (London: 1951), p. 419.

have been earned, if the trade had been opened to the free competition of all Englishmen, and consequently excluding privileges were essential to the success of these companies."

National colonization companies likewise had to sustain high costs of transport, settlement and protection, "Had the English government been in a position to undertake the work of colonization," Beer concludes, "it would have been possible to avoid granting these monopolistic trading privileges, The Crown's revenue, however, was totally inadequate even for domestic purposes ..."[11] Imperial-nation governments therefore granted monopolies with a view toward the long-term national interest, which sometimes turned against those of the monopolies in question (as witnessed by the long debate over whether to renew the monopoly powers of the British East India Company).

Lenin held that governments had become servants of private enterprise rather than the other way around. Even so, he believed, private enterprise would develop the world in a technologically rational way, paving the way for a relatively easy transition to industrial socialism.

> When a big enterprise assumes gigantic proportions, and ... organizes the supply of primary raw materials to tens of millions of people; when the raw materials are transported in a systematic and organized manner to the most suitable places of production ... when a single center directs all the consecutive states of processing the material right up to the manufacture of numerous varieties of finished articles; when these products are distributed according to a single plan among tens and hundreds of millions of consumers (the marketing of oil in America and Germany by the American oil trust)—then it becomes evident that we have socialization of production, and not mere "interlocking"; that economic and private property relations constitute a shell which no longer fits its contents, a shell which must inevitably decay ...[12]

Luxemburg agreed that

> the achievement of capitalist autonomy in the *hinterland* and backward colonies is attained amidst wars and revolutions. Revolution is an essential for the process of capitalist emancipation. The backward countries must shed their obsolete political organizations, relics of natural and simple commodity economy, and create a modern state machinery adapted to the purposes of capitalist production.[13]

Governments need not intervene to change the investment and trade patterns sponsored by international investment capital. Large mineral and industrial cartels would install a productive infrastructure throughout the world. In sum, the effect of foreign investment would be to put in place the infrastructure for a ripening, increasingly competitive capitalism.

---

[11]  George Louis Beer, *The Origins of the British Colonial System: 1578–1660* (New York: 1922), p. 222.

[12]  Lenin, *Imperialism*, pp. 302f.      [13]  Luxemburg, *The Accumulation of Capital*, p. 419.

Unlike the case with free-trade imperialism discussed in chapter 4, there was no theory as to how free international investment might retard the development of less populated regions. From Marx, Hobson and Lenin through Keynes and his followers, the major economists did not address the problem of underdevelopment and the emergence of impaired dual economies. Rather, they held that international investment would stimulate the overall development of less industrialized countries, bringing them toward a state of economic and political similarity with the industrial economies, despite the fact that international investment was concentrated (at least initially) in their raw-materials export sectors.

It therefore is appropriate to examine more closely the consequences of international investment over the centuries in order to explain why less developed economies have failed to modernize their domestic subsistence sectors, resulting in widening productivity gaps and balance-of-payment disparities between the industrial nations and the periphery. It also is necessary to explain why trade and investment have grown primarily among the industrial nations themselves (that is, among erstwhile rivals) while colonial trade and investment was stagnating already in 1902 when Hobson published his book. Indeed, as Hobson himself noted, mother countries were purchasing a declining share of their own colonies' exports.

International investment (and hence debt) has been concentrated among the industrial nations because they are the most thriving and creditworthy economies. As Ragnar Nurske has remarked: "Had [Hobson] tried to do what he did for trade, that is, to show the geographical distribution of overseas investment, he would have found that British capital tended to bypass the primitive tropical economies and flowed mainly to the regions of recent settlement outside as well as inside the British empire."[14]

By the 1940s, colonial empires, particularly the backward tropical areas of the world, long since had ceased to be paying propositions. Despite such institutions of colonial privilege as Britain's Imperial Preference System and the

[14] D. K. Fieldhouse, "Imperialism: A Historiographic Revision," *Economic History Review*, 2nd Ser., XIV (1961), p. 199, quoting Ragnar Nurske, *Patterns of Trade and Development* (Stockholm: 1959), p. 19, and referring to Hobson, *Imperialism*, pp. 23, 369, 32–39, 67 and 78. George Paish, "Great Britain's foreign investments," *Journal of the Royal Statistical Society*, LXXIV (1911), p. 186, published statistics demonstrating that most of Britain's investments (to quote Fieldhouse's summary) lay in the United States (£688 m.) followed by "South America, £587 m.; Canada, £382 m.; Australia, £380 m.; India and Ceylon, £365 m.; and South Africa, £351 m. By contrast, West Africa had received only £29 m., the Straits and Malay States, £22 m., and the remaining British possessions £33 m. ... Hence, to maintain that Britain had found it necessary to acquire these territories because of an urgent need for new fields for investment is simply unrealistic."

Sterling Area, its colonial markets and those of other European were being won by the most efficient industrial nations, headed by the United States.

Nearly all the theories of international investment voiced prior to the 1950s indicated that such investment would help less developed countries catch up with the industrial nations. Instead, the Latin American, African and Asiatic peripheries tended to become service economies to the industrial nations. The impact of international investment turned out to be as one-sided as earlier, more politically overt forms of mercantilist and colonialist control. Productivity has increased much more in the export sectors than in the domestic economy.

### From trade and investment rivalries to war

Liberal economists in the mid-nineteenth century believed that the growth of commerce would render wars a thing of the past. Trade and investment were supposed to replace the rivalries that hitherto had governed humankind with enlightened and peaceful self-interested linkages. But it was precisely in their rivalry to create such linkages between core and periphery that international investors prompted new forms of rivalries.

Recognizing that competition among industrial nations to expand their colonial empires and spheres of influence had been gaining momentum since the 1870s, Hobson hoped to see England develop an alternative by building up its home market based on growth of domestic consumption standards rather than one based on exploiting less developed countries and leading to international wars. Income redistribution at home could supply the needed investment and sales outlets.

Lenin replied that if capitalism gave workers a higher standard of life, it would no longer be capitalism. He claimed that imperialism and its wars were an intrinsic feature of capitalism, not a discretionary policy choice. Governments were less able than private corporations to reach businesslike compromises on how to carve up and renegotiate world markets. Corporate cartels might be flexible when necessary, but governments were not. Competition for investment outlets in less developed countries would culminate in imperialist wars among the industrial nations as the Law of Uneven Development would impose strains on whatever political arrangements governments might negotiate. Lenin thus depicted as a utopian dream Karl Kautsky's view of "ultra-imperialism" or "super-imperialism" in which governments would administer a peaceful centralization of world relations.

### Keynes's synthesis of trade and investment processes

The financial convulsions following World War I and the a debate over Germany's capacity to pay reparations (analyzed in Chapter 16) inspired John Maynard Keynes to develop a structural analysis of Germany's balance of payments by integrating the theory of international investment with that of the overall balance of payments and domestic economic balance. In his 1930 *Treatise on Money*, Keynes pointed out that the factors determining the trade balance were different from those determining the balance on capital account. Trade was a function of relative production costs, elasticities of demand and price levels, while international investment depended largely on relative interest and profit rates. *There was no intrinsic reason why these disparate factors should result in precisely offsetting balances.* Attempts to improve the long-term trade balance by spurring domestic investment called for a policy of low interest rates. But this would spur capital outflows in the short run. Hence, economists could not simply assume that the trade balance automatically should equate with the balance on capital account, especially when the latter was defined to include monetary movements, reparations and debt payments.

The problem was not simply one of how to balance trade and investment functions with each other, but how to balance the international accounts as a whole with domestic production and employment functions. One could not simply assume that the price changes and interest-rate adjustments that balanced international payments would just happen simultaneously to promote domestic full-employment equilibrium. This perception inspired Keynes to recommend economic nationalism to subordinate balance-of-payments considerations to domestic employment and investment objectives.

Over and above the tendency for profits to be higher in less developed countries, attracting capital from the industrial nations, Keynes pointed out that matters would be further complicated if less developed economies stimulated their industrial self-sufficiency by the kind of protectionist policies that Europe, the United States and Japan had employed during their own formative industrial periods. He worried about the "pickle a country might get into if a higher rate of interest abroad than can be earned at home leads to most of its savings being lent abroad, whilst at the same time there are tariffs abroad against most of its exports and a tendency to raise these tariffs from time to time to balance the gradually rising level of costs in the protected countries due to the outflow of gold from the lending country."[15] Labor-union pressures for higher wages in the industrial nations would exacerbate this problem.

---

[15] J. M. Keynes, *A Treatise on Money* (London: 1930) Vol. I, p. 347. See also Vol. II, p. 185.

These nations for their part needed to sustain direct investment outflows to less developed countries to ensure the continued supply of abundant low-priced raw materials. This investment would have to be financed by a corresponding trade surplus at least the return flow of foreign earnings sufficed to finance new investment outflows. However, a trade surplus for the industrial nations might not be achievable if less developed countries adopted a counter-vailing protection of their own. If that occurred, their self-feeding development would drain monetary and gold resources from the industrial nations, producing monetary deflation and economic depression. A new kind of cumulative decline in the economic activity of the industrial nations seemed imminent, especially for England, because

> the business losses resulting from the Profit Deflation served to increase still further the relative attractiveness of foreign investment, thus making it still more necessary to maintain an artificially high rate of interest and so riveting still more firmly on our necks the Profit Deflation, consequent on the deficiency of total investment relatively to savings, and the Unemployment which Profit Deflation brings.[16]

The inference was that England and other industrial nations seemed destined to lose their favored historical position. Monetary authorities could avert investment outflows only by abandoning the gold standard in favor of managed currency systems subject to strict capital controls. Keynes believed that this would occur, signalling the end of laissez faire.

It seemed clear to him that the balance of payments no longer could be stabilized simply by interest rate adjustments. Rising rates would destabilize domestic saving, investment and employment over the intermediate and longer term. Higher domestic investment was needed to produce more exports, displace imports and cut costs generally. The financing of such investment required favorably low interest rates. This easy-money policy would create a profit inflation—but would tend to impair the trade balance and spur capital outflows (in the absence of capital controls). The high interest rates required to ensure balance-of-payments equilibrium thus threatened to exceed the going profit rate on direct investment, curtailing it as industrial companies hardly could be expected to borrow at interest rates in excess of their prospective earnings.

The financial dilemma for England was that the conditions required for short- and long-term stability seemed to be at odds with each other. Stabilizing the balance of payments by the traditional policy of raising interest rates would undermine the long-term trade balance by discouraging new direct investment. But if England did *not* raise rates and even prohibit investment outflows, it

---

[16] Keynes, *ibid.,* Vol. II, pp. 185f.

would lose gold and experience monetary stringency, pushing the economy into depression.

Four policies suggested themselves, each beset by its own inner contradictions. First, higher productivity might come to the rescue, improving the balance of trade for industrial nations. But would technical innovation occur more rapidly at home than abroad? This seemed to be a precondition for wage rates and living standards in the industrial nations to remain intact. New investment required relatively low interest rates, or subsidies (Keynes's second proposal), as well as tariff protection (his third policy), and possibly restrictions on capital outflows to keep savings at home.

Keynes felt that the problem with all these policies was that they would inspire less developed economies to make their own countervailing moves toward autonomy, perhaps to an even greater extent than the industrial nations could match. Protective tariffs and subsidies enacted by less developed countries would likely attract foreign investment from manufacturing companies in the industrial nations as these firms sought to relocate behind foreign trade barriers. As for capital controls, they were a tricky game that could backfire.

As events have worked out, Europe and America have played the game quite adroitly. Third World policy consciousness has been instilled with a free-trade view that existing world relationships are natural rather than subject to change. This indoctrination has effectively denationalized their economic perspective, subordinating it to lead-nation nationalism. This is why Keynes's fourth suggested policy has not had to be called into play: an international cheap-money policy encouraging world inflation. This was what Keynes believed would be the most likely ultimate outcome.

In the context of these policy alternatives Keynes reviewed the classical scenario for England's long-term economic prospects: "Great Britain is an old country with a higher standard of working-class life than exists in most other parts of the world. The population will soon cease to grow."[17] England thus faced the prospect of what Mill had called the stationary state. It saved about 10 per cent of its income—high enough to result in low domestic interest rates and to prompt investment in less developed countries. Keynes concluded that "equilibrium under *laissez-faire* will, therefore, require that a large and increasing proportion of our savings must find its outlet in foreign investment."

The only hope was that England's investment earnings might suffice to finance its trade deficit. In fact, a silver lining to the industrial nations' trade dependency was that British investors had established themselves solidly throughout their empire and in other less developed countries, and thus would

---

[17]  Keynes, *ibid.*, p. 188.

secure most of the earnings on any shift in the terms of trade favoring these countries. Britain's low domestic interest rates would help it retain its comparative advantage in capital-intensive manufactures. Still, the rate of interest that would balance the capital account with the trade balance probably was higher than that which would equate domestic savings and investment at full employment levels. Keynes believed that this problem would spell the end of laissez faire.

Six years after his *Treatise on Money*, Keynes developed his income analysis in his *General Theory of Employment, Interest and Money* (1936). There seemed some hope that investment outflows might "multiply" foreign incomes to spur a demand for imports from England and other investor nations. This perception underlay Fritz Machlup's observation that "the use of multiplier theory [afforded] an argument for generous foreign lending," a policy implemented following World War II by the International Monetary Fund, the World Bank, and bilateral foreign aid programs by the United States and other nations.[18]

However, loans were extended to less developed countries to build them up as markets (especially for grains and arms), not as competitors, that is, to steer them to become raw-materials satellites, not to promote their evolution into self-reliant industrial rivals. This investment helped produce an oversupply of raw materials, contributing to steady downward pressure on the terms of trade of "capital-recipient" economies. Keynes's fears of foreign moves toward economic nationalism did not materialize. The industrial nations not only maintained their technological superiority but extended it to agriculture behind high trade barriers, without spurring similar moves abroad, except where the protected sectors happened to be foreign-owned.

### *Where trade theory went wrong*

None of the international scenarios developed from Hume and Ricardo through Lenin and Keynes have materialized. Fears voiced by economists in the industrial nations regarding competition from less developed countries have proved to be unjustified. Instead of catching up with the industrial nations as in the scenarios drawn by Hume and subsequent free traders, the experience of these countries has been closer to what Tucker and Steuart anticipated. Theories describing how less developed countries might benefit from world trade and investment trends resemble the probability models designed to analyze the struggles of Pizarro and Cortes against the Incas and Aztecs. Herman Kahn once told me that in every model the Spaniards lose, the natives win. Today's trade models likewise predict the wrong outcome.

[18] Fritz Machlup, *International Trade and the National Income Multiplier* (Philadelphia, 1943), p. 216.

What has happened? Instead of the industrial lead nations letting their trade surpluses and consequent monetary inflows inflate their prices as Hume anticipated, they have used these inflows to purchase ownership of world raw-materials resources and to make other profitable investments abroad. Instead of diminishing returns in European agriculture and mining leading to widening trade deficits with less industrialized countries as Ricardo believed, the industrial nations have become growing net grain exporters. And instead of their higher incomes spurring proportionally higher rates of population growth as forecast by Malthusian models, rising incomes and living standards have universally been associated with declining rates of population increase.

Domestic investment in the industrial nations has not been dried up by capital outflows to less developed economies. Rather, the flow of capital, interest and earnings in recent years has been from these countries to the industrial nations, largely in the form of debt service and flight capital).[19] Even in the case of foreign aid, repayment by debtor countries on past aid lending (mainly export-financing) exceeds the inflow of new liquid U.S. and European foreign-aid credits."[20]

Economic orthodoxy has not troubled to explain these "surprising" developments. It has not replaced the economics of "pessimism" (from the vantage point of the industrial nations—or "optimism" from the Third World's point of view) with an explanation of why the industrial capital-rich, high-wage nations have extended their lead over less developed debtor countries. Economists prefer to deal merely with shifts at the margin. The future of the world economy is supposed to retain the same basic general structure as the present, merely to be larger—and somehow to be in an increasingly equitable global economic and political convergence.

A major dimension of reality whose neglect contributes to this orthodox misassessment concerns the impact of multinational firms on world trade and investment. Third World exports are produced largely by foreign owned

[19]   Speech of World Bank President A. W. Clausen, January 25, 1984, reported in *The New York Times*, Jan. 26, 1984: "in 1982 the net transfer [from Third World countries to the rest of the world] was a negative $7 billion, and this expanded to a negative $21 billion in 1983." Meanwhile, private sector direct investment in Third World countries declined from $14 billion in 1981 to $13 billion in 1982 and $10 billion in 1983. On balance, Third World foreign debt climbed to $810 million in 1983, up 33 per cent in a year. By 1989 it had reached $1.3 trillion, largely the result of accruing interest charges.

[20]   Statistics on the net balance-of-payments effect of U.S. foreign aid are published quarterly in Table 5 of the reports on the U.S. balance of payments published in the Commerce Department's *Survey of Current Business*. I have discussed the balance-of-payments drain on Third World economies by U.S. foreign aid in *Super Imperialism: The Economic Strategy of American Empire* (1972), *The Myth of Aid* (1971), and "A Payments-Flow Analysis of U.S. International Transactions: 1960–1968," New York University, Graduate School of Business Administration, *The Bulletin*, Nos. 61–63 (March 1970).

companies with imported capital goods, foreign managerial labor and leased technology. Prices for these exports are fixed in dollars (sometimes in sterling) by the world minerals and plantation product cartels. When countries devalue their currency, they do not necessarily lower the price of these exports, because *copper, oil, grains and other raw materials are priced in dollars or other key currencies*. No matter how great the deflation or inflation in Third World countries, devaluation has little direct impact on the export pricing of these commodities. Even domestic costs are affected only minimally, because a large component of minerals exports represents imported capital equipment and payments for imported fuels and other hard-currency operating costs.

It is a paradox of free-trade orthodoxy that international trade and investment have been an "engine of growth" only for the industrial lead nations, not for the primary commodity exporters whose international trade and investment has warped their overall development. Each country is supposed to have a fixed set of transformation curves between industry and agriculture, "cloth" and "wine." No adverse impact of foreign trade on the evolution of these productive powers is recognized, no resource depletion or are other ecological considerations. There are no external economies or diseconomies, no contradictions between short- and long-term objectives, or between profitability for private-sector investors and the physical growth of the economy as a whole. Capital inflows or outflows are assumed to relate exclusively to direct investment, not to lending and subsequent debt service. In sum, this academic theory portrays international investment and lending in an exclusively favorable light by compartmentalizing the scope of analysis rather than acknowledging how broad global reality is and the extent of the Third World's economic devastation.

### The debt legacy of foreign trade and investment

International lending and investment, foreign aid, trade dependency and wars have given birth to foreign debts that have come to far exceed the ability or willingness of countries to pay. This poses the question of structural limits to the payment of debt service in this long legacy of economic imbalance. Most textbook depictions of international economic relations ignore this problem. Balance-of-payments equilibrium is treated simply as a problem of establishing an appropriate exchange rate to spur the trade balance by enough to cover the outflow for debt service, capital flight and military spending.

The problem is that *debt service is unlike import and export trade. It is not responsive to changes in price and income levels*, but has become built-in as a structural fact of life that can be alleviated only by debt rescheduling or outright cancellation. The former is a highly political process requiring negotiations with the International Monetary Fund, the U.S. Treasury and other industrial-nation governments. Creditor-nation officials insist that debtor governments shift resources and the tax burden off raw-materials exports, even at falling world prices. "Aid" recipients and borrowers are told not only to provide a friendly environment for foreign investment, but since 1980 to start selling off their public domain and natural monopolies to creditor-nation investors in what is essentially a bankruptcy sale.

The volume of debt currently owed by Third World countries far exceeds their foreseeable ability to pay out of export earnings. This explains the demand that these countries sell off their public enterprises. As long as they remain part of the world's "market economy," they must capitulate to commercial policies handed down by industrial-nation governments. Debtor countries that do not go along with this approach face exclusion of the sort imposed on the Soviet Union after 1917 and Cuba after 1959. If they start to deviate from free-trade policy (as economists from Tucker and Steuart through Keynes feared they someday would do), the industrial-nation retaliation is typified by the U.S. denial of favorable tariff treatment to Venezuela and other Latin American oil-exporting countries until such time as they agreed to withdraw from OPEC.

Today's terms of debt refinancing require countries to export the raw materials desired by creditor nations, and even (under the kind of regime dictated by World Bank President Robert McNamara in the early 1970s) to curtail their rates of population growth to minimize consumption of their own resources. They must not subsidize industries to compete with those already established in the creditor nations, but must submit to monetary austerity blocking new investment in social infrastructure and domestic industries that would work up their own raw materials into finished manufactures. They must not protect their agriculture or undertake meaningful land reform or associated rural modernization. Only under these conditions will industrial-nation governments, the World Bank, the IMF and major commercial banks agree to further debt rescheduling or "development funding."

This kind of non-military lending among governments has become a new form of international control in steering the world's resource allocation. The calculated political terms on which official loans and debt rescheduling are negotiated rarely are acknowledged, nor is the burden of debt service on payments-deficit economies. To explain the workings of this debt burden, the balance of Part III concentrates on this financial context for international trade and development.

# 13

## Structuralist vs. Monetarist Financial Analysis

"Free market" theorizing overlooks the degree to which political factors under-lie world trade, investment and debt relationships. Part I has shown that "factor endowments," capital formation and economic infrastructure have been brought into being more by policy than by nature. Among the industrial nations, debts have arisen primarily from wars. Debts for the less developed economies stem increasingly from their trade dependency and capital flight resulting from the backward institutions associated with their legacy of colonialism and its sequel, export monocultures.

Since World War I the buildup of foreign debt has been coordinated by three highly politicized international agencies: the IMF and the World Bank (founded in 1944 as World War II was drawing to a close) and the Bank for International Settlements, founded in 1929 to handle the transfer of German reparations. Also playing major bilateral roles are the U.S. State Department and its Agency for International Development (AID), the Treasury, Federal Reserve System and their European counterparts. Acting in concert, these institutions impose economic austerity on debtor countries.

Refinancing debt obligations serves as a lever to limit Third World options via today's array of "market forces." As a condition for extending foreign credit, they oblige these countries to service their foreign liabilities by reducing domestic incomes. Since 1980, debtor economies have been told to sell off their public enterprises and other assets and to steer their production and export patterns to benefit of the creditor-investor nations.

Given the tendency of international finance to reinforce world trade and dependency patterns, it hardly is surprising that monetarism should join forces with laissez faire economics. The common motto is that "what is, is natural," whether referring to labor/capital ratios, assets or debts. All countries should "adjust" to be "in equilibrium" with the existing status quo.

The remaining chapters of Part III therefore examine international financial orthodoxy as it has paralleled the narrowness of free-trade doctrine. By no accident, Ricardo and Ohlin, two of the leading free-trade advocates dis-cussed in Part II, reappear here as creditor-oriented monetarists, along with Milton Friedman as spokesman for the Chicago School of laissez faire, Jacob

Viner and Harry Johnson. Conversely, Thomas Malthus, an early opponent of Ricardo's theory of comparative costs, appears also as one of the most trenchant critics of his bullionism, just as Keynes criticized the monetarist and free-trade views of the 1920s and '30s. For that matter, the alignment of protectionism and anti-monetarism goes back to James Steuart in his 1767 critique of Hume.

If the views of these critics are not better known, it is because most surveys of international economics neglect to report that historically, in every epoch, free-trade theories and their associated creditor-oriented monetarist doctrines have been controverted by more comprehensive and dynamic theories that place financial and trade variables in the context of the economy's technological, demographic and political dimensions. Yet since the 1930s anti-monetarist views have been unable to get a hearing, save for Keynes's 1936 General Theory. And even the latter's income approach has been mobilized in recent years by austerity theorists in a spirit opposed to that of Keynes.

The non-aligned nations have formally opposed the philosophy of economic austerity since their 1979 Havana meeting. But they have not put forth an alternative doctrine to explain why monetarist programs do not work. It is as if the world has forgotten the long history of anti-monetarist theorizing, which reached its most recent high point in the 1920s in the debate over German reparations and inter-Ally debts. (So much for the idea that circumstances invariably call forth appropriate bodies of theory to deal with them!)

Thanks largely to the academic endowment of Ricardian-type monetarism, the creditor nations have been able to thwart attempts by less developed economies to meaningfully renegotiate their debts in the interest of modernizing and upgrading their agriculture, industry and labor force. The result is that an advanced protectionist center—the United States, Europe and Japan –juxtaposes itself to indebted low-technology economies. Debt pressures tie a financial strait-jacket imposing social and technological poverty on the Third World, forcing it to live in the short run under a chronic emergency program of high interest rates and fiscal austerity. The associated currency devaluations do not make Third World products more competitive, but merely shift resources to the export sector in such a way that products of low-wage labor and high-interest capital are exchanged for goods produced by high-wage labor and low-interest capital in the lead nations. All this is depicted as part of economic nature, and as such, as more efficient than the alternative of government tariff policies and capital controls to change the terms of trade, productivity and debtor/creditor relationships.

## Nine shortcomings of monetarist analysis

Before turning to a chronological review of capital-transfer theory (the jargon masks the subject's political impact), it may help to put the discussion in perspective by alerting readers to some of the tacit and hidden assumptions that monetarist economists make, and to point out why they are unrealistic.

1. *Monetarism ignores the polarization between creditor and debtor economies that occurs as the latter fall into debt-ridden austerity.* It thus suffers from the same prejudice as free-trade orthodoxy in assuming that if only governments refrain from intervening, the balance of payments and exchange rates will settle at a fair and stable equilibrium. The balance of payments is supposed to return automatically to equilibrium if disturbed, along the same lines that are postulated by the price-specie flow mechanism's monetary, price and income adjustments. These adjustments are supposed to generate a trade surplus capable of balancing the capital outflow by debtor countries.

Refusing to concede that debt service, military spending or other capital transfers can create more than marginal problems, monetarists deny that there is a valid logic for governments to impose capital controls, subsidize investment, refuse to submit to IMF austerity programs or negotiate a moratorium on their foreign debt service. Debtor-country governments are advised to tighten the money supply and raise taxes on labor so as to reduce consumption and hence prices, and raise interest rates to attract short-term capital until such time as trade balance is restored. The fact that this happy outcome rarely materializes has not dented creditor ideology.[1] The buildup (or perhaps we should say "endowment") of debts involves onerous transfers of interest and principal, pushing the balance of payments into chronic deficit, impairing the terms of trade, stripping economies of already scarce capital resources, and imposing domestic austerity and its Economy of Low Wages trap. Debtor economies can retain borrowed money only by keeping their interest rates high. This discourages new investment and employment, aggravating foreign dependency and tending ultimately to raise rather than lower prices.

2. *The monetary sector is held to be merely a veil for the "real" goods-and-service-producing sectors.* The terminology of "real output" suggests that financial considerations are somehow *less* real. *Money is assumed to influence only prices, not output.* Even deflationary austerity or a currency collapse is not acknowledged to derange direct investment and employment. If anything, such distress conditions are assumed to make exports more attractive by lowering prices.

---

1  See for instance Haberler, *Theory of International Trade*, p. 58.

3. *Monetarism fails to acknowledge how capital outflows adversely affect productivity.* Just as orthodox trade theory neglects the feedback between rising wage levels and labor productivity, so monetarism recognizes no impact of monetary expansion (or contraction) on the level of investment and output. All that is supposed to change are the "counters," not the goods and services and resources being counted.[2] Countries are supposed to produce and export more by keeping their prices and incomes low through a program of financial stringency and curtailed infrastructure spending, not by more abundant credit, rising wage levels, educational upgrading, infrastructure spending and subsidized technological innovation.

The reality is that countries submitting to austerity are unable to free themselves from international dependency. Their low wage levels are unable to provide them with the promised competitive parity with high-wage, capital-intensive economies. Currency depreciation destroys purchasing power and transfers income from debtors to creditors, lowering the rate at which labor exchanges for products and capital. High interest rates with relatively short debt maturities make Third World capital even higher priced than comparable investments financed on more favorable debt and stock-market terms in the United States, western Europe and Japan.

4. Monetarism shares with free-trade orthodoxy the belief that *merely marginal monetary, price and income adjustments can rectify payments deficits or other forms of economic imbalance,* regardless of their magnitude. In reality, price adjustments are able to work only within fairly narrow limits, and cannot overcome underlying structural problems.

5. *Monetarism fails to recognize how capital transfers impose a terms-of-trade penalty and are subject to limits to the capacity to pay.* Monetarists argue that a country can transfer abroad an amount equal to *however much it can tax or borrow from its residents in domestic currency.* No transfer problem is recognized independently of this domestic budgetary problem. As long as governments can limit purchasing power by taxing incomes or reducing the money supply, goods will be "freed" for export, *presumably at stable terms of trade and without impairing current production.* This is the theory of Ricardo, Ohlin, Rueff, and today's Chicago School monetarists.

Yet as early as England's Napoleonic Wars, economists such as Henry Thornton (1802) and Malthus (1811), followed by Mill (1829 and 1844), showed how capital transfers adversely affect the paying country's terms of trade. This

---

[2]   The free trader Frank Taussig (*International Trade* [New York: 1927], pp. 339–40) acknowledged that the Ricardians "regarded monetary disturbances as of little substantive importance, whether for domestic or international trade; the only significant consequence of inflated prices was that a new set of counters came to be used."

poses a transfer problem over and above the domestic budgetary problem. *At going prices, markets may not exist for the added exports needed to finance the capital transfer.* This is especially the case if creditor nations erect tariffs against the anticipated exports, as the United States has done in recent decades.

6. *Monetarist policies lead to economic crisis and government repression.* Ostensible stabilization programs disrupt economies with a plague of what orthodox economists dismiss as "exogenous" phenomena—strikes and political upheavals, "IMF riots" and a collapse of domestic investment. Democratically elected governments imposing such austerity programs rarely are able to remain in office as large-scale unemployment, escalating inflation rates, capital flight, a collapse of currency values and chronic political crisis call forth emergency measures that centralize authoritarian power, usually in the finance department and central bank acting on behalf of the IMF and World Bank.

7. *Monetarism views economic activity as limited to current production and trade,* which are assumed to respond quickly to market shifts. In reality, lead times are required for output to respond to prices. For raw-materials production these lead times typically extend up to five or six years for exploration, development, refining and transport. This means that balance-of-payments adjustment in the short run must come in some form other than that of higher exports, because it often is difficult to divert current output to foreign markets. In many cases new international distribution systems must be put in place.

High interest rates increase the break-even points and "costing" of capital, making it all the harder to compete with creditor nations in world markets. A falling currency and/or rising interest rates may prompt foreign takeovers of domestic companies, real estate and movable assets, as stock and bond prices collapse and assets are sold under distress conditions.

8. *Monetarism ignores how currencies are used for reasons other than to buy exports.* Debt service has come to dominate the balance of payments of many countries, just as military spending periodically swamped the economies of industrial nations in the past. Foreign debt service causes currency values to diverge from international purchasing-power ratios.

9. *Monetarism holds that international transactions are voluntary and a matter of choice, free of prior commitments.* Raw materials exports face a price-inelastic world demand, and many debtor economies are absolutely dependent on imported necessities. Foreign debt has become the dominant *a priori* constraint. It must be paid regardless of shifts in currency parities and relative prices. In general, every economy's balance of payments is constrained by such basic needs and commitments, including contractual debt service and long-term purchase contracts at fixed prices. Many countries are dependent on food, replacement parts and other essentials that must be imported regardless of cost.

## WHAT A MONETARIST BELIEVES

1. *Elasticity optimism*

All international transactions are price-elastic, and prices are a direct function of the rate of money creation. Hence, if the balance of payments falls into deficit, an appropriately deflationary monetary policy can restore balance.

2. *Disturbances are merely marginal*

Most problems can be solved by marginal price and income adjustments without needing to restructure production functions or cancel unpayable debts. The economy has a high degree of flexibility, few rigidities.

3. *Emphasis on (short-term) monetary solutions*

The rate of money creation is the source of any country's inflation. Hence, financial austerity can cure payments imbalance by reducing price levels and freeing domestic output for export. If an economy lives in the short run in this way, the long run will take care of itself.

4. *Doctrine of austerity*

The way to stabilize international payments is to hold interest rates high enough to attract foreign capital, and to hold incomes low enough to free output for export and discourage imports.

5. *Laissez faire*

Things will lake care of themselves if market forces are left alone. Government action can only be counterproductive. Equilibrium will automatically be ensured by price, interest-rate and income adjustments.

## WHAT A STRUCTURALIST BELIEVES

*Elasticity pessimism*

Debt service must be paid irrespective of price and income levels, and essential imports must be purchased whatever the monetary state of affairs. This is why international trade and payments imbalance is increasingly structural in character.

*Structural problems are more serious*

Structural constraints limit the degree of choice. Trade and debt dependency may require a higher volume of imports and debt service than export earnings can cover.

*Emphasis on (long-term) productive powers*

Inflation is caused largely by currency depreciation as debt service and other capital transfers are the price to be paid for past trade dependency. These payments put downward pressure on exchange rates, leading to higher domestic prices for imported commodities. Short-term policies to attract foreign loans by raising interest rates deter long-term investment that self-reliance requires.

*Doctrine of prosperity*

High interest rates discourage new investment, slowing growth in productivity and output, leading to import dependency and pushing the trade balance into chronic deficit.

*Intervention*

A long-term cure for most countries' economic problems involves restructuring their production functions and institutions. It also may require debt suspension. These policies require active government efforts, as well as tariffs and subsidies to shape the economic environment in which market incentives operate.

Balance-of-payments projections for debtor countries typically start by analyzing volume trends in commodity trade, and then factor in expected prices for the major imports and exports, based on anticipated worldwide supply and demand. Contractual debt service and more or less stable trends in service payments for passenger travel, immigrants' remittances or retiree income, licensing fees and so forth are then added on. The question is how much the economy can export (and earn on its foreign investments) to service its debts, pay for necessary imports and cover normal trend levels of international payments for transport and other services.

Usually these trends and scheduled debt service are in net deficit, which must be financed by satisfying the political conditions laid down by creditor nations and their multinational agencies to extend new short-term loans. The deflationary conditions imposed by this financial dependency increases the need to borrow yet more in future years to pay the mounting debt service. The effect is to put chronic downward pressure on the currency, causing a deteriorating spiral of payments deficits, austerity and deepening international dependency.

The monetary debates reviewed in the following chapters have been fought over the question of just what *causes* gold prices and other international indices to rise (or stated the other way around, what causes the currency to fall) relative to domestic prices. The answer to this question is the starting point, for the supposed "cause" dictates the recommended policy "cure."

There are two schools and two directions of causation at work, not just one. Monetarism tends to be reductionist in asserting that any economic imbalance, whatever its causes, can be cured by rolling back the money supply and hence income and price levels. All problems supposedly have a common cause in inflationary money creation. Deflation is supposed to save a corresponding amount of foreign exchange—without shrinking the level of economic activity.

Structuralist analysis is based on long-term growth models that see the basic problem in terms of inadequate investment, productivity, output and domestic credit creation. Imbalance in an economy's international accounts stems characteristically from domestic production shortfalls in essentials (above all food production) and contractual obligations such as foreign debts (or military spending) relative to international earning power based on the ability to prouduce exports and replace imports with domestic output. These types of transaction tend to operate independently of domestic money creation, fiscal policy or price developments.

## *What causes payments deficits and inflation?*

In recent years there has been a tendency to view international trade and finance as a passive residual of the domestic economy. Falling exchange rates are attributed to unwarranted domestic money creation or government budget deficits, or to foreign borrowing to finance domestic spending—but rarely to the burden of foreign debt service or trade dependency. The economic "problem" is defined so as to recognize only the monetary variable. The result is a "one-size-fits-all" monetary solution.

At issue between structuralists and monetarists is not merely whether payments imbalance stems from causes associated with external obligations rather than domestic monetary overissue, but whether foreign problems can be cured by treating their purely domestic monetary symptoms.

Monetarists claim that payments deficits could not have been sustained without central banks creating the money to spend, or governments failing to tax incomes which then are paid abroad. This point is true as far as it goes (much like the point that economic activity could not be created without oxygen in the air), but it does not penetrate to the heart of matters. The basic issue is one of whether to attack the cause (the balance of payments and its associated trade and debt structures) or the symptoms (domestic money creation and budget deficits).

Was it always domestic monetary over-issue that impaired the balance of trade (and hence the exchange rate) by forcing up prices to discourage exports and encourage imports? Or, might export proceeds decline because of autonomous changes in foreign demand unrelated to economic conditions at home?

England's bullion debate (reviewed in Chapter 14) is a case in point. It concerned whether gold prices rose (and hence sterling's exchange rate fell) because the nation's military subsidies abroad in the war against Napoleon overwhelmed the balance of payments, or because the Bank of England over-issued paper money after the gold cover was removed in 1797. A century later the German reparations debate (summarized in Chapter 16) argued over whether the German mark's collapse stemmed from the attempt to make reparations payments far in excess of the ability of German export earnings to cover, or merely from domestic credit overissue and foreign borrowing. All observers agreed that money creation, price increases and falling exchange rates were related, but they differed as to the causal sequence at work. Anti-monetarists claimed that more money was created simply to pay for the higher valuation of transactions, and hence was a response, not a cause. A falling exchange rate forced up domestic prices, requiring more money and credit merely to transact business. A balance-of-payments deficit thus might *spur* a domestic monetary expansion rather than the other way around. In all documented statistical studies, the decline in the exchange rate exceeds (and leads) the rate of domestic price inflation, which in turn exceeds (and leads) growth in the money supply.

No greater error can be made than to imagine that an inflation stemming from domestic monetary overissue produces the same specific pattern of price increases as does a fall in the currency's foreign exchange value. The pattern of hyperinflation stemming from capital transfers differs basically from domestic monetary overissue stemming from local-currency budget deficits. The inability of foreign exchange receipts to cover payments leads to a decline in the currency's value, making import prices higher. This makes domestic goods more attractive—just the opposite from what happens in the case of domestic monetary overissue! If the inflation were a purely domestic monetary or fiscal phenomenon, it could be stopped before it became "hyper." But it cannot be stopped nearly as readily when it stems basically from external factors.

It is characteristic of classical hyperinflations that *an increasing money supply tends to be a response to the more fundamental balance-of-payments problem of currency depreciation*. The theory of hyperinflation accordingly analyzes how an adverse balance of payments causes domestic monetary and fiscal *responses*.

## The price-inelastic character of debt service

Creditor-oriented economists insist that monetary deflation can solve structural trade deficits and meet any level of contractual debt service. For two decades IMF austerity programs based on this assumption have aggravated rather than stabilized the balance of payments of debtor countries. This has not deterred Milton Friedman from defending flexible (that is, falling) exchange rates on the ground that devaluation will alter market preferences so as to reduce *all* outflows, including even debt service denominated in foreign currency!

> Holders of foreign currencies *want* to exchange them for the currency of a particular country in order to purchase commodities produced in that country, or to purchase securities or other capital assets in that country, *or to pay interest on or repay debts to that country*, or to make gifts to citizens of that country, or simply to hold for one of these uses or for sale. ... Other things the same, the more expensive a given currency, that is, the higher the exchange rate, the less of that currency will in general be demanded for each of these purposes.[3] (Italics added.)

This suggests that countries elect to pay less on their foreign debt as the currencies in which it is denominated become more expensive. But do they

---

3   Milton Friedman, "The Case for Flexible Exchange Rates," *Essays in Political Economics* (Chicago: 1953), reprinted in Caves and Johnson, eds., *Readings in International Economics* (Homewood: 1968), p. 415.

really have a choice? They cannot pay less without being held in default and confronted with international sanctions including a cutoff of future credit and probably trade barriers and consequent loss of foreign markets.

Of all the price-inelastic categories of international payments, debt service has become the least voluntary and most inexorable class of payments. Steuart perceived this two centuries ago in classifying payments according to their relative price elasticity: "It is only the circulation of the industrious, of the rich, in short buying, that is to say, *voluntary circulation*, which is stopped for want of currency: paying, that is, *involuntary circulation*, never can be stopped; debtors *must* find money, as long as there is any in the country, were they to give an acre for a shilling, or a house for half a crown."[4]

### *What the purchasing-power parity theory of exchange rates leaves out of account*

If domestic money creation occurs in the context of balanced international payments, domestic goods are the first to rise in price, making foreign goods more attractive. The price inflation thus leads rather than follows the adverse shift in the terms of trade and the balance of payments. But when a currency comes under pressure because international payments exceed current receipts (without there necessarily being any domestic monetary overissue), the price of imports rises first, making them become more expensive in domestic currency. In both cases import prices and domestic prices rise, but the causal sequence is reversed. As John Williams observed with regard to Germany's hyperinflation of the early 1920s:

> The German price situation thus bears out the view that in a period of depreciating exchange export and import prices rise first and in close sympathy with the exchange, whereas the rise in internal prices follows more slowly, the gap between the two providing a stimulus to exports and a burden upon imports. It indicates unmistakably also that the price changes *follow* the changes in the exchange rate. It is equally clear that in this instance the increase in note issue has *followed* the decline in exchange and the consequent rise of prices. ... The greatest rate of increase in note issue yet recorded was in the first half of 1920, when the circulation rose from 49,807,000,000 marks to 67,608,000,000; yet in those six months the mark exchange rose from 50 to 38 for the dollar, and between the end of January and the end of May when inflation was most pronounced of all the mark recovered from 104 to 35. ...
>
> So far as the German case is concerned, it is evident that to demand restriction of inconvertible paper as the fundamental cure for depreciating exchange is to beg the question: the Reichsbank has not inflated for its own amusement. The same may be said of the view that the fundamental cure must be to "balance the budget"; that budgetary deficits necessitate further note issue to cover the

---

4   Steuart, *Principles of Political Oeconomy*, Vol. II, p. 181.

deficit, and that the increased issue causes further increase of prices and hence depreciation of exchange. The first part of the statement is true so far as it goes, but it does not start far enough back. What causes the budgetary deficit?[5]

In the summer of 1926, Hjalmar Schacht attributed the entire increase in Germany's note circulation (some 300 million marks) to an increased conversion of foreign borrowings into domestic currency, with consequent inflationary effects.[6] Similarly with regard to France, James Rogers concludes:

> The general tendency of prices to lag slightly behind exchange rates would seem to signify that during much of the [1924-26] period the exchange value of the franc was moving under influences unconnected directly with internal price movements in France and that the changing rates of exchange, on the contrary, were causing prices to adjust themselves to new international values of the franc.[7]

The free trader Frank Taussig acknowledged that structural payment deficits were the major cause of monetary inflation, in a statement akin to the anti-bullionist position of 1810–11:

> merchandise movements, instead of following variations in the foreign exchanges, may set in of their own accord; they may precede the exchange variations ... The essential point is that the price of foreign exchange, the purchasing power of one currency in terms of the other, depends at any given time on the respective volumes of remittances... The price of foreign exchange thus may change without any movement in the general range of prices in either country.[8]

Ignoring the leads and lags at work, the purchasing-power parity theory of exchange rates holds that currency values change in direct proportion to their general domestic price levels. Haberler traces this idea back to Ricardo, in whose writings "there seems nowhere to be a hint that price-movements and movements of the exchange may temporarily diverge."[9] But that is what occurs when foreign currency is needed for purposes that have nothing to do with current relative prices, *e.g.*, to pay foreign debts or make military transfers. Haberler concludes that "One should not say—as supporters of the theory of purchasing-power parity are fond of doing—that the rise in prices is the primary phenomenon, and that the depreciation of the exchange is merely an effect on this."[10]

---

5  Williams, "German Foreign Trade and Reparations Payments," *Quarterly Journal of Economics*, XXXVI (May 1922). pp. 501f. See also his article on "Foreign Exchange prefer Depreciated Paper: A criticism of Cassell's doctrine of purchasing power parity," *Journal of the American Bankers Association*, January 1922.
6  Salomon J. Flink, *The German Reichsbank and Economic Germany* (New York, 1930), p. 189.
7  James Harvey Rogers, *The Process of Inflation in France* (New York: 1929).
8  Taussig, *International Trade*, pp. 363, 45.
9  Haberler, *Theory of International Trade*, p. 60n.
10  *Ibid.*, p. 60. But Haberler still insists that "the two changes bear a functional relation so one another and are both effects of the same cause. This is the increase in the quantity of money, which in its turn is the effect of the budget deficit."

Germany's hyperinflation stemmed from reparations payments and the consequent plunge in the mark's exchange rate, not the other way around. Haberler quotes with approval Helfferich's observation:

> In considering the monetary conditions in Germany, the view widely held, especially abroad, is based on the pure quantity theory, and accordingly regards the increase in the circulation of paper-currency in Germany as the cause of the rise in the level of German prices and of the depreciation of the currency. On closer examination, however, we find that cause and effect are here interchanged, and that the increase in the amount of paper money circulating in Germany is not in fact the cause but the result of the fall of the German exchanges and of the consequential rise in wages and prices.[11]

Recognizing that during a domestic monetary inflation the prices of home goods rise most, and import prices the least, Viner and Wu follow Taussig and Haberler in distinguishing between "domestic," import" and "export" price levels.[12] Yet Friedman states stubbornly that all prices change at the same rate during inflations and devaluation:

> In principle, changes in internal prices could produce the same effects on trade as changes in the exchange rate. For example, a decline of 10 percent in every internal price in Germany (including wages, rents, etc.) with an unchanged dollar price of the mark would have identically the same effects on the relative costs of domestic and foreign goods as a decline of 10 percent in the dollar price of the mark, with all internal prices unchanged.[13]

But Germany's internal incomes, costs and prices do *not* all respond equally, nor does such symmetry occur when the mark rises against the dollar. In the latter case of upward revaluation (more typical over the past 40 years), Germany's import costs fall (in mark terms) by the amount of the revaluation. (In theory there may be a marginal adjustment if this spurs more German demand for imports.) The price of domestic import-competing goods, especially grain and other farm products, should come under downward pressure, although in practice Germany protects farm incomes via the European Community's Common Agricultural Policy.

Appreciation of the mark may or may not oblige German exporters to lower their prices to hold onto foreign markets. It all depends on the elasticity of international demand for Mercedes, Volkswagen and other German exports. Mark prices for luxury cars tend to hold steady, especially if they are held abroad as appreciating stores of value in an inflationary world. Demand for these high-priced status symbols may even increase as the mark rises, although Volkswagen

---

[11]  *Ibid.*, quoting Helfferich, *Money*, pp. 598f.
[12]  Chi-Yuen Wu, *An Outline of International Price Theories* (London: t939), p. 84.
[13]  Friedman, "Flexible Exchange Rates," p. 419.

sales may come under pressure. In any case, mark prices for exports are unlikely to fall fully in keeping with import prices. To the extent that they may decline, they reduce the profits of German exporters, shifting the nation's investment functions toward satisfying the home market.

As for the capital account, if Germans have borrowed funds denominated in U.S. dollars, the domestic mark-costs of servicing these debts will decline in keeping with the mark's revaluation. Foreign funds may move into German stocks, bonds and bank deposits precisely to benefit from mark appreciation. These ways tend to make currency appreciation a cumulative self-feeding phenomenon.

When the U.S. dollar declines against the mark or yen, prices for U.S. imports from Europe and Japan are the first to rise, but not prices for raw materials, which are denominated in dollars. From the 1960s through the 1970s the decline in the dollar's international value reduced the purchasing power of Third World exports, irrespective of changes in their own domestic money supply and price levels. Dollar depreciation made oil and metals cheaper in German marks and Japanese yen—and increased the cost of servicing borrowings denominated in currencies that were appreciating. Meanwhile, in the United States, rising import prices for manufactured goods acted as an umbrella to increase the prices (and hence profits) for competing local products such as cars. This increased domestic investment in import-competing industries.

Friedman and his fellow monetarists try to explain away the fact that increases in the money supply are not as large as price increases (which in turn are not as large as the foreign-exchange depreciation) by focusing on domestic financial lags. As prices rise, people naturally try to economize on their money balances. This increases the velocity (that is, turnover) of money, in accordance with the formula $MV=PT$ (see Chapter 3), with $V = f(\Delta P)$. Prices therefore rise more rapidly than the money supply. Depreciation of the foreign exchange rate is attributed tautologically to "anticipations," covering or hoarding. Everything is made to turn on domestic money creation as causal.

### Monetarist vs. structuralist policy responses to payments deficits and price inflation

Why is "too much" money created? To finance domestic budget deficits, says Friedman. During the Great Depression of the 1930s Latin American governments found that as their raw materials exports declined in price and volume, their tax revenues based on these exports also fell. They did not cut back on their spending proportionally, because it had become a political and economic necessity. Latin American governments simply printed the money to cover expenditures in excess of tax revenues. Monetarists conclude that if only these governments had been willing to live within their (shrinking) means, there would have been no such deficits to monetize. Hence, there would have been that much less money available to spend on imports. Recent budget deficits in the United States likewise have been attributed to structural rigidities on which inflation is blamed.[14]

This logic does not ask whether it is counterproductive to cut back public spending on education and other basic infrastructure needs. To reduce food subsidies and other transfer payments may lead to strikes and food riots in many countries, further impairing the economy's overall position. Such questions are dismissed as "exogenous" to the monetarist monomania of focusing only on a few variables that can be used to rationalize their tight-money policy of financial austerity.

In many cases the initiating disturbance causing budget deficits stems from international forces altering the balance-of-payments position beyond the control or range of domestic options. Latin America's fiscal problem of the 1930s stemmed primarily from less tax revenue being collected from the minerals sector. Domestic price increases resulted largely from falling exchange rates as exports shrank. The domestic inflation and budget deficits were mainly a response to the payments deficit, not the other way around.

If a problem's cure should address its cause, then the solution to domestic inflation stemming from chronic payments deficits should lake the form of restructuring trade and payments. Monetary deflation discourages investment to upgrade productivity and replace imports, to upgrade the educational and general economic level of the labor force, and to provide the basic infrastructure needed to minimize domestic costs across the board. Such investment is not indicated if the root causes of balance-of-payments deficits are attributed only to excess credit creation and government spending.

Historical explanations often clarify economic understanding. During World War II most Latin American countries became self-sufficient in food and other essentials under force of necessity resulting from the interruption of trade. Indeed, they built up dollar and sterling balances by supplying raw materials to the Allies. But upon the return to peace they lapsed back into the specialization pattern of increased dependency on imported food and other essentials. Their raw-materials exports rose in volume, but their food deficits widened even more. Foreign borrowing financed the resulting trade deficits, subsidizing the failure to modernize their agriculture. As interest rates rose

---

[14]   See for instance the 1984 *Economic Report to the President of the United States* (Washington: 1984), pp. 35f. For the monetarist position on budget deficits see Philip Cagan, "The Monetary Dynamics of Hyperinflation," in Milton Friedman, ed., *Studies in the Quantity Theory of Money* (Chicago: 1956), pp. 25–117.

steadily from 1945 to 1980, the cost of servicing foreign debt has imposed increasingly severe burdens on the balance of payments, to the point where it became a major cause of hyperinflation from Latin America to Africa.

Harry Johnson recognizes two basic approaches to curing payments deficits. The problem can be posed "as a *real* problem or as a *monetary* problem." The long-term "real" approach is to increase output. This may involve restructuring the economy to make it more competitive. The short-term approach is just the opposite—to reduce expenditure, specifically federal spending and the money supply that are most directly under the control of policy makers. This policy involves tight credit, discouraging the direct investment which holds the only long-term promise of increasing exports, displacing imports and hence balancing international payments by growth and development rather than economic shrinkage.

However, Johnson and his fellow monetarists prefer short-term "demand management" to investment to increase productivity, especially if the latter involves subsidized long-term credit for capital-intensive industries: "Since output is governed by demand for it, a change in output can only be brought about by a change in the demand for it: a policy of increasing domestic output can only be effected by operating on expenditure (either foreign or domestic) on that output."[15] But demand does not automatically call forth output, especially if local producers are not internationally competitive. Neither Johnson nor other monetarists inquire into just what the conditions of competitive advantage are in today's capital-intensive world, particularly in the financial area of capital costing.

When Friedman commented in the early 1970s that "we are all Keynesians," he meant this in the macroeconomic sense of translating income trends into their monetary preconditions or effects. Economic activity obviously needs money and credit to expand, and even to be transacted, as John Law emphasized early in the eighteenth century. How then can monetary deflation automatically cure chronic payments deficits? It certainly can curtail domestic spending and investment. But will this reduce imports by an equivalent amount (that is, by reducing the apparent gap between domestic purchasing power and output)? If demand for imports is price-inelastic—as in the case of food, replacement parts and (so it seems) arms—then what is curtailed will be primarily spending on the domestic output, not spending on imports. It hardly can be assumed that all such output not bought at home will automatically be exported.

---

[15] Harry G. Johnson, "The Transfer Problem of Exchange Stability," *Journal of Political Economy,* LXIV (June 1956), in *International Trade and Economic Growth: Studies in Pure Theory* [1958] (Cambridge: 1967), p. 169, and "Towards a General Theory of the Balance of Payments," *ibid.*, pp. 161f.

Chapter 3 has described how additional money and spending tends to increase output more than prices when labor and other resources are unemployed—and the corollary principle that monetary deflation in unemployment conditions tends to curtail output more than imports. By destabilizing economic life it leads to higher import dependency. As Salomon Flink noted with regard to the German experience of the 1920s, "credit restriction ... results in credit crises."[16] Businesses that have financed their capital requirements with short-term funds are unable to meet their debts. If they cannot increase their credit lines, they must liquidate their reserves and inventories, sell out, or declare bankruptcy. The monetarist austerity solution thus creates an even larger problem.

The process of deflation thus is asymmetrical with that of inflation. While inflation represents a transfer of income from creditors to debtors, deflation represents a transfer of *property* from debtors to creditors, via the foreclosure process. Phenomena much more important than mere "counters" are affected by these asymmetries.

The following chapters describe how the primary issues in monetary debates for two centuries have concerned the cause of inflation and deflation, and whether the domestic money supply or the balance of payments is responsible. Also at issue are the proposed solutions: monetary deflation or a restructuring of trade and investment.

It should be noted that wars have been the major "exogenous" phenomena transforming trade and financial relations over the centuries. In the monetary sphere, history's major inflations have been associated with wars—and also the major deflations. Foreign military spending throws the balance of payments into deficit and forces the currency off gold, while monetization of wartime budget deficits tends to produce inflation. The major deflation have resulted from postwar attempts to re-establish the convertibility of paper into gold, while the reopening of foreign commerce under peacetime conditions threatens high-cost domestic industry and agriculture established during the years of wartime isolation. Repaying national and international debts alters the distribution of income and wealth between taxpayers and bondholders. Debtor interests and protectionism have tended to go together, just as creditor interests usually advocate laissez faire. The result is that debates in international finance have been linked closely to those concerning foreign trade, with the same sets of economic writers arguing with each other.

Wars brought into being the largest early domestic and foreign debts—along with capital markets to fund them. Wars also have been the major vehicle forcing governments to suspend laissez faire. The Bank of England suspended

---

[16]   Flink, *The German Reichsbank and Economic Germany*, pp 115f.

convertibility of sterling in 1797, and after the war the great fight was to repeal the Corn Laws that protected the vested agricultural interests that grew during the Napoleonic Wars. Meanwhile, England suffered a postwar deflation by (needlessly) restoring the price of gold to its pre-war level—as the United States would do in a similarly painful exercise after its Civil War.

During the Vietnam War years 1960–72, foreign military spending represented the entire U.S. balance-of-payments deficit. This was reflected in a $100 billion debt run up by the U.S. Treasury to foreign central banks. It became the lever that transformed international financial relationships after 1971 when the U.S. Treasury-bill (public debt) standard replaced the international gold (asset) standard. All these developments transformed the underlying structure of the international financial system.

# 14

## The Napoleonic Wars and England's Bullion Debate

Wars consume more resources than they generate. Quite apart from the lives lost and the money spent on armaments, the financial impact usually lasts long after military hostilities are over. Having thrown the balance of payments for belligerent powers into deficit and forced their currencies off gold, wars leave a legacy of domestic and international debt to be paid off. Postwar economies are further burdened if countries roll back their price levels and exchange rates to their prewar (allegedly natural) level. This currency deflation and appreciation of exchange rates to repay the debts run up during the war tend to be much more traumatic than the wartime inflation.

England's war with France following the latter's 1789 Revolution affords a classic example of these war-related strains and postwar financial realignments. In February 1793, almost immediately after executing Louis XVI, France declared war on England, Prussia and Austria, which had formed an anti-French alliance the previous year. For two decades Europe was embroiled in its most intensive war yet, highlighted by the French blockade of England (called the Continental System), widespread seizure of the ships of non-belligerent countries, and troop movements on an unprecedented scale.

England's subsidies to its continental European allies drained its gold reserves and pushed its national budget more than £30 million into deficit during 1795 and 1796. Meanwhile, two successive crop failures helped push grain prices 25 per cent above their 1794 levels. This paved the way for monetary crisis in February 1797, when rumors of an imminent French invasion of the British Isles triggered a run on country banks (an "internal drain" of gold). The Restriction Act suspended Sterling convertibility, and remained in effect until 1821, six years after hostilities ended.

Through the centuries a major objective in suspending convertibility has been to conserve gold for overseas military spending and subsidies. (This was, after all, what forced the United States off gold in 1971, and with it the entire world economy.) A domestic effect of the suspension was that the Bank of England could create paper credit without being obliged to convert its bank notes into gold on demand. They sold at a discount against gold after 1799, when Napoleon came to power and hostilities escalated.

The ensuing inflation, in particular the rising price of gold, inspired a debate over whether the rise in gold prices was caused by a domestic overissue of paper money or by the extraordinary demand for gold to settle balance-of-payment deficits stemming from Britain's military subsidies, other capital transfers and unusually high imports. The early literature was headed by Henry Thornton's *Enquiry into the Nature and Effects of the Paper Credit of Great Britain* (1802) and less monetarist pamphlets such as Walter Boyd's *Letter to … William Pitt* (1801) and Peter King's proto-Ricardian *Thoughts on the Effects of the Bank Restriction* (1803).

The discussion subsided as the price of gold fell back near normal during 1804-08, but broke out anew in the autumn of 1809 when the largest trade deficit since 1799 pushed up gold prices once again. By 1810, France's blockade against England was at its peak, throwing the country back on its domestic resources and forcing it to become more agriculturally self-sufficient. General prices rose more than the price of gold, which increased by 13.5 per cent. Acceptable index numbers were not yet compiled for English commodity prices in general, so the discussion focused on the price of gold. Meanwhile, the annual budget deficit receded to "only" £10 million—a level that had proved quite tolerable during 1793–94. The inflation was mild by modern standards—mild enough to confuse the issue of just what factors caused it. Parliament issued a report in the midst of the bullion debate in 1810, and the following year Malthus summarized the pamphlet literature emerging from the controversy.[1]

---

[1]    The new controversy was touched off by a series of letters from Ricardo in the *Morning Chronicle* in September 1809, followed by his 1810 pamphlet on *The High Price of Bullion, a Proof of the Depreciation of Bank Notes*. Parliament issued the *Bullion Report* on June 8, 1810, composed by Francis Horner, William Huskisson and Henry Thornton, who had come to believe that an overissue of paper currency had become a more pressing threat to economic stability than the balance-of-payments pressures and other non-monetary causes he had stressed in his 1802 *Paper Credit of Great Britain*. Both in the *Bullion Report* and in his speeches during the parliamentary debate over this report (which occurred in 1811, a year after its release), Thornton emphasized that price levels and exchange rates were determined by autonomous balance-of-payments functions as well as by increases in the money supply.

Edwin Cannan's *The Paper Pound of 1797–1821* (London: 1919) reprints the *Bullion Report*. Charles Rist, *History of Monetary and Credit Theory, from John Law to the Present Day* (London: 1940), and Joseph Schumpeter, *History of Economic Analysis* (New York: 1954), Chapter 7, provide excellent background material and a summary of the debate in the context of its times.

The more broadminded Malthus criticized Ricardo's metallist views in the February and August 1811 issues of the *Edinburgh Review*. Ricardo answered these criticisms in an appendix to the fourth edition of his *High Price of Bullion*. During the course of this debate Malthus introduced himself to Ricardo, paving the way for a long friendship that has left a rich correspondence detailing their points of disagreement.

The anti-bullionists in Parliament were led by Nicholas Vansittart and Prime Minister Spencer Perceval, who also was Chancellor of the Exchequer. They acknowledged that

The Bank of England avoided a shortage of money by issuing more than enough paper to take the place of the gold flowing out of the economy. Country banks also stepped up their currency issue, enabling trade to continue. Meanwhile, the most visible factor depressing exchange markets was England's military subsidy to its allies, financed by selling Exchequer bills on world markets. These subsidies were independent of relative prices, the money supply or other purely market-related factors.

England's balance of trade and payments was deteriorating both for monetary and non-monetary reasons. The bullionists blamed the increase in gold prices on the Bank of England for increasing the money supply while the volume of gold support was shrinking. The anti-bullionists defended the Bank of England for acting as responsibly as it could in the face of wartime government borrowing and domestic credit needs. They attributed the rise in gold and commodity prices to England's balance-of-payments deficits resulting from military spending and subsidies to its allies, as well as to a few bad harvests. Food had to be imported irrespective of monetary and price considerations. Gold accordingly rose because it was used to settle the resulting payments deficits.

Both parties acknowledged that resumption of convertibility at the 1797 rate would require a deflation of the currency, inasmuch as there was not enough gold to cover the existing note issue. Monetary deflation meant economic austerity and lower prices. This threatened to transfer wealth from taxpayers and debtors to creditors.

The policy issue was whether the return to gold convertibility should occur upon the return to peace or be deferred. Would monetary deflation cure England's payments deficits by reducing prices? Or, would it impair production and hence export functions by even more than it would curtail imports?

What makes this debate so relevant to modern times is that the same issue is being debated today with respect to the IMF's monetarist rationale for deflation. The bullionist principles set forth by Ricardo are the direct antecedents of those which Milton Friedman and his monetarist followers have enunciated in recent decades. In this respect Ricardo's bullionist writings of 1809-11 represent the starting point for today's monetarism. They stripped away from the analysis of prices and the balance of payments all elements except changes in the money supply, urging repeal of the 1797 Restriction Act so that the paper currency would be covered 100 per cent by gold.

---

resumption should be approved as soon as it was practical, but they opposed it in 1810. Parliamentary majorities of about two to one upheld their position. Vansittart's resolutions defeated those of the bullionist Horner, and resumption of specie payments was deferred. Vansittart himself was appointed Chancellor of the Exchequer during 1812-23. Yet from the attention lavished on them by many one-sided monetarist historians, one would get the impression that the bullionists won the debate!

## The bullionist position

Bullionists—who also were called metallists, and today would be called monetarists—were so named because they insisted that paper currency should be
limited to the volume of bank notes that could be converted into gold bullion
on demand. This was supposed to stabilize prices and thereby balance England's
international payments by preventing a credit superstructure. Like most defla-
tionists, the bullionists were what Schumpeter called "monetary monomaniacs."
They believed that prices rose for one reason only: "an Excess of Paper
Currency" (in the words of the *Bullion Report*), which could be "cured by the
resumption of Cash Payments by the Bank." This made them the hard-money
party. As Ricardo summarized his diagnosis in *The High Price of Bullion* (1810):

> The only legitimate security which the public can possess against the indiscretion
> of the Bank is to oblige them to pay their notes on demand in specie; and this
> can only be effected by diminishing the amount of bank-notes in circulation till
> the nominal price of gold be lowered to the mint price.[2]

To today's monetarists, the key ratio is the supply of money relative to the
quantity of goods and services available to absorb this purchasing power.
Lacking a suitable measure of the economy's overall volume of output (national
income and product accounts were not yet compiled), England's bullionists
focused on the surplus of paper money over what could be covered under a
convertible gold standard. Their position would agree with that of today's
monetarists if gold supplies happened to increase by precisely enough to enable
economic activity to expand in the context of stable price conditions and balanced international payments. This coincidence was taken for granted rather
than demonstrated. Each country was supposed to have a natural proportion of
the circulating medium to output.[3]

Ricardo and his fellow bullionists took gold prices as a proxy both for the
general price level and for the foreign exchange premium. They assumed that
exchange rates directly reflected international price levels, which in turn were a
direct function of each country's money supply. The gold premium was
supposed to reflect the general exchange rate, which in turn reflected the
general domestic inflation, as in the purchasing-power theory of exchange rates.

---

2  Schumpeter, *History of Economic Analysis*, p. 712, *Bullion Report*, p. 52, and Ricardo, *The High Price of Bullion, A Proof of the Depreciation of Bank Notes* (London: 1810), reprinted in *Works*, III: *Pamphlets and Papers, 1809–1811* (Cambridge: 1951), p. 99.

3  *Bullion Report*, pp. 52f.: "When the currency consists entirely of the precious metals, or of paper currency convertible at will into the precious metals, the natural process of commerce, by establishing Exchanges among all the different countries of the world, adjusts, in every particular country, the proportion of circulating medium to its actual occasion, according to the supply of the precious metals which the mines furnish to the general market of the world."

This implied that exchange rates were not influenced by autonomous capital movements such as the need to purchase foreign exchange to make military payments, or trade movements deriving from autonomous demand such as crop failures or other inadequate production powers. It was as if general prices, gold prices and foreign exchange rates moved together in parallel motion.[4]

Ricardo wrote to Francis Horner that foreign exchange rates were the result of two functions. The first was the quantity theory of money as it appeared in the price-specie flow mechanism, so that "an apprehended alternation, in the relative prices of commodities in the two countries … is in most cases to be traced to some augmentation or diminution in the amount of the currency of one of them." The second factor at work was "an increased or diminished difficulty and expense (or the anticipation of such), attending the transmission of money." This factor, representing "the difficulties which our enemy has interposed in the way of exportation," was responsible for the excess depreciation of the currency, that is, the rise in general commodity prices beyond that of the price of gold.[5]

This is as close as Ricardo came to recognizing a terms-of-trade shift. No-where in his published writings did he acknowledge this awareness. He criticized Horner for acknowledging that "other factors besides the superabundance of the paper circulation had contributed to the high price of gold," and that the combination of England's interrupted export trade and the suspension of gold shipments from South America had driven up world gold prices independently of the increase in England's money supply. He insisted that "no point can be more satisfactorily established, than that the excess of the market above the mint price of gold bullion, is, at present, wholly and solely, owing to the too abundant quantity of paper circulation."[6] The only qualification he granted to the purchasing-power parity theory of foreign exchange values was the role played by transport costs, which functioned like a *de facto* tariff. Even here he had no idea of the incidence of transport costs discussed in Chapter 6.

Horner acknowledged that "the adverse circumstances of our Trade, together with the large amount of our Military Expenditures Abroad, may have

[4]  To be sure, Ricardo acknowledged to Malthus (July 17, 1811, in *Works*, VI: *Letters: 1810–1815* [Cambridge: 1952], p. 39, hereafter referred to as *Letters*), "I do not mean to contend that a convulsed state of the exchange, such as would be caused by a subsidy granted to a foreign power, would accurately measure the value of the currency" in terms of commodities produced and traded. However, England's demand for foreign currency would "have the effect of forcing the exports of commodities by means of the bounty which the exchange would afford." In other words, the capital transfer would somewhat impair Britain's terms of trade, but this shift would work to maintain equilibrium.

[5]  Ricardo to Horner, January 4, 1812, in *Letters*, pp. 79f.

[6]  Ricardo to Horner, February 5, 1810, in *Letters*, pp. 1f.

contributed to render our Exchanges with the Continent of Europe unfavour-able." Still, the Bullion Report insisted that "no increased demand for Gold from other parts of the world, however great, or from whatever cause arising, can have the effect of producing here, for a considerable period of time, a material rise in the market price of gold."[7] Only an increase in the money supply could do this. If there indeed were an extraordinary demand for gold, its command over other commodities would rise. But this had not been the case: general prices had risen by considerably more than the price of gold.

## The anti-bullionist position

Anti-bullionists pointed out that England's overseas military spending and crop failures were unrelated to the volume of note issue or price movements, except to cause them by turning the balance of payments against England. Price increases for gold and other commodities thus were independent of increases in the domestic money supply. Hence, the quantity theory of money could not explain either the fall in the price of sterling or the rise in the price of gold.

Nicholas Vansittart, head of the Parliamentary anti-bullionists, noted that gold prices normally rose to a premium in periods of balance-of-payments deficits, "and that such circumstances have usually occurred when expensive Naval and Military operations have been carried on abroad, and in times of public danger or alarm, or when large importations of grain have taken place."[8] The extraordinary need for gold to cover such foreign payments was respon-sible for the premium of gold over paper, not the latter's overissue. Already in 1802, Thornton had observed that quite independently of domestic monetary developments and price levels, "numerous stores were shipped during the war, for the support of our navy and army in foreign parts. Remittances were made, in the way of loan and subsidy, to our allies. Some dividends may be supposed to have been transmitted to the foreign proprietors of British stock," as well as foreign investment leaving England for the East and West Indies and other parts of the world.[9]

What forced sterling off gold was military-related capital transfers not initially connected with the monetary, price and trade movements emphasized

<hr>

[7]  Horner's 13th Resolution, and the *Bullion Report*, p. 6.
[8]  Vansittart's 4th Resolution, introduced in answer to those of Francis Horner (repr. in the *Bullion Report*). Vansittart cited "the wars carried on by King William the Third, Queen Anne, the Seven Years War, the American War, and during the War and Scarcity of grain in 1795 and 1796."
[9]  Thornton, *An Enquiry into the Nature and Effects of the Paper Credit of Great Britain* (London: 1802), pp. 144, 157, 147f., citing Smith, *Wealth of Nations*, Book II, ch. ii (Canaan ed., p. 320).

by the price-specie flow mechanism. The currency crisis peaked when international investors started a run on sterling by calling in their loans and selling their investments in English securities, much like the run on America's gold stock as the Vietnam War pushed the U.S. balance of payments deeper into deficit in the late 1960s. Under these conditions the balance of payments (and hence the rise in the price of gold) hardly could be blamed on domestic monetary policy, and Adam Smith had been unfair in criticizing the Bank of England for having "issued too many notes" in similar earlier periods.

Malthus protested to Horner that he remained "quite unconvinced—indeed there is no point on which I feel more sure than of the incorrectness of attributing the variations of the exchange exclusively to redundancy or deficiency of currency."[10] He wrote to Ricardo (apparently to no avail) urging him to read Steuart's *Principles of Political Oeconomy*, Book II, Chapter 18 for an example of "a comparative rise of prices not occasioned by a comparative redundancy of currency." Steuart had written that food and other necessities tended to rise relative to other goods as a result of industrialization, just as the rise in labor productivity and the introduction of machinery tended to reduce prices quite independently of changes in the money supply.[11] Ironically, this was the economic rent argument Ricardo used against Malthus to urge abolition of the Corn Laws after the war ended.

In his published review of the bullion debate, Malthus singled out Ricardo for taking the most extreme position and attributing "a favourable or an unfavourable exchange exclusively to a redundant or deficient currency, and overlook[ing] the varying desires and wants of different societies, as an original cause of a temporary excess of imports above exports, or exports above imports."[12] But Ricardo insisted (in a personal letter) that all fluctuations in the value of gold and silver were ultimately the result of

> one cause, namely, a redundancy of currency ... and not ... the demand for particular commodities. These demands ... are not causes but effects ... you admit that a relatively redundant currency may be and frequently is a cause of an unfavourable balance of trade but you contend that it is not the only cause. Now I ... contend that it is the invariable cause.

In his published answer to Malthus's criticisms (the appendix to the fourth edition of his *High Price of Bullion*), Ricardo insisted that "a bad harvest will not occasion the export of money, unless money is relatively cheap in the

10   Malthus to Horner, April 7, 1810, and to Ricardo, July 14, 1811, in *Letters*, pp. 12, 134.
11   Steuart, *Principles of Political Oeconomy*, Vol. I, pp. 283–300.
12   Article V in the February 1811 issue of the *Edinburgh Review*, republished in the *Occasional Papers of T. R. Malthus, on Ireland, Population and Political Economy*, Bernard Semmel ed. (New York: 1963), p. 75.

exporting country." *If the price of grain rose relative to other commodities as a result of a crop failure, the country would export these other products in exchange for food.* Included among these other products was monetary gold, in the same proportion to which it circulated domestically (about one-fiftieth). To export gold in excess of this average proportion to other products would signify an excess rate of money creation in the payments-deficit country:

> If we consent to give coin in exchange for goods, it must be from choice, not necessity. We should not import more goods than we export, unless we had a redundancy of currency, which it therefore suits us to make a part of our exports. The exportation of the coin is caused by its cheapness, and is not the effect, but the cause of an unfavourable balance.[13]

The monetary metals were merely commodities, not the tools of trade. Even as commodities they had little real importance. Ricardo quoted with approval Adam Smith's claim "that the most abundant mines of the precious metals would add little to the wealth of the world. A produce of which the value is principally derived from its scarcity is necessarily degraded by its abundance."[14] He did not acknowledge any favorable "real" economic impact to the result from new gold discoveries or other monetary inflows. When monetized, he insisted, "gold (or silver) is not productive to us nor does it augment our riches—but to obtain this unproductive commodity we should in return export commodities which may be considered as really effective capital." He reiterated that

> Money is precisely that article which till it is re-exchanged never adds to the wealth of a country: accordingly we find, that to increase the amount is never the voluntary act of any country any more than it is that of any individual ... the augmented currency ... will be of no more real value than the original amount of currency. Thus then will this industrious nation become tributary to those nations which are in possession of the mines, and will carry on a trade in which it gains nothing and loses everything.[15]

A more extreme statement would be hard to find. It recognized no positive or negative influence of monetary movements on the level and structure of economic activity. Ricardo approached the financial sector in a spirit of barter based on relative supply and demand—the supply of money relative to

---

[13] Ricardo to Malthus, June 18, 1811, in *Letters*, p. 26, and *The High Price of Bullion*, pp. 100, 61.

[14] *The High Price of Bullion*, p. 53, quoting Smith, *Wealth of Nations*, Book I, ch. xi, part ii (Cannan ed., Vol. I, p. 173).

[15] Ricardo to James Mill, January 1, 1811 (*Letters*, p. 17) and *The High Price of Bullion*, pp. 108f. (See also pp. 555 and 61.) In addition see Malthus to Ricardo, February 23,1812, and Ricardo to Malthus, June 18, 1811, March 22, 1813, and March 24, 1813 (*Letters*, pp. 83, 24, 90f.).

output. The price of bullion was held to be subject to the same laws that governed commodities in general. He refused to acknowledge that gold functioned as a monetary institution supporting the credit superstructure, having an institutional demand that made it critically important in settling balance-of-payments deficits or runs on the banking system (the "external" and "internal" monetary drains, respectively).

## Capital payments, the terms of trade and income adjustments

In refusing to attribute food imports to absolute need, Ricardo reasoned as if the supply and demand of all commodities were highly elastic. This meant that their purchase was simply a matter of price, and hence of choice. Increased English exports to pay for food, or foreign exchange to make military payments, would not entail a terms-of-trade penalty. Trade would remain in balance, assuming no problem of relative elasticities of international demand.

Ricardo never understood this elasticities problem, which remained for Mill to elucidate, and which Thornton and Malthus began to explain. Even in the case of military subsidies, Ricardo believed, "money would not be exported whilst there were any goods which could more cheaply discharge the payment. The interest of individuals would render the exportation of the money unnecessary." He asked whether,

> After comparing the relative value of coffee, sugar, ivory, indigo, and all other exportable commodities in the two markets (England and France), if I persist in sending money, what further proof can be required of money being actually the cheapest of all these commodities in the English market, in relation to the foreign markets, and therefore the most profitable to be exported?[16]

Foreign countries indeed might be willing to purchase more English exports, but at what price? Thornton posed the case of foreigners only being interested in buying English exports at a severe price discount. Ricardo denied that this was realistic. If they took gold, it was because this was the commodity in greatest over-supply relative to other products, not because it was what Steuart had called the money of the world. This begged the question of price and income elasticities for specific commodities, as Thornton pointed out:

> At the time of a very unfavourable balance produced through a failure of the harvest a country has occasion for a large supply of corn from abroad … but the goods which the country is able to furnish as means of cancelling its debt are not in such demand as to afford the prospect of a tempting or even of a

---

[16] Ricardo, *The High Price of Bullion*, pp. 63, 105.

Table 14.1  Contrast between the Bullionist and Anti-Bullionist Positions

| BULLIONISTS (Ricardo, Horner, Wheatley) | ANTI-BULLIONISTS (Vansittart, Malthus, Thornton in 1802) |
|---|---|
| 1. Reductionist: Price increases are caused by issuing money beyond the volume of bank notes that could be converted freely into gold. | Price increases frequently result from non-monetary causes, including crop failures, foreign military spending, capital transfers and debt service. |
| 2. A Purchasing-Power Parity theory of foreign-exchange rates (subject to transport-cost margins). Changes in the price of gold and foreign exchange reflect domestic inflation rates. | A balance-of-payments explanation of exchange rates. Gold prices tend to vary independently of money-supply changes and general commodity prices. |
| 3. If international payments fall into deficit, a "typical cross-section" of money and goods is exported. | Trade imbalances must be financed mainly in gold, creating an extraordinary demand for that metal. |
| 4. International payments will remain in balance even in the face of crop failures, military spending and subsidies if sound monetary policies are followed. | Foreigners may not purchase enough of England's exports to cover its capital transfers, except at highly unfavorable terms of trade to England. |
| 5. Gold is a *commodity* subject to the same laws that determine the value of any other commodity. | Gold functions as a financial *institution* with its own demand, over and above its use as an industrial commodity. |
| 6. No terms-of-trade penalty is recognized for increased commodity exports. | If capital transfers are settled by commodity exports, export prices will fall. |
| 7. Gold inflows do not add to the wealth of nations. Just the opposite, they *absorb* this wealth by being a sterile form of capital. | Gold adds to the wealth of nations and is a precondition for this wealth by enabling more investment, credit and economic activity to be financed. |
| 8. Reducing the money supply can cure inflation, and also balance-of-payments deficits. Austerity smoothly reverses the inflationary process. | Deflation tends to derange economic activity, reducing output by even more than the money supply. This spurs shortage-induced price increases and payments deficits. |
| 9. All imports and foreign payments, including debt service, are a matter of choice based on price differentials, which are a direct function of relative international rates of money creation. (There is no recognition of price-inelastic trade and payments.) | Some foreign payments—in particular, debt service—are based on structural needs, rather than a matter of free choice, *e.g.*, food imports during crop failures. (If England tries to export more, it may have to lower its export prices.) |
| 10. Debts improve a nation's economic position; otherwise, they would not be contracted. Debt service does not impair a nation's terms of trade. | Once a debt is entered into, debt service no longer is a matter of free choice. It may impair a nation's terms of trade, requiring more exports. This causes domestic shortages, spurring price inflation. |

tolerable price. ... In order then to induce the country having the favourable balance to take all its payments in goods and no part of it in gold it would be requisite ... to render them excessively cheap.[17]

Malthus followed in Thornton's steps by observing that to sustain military spending and subsidies (or to pay for urgently needed food imports after a bad harvest), England was obliged to export goods for which markets might be lacking unless export prices fell sharply. Thus, "The prices of commodities are liable to great depressions from a glut in the market."[18] A growing supply of English exports might force down their prices so far that gold might be the most economic product to transfer, especially inasmuch as it was the accepted money of the world. In this line of reasoning Malthus anticipated Mill, whose views will be discussed in the next chapter.

Ricardo had dismissed this terms-of-trade argument with the comment that "No mistake can be greater than to suppose *that a nation can ever be without wants for commodities of some sort* ... no country ever possessed a general glut of all commodities." He insisted that it was only paper money glutting the domestic market, not goods in foreign markets: "money will never be exported, unless it's relatively abundant with commodities, as compared with other countries."[19] If international payments happened to fall into deficit, the balance would be settled almost entirely in commodities via a *pro rata* volume of goods, including *some* aliquot portion of money, namely—the amount of monetary gold nor- mally needed to satisfy the transactions demand for these exports:

> If the circulating medium of England consisted wholly of the precious metals, and were a fiftieth part of the value of the commodities which it circulated, the whole amount of money which would under the circumstances supposed be exported in exchange for corn, would be a fiftieth part of the value of such corn: for the rest we should export commodities, and thus would the proportion between money and commodities be equally preserved in both countries. England, in consequence of a bad harvest, would come under the case ... of a country having been deprived of a part of its commodities, and therefore requiring a diminished amount of circulating medium. The currency which was before equal to her payments would now become superabundant and relatively cheap, in the proportion of one-fiftieth part of her diminished production; the exportation of this sum, therefore, would restore the value of her currency to the value of the currencies of other countries. Thus it appears to be satisfactorily proved that a bad harvest operates on the exchange in no other way than by

[17]   Thornton, *Paper Credit of Great Britain* (London: 1939), p. 151.
[18]   Ricardo, *The High Price of Bullion*, p. 101, referring to Malthus's criticism in the *Edinburgh Review* (*Occasional Papers*, p. 77). See also pp. 112f.
[19]   Ricardo, *Letters*, p. 108, and *The High Price of Bullion*, p. 61.

causing the currency which was before at its just level to become redundant, and thus is the principle that an unfavourable exchange may always be traced to a relatively redundant currency most fully exemplified.[20]

According to this view, gold would represent only one-fiftieth of the required military subsidy or other capital transfer. A crop failure would result in fewer bushels of wheat ("transactions") having to be financed by money, which therefore could be exported. *Ricardo assumed that countries receiving subsidies or export proceeds automatically would increase their demand for imports from the nation making these payments, at the existing terms of trade.* This assumed a 100 per cent marginal propensity to import for all increases in their purchasing power. (Chapter 18 shows how a similar assumption underlies today's IMF austerity programs.)

Malthus followed Steuart and other earlier writers in emphasizing the favorable impact of an increasing money supply on spurring production. He described how

A merchant, or manufacturer obtains a loan in paper from a bank; and, with this loan, he is able to command materials to work upon, tools to work with, and wherewithal to pay the wages of labor; and yet, he is told (by the bullionists) that this transaction dues not tend, in the slightest degree, to increase the capital of the country.

In reality, not only did increases in the money supply spur output (as long as labor and capital resources were available), but the inflation, if and when it did make place, served indirectly to spur capital accumulation, as long as wages lagged behind profits. The result of monetary inflows on balance was frequently to give

---

[20]  Ricardo, *The High Price of Bullion*, pp. 106f. Today's monetarists have gone so far as to cite his authority for the view that payments deficits should be settled by an income-transfer mechanism not requiring any gold or foreign exchange to be transferred at all! Ohlin (*Interregional and International Trade*, pp. 403f.) claimed that Ricardo alone among the prominent classical economists "never accepted the orthodox price level variation mechanism in the case of subsidies and crop failures, but attempted to show that a more automatic and smoother adjustment would take place. Although he was not very explicit on has question and made certain untenable statements, it seems probable that he had in mind that reactions on the demand side would reduce the need for gold flows and price level changes."

Chi-Yuen Wu (*An Outline of International Price Theories*, p. 274) says that Ricardo insisted that even in the short run "there was no reason to expect a transfer to cause an outflow of gold from the paying country." Although Ricardo did not go as far as Ohlin and Wu have claimed (in particular he did not refine his view of international income demand), he denied that gold would be exported for any reason other than its relative oversupply or "redundancy." Bastable later followed Ricardo's reasoning rather than the terms-of-trade analysis of Thornton, Malthus and Mill.

such a stimulus to the productive powers of the country, that, in a short time, the balance between commodities and currency is restored, by the great multiplication of the former—and prices return to their former level. We cannot help thinking, that an effect of this kind took place in Scotland in the interval of two periods alluded to by Hume and Smith. In 1751 and 1752, when Hume published his Political Discourses, and soon after the great multiplication of paper money in Scotland, there was a very sensible rise in the price of provisions; and this was naturally, and probably justly, attributed by him, in part, to the abundance of paper. In 1759, when the paper currency had probably not been diminished, Dr. Smith notices a different state of prices; and observes that, for a long period, provisions had never been cheaper. The dearness at the time that Hume wrote, he attributes carelessly, and without any inquiry about the fact, to the badness of the seasons; and intimates, that it could not be occasioned by the multiplication of paper money. The probability, however, seems to be, that the high prices of 1751 and 1752 were influenced by the paper—as we do not see how it is possible for the substitution of paper for coin to take place, without an increase of prices; but that the new stimulus given to industry by this increase of capital, had so increased the quantity of commodities in the interval between 1752 and 1759, as to restore them to a level with the increased currency.[21]

## Thornton's synthesis of the monetarist and balance-of-payments positions

By 1810 the anti-bullionists had become so antagonistic to the one-sided Ricardian arguments that they swung to the opposite extreme. Vansittart went so far as to neglect altogether the monetary causes of price inflation and payments deficits. Thornton, who had originated many of the anti-bullionist arguments in 1802, acknowledged that during the intervening decade an inflationary overissue of paper credit had become a problem, and that at the very least, the quantity theory of money came into play once full employment was reached. One certainly could not claim "that indefinitely to increase our paper, was the way indefinitely to improve its value in exchange for the circulating medium of other countries, as well as in exchange for bullion and for all commodities." Yet of the

---

[21] Malthus, *Occasional Papers*, pp. 95, 98. Malthus saw (p. 101) that this line of reasoning might remind one of John Law, whose *Money and Trade Considered* (Glasgow: 1750, p. 167) held that if money were lent out against "real bills," that is, commercial paper, no inflation could take place, because M/O would remain constant (higher money responding to and spurring more output). Malthus pointed out that

This … is precisely the language of the present Bank Directors; and they in no respect fall short of Mr. Law in the grand mistake, of confounding the quantity of good security in the country, and the quantity of money which people may want to borrow at the legal interest, particularly during a time of mercantile speculation or distress, with the quantity necessary for the circulation, so as to keep it on a level with the precious metals, and the currencies of the surrounding countries.

various circumstances to which Vansittart looked for the means of producing an improvement of the exchange, none included monetary policy. He cited "first, a continental peace: secondly, a better understanding, and, consequently, an open trade with America; thirdly, some extension of our commercial intercourse with Europe … but it was remarkable that he totally omitted any mention of a limitation of paper, in this enumeration of the means of meliorating our exchanges."[22]

Already in 1802 Thornton had warned that to push the anti-bullionist principle to the extreme of neglecting the potentially inflationary influence of domestic money creation, would provide a rationale to overissue domestic paper.

> The evil of an unfavourable exchange, and of a consequent high price of gold arises from an unfavourable balance of trade, and from that cause only. The true mode of preventing this evil, or of remedying it, if unfortunately it exists, is to increase the national industry. The way to encourage industry is to give full scope to trade and manufacturers by a liberal emission of paper. The balance of trade will not fail to be rendered favourable by that abundance of exportable articles which the labor thus excited must necessarily create. The course of exchange will, consequently, be supported … and thus the value of our paper will be sustained by the very means of its increase.[23]

By 1810 this indeed had become the approach of Lord Castlereaigh and others. Although it contained an important kernel of truth, it was dangerously one-sided.

The fact of the matter was that the balance of payments, and hence the depreciation of paper relative to gold, stemmed from two causes: on the one hand, the balance of trade reflecting in turn the state of Britain's productive powers (output) relative to its consumption needs, and on the other hand the rate of domestic money creation relative to output. This dual set of relationships recalls the two-phase economic models used by Steuart, Tucker, Hume and their late eighteenth-century contemporaries to distinguish between underemployment and full employment conditions (Chapter 3). In this more general theory of money, prices and exchange rates, more money excites industry at first, but its productivity effect dwindles as full employment conditions are approached and prices begin to rise. The anti-bullionist principle, according to which more money increases output rather than prices, thus is limited to underemployment situations:

---

[22]  Thornton's speech of May 14, 1811, reprinted in *Paper Credit*, ed. Friedrich A. von Hayek ed. (London: 1939), p. 347.
[23]  Von Hayek, *Paper Credit*, p. 231. See also Thornton's speech of May 14, 1811, p. 353.

... it is obvious, that the antecedently idle persons to whom we may suppose the new capital to give employ, are limited in number; and that, therefore, if the encreased issue is indefinite, it will set to work labourers, of whom a part will be drawn from other, perhaps, no less useful occupations. It may be inferred from this consideration, that there are some bounds to the benefit which is to be derived from an augmentation of paper.[24]

To sum up, trade surpluses often went hand in hand with monetary increases. In 1811 Malthus criticized the bullionists for being unable

to explain an improving exchange (that is, a favourable balance of payments) under an obviously increasing issue of notes; an event that not infrequently happens, and was much insisted upon by the Deputy-governor of the Bank, as a proof that our foreign exchanges had no connexion with the state of our currency.[25]

As for autonomous trade developments not caused by price differentials or antecedent changes in the money supply—such as imports after a domestic crop failure, or the opening of new export markets—"the exportation (or importation) of bullion was the *effect of a balance of trade*, originating in causes which may exist without any relation whatever to redundancy or deficiency of currency."[26]

Schumpeter has called this position the Balance-of-Payments Theory of foreign exchange, in contrast to Ricardo's Relative Inflation explanation focusing on "variations in the value of a country's monetary unit, in relation to the value of other countries' monetary units." The bullionist theory attributed payments deficits to the overissue of money. But what about the case where the trade deficit resulted from the production side of the equation, as in a crop failure? And could monetary deflation alone really ensure trade surpluses?

Wheatley and Ricardo denied that a crop failure will create "redundancy" of currency, though Ricardo admitted this in a letter to Malthus. But Wheatley ... said boldly that, in spite of all the subsidies and other sums sent abroad during the Napoleonic Wars, it would have been possible to enforce "influx of money to any extent,"[27]

simply by monetary deflation of England's domestic economy. This assertion contains the basic thrust of the IMF austerity programs since the 1960s.

Thornton inverted Ricardo's monetarist line of causation: payments deficits led to currency depreciation, rising import prices, higher domestic prices in general and hence a need for more money as a means of payment. In his

---

[24] Von Hayek, *ibid.*, p. 236.
[25] Malthus, *Occasional Papers*, p. 91.
[26] Malthus, *ibid.*, p. 74.
[27] Schumpeter, *History of Economic Analysis*, pp. 735, 737, quoting Wheatley, *Essay on the Theory of Money*, Vol. I, p. 194.

words the bullionists mistook "the effect for the cause ... the encrease of Bank of England paper [is] the effect and not the cause of an advanced price of commodities."[28] More money was needed to finance commerce at higher price levels. The inference that "an excess of the market price above the mint price of gold" is always caused solely by

> a too great issue of paper ... is one which ... should always be very cautiously made; for it is to be borne in mind, that the excess may arise from other causes besides that of a too great emission of paper.

The balance of payments was much more than the trade balance, and Thornton emphasized that both balances were affected by numerous factors other than relative prices. *In particular, exports and imports reflected relative productive powers among nations, whose balance was thrown into disequilibrium by England's two major crop failures in the mid-1790s.* On this ground he concluded that deficits in England's balance of payments "may arise when there is no encrease of bank paper." These deficits would be

> the more obvious causes of a fall an our exchange, and, therefore, also of a high price of bullion.
> We are thus led back to the point (that) our two defective harvests, and the interruptions experienced in our export trade, very sufficiently account for the later fluctuation of our exchanges ... while there has been nothing which ought to be deemed extraordinary in the quantity of paper issued by the Bank of England?[29]

### Arguments against monetary austerity

"There is no unfavourable exchange which may not be corrected by a diminution in the amount of currency," Ricardo wrote to Malthus in 1812, looking forward to a postwar deflation and its consequent rise in bond prices.[30] Ever since, one of the most perverse applications of the quantity doctrine of money has been its attribution of economic recovery, especially following wars, to financial austerity rather than to modernization and prosperity.

The quantity theory's limited number of variables left no room to acknowledge the productivity improvement that enabled a rising stream of English exports of textiles and other products of industry to earn sufficient gold to enable convertibility to be resumed. Nor did Ricardo's bullionist theory acknowledge the adverse impact of monetary deflation on the country's production functions. England's recovery was as needlessly deflationary and poverty-ridden as was that following World War I.

28  Thornton, *Paper Credit*, pp. 221, 230.
29  *Ibid.*, pp. 225f.
30  Ricardo to Malthus, December 17, 1812, in *Letters*, p. 88.

Such recovery as occurred was not he result of a curtailed issue of domestic paper money leading to fewer imports. Growth in industrial exports in fact required rising imports of raw materials. "And what had the Bank done to attract gold, or to raise the value of its notes?" asks the French historian of economic thought Charles Rist. "Nothing at all!" Thus, what

> many prominent economists have adopted (as) an "orthodox" truth … is, in fact, nothing but a legend! … It was through the foreign exchange market—and not by a policy of intense deflation—that Great Britain returned to the gold standard, as the United States was to do later,

after the Civil War, when "it was not reduction in the quantity of paper money which brought the famous 'greenbacks' up to parity with gold, but an influx of gold."[31]

Determination of whether a payments deficit was caused by structural factors or by monetary inflation is always crucial for diagnosing the appropriate mode of adjustment. Monetary deflation would be called for only if a domestic overissue of paper money alone were responsible for pushing up domestic prices relative to foreign prices. But a trade deficit in itself was not sufficient indication of an overissue of paper. In any event, deflation would not be an appropriate response to trade deficits that resulted primarily from inadequate productive capacity such as crop failures. It would not substantially reduce food imports during such periods. Basic subsistence needs would have to be met regardless of how low England's domestic prices fell relative to international levels.

Monetary deflation threatened to cause more problems than it cured, by reducing prices at the cost of impairing trade and production. The danger was that output and exports might fall by even more than the money supply was reduced. Thornton thus warned that "in proceeding to limit our paper with a view to the improvement of the exchange, we ought to avoid that severity of pressure by which manufacturing industry might be seriously interrupted."[32]

In short, inflation and deflation posed different sets of problems: "We have been lately placed between two dangers; between that of a depreciated paper currency on the one hand, and that of an interruption of our paper credit, and consequent stagnation of our commerce and manufacturers on the other." Faced with this Hobson's choice between inflation and deflation, the directors of the Bank of England had shown themselves courageous in bucking "political and popular (monetarist) prejudices on this subject" and refusing to deflate the volume of paper currency as called for by the bullionists.[33]

---

[31] Charles Rist, *History of Monetary and Credit Theory,* (London: 1940), pp. 193, 195, 157.
[32] Thornton, *Paper Credit*, p. 353.
[33] Thornton, *ibid.*, p. 226.

Additions to the money supply might set industry in motion if unemployment existed, or they might push up prices under full employment conditions. But monetary deflation generally tended to impair production, quite apart from whether or not it reduced the puce level. It could work only within narrow limits before it began to stifle the economy's production functions and hence export potential. If the central bank attempted to stabilize domestic prices by contracting the money supply in the face of higher import prices for grain and other raw materials, this might derange the financial system before it reduced consumption levels (which were not very price-elastic to begin with, at least in economies whose workers lived near subsistence levels, as they did in England). Thornton warned that if England adopted the monetarist policies advocated by Ricardo, commodity prices would fall as a result of distress. The long-term impact would be one of international dependency and higher prices.

Domestic monetary policy, prices and the foreign exchange rate might not be able to restore equilibrium no matter how low they fell if the problem lay either in production functions or in capital-transfer needs. If the Bank of England imposed financial austerity in the belief that this would have no other effect than to reduce prices,

> then there will arise those other questions, which Dr. Smith leaves totally out of his consideration namely, whether the bank, in the attempt to produce this very low price, may not ... so exceedingly distress trade and discourage manufacturers as to impair ... those sources of our returning wealth to which we must chiefly trust for the restoration of our balance of trade, and for bringing back the tide of gold into Great Britain.

On this basis Thornton concluded that "the bank ought to avoid too contracted an issue of bank notes."[34] But Ricardo advocated precisely this when he wrote to Prime Minister Perceval to allay fears that a reduction in the volume of bank notes "could not be effected without impairing our resources, cramping our trade, and distressing our commerce."[35]

The monetarist views of Ricardo were controverted long before Milton Friedman and his followers revived them in modern times. As far back as 1767, Steuart rejected the doctrine that banks should respond to balance-of-payments deficits by reducing the money supply or, what was virtually the same thing, their loan volume: "It is inconsistent with their principles and interest," he wrote, "to withhold lending and giving credit, so far as is necessary for keeping up the fund of circulation to that standard which alienation and ready money demands require." Money that was lent out tended to create its own demand,

---

[34]  Thornton, *ibid.*, pp. 151ff.
[35]  Ricardo to Perceval, July 27, 1811, in *Letters*, p. 43.

for by increasing employment and output it led to more goods being produced to absorb the money. By contrast, a monetary outflow reduced bank loans and output, and hence *seemed* to lessen the need for money, but only because the country suffered from unemployment and below-potential production. This hardly was the way to improve its long-term balance of trade and payments. Monetary deflation, Steuart concluded, was a self-defeating policy. By refusing credit the central bank prevented the means to set labor and industry in motion. By calling in bank loans "it is active in destroying both itself and the country." And by letting an adverse balance of payments strip the economy of money, the central bank "only appears passive in allowing natural causes to destroy both the bank and the nation." Of what possible benefit could monetary deflation be to the economy, Steuart asked; "nay, what benefit can it ever reap from withholding its notes from those who can give good security for them! Every penny it borrows, or calls in, circumscribes its own profits, while it distresses the country."[36]

The indicated strategy for improving England's balance of trade and payments after 1815 was to lower its cost structure by increasing productivity. Enhancing production functions was the only lasting way to overcome a structural payments deficit. The idea was that new money would be created primarily to finance new means of production. And as matters worked out following the Napoleonic Wars, it was through industrial innovation that England stabilized its international payments. Upon the reopening of foreign markets, the export surge was led by textiles, whose production costs had been dramatically lowered by the steam-powered mechanization of production. Improved technology and higher output was reflected in higher unit earnings (that is, the factoral terms of trade) despite the fall in money prices for English exports. However, this price decline was utterly different from the monetary deflation and falling terms of trade implicit in the price-specie flow mechanism. By leaving productivity out of account, the latter tacitly implied that incomes in the export sector would have to decline in proportion to money and prices. No attention was paid to how money and bank credit for industrial innovation would lower long-term production costs or enable more favorable terms of export credit to be extended. Higher credit availability was supposed to increase prices, not lower them.

On the other side of the international equation, England's export surge pushed foreign economies into a postwar depression, aggravated by the general worldwide deflation. Economic recovery was achieved only by protectionism, most notably in the United States. Countries failing to protect the industries that had begun to flourish during the war became skewed into raw-materials suppliers. None of this was acknowledged by bullionist-monetarist doctrine.

---

[36] Steuart, *Principles of Political Oeconomy*, Vol. II, pp. 179, 181, 184.

Even the monetarist von Hayek has criticized Ricardo's "unwillingness to recognize that the excess of the circulation might be an effect as well as a cause of the unfavorable balance of trade." This insistence "caused the theory to remain for a long time in a much more rigid and unsatisfactory" form than that which it had originally received at the hands of Thornton."[37] Rist has gone further:

> There are few more striking examples of the persistence of a theory that has been exploded by the facts, simply because it appears to be supported by logical reasoning. Cannot deflation undo what inflation has done? Those who reason on these lines forget one important fact, that economic phenomena are "irreversible." After inflation has raised prices to a far higher level than they were before, it is impossible to return to the starting point except by destroying the income represented by the money withdrawn from circulation.[38]

Ricardo and his followers neglected the "arrow of time" and its associated irreversibility of economic process. This blindness has crippled monetarism in Britain and the United States for more than a century and a half. Austerity in England, France and other countries after World War I was as disastrous in its day as are IMF programs today. "In all these cases," evaluates Rist, "attempts were at first made to apply Ricardo's policy, only to be given up in the face of the obstinate refusal of the facts to accommodate themselves to this policy."

To Ricardo, cheap gold (that is, a high international currency value) meant scarce paper currency. This was something quite different from the effects of overly abundant gold stemming from a trade surplus, new discoveries or technological innovation in gold production. Expensive gold meant simply that the metal was scarce relative to paper money, not to commodities in general. Ricardo attributed gold exports exclusively to the relative abundance" of gold bullion or to paper money driving gold out of circulation. But this was only an after-the-fact rationalization achieved by tautologies. As noted above, Ricardo did not trace its high price to balance-of-payments deficits draining gold. "The fact that Ricardo made no distinction between … dearness or cheapness, and scarcity or abundance, is very important," points out Rist. It "vitiates his entire theory of the distribution of the precious metals."

Rist attributes this narrowness to Ricardo's position as a foreign exchange broker. Rather than making him a man of broad experience, Ricardo's position led him to take a narrow broker's-eye view of the world.

As a broker, Ricardo was correct in saying that gold exports always originate in a rise on the exchange, that is to say in a rise in the price (in national currency) of gold in other countries. But as an economist he was mistaken in thinking that there is an equilibrium—impossible to imagine or to define—

[37] Von Hayek, introduction to Thornton's *Paper Credit*, pp. 48f.
[38] Rist, *Monetary and Credit Theory*, p. 195,

between a country's gold "requirements" and the actual quantity of gold which that country acquires.[39]

In his monetary theory Ricardo was guilty of precisely what he accused Malthus of doing in the realm of trade theory, namely, taking a simplistic supply-and-demand approach without peering beneath the surface into the factors underlying supply and demand—especially demand. "The concept of quantity completely dominates Ricardo's monetary theory," continues Rist:

> ... the level of prices depends on the quantity of money, whether that money is metallic or paper ... Exchange rates are determined solely by the quantity of paper money issued in a country with a paper currency, the changes in the rate being an exact measure of the depreciation consequent upon an increase in quantity.[40]

Ricardo left out of account the causes of why the money supply changed in the first place. Rist suggests that the quantity theory of money and its associated notion of balance-of-payments adjustment should be called the Ricardian rather than the classical theory, because it was an "astonishing digression" from the truly classical thought of Thornton and Thomas Tooke. "After Ricardo one rigid conception—the quantity of money in circulation, and the limitation of that quantity—took the place of all others in the explanation of monetary phenomena."[41]

The extreme spirit that characterized both bullionists and anti-bullionists was perhaps best summed up by Malthus in the introduction to his 1820 *Principles of Political Economy*:

> The principal cause of error, and of the differences which prevail at present among the scientific writers on political economy, appears to me to be a precipitate attempt to simplify and generalize ...
>
> In political economy the desire to simplify has occasioned an unwillingness to acknowledge the operation of more causes than one in the production of particular effects; ... I have always thought that the late controversy on the bullion question presented a signal instance of this kind of error. Each party being possessed of a theory which would account for an unfavourable exchange, and an excess of the market price above the mint price of bullion, adhered to that single view of the questions, which it had been accustomed to consider as correct; and scarcely one writer seemed willing to admit of the operation of both theories, the combination of which, sometimes acting in conjunction and sometimes in opposition, could alone adequately account for the variable and complicated phenomena observable. ...

---

[39] Rist, *ibid.*, pp. 163, 165. Rist was particularly sensitive on this latter point, noting that countries might peg their currencies at low enough levels to attract gold, as France did in the 1920s and the United States in the 1930s.
[40] Rist, *ibid.*, p. 170. See also pp. 345. 349f.          [41] Rist, *ibid.*, pp. 173, 180, 175.

The same tendency to simplify and generalize, produces a still greater disinclination to allow of modifications, limitations, and exceptions to any rule or proposition, than to admit the operation of more causes than one. ...

The tendency to premature generalization occasions also, in some of the principal writers on political economy, an unwillingness to bring their theories to the test of experience. ... A theory may appear to be correct, and may really be correct under given premises; it may further appear that these premises are the same as those under which the theory is about to be applied, but a difference which might before have been unobserved, may shew itself in the difference of the results from those which were expected.[42]

### Monetary reasoning alter the bullion debate

Following in the steps of Thornton, Ricardo, Malthus and their contemporaries, the major bearer of the anti-bullionist tradition was Thomas Tooke. His anti-Ricardian financial principles demonstrated how the supply and demand for English and foreign currencies were functions not only of trade movements resulting from price changes, but also of trade that was not price-responsive (that is, where structural dependency existed or trade was monopolized), as well as capital transfers such as foreign military spending, investment and debt service. As Tooke summarized his balance-of-payments orientation, "it was gold that, by increased demand departed from the paper, and not the paper by increased quantity from the gold." The destabilizing impulse came from the balance of payments, not from the domestic money and credit system. Tooke's follower Newmarch added that one cannot usefully take a *caeteris paribus* view of the price effects of changing quantities of money, because

it is precisely these omitted elements which constitute the essence of the question ... we have found ... that by the process of the Diffusion there are brought into operation causes which go very far to invalidate the *a priori* inferences adopted on abstract grounds.[43]

Rist has criticized the errors of monetarism even more clearly. It "made the mistake of regarding money as the mechanism which is *superimposed* on a pre-existing exchange system, whereas in fact it constitutes an integral part of the economic system."[44] The result is a travesty of scientific method inasmuch

---

[42]  Malthus, *Principles of Political Economy* (London: 1820), pp. 4ff., 8f.

[43]  Rist, *Monetary and Credit Theory*, pp. 189, 191, 243, citing Tooke and Newmarch, *A History of Prices*, Vol. VI, pp. 194f. As Rist has summarized Tooke's position: "The rise in prices is thus effected not through one channel alone, as Ricardo imagined, but through two different channels—expansion of the home demand for goods due to successive increases in the amount of paper money put into circulation, and a rise in the price of goods imported due to the depreciation of the *paper money on the foreign exchange market*, the latter deriving from many causes independent of the quantity of money."

[44]  Rist, *ibid.*, p. 162.

as it is based on a partial rather than a holistic view of the economic system. Schumpeter criticizes the methodology of monetarism in similar terms. His own discussion begins by "building up the analysis of money, currency and banking" and then adding complications in the credit and paper-money superstructure. "But logically, it is by no means clear that the most useful method is to start from the coin ... practically and analytically a credit theory of money is possibly preferable to a monetary theory of credit."[45]

The reasons *why* money is created, and the conditions under which it is created, are as important as the bare fact of its creation. If credit is extended to increase output, it tends to be self-justifying and self-amortizing. It need not inflate prices if it is issued under conditions of unemployed resources. Only if it is issued for consumption purposes or under full employment conditions is it likely to be inflationary in the manner the monetarists anticipate. Gold may be drained from the monetary system for reasons unrelated to price changes, for example to finance structural payments deficits or capital transfers. Schumpeter concludes:

> The commodity-trade theory of international finance is thus open to the criticism—as is the theory of international values—that its conception of the phenomena with which it undertakes to deal is much too narrow. ... A theory of international finance that pivots on commodity trade will naturally emphasize the equilibrating role of variations in relative prices.

By contrast, the role of capital transfers

> such as the South American loans and mining stocks, for instance, that were being issued in 1824 and that for the time being dominated the London money market left no footprints in basic theory. For us, the exactly opposite approach seems more natural: we are likely to look upon international capital transactions as the basic phenomenon to which commodity trade is subsidiary, by which it is controlled, from which it must be understood. And this point ... would suffice in itself to divorce modern analysis from what may be described as the Commodity-Trade Theory of international finance (or of international payments or of international gold movements).[46]

Why did monetarism make these oversimplifications? Why were they accepted and popularized to the exclusion of more realistic analysis? The theory's self-justification has been that its methodology is the logical step-by-step way to proceed. But it was not logic applied to the real world, merely to the parallel universe in which Ricardo and other creditor spokesmen wanted to believe. It is a caricature of scientific method, as Malthus perceived in the passages quoted above.

---

[45] Schumpeter, *History of Economic Analysis*, p. 717.
[46] *Ibid.*, pp. 732f.

The explanation for monetarism's success lies mainly in the extent to which it has served creditor interests and opponents of state intervention. As Part II has traced, the key to the spirit of laissez faire—of which monetarism is a major anti-government branch—is to assume that economic intervention can only aggravate society's problems, and that more money can only inflate prices and worsen the trade balance. Starting with this conclusion—one that leads in practice to world polarization rather than convergence—monetarism works backwards logically to construct a set of assumptions and theories that will support its argument.

In assuming that changes in the money supply cannot influence the level of employment and output (save in exceptional depression situations) the bullionist theory implies that money creation can only influence prices. Assuming velocity and output to remain stable, money and prices are held to move together. This approach reflects the build-up of productive powers. It leaves less developed countries in the unenviable position of being credit-starved raw-materials exporters who must sell off ownership of their resources to pay their foreign debts.

The reason why monetarism achieves in practice just the opposite of what it promises to achieve in principle is that it takes for granted society's existing technological and institutional structure rather than recognizing that this is subject to transformation, given adequate financing and protection. Monetarism assumes full employment to occur automatically, and to maintain itself at equitable world levels without any need for government action.

Why should anyone accept these narrow assumptions? The alternative view, that a growing money supply may spur higher output, provides a motive for nations to regulate their economic activity and foreign trade so as to run balance-of-payments surpluses which in turn will support their money and credit systems. This though is anathema to free traders, who urged governments to leave business—and especially finance—alone.

# 15

## Debt Service and the Terms of Trade

The hundred years spanning the end of the Napoleonic Wars in 1815 and the outbreak of World War I in 1914 were unique for their military and financial tranquility. The world's monetary and balance-of-payments needs were satisfied by major new gold discoveries beginning in the 1840s, and by a rising flow of international lending.

At the Congress of Vienna in 1815 England did not demand repayment of the loans and subsidies it had granted its allies. The Treaty of Paris did not even impose damages on France. But the allies did levy reparations after Napoleon broke the peace. Occupying France with 150,000 troops, they obliged France to pay support costs for the military force. Although its treasury was bare, France was able to handle the situation by turning over bonds for the entire sum to the allied powers after a reparations conference held in January 1817. Alexander Baring and the Hopes banking family then sold these bonds to the public in London. Prices started at 55 per cent of par in February 1817 and rose to 74 percent by October 1818 as the idea of funding international obligations gained acceptance. By servicing these bonds conscientiously, France helped establish a market for international loans that expanded throughout the remainder of the century. After all, if nearly bankrupt France with its historically bad payments record could handle such loans, so could other countries, it seemed.[1]

Within domestic economies, paper money and bank credit supplemented gold and silver to a growing degree. The role of stock and bond markets expanded along with that of the banks, which extended loans—at least in principle—for self-amortizing projects capable of generating the funds to pay off the loans with interest. When such payment could not be made, corporate and personal debtors were permitted to wipe their obligations off the books by declaring bankruptcy. Debtors' prisons were phased out, making palatable the dissolution of anti-usury laws. Institutionalized saving and investment developed on an unprecedented scale through such new facilities as savings banks and, in the latter half of the century, industrial investment banks.

---

[1] On Britain's willingness to cancel its wartime loans see J. H. Clapham, "Loans and Subsidies in Time of War," *Economic Journal*, XXVII (1917), pp. 495–501. For a description of how France handled its reparations see Otto Wolff, *Ouvrard: Speculator of Genius, 1770–1846* (New York: 1962), pp. 133–46.

A large proportion of savings was lent abroad, enabling capital-importing countries to finance their trade deficits and public infrastructure. An expansion of productive powers throughout the world economy helped carry a growing volume of international as well as domestic debt.

Raw-materials exporters had not yet fallen into chronic food and energy deficits. Many, such as Canada, supplied savings to their mother countries as their export income exceeded domestic investment opportunities. Egypt, Turkey and Persia were despoiled, but that was largely because their rulers were more willing to accept creditor demands than, say, the American states that defaulted. Most debtor economies were not as readily sacrificed to meet their foreign obligations as is the case today.

Only after World War I did nations begin to compile systematic balance-of-payments statistics on foreign direct and indirect investment, the remission of earnings and interest to foreign investors, and the repatriation of funds by immigrants. John Williams of Harvard worked with some of the leading New York international banks in the 1920s to pave the way for the Commerce Department to assume responsibility for collecting U.S. data. Prior to this time the lack of statistics, along with an absence of serious debt-servicing problems, fostered a neglect of the impact of foreign lending, debt service, military spending and other capital transfers. But economists could ignore the phenomena only as long as they remained relatively unproblematic.

### The causes and consequences of postwar monetary deflations

As countries returned to gold convertibility after the Napoleonic Wars, the world economy suffered from a general deflation. Instead of restoring gold convertibility at its postwar 1815 value, England targeted the prewar gold parity (as it would do again after World War I). This benefited creditors—Ricardo's class—as prices for goods and labor declined by a quarter to a third of their wartime levels. This price deflation increased the purchasing power of bonds, but stifled credit creation in the face of the burgeoning Industrial Revolution.

Depressed conditions plagued England, save for industrial spurts in 1817, 1824 and the early 1830s. This was the result of "real", that is physical, causes as well as purely monetary ones. Thomas Tooke cited six factors as operating during the years 1814-37: "good harvests [lowering crop prices], favourable foreign exchange, removal of obstructions to foreign supplies and the emergence of new sources of raw materials, falling rates of freight and insurance, technological progress, increasing supply of capital, hence lower rates of interest."[2]

---

[2]   Schumpeter, *History of Economic Analysis*, p. 713, citing Tooke, *History of Prices*, Vol. II, pp. 348–49.

Parallel to the debate between free traders and protectionists over England's Corn Laws was that between advocates of monetary deflation and proponents of the policy they called "inflationary" because it did not advocate rolling prices back to their 1797 position. Malthus pointed out that Tooke's data on wartime economic activity showed that "the products of the land, the labour and the capital of this country, never in any period of our history increased for twenty-two years together with the same rapidity as in the twenty-two years from 1793 to 1814 inclusive." Population had grown between 25 and 33 per cent, and agricultural output rose proportionally as capital was applied to the land with growing efficiency. Exports of manufactures actually doubled during these years, accompanied by an unprecedented "increase of draining and inclosures, roads and bridges, canals and harbours, paving and other local improvements, machinery, shipping and exciseable commodities."[3] But despite the return to peace after 1815, the volume of British exports diminished, except for the products of cotton and wool "for which new and increasing markets have been opened." Imports also fell.

The bullionists and their successors, the Currency School, refused to acknowledge any unfavorable economic impact resulting from shrinking the money supply. Ricardo went so far as to deny that the financial sector had any impact on business conditions. Commercial crises, he insisted, resulted from allocating resources along more efficient lines as trade patterns shifted: "The commencement of war after a long peace, or of peace after a long war, generally produces considerable distress in trade. It changes in a great degree the nature of the employments to which the respective capitals of countries were being devoted." Prosperity would resume once resources were diverted to their most efficient peacetime channels.

Ricardo rationalized that industrial nations suffered more from business crises than agricultural societies because their physical capital and industrial labor force were less flexible than was labor working with simple tools, not because their industries were more capital intensive and their credit systems more highly leveraged. The severity of business crises would tend to increase as the division of labor proceeded, making labor and capital less mobile from one sector to another.

> In rich and powerful countries, where large capitals are invested in machinery, more distress will be experienced from a revulsion in trade, than in poorer countries where there is proportionally a much smaller amount of fixed, and a much larger amount of circulating capital, and where consequently more work is done by the labour of men. It is not so difficult to withdraw a circulating as a fixed capital, from any employment in which it may be engaged. It is often impossible

---

[3] Malthus, "Tooke on High and Low Prices," *Quarterly Review*, April 1823, reprinted in *Occasional Papers*, pp. 158–59.

to divert the machinery which may have been erected for one manufacture, to the purpose of another; but the clothing, the food, and the lodging of the labourer in one employment may be devoted to the support of the labourer in another. ... This, however, is an evil to which a rich nation must submit; and it would not be more reasonable to complain of it, than it would be in a rich merchant to lament that his ship was exposed to the dangers of the sea, whilst his poor neighbour's cottage was safe from all such hazard.[4]

This view ignored the financial complications with which Ricardo should have been most familiar in his profession of stockbroker. The Currency School followed his doctrines in promising that countries could overcome business cycles or "overbanking" and enable economic growth to proceed smoothly if they only would refrain from "overissuing" money and causing gold prices to rise.

It was widely recognized that trade and payments deficits occasionally might oblige countries to borrow, but the general impression was that such indebtedness was not problematic. According to Thornton, it could not continue for long. "To suppose large and successive balances to be formed into a debt, is to assume an accumulation of debt, which is almost equally incredible."[5] Creditor nations would not lend unless they were convinced that debtor countries could pay. Inasmuch as foreign loans were less secure than domestic investment, Thornton believed that prosperous nations would prefer to invest their growing wealth at home rather than lend it abroad. Payments-deficit countries for their part had a healthy "disinclination to borrow" in the face of their limited ability to service foreign debts.

Ricardo made no mention of borrowing to import food to feed people who otherwise would starve, and also ignored war spending and reparations debts. Borrowing was supposed to be contracted only for sound business purposes. Whereas Malthus insisted to Ricardo that debt service and other capital transfers could depress exchange rates (and hence gold prices), Ricardo assumed that such transfers were for productive loans invested in projects that generated the revenue to repay the creditor with interest, so there would be no debt problem. As he put the crux of his argument with Malthus:

> You appear to me not sufficiently to consider the circumstances which induce one country to contract a debt to another. In all the cases you bring forward you always suppose the debt already contracted, forgetting that I uniformly contend that it is the relative state of the currency which is the motive to the contract itself. The corn, I say, will not be bought unless money be relatively redundant; you answer me by supposing it already bought and the question to be only concerning the payment. A merchant will not contract a debt for corn to a foreign country unless he is fully convinced that he shall obtain for that corn

4   Ricardo, *Principles of Political Economy*, p. 265.
5   Thornton, *Paper Credit of Great Britain*, p. 142.

more money than he contracts to pay for it, and if the commerce of the two countries were limited to these transactions it would as satisfactorily prove to me that money was redundant in one country as that corn was redundant in the other. It would prove too that nothing but money was redundant.[6]

Thornton recognized that for borrowings that were *not* self-amortizing in a relatively short period of time, payment in the form of gold would, beyond a point, impair the credit foundation of domestic production. Whereas monetary inflows—or a domestic credit inflation—might push up prices, monetary out-flows or deflation tended to reduce output and income. while payment in the form of exports would impair the terms of trade, as the goods "which the country is able to furnish as means of canceling its debt are not in such demand as to afford the prospect of a tempting or even of a tolerable price." In the passage quoted in the preceding chapter (fn 17), he pointed out that in order to sell more exports, the capital-paying country might need to lower its prices by so much as "to render them excessively cheap. It would be necessary, therefore, that the bank [of England] should ... very greatly diminish" its paper circulation. "But the bank in the attempt to produce this very low price may so exceedingly distress trade and discourage manufacturers as to impair ... the restoration of our balance of trade."[7]

Paying foreign debts in gold would reduce the money supply. Paying in England's own currency would depreciate the price of sterling, lowering the gold value of sterling-denominated export prices. *The supply and demand situation in foreign exchange markets thus threatened to overshadow comparative-cost disparities*, making currency shifts increasingly important in determining international prices.

### Mill's theory of how capital transfers influence the terms of trade

John Stuart Mill developed the theoretical basis for analyzing the impact of debt payments along these lines. Following Malthus in emphasizing supply conditions, he traced how capital transfers led currency values to diverge from their relative purchasing-power ratios, he demonstrated how financial payments ("capital") from one country to another influenced comparative prices *by over-laying a mutual demand for commodities with an extraordinary demand for currencies by debtor countries to meet their foreign obligations*. Instead of commodities being exchanged for one another in accordance with their relative labor content, they were sold for money, which also was being used to pay debts, for military purposes and for other non-trade transactions. These transactions often were not subject to price considerations, and did not involve any labor content.

---

6   Ricardo to Malthus, June 18, 1811, in Ricardo, *Letters*, p. 27.
7   Thornton, *Paper Credit of Great Britain*, pp. 151–52.

In keeping with the wine/cloth example so often used for expository purposes, Figure 15.1 illustrates Portugal's and England's offer curves. As Chapter 5 has reviewed, $OE$ represents England's offer curve of cloth for wine, while $OP_1$ represents Portugal's offer curve of port for English cloth. As Portugal exports more wine, it will receive less and less cloth (or English sterling) per unit of wine as markets become glutted.

Matters are complicated by the fact that products are not really bartered, but are sold for foreign currency or on credit $(OP_2)$. Countries no longer need to stop importing when they run out of goods to export. By throwing more escudos onto international currency markets, Portugal may keep buying English cloth in the face of falling sterling receipts for its wine exports. This will depress the price of escudos, to be sure. Also making escudos cheaper relative to sterling would be Portugal's need to pay debts to England. This lowers the sterling price of escudo-denominated wine exports. To pay in sterling, Portugal must export an extra $(OW_2-OW_1)$ worth of port.

Figure 15.1 Portugal's and England's Offer Curves

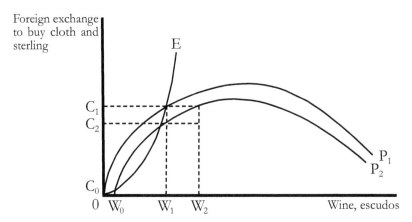

Sales on credit lead to settlement payments less than the nominal value of the wine and cloth being exchanged, but will reappear at some future time, at a level that includes interest charges (about which financier Ricardo was silent). Matters are further complicated if Portugal services debts stemming from past borrowings, or if it must remit profits to English investors on their ownership of Portuguese vineyards or other assets. Portugal must finance these transfers by either exporting more wine $(OW_2-OW_1$, turning the terms of trade against itself) or by curtailing its cloth imports and thus losing the gains from trade.

Portugal may transfer capital directly in the form of gold, or may supply its currency to be converted into gold or creditor-nation currency. Either of these alternatives tends to turn the terms of trade against it. "Let us suppose a supply exceeding the demand," wrote Mill in his 1848 *Principles of Political Economy*. The extra quantity of commodities or currency can find a market only by generating an additional demand at lower prices. "The value falls, and brings the article within the reach of more numerous customers, or induces those who were already consumers to make increased purchases."[8] But will this enable the country to balance its international payments in the face of substantial capital transfers? Mill assumed that it would *if* a relatively mild price decline substantially extended the market (that is, if this trade remained highly price elastic). But this itself was a special condition.

Under normal conditions, payment in gold has a deflationary monetary effect on internal prices, lowering export prices. Payment in paper currency may be inflationary domestically, but on international currency markets it tends to depress the value of Portugal's escudo relative to that of sterling. This glutting of currency markets makes Portuguese exports less costly in international terms, and imports more costly in domestic escudo-prices.

The upshot is that Portuguese winemakers must work longer to produce more exports to exchange for given quantities of English cloth or currency to make capital transfers. As the escudo is devalued, a widening foreign demand may support the price of Portugal's exports somewhat, so that they need not fall by the entire depreciation rate. But Mill's analysis showed that the added export volume falls in price to some degree, and in some cases dramatically. Domestic prices—and hence the terms of trade—will shift until they produce equilibrium in the balance of payments. Unless Portugal enacts protective tariffs to reduce its demand for imports or promotes import substitution, making capital transfers will depress its terms of trade.

In his earlier *Essays on Some Unsettled Questions of Political Economy*, Mill used the example of German linen instead of Portuguese wine. He supposed that England had to pay money to Germany, and that it raised the money by selling gold. This would deflate its domestic prices, including the price of cloth, enabling England to export the latter instead of money. Mill pointed out that this decline in English cloth prices also would reduce the price of cloth in Germany, while the rise (in sterling terms) of German linen prices would increase linen prices

> in England also, and the demand for it will diminish. Although the increased exportation of cloth takes place at a lower price, and the diminished importation of linen at a higher, yet the total money value of the exportation would probably increase, that of the importation diminish. As cloth fell in price and linen rose, there would be some particular price of both articles at which the cloth exported, and the linen imported, would exactly pay for each other. At this point prices would remain, because money would then cease to move out of England into Germany.[9]

---

[8]  Mill, *Principles of Political Economy*, p. 447.
[9]  Mill, *Essays on Some Unsettled Questions of Political Economy*, pp. 15–16.

However, Mill then cast doubt on the happy assumption that a price adjustment by itself would suffice to balance international payments. If trade were relatively price-inelastic—as much trade is in practice—international payments might achieve balance only with a great sacrifice by the capital-paying country (England in this case):

> If the fall of cloth did not much increase the demand for it in Germany and the rise of linen did not diminish very rapidly the demand for it in England, much money must pass before the equilibrium is restored, cloth would fall very much, and linen would rise, until England, perhaps, had to pay nearly as much for it as when she produced it herself.

"The greater the efflux of money required to restore the equilibrium," Mill concluded,

> the greater will be the gain of Germany; both by the fall of cloth [prices], and by the rise of her general prices. ... The result to the tributary country is a diminution of her share in the advantage of foreign trade ... she pays dearer for her imports, in two ways, because she pays more money, and because that money is of higher value, the money incomes of her inhabitants being of smaller amount.[10]

Ireland afforded an example of a tributary country that "pays dearer for her imports in consequence of her [landlord] absentees" who remitted their rental income back to England. Commenting on this phenomenon already in 1804, Leslie Foster contrasted the behavior of absentee English landowners to Irish landlords who tended to spend more of their rents at home:

> Perhaps the most correct mode of considering the effect of the absentees in the abstract would be, that, had they continued in Ireland, they would have given birth to a quantity of produce equal in value to their rents, and consumed it in Ireland; but that living in England, they still gave birth to an equal amount of Irish produce [which was exported], but consume it in England ... but though the quantities produced and consumed in both cases appear to be the same in value, they are certainly different in the nature of the items of which they are composed.
>     The Irish produce which would have been consumed in Ireland, had the proprietor remained at home ... on his emigration ... become such as the foreign market shall demand. The consumers also are different; for it is not to be supposed that the absentee spends his income in the purchase of Irish commodities: on the contrary, he spends his Irish rents in the encouragement of English industry; but then he is the cause that others become the consumers of Irish produce of another description, and to an equal amount. The Irish producers are also different. Had the proprietor remained at home, he would have called forth industry probably on his own estate, and in its immediate neighbourhood, but when settled in England, the proprietor of an estate in Munster may per-

---

[10]  *Ibid.*, pp. 17, 43.

haps, to a much greater degree, encourage the industry of Ulster. ... It is this circumstance, perhaps more than any other, which has made the absentee the object of jealousy in Ireland.[11]

The parallel with today's Third World countries hardly can be missed. *Capital transfers depress the terms of trade.* The more international funds a nation borrows today to finance its trade and payments deficit, the more costly it will be to pay these debts by exporting relatively price-inelastic raw materials in years to come.

In Figure 15.1, in addition to purchasing sterling to pay for its cloth imports ($OE$), Portugal must make capital transfers. At an initial zero-import position it must give $OW_0$ in wine to pay for the capital transfer. But if it already is exporting $OW_1$ in wine for $OC_1$ of cloth, it now must provide $OW_2$ worth of wine. This payment typically would increase the price of sterling (or depreciate that of the Portuguese escudo) *beyond* the commodity-price "barter" effects, *leading the two countries' exchange rates to diverge from their comparative purchasing-power ratios.* The goods of the capital-paying country would become a buy.

Neither Mill nor his contemporaries addressed the unemployment conditions raised by Tucker and Steuart a century earlier. Their logic implied that if English labor and capital were unemployed, Portugal's capital transfer might increase English employment, investment and output without pushing up prices or reflecting itself in higher import demand. If England used its receipt of debt service to modernize its capital plant and increase output, no inflationary pressure need occur.

A kindred example occurred in the United States in the 1950s. Foreign investment inflows into the stock market provided easy financing for corporations, higher levels of domestic investment, more rapid productivity gains and technological leadership, and hence falling rather than rising prices for domestic and export goods. The effect was to improve the balance of trade and payments on private-sector account, although rising military spending pushed the overall balance of payments into deficit after 1951. Overseas military spending was undertaken partly to provide the world economy with more dollars to alleviate the dollar shortage in international reserves. Adjustment thus came by government policy, not by "automatic market forces."

Mill's analysis casts doubt on the ability of the classical adjustment mechanisms—monetary deflation, currency depreciation and diverting production from domestic to foreign markets—to restore equilibrium in international

---

[11] Leslie Foster, *An Essay on the Principle of Commercial Exchanges, and more particularly of the Exchange between Great Britain and Ireland* (London: 1804), pp. 23–46, excerpted in John Ramsay McCulloch, *The Literature of Political Economy* (London: 1845), pp. 171–72. In 1825 the House of Commons appointed a committee to discuss the problem of absentee expenditure.

payments to virtually any degree. These three equilibrating mechanisms assume what has become known as "elasticity optimism" (see Chapter 13, p. 256), a belief that demand for a country's exports remains sufficiently elastic that increased foreign purchases will *more* than compensate for a fall in the capital-paying country's export prices. A modest lowering of a country's prices will substantially increase world demand for its exports and/or substantially reduce its own demand for imports.

Only on this condition can international equilibrium be achieved. But each of these adjustment processes has a limit—the point beyond which export demand becomes inelastic. When the increase in foreign demand for exports is *less* than the decline in their prices (that is, as long as foreign demand elasticity for exports is less than unity), the balance of payments will be impaired rather than aided. Once exports (or paper currency issues) reach this point, further export production (or supply of currency on exchange markets) will not raise more foreign exchange, but will set in motion a spiral of collapsing economic fortunes.

This explains the debt and import dependency that burdened many countries. But Ricardian theorists assumed that monetary movements, price and cost shifts were merely marginal. The happy and optimum balance was not supposed to be disturbed except temporarily. Neither debt overhead nor structural dependency mattered, and hence were deemed "exogenous."

### How international payments were balanced prior to World War I

Not until the 1920s were the limits to capital-transfer capacity for industrial nations probed. Until then, monetary and financial developments did not pose severe problems of currency depreciation, inflation or deflation. As Rist has observed, Ricardo "has nothing to say about the influence of precious metals on the general prosperity of the world, a matter to which eighteenth-century writers gave considerable thought; as far as the abundance or scarcity of the precious metals is concerned, his attitude approaches one of complete indifference; this was to become the gospel of his followers and was strongly criticized by Newmarch when the Californian and Australian gold discoveries were made."[12] Countries were assumed to be capable of running ongoing payments surpluses that would draw gold into their domestic monetary systems at a rate sufficient to finance new investment and economic expansion under full employment conditions. The major new gold discoveries made after 1849 ensured that economic activity and its necessary superstructure of paper credit would not suffer from a lack of gold backing.

---

[12]  Rist, *History of Monetary and Credit Theory*, p. 160.

The nineteenth century's largest capital transfer was France's $3 billion indemnity to Prussia in 1871 at the end of the Franco-Prussian War. France raised the funds neither by major increases in exports at falling prices nor by currency collapse as money flowed out. The government simply borrowed the funds (this time in large part domestically), in addition to selling off French foreign investments, much as it had done after the Napoleonic Wars. The adjustments associated with this capital transfer were concentrated in the financial markets in the form of high interest rates, not in the commodity markets via price responses. Germany invested its receipt of capital in economic infrastructure, so that the capital inflow increased its productivity.

Most adverse international balances were settled by borrowing. This required higher interest rates to attract short-term funds from abroad, a policy described by Thornton in 1802 and Tooke in 1838. One reason why the adjustment came on capital account rather than on trade account was that price adjustments took too long to lead to increased exports, as Malthus pointed out in 1811:

> The real state of the case seems to be, that though the effects of a redundancy of currency upon the exchange are sure, they are slow compared with the effects of those mercantile transactions not connected with the question of currency; and, while the former of these causes is proceeding in its operations with a steady and generally uniform pace, the more rapid movements of the latter are opposing, aggravating or modifying these operations in various ways, and producing all those complex, and seemingly inconsistent appearances, which are to be found in the computed exchange.[13]

Schumpeter notes that in 1832, J. Horsely Palmer, bullionist governor of the Bank of England, pointed to the key role played by interest-rate adjustments in the workings of the price-specie flow mechanism. "Accepting an unfavorable turn in foreign exchanges as a sign of an 'unduly' great expansion of credit, he averred that the Bank could prevent or stop an outflow of gold by raising its rate: the increased rate would reduce borrowing; reduced borrowing would mean a smaller volume of transactions and employment, and lower prices; reduced prices would increase exports and decrease imports; and this would turn the balance of payments, hence exchange rates."[14]

But the price-specie flow mechanism remained out of favor until it was re-popularized around the turn of the twentieth century by Frank Taussig of Harvard University. Frank Fetter has described how Taussig established it as "part of the oral tradition in the United States," representing the mechanism as

---

[13]  Malthus, review of the bullionist literature, *Quarterly Review*, February 1811, in *Occasional Papers*, p. 92. See also Malthus's letter to Ricardo, February 23, 1812, in Ricardo, *Letters*, p. 82.

[14]  Schumpeter, *History of Economic Analysis*, p. 698.

"the accepted classical analysis" and associating it indelibly with the name of Hume (neglecting to note how Tucker, Steuart and other contemporaries of Hume had qualified the bare theory). The mechanism was not accepted outside of academic circles in England or America, much less in continental Europe. "Witnesses before the [Parliamentary] committees of 1848, 1857, and 1858, and articles in the *Economist* and *Bankers' Magazine* … stressed not commodity price changes but interest rate changes as the cause of international adjustment," influencing short-term banking and financial movements by borrowing on capital account. "The closest approach of any witness to an organized presentation of the familiar stereotype of specie-flow price-adjustment came from J. G. Hubbard, governor of the Bank [of England] in 1853-1855, to the Committee on Bank Acts of 1857. But Hubbard presented the analysis simply to ridicule it. Much of what he said is suggestive of modern criticism, based upon elasticity assumptions, that monetary policy cannot influence favorably the relation of the value of exports and imports of goods and services."[15]

Hubbard testified that the problem was not so much that declining prices and rising exports took time to respond to reductions in the money supply, but that *price declines would not necessarily have a favorable impact on the net balance of trade at all.* International demand was limited by the fact that so many exports were price-inelastic:

> If a drain of bullion does take place, and if, according to their theory, the value of all commodities were affected, the result would be, according to their idea, an export of goods in order to restore the amount of our claims upon the rest of the commercial world, and to recover our treasure; but if you measure the effect of a fall of prices upon the value of such commodities, you will find that it has the contrary effect, lowering the amount of our claims upon the rest of the world, instead of increasing it.
>
> Imagine, for instance, that our exports were £100,000,000. annually, and that a fall of prices of 10 per cent took place in consequence of the export of bullion, according to the prices theory, so far from our having a larger claim upon foreigners we should have a less claim, because we should reduce pro tanto the amount of value of the goods sent to them. And supposing that the prices of our exports would be lessened, the effect which took place here (according to that notion of a fall of prices by the export of bullion) is reversed abroad. There they have got our bullion, and therefore their prices would be higher … so that the theory appears to me really to break down with reference to the effects which are supposed. I believe that the effect of the export of bullion upon the rate of prices has no reference whatever to the prices of commodities. It has an effect, and a very important one, upon the price of interest-bearing securities, because, as the rate of interest varies the value of commodities which embodied

---

[15]  Frank W. Fetter, *Development of British Monetary Orthodoxy: 1797–1875* (Cambridge: 1965), pp. 228–29.

that interest is necessarily powerfully affected. ... But the action upon prices I totally disbelieve; I think it is untenable in theory, and irreconcilable with facts.[16]

It thus seemed plausible that payments-deficit countries might balance their accounts by raising their interest rates to attract foreign short-term money, while nations experiencing payments surpluses (and hence additions to their supply of loanable funds) would experience downward pressure on their interest rates, spurring capital outflows. This apparently equilibrating process might destabilize payments if trade-surplus economies also experienced an influx of long-term investment capital. That would increase their production and export functions, while trade-deficit countries found that paying high interest rates to stabilize their exchange rate discouraged new domestic investment. This kind of problem became clearer after World War I, as Williams observed in 1932:

> A rise of prices in one country relative to others ... may in fact attract capital from abroad. Rising prices usually mean rising profits [at least, early in the business cycle], which attract capital, which in turn is likely to cause further rise of prices, and hence more profits, and hence more capital inflow. This cumulative movement is more apt to be accompanied by gold inflow than by gold outflow, and the gold inflow provides a monetary basis for still further expansion. Recent investigations of the prewar movements of gold show, in the case of both England and the United States, a clearly defined tendency for gold to flow inward during prosperity and outward during depression.[17]

Monetary inflows in boom conditions may become cumulative and self-feeding in a financially sophisticated economy. Interest rates fall and prices rise for stocks and bonds, attracting foreign capital, often in excess of the amount by which commodity-price inflation may impair the trade balance. These capital inflows spur new investment, lowering production costs. Even if commodity prices do respond, rising export prices may improve rather than reduce the balance of trade if foreign demand for exports is price-inelastic.

It may take a number of years for inflation to erode profits and spur a market outflow. For one thing, countries receiving payments inflows could choose to not monetize them. Taussig reminded his students that the Federal Reserve System

> was expected to protect the country's financial and industrial structure against the impact of international gold movements. ... A great reserve in the Federal Banks obviously can serve as a buffer against external strain. Pressure from an inflowing gold supply may be easily absorbed by it. ... Conversely, an outflow may simply diminish the store held by them, again leaving the country at large undisturbed.[18]

[16]  Fetter, *ibid.*, pp. 228–29.
[17]  John Williams, "The Crisis of the Gold Standard," *Foreign Affairs*, January 1932, reprinted in *Postwar Monetary Plans and Other Essays* (3rd ed., New York 1947), p. 156.
[18]  Frank Taussig, *International Trade* (New York: 1827), pp. 213-14. See also pp. 331–32.

As nations managed their domestic monetary systems with increasing skill, they insulated the domestic monetary base from foreign trade and payments. Williams explained how the Federal Reserve offset the Treasury's receipt of foreign gold by "sterilization," selling government securities in the open market to absorb enough funds to offset the nation's gold inflow.

> Our gold holdings are so large that the [Federal] Reserve banks can afford to ignore the effect of gold movements upon themselves. By offsetting the gold flow we keep our domestic price level stable and throw the entire strain of trade adjustment upon foreign price levels. ... In 1925–29 [a period of inflation, led by U.S. stock-market prices] our gold holdings did not increase, though there were some rather violent inward movements. From October 1929 to July 1931, we imported $573 million of gold [in the face of a sharp deflation].[19]

The Fed reasoned that most of the subsequent inflow in the 1930s was refugee capital seeking a safe haven in anticipation of World War II rather than resulting from America's price competitiveness. As a result of such sterilization practices, the money supply of one country no longer is tied directly to that of others.

### Tendency for the capital account to finance the trade account

The above caveats made theories of automatic trade balance quite tenuous. At best there was a rough pragmatic faith that capital inflows would finance trade deficits. In the 1920s this faith took the form of the so-called Law of Promotions and Detractions. International payments in any given sector were supposed to generate compensating flows elsewhere. The receipt of interest and principal from Europe on its war debts to the United States, for instance, was held to "absorb" (that is, detract from) Europe's ability to purchase U.S. exports. Conversely, American investment abroad was supposed to promote Europe's international purchasing power for U.S. goods and services.

This theory was developed primarily to evaluate whether the U.S. trade balance would remain in surplus or move into deficit in response to the receipt of inter-Ally debt service. Commerce Department economists held that America's trade surplus since 1873 had been "promoted" mainly by U.S. payments to European investors on their capital holdings in the United States. Balancing the receipt of new investment funds from Europe against the reciprocal flow of remitted earnings on existing investments in America, the economists hypothesized that this measure "has had more influence than any other in determining the nature and amount of our trade balance."[20]

---

[19]  Williams, "The Crisis of the Gold Standard," *op. cit.*, pp. 159–60. See also Taussig, *International Trade*, pp. 213–14.

[20]  U.S. Department of Commerce, "The Balance of International Payments of the United States in 1922," p. 22. For greater detail on the Law of Promotions and Detractions in the context of its time, see Appendix A to Hudson, "A Financial Payments-Flow Analysis of

The promotions and detractions theory governed U.S. official thinking for a number of years. Arms and raw-materials shipments and loans during World War I had enabled the United States to liquidate its net indebtedness to Europeans. The nation had entered the war a net debtor of some $3.7 billion and emerged a net creditor by this same amount. By 1924 it had increased its net investment position to $7 billion. There was general belief that the United States must either move into trade deficit or increase foreign investment to provide Europe with funds to service its debt to the United States. (Only in unofficial circles was it recommended that the United States solve the problem simply by suspending the inter-Ally debts, which finally occurred in 1931 under crisis conditions.) "If the European Governments that have not yet started to pay their debts to the United States Government should do so," the 1923 report speculated, "there can be little doubt that imports of merchandise would regularly equal or exceed exports, as is usually the case with creditor countries."[21]

The U.S. trade balance did indeed decline from $4 billion in 1919 to $0.7 billion in 1922 and $0.4 billion in 1923. Thereafter, however, it increased, and by 1926 the Department of Commerce began to challenge the earlier view "that our Nation will presently enter a long era characterized by a constantly unfavorable trade balance ... when the yield of our foreign investments actually does exceed the volume of our new investment abroad."[22] The Commerce Department acknowledged that "so-called creditor nations have usually had unfavor-

---

U.S. International Transactions: 1960-1968," in New York University: Graduate School of Business Administration, *The Bulletin*, triple issue Nos. 61-63 (March 1970).

It hardly is surprising that American protectionists had a different view of matters. In the mid-1880s, Congressman John A. Kasson of Iowa viewed the nation's balance on capital account (including monetary transfers of gold) as a residual of its trade balance and hence as a function of national tariff policy. In "Free Trade not the International Law of the Almighty," published by the American Iron and Steel Association (*Tariff Tract* No. 3 [1884], p. 7), he observed that "If money is not real wealth it is an enormously powerful instrument in the production of wealth." He traced how

> the change in our balance of trade with foreign countries ... has caused a cessation in the payment of interest to foreign countries, has swollen the contents of our savings banks and the credit balances of our depositors, has enabled us to resume speccic payments, has reduced interest to the lowest point ever known in the history of the country, both for governments and individuals ... and has so magnified the capital of the country that borrowers have ceased to seek lenders ...

America's trade surplus freed the country from having to borrow from England. Its gold output could be monetized at home to finance increasing prosperity as abundant credit and low interest rates would finance increasing domestic investment, employment and wage levels.

[21] U.S. Department of Commerce, "The Balance of International Payments of the United States in 1923," p. 19.

[22] U.S. Department of Commerce, "The Balance of International Payments of the United States in 1926," p. 47.

able balances of trade" (the outstanding case being England), but pointed out
that by contrast, the United States traditionally ran a deficit in services. Its
merchant marine was not as remunerative as that of Britain, showing a modest
net deficit from 1925 onward. U.S. residents traveled and spent more abroad,
resulting in a travel and tourism deficit of about $500 million annually. Its
immigrants remitted about $250 million annually back to their families abroad,
and U.S. enterprises paid a substantial flow of dividends and interest to foreign
investors. The Commerce Department report concluded that "When our
investments abroad yield us more than we relend—and the time may or may not
be soon—… the effect may again be absorbed entirely by other invisibles or it
may not. It is therefore impossible to predict with assurance that the United
States will ever have an unfavorable balance of trade."

Some attempts were made to project these international payments trends
in terms of what Keynes called the "theory of solids," that is, fixed trends with
an economic inertia not very responsive to marginal changes in prices and
interest rates.

In fact, the Law of Promotions and Detractions sought to relate the capital
account to the trade account without any reference to interest-rate or price
adjustments. It also neglected credit creation and how the exponential growth
of international debt involved carrying charges that required debtor counties to
run increasing trade surpluses. Like the marginalist approach, the Law of
Promotions and Detractions assumed that the gold reserves of all countries
would increase at a fairly steady albeit modest rate, seemingly automatically.

What was not perceived was that imbalances in net payments or receipts
among the basic categories of trade, services and capital movements might set
in motion a cumulative disequilibrium deriving largely from short-term banking
movements. By 1932, in the face of America's rising protectionism with the
Hawley-Smoot tariff, it became apparent that service transactions, investment
outflows or a movement into trade deficit would not offset net U.S. receipts of
income from abroad. European flight capital and gold moved at an accelerating
pace into the United States after devaluation of the dollar in 1934, accelerating
as the storm clouds of war gathered.

### How capital outflows impair investment and productive powers

In order to finance trade deficits, overseas military spending, debt service or
capital flight by borrowing, it is necessary to offer international lenders higher
interest rates than they can get in their own economies. The problem is that high
interest rates discourage domestic investment, as England discovered in the
1920s. Strapped for funds because it had re-established the value of sterling at
high prewar levels that brought on an industrial depression and general strike by

1926, England found its export abilities limited. It kept its interest rates high enough to attract foreign capital, but this became increasingly difficult as U.S. interest rates rose as a result of boom conditions.

When neither America's export trade nor its capital inflows reversed themselves as envisioned by the classical adjustment mechanisms, adjustment once again came in the form of government intervention. In 1927 the Bank of England asked the U.S. Federal Reserve to pursue an easy money policy so that the United States would not bid funds away from England. Low U.S. interest rates would encourage the triangular flow of U.S. lending to German cities and other borrowers, which would turn the proceeds over to the Reichsbank to use in paying German reparations to England. The latter then turned all of *its* reparations receipts over to the U.S. Government as inter-Ally debt service.

What broke this triangular flow of payments was that easy U.S. credit conditions (largely to accommodate England) fueled a stock-market boom, which attracted U.S. savings away from lending to Germany and other European countries. This made it impossible for the major nations to keep their payments in balance simply by raising their interest rates.

Today, the problem still exists that high rates discourage domestic investment, preventing debtor countries from being able to produce the exports that are the only way they can work their way out of debt over time. Deflation and economic recession impair rather than help the payments position as domestic as well as foreign investors dump their stocks and withdraw their money from markets that are not growing. The foreign debt burden grows larger, imposing a financial overhead that aggravates trade dependency.

## Summary: *The international economy's financial context*

Mill explained how making payments involved foreign currencies, not just the direct barter of exports for foreign products. Unless debtor countries could sell more to creditor nations at unchanged (or even higher) prices, their larger export volume would tend to lower unit prices. Debt service thus involved a terms-of-trade penalty under normal conditions, in contrast to Ricardo's assumption that income shifts by themselves would handle the adjustment. Indeed, matters were aggravated by the fact that investment in such countries tended to be biased toward raw-materials production, which tends to glut markets in the manner demonstrated by Mill, Edgeworth and Marshall.

Just as differing rates of labor productivity among nations rendered the world economy "international" according to the Ricardian theory of comparative costs, *so differing rates of domestic inflation and currency depreciation—* resulting largely from capital transfers and their terms-of-trade effects—*rendered it international in the financial sense.* In the twentieth century Carl Iversen grasped that this monetary consideration remained the major reason for dealing with nations "as the main regional concept. … International trade may be defined, therefore, as *trade between regions maintaining currency systems of their own.*"[23] However, neither Iversen nor his contemporaries defined this specifically as involving a disparity between international exchange rates and the evolution of domestic prices and incomes.

Financial orthodoxy remained characterized by what Gustav Cassel called the purchasing-power parity theory of prices and foreign exchange. This theory stated that prices and exchange rates moved together, despite all the statistical demonstration to the contrary and the fact that Mill had disproved this by tracing how capital transfers led exchange rates to diverge from domestic inflation (or deflation) rates.

One consequence of the tendency of inflation to lag behind the rate of currency depreciation has been that the purchasing power of wages falls as imported consumer goods become more expensive (as John Barton recognized early in the nineteenth century; see Chapter 18, note 16). This is a major reason why the IMF has endorsed hyperinflation and corresponding depreciation of Third World currencies. The idea is to shift incomes away from consumers, in the belief that this will "free" output for exportation. But not all output is exportable, and incomes are not shifted to the investment sector, because capital flight is a major consequence of chronic depreciation and depression.

Non-structural theories of capital transfers assume that automatic adjustment processes will keep international payments in balance. All disturbances are merely marginal, so that balance-of-payments disequilibrium will not exceed the ability of price and monetary adjustments to cure. Boom conditions in capital-recipient economies lead to high prices and incomes (and hence, to higher demand for imports) or to investment outflows and trade deficits vis-à-vis the debtor economies. Exchange rates for countries operating on an inconvertible paper or floating-currency standard are supposed to shift in parallel with their domestic price levels (or somewhat more if they have to make capital transfers), until payments equilibrium is restored.

Pressed to its logical conclusion, Mill's theory of capital transfers implies that industrial nations benefit in two extraordinary ways from world economic evolution. As exporters, they may monopolize the gains from trade, thanks to their favorable growth in industrial (and as matters have turned out, agricultural) technology, enjoying the world's positive income-elasticity for their output. As

---

[23] Carl Iversen, *International Capital Movements*, p. 5. Iversen cites as defending this concept Gustav Cassel, in *Theoretische Sozialöconomie*, 4th ed. (Leipzig: 1927), p. 609.

creditors, they reap further terms-of-trade benefits as debtor countries are obliged to export more raw materials to raise the foreign exchange to pay off their debts. These raw materials fall in price as a result of relatively income-inelastic demand on the part of the industrial nations.

The implication is that countries should specialize in commodity lines that promise to enjoy rising terms of trade and achieve technological breakthroughs over time. This normally involves restricting imports so as to avoid falling into foreign debt and suffering the terms-of-trade penalty associated with paying interest and principal transfers. It also entails staying out of war, or at least not being on the losing side. The alternative is exemplified by Germany's tragic experience, discussed in the next chapter.

# 16

## The German Reparations Debate

Constraints on capital-transfer capacity were not clearly apparent prior to World War I. Industrial progress was so strong that most countries were able to carry a rising volume of debt without seriously impeding their development. By and large, world debts seemed to take care of themselves. Egypt and Turkey were ruined, but that was attributed to their political and social backwardness. The idea of structural limits to debt-paying capacity hardly could be developed until a major attempt was made to exceed such limits by major industrial nations.

Only after World War I did the most pressing economic problems become monetary. German reparations and inter-Ally war debts caused an unprecedented financial crisis which prompted a dispute between creditor and debtor interests that made the theory of capital transfers (debt service) as politically charged as the earlier debate between free traders and protectionists had been.

Inasmuch as France had paid Germany the heaviest reparations bill in the nineteenth century, it seemed only natural to seek even higher reparations from Germany after World War I. Its fellow Allies wanted to share, especially in view of their heavy debts to the United States, whose government insisted that it be paid for the $12 billion in arms it had supplied the Allies prior to its entry into the war and for its postwar reconstruction lending. The Allies turned to Germany to bear the cost of their debts and for the property destroyed in France and other countries—and even for the price paid for waging the war, which had cost $209 billion. The question was, just how much could Germany pay, and how much could the allies afford to pay America.

The Allied governments acted as experimenters, with defeated Germany their economic laboratory, making it a dress rehearsal for the austerity programs that the International Monetary Fund's imposes on today's Third World debtor economies. Germany was burdened with reparations so vast that their amount was not even specified by the Treaty of Versailles. The intention of the Allies as phrased by Eric Geddes, head of Britain's Admiralty, was to "squeeze Germany until the pips squeaked."

Its indemnity was the first levied in excess of a defeated country's ability to pay on the spot. Liquidating Germany's portfolio of foreign investments and colonial possessions, transferring its land and capital goods and borrowing the balance—as France had done in 1817 and again in 1871 by raising interest rates—was the first step in what became a program to stripping Germany to such an extent that it led to collapse of the mark and hyperinflation by 1921.

Germany's liability remained unlimited. "The Dawes Plan merely fixed what Germany should pay every year; it did not fix the total debt, or for how many years she had to go on paying, or what amount represented interest and what amount represented repayment of capital."[1] The economic question seemed simply to be how large a foreign-exchange surplus Germany could generate.

Did any limit exist? Europe had adjusted its economic life to the demands of war beyond anyone's imagination. Many economists made fools of themselves in the early months of the war by predicting that hostilities could not last long before Europe's economic resources were exhausted. But taxes were raised, government spending was monetized and massive shipments of arms were transferred on unparalleled amounts of credit. In view of this seemingly unlimited ability to wage the Great War, it appeared that defeated Germany's ability to pay reparations might likewise rise to meet the challenge of whatever sum was imposed. Most Germans initially shared the belief that their economy could make the appropriate adjustment to pay for the damage the nation had caused.

The economic disruptions of the 1920s laid bare the financial skeleton of international relations as the Allies pursued incompatible policies toward Germany. To prevent its further aggression they dismantled it economically and geographically. Stripped of its foreign investments, its colonial possessions, its Saar mining and manufacturing complex, its international financial reserves, much of its rolling stuck and other resources, the nation was granted virtually no time in which to adjust its industry to the realities of postwar export markets. Yet the Allies insisted that Germany pay reparations as if its economy had not been dismantled.

The only kind of economic theory that could have developed to justify this situation was one that denied the existence of any limit to the amount of debt that could be paid. This is what the leading creditor-oriented (essentially anti-German) monetarists in the Allied countries claimed. Bertil Ohlin, Jacques Rueff and Carl Iversen asserted that no export-revenue limit existed *apart from the ability of Germany's government to tax its citizens.* The limit to capital transfers thus represented nothing less than the totality of income generated within Germany—presumably over and above minimum necessary subsistence costs, which might be ground down quite low indeed. Germany could pay reparations by taxing its citizens in domestic reichsmarks and converting them into the foreign currencies in which the country's reparations and debt service were due.

---

[1]    Quoted in R. H. Brand, "The Reparation Problem," *Journal of the Royal Institute of International Affairs* (May 1929), pp. 204–07. For a general discussion of German reparations and inter-Ally debts see Hudson, *Super-Imperialism* (2nd ed., London 2002).

Foreign exchange had to be earned by making exports, but Mill's terms-of-trade analysis (above, pp. 221ff.) implied that the more Germany exported, the less it would earn. Beyond a certain limit its export revenue would begin to decline as export prices fell more rapidly than their volume increased. Keynes pointed out that one way out of this constraint was for Germany to restructure its economy to diversify its exports and increase its productivity. This would cost money, making it unavailable to pay reparations and other foreign debts.

Monetarists denied that countries making debt payments would suffer a terms-of-trade penalty, or that there was any need to invest in restructuring economic activity. Retaining an unwavering faith in automatic adjustment mechanisms, they claimed that no transfer problem existed, if only Germany would tax its citizens heavily enough. The economy was supposed to face only the budgetary problem of reducing its domestic incomes by the Reichsmark equivalent of whatever it owed. A million dollars worth of forgone German consumption of goods could realize a million dollars when these commodities were "freed" for sale on world markets. No downward price adjustment need be suffered by these increased exports, because Germany's capital transfer would increase the demand for goods (including German exports) in the capital-receiving economies by the amount needed to enable it to make its capital transfers!

This income-demand effect of capital transfers was essentially Ricardo's position in the bullion debate a century earlier. The monetarists of the 1920s held that incomes would fall by however much was necessary to free enough exports to finance foreign debt service to virtually any degree called for, without the economy breaking stride. Even in the face of the hyperinflation to which the German and French economies succumbed in the early 1920s, every country's export level was supposed to adjust to whatever capital-transfer needs might he imposed on it—assuming that creditor nations were willing to accept such exports. America's protectionist tariff policy showed this assumption to be erroneous.

German manufactures were thrown onto world markets in a desperate attempt to raise foreign exchange to pay reparations far beyond the nation's capacity to pay except by bankrupting its economy and reducing investment below basic replacement levels. Its economic collapse showed the assumptions of monetarism to be extreme in restricting themselves to problems calling for merely marginal adjustments. The immense sums of foreign exchange needed to meet Germany's reparations liability and the inter-Ally war debts were beyond the capacity of marginal adjustments to generate. What was called for was for payments to be reduced in recognition of existing productive powers and export capacity, subject to domestic consumption and investment needs, while trade and production (along with foreign tariffs) were restructured. Only this would have enabled Germany to transfer a higher level of net exports to its creditors.

Germany's productive capacity was insufficient to create an export surplus of the magnitude needed to finance its scheduled reparations. And when the nation imposed austerity in the hope that this would free more output for export, it only stifled necessary industrial investment. Like today's Third World countries, the only option Germany could find was to borrow abroad to cover its balance-of-payments shortfall. But the more Germany borrowed, the more interest and principal it would have to pay in future years, putting even more downward pressure on its long-term payments position. As in today's world, German political instability led to an emigration of skilled labor and capital flight, creating bottlenecks that made it even more difficult to increase productive powers. The nation was bankrupted in a futile attempt to pay. In the ensuing shambles Germany succumbed to authoritarian rule under the National Socialists and their program of repudiating foreign creditor control. This was a major economic platform on which Hitler campaigned and was elected.

Yet throughout the 1920s, successive German governments strove obediently to make the scheduled reparations payments without regard for its capacity to earn the funds. The Reichsbank simply printed marks to purchase the foreign exchange to pay. Its currency soon collapsed more drastically than any other in history, succumbing to hyperinflation. The currency's falling value was supposed to discourage imports and other payments to foreigners and to spur exports. But Germany's essential import needs and scheduled debt service were so high that currency depreciation did not succeed in balancing the country's international payments. By the time the mark was devalued a billion fold, the fallacy of the liberal faith in purely financial adjustment mechanisms was demonstrated irrefutably. Instead of promoting payments equilibrium at a higher level of German exports and capital transfers, the economic collapse impoverished Germany and threw its balance of payments ever further into deficit. This was just the opposite of what was supposed to occur according to the price-specie flow mechanism and the Ricardian income-transfer theory.

Payment of Germany's reparations debt called for much more than merely marginal adjustments to transfer capital under the conditions that Ricardo had described. The scheduled payments were so huge, Taussig observed,

> so vastly greater than had ever been imagined, that the theory of the case ... must be revised and modified. ... the ordinary mechanism of international trade—specie outflow, price changes and consequent changes in exports and imports—cannot cope with transactions so huge.

> If the German government were to undertake remittance by purchasing bills of exchange in the market, then allowing specie outflow to set in and to last until automatically brought to a close, Germany's circulating medium would be completely drained in a few months, at most in a year. Exports and imports of merchandise could not possibly accommodate themselves in short order to such

overwhelming changes. ... It could be doubtless argued that eventually there must come a readjustment in accord with the fundamentals of theory. But such drastic adjustment could be reached only after a period of monetary revolution and credit collapse that would affect not Germany alone, but the entire world. It would be idle to speculate on possibilities of this sort.[2]

Yet this was precisely the policy advocated by the monetarists Rueff and Ohlin as late as 1929, and their successors ever since. "Bad theory has crowded out good," attesting to the ability of creditor interests to impose their worldview on an erstwhile scientific economics discipline.

Appearances seemed to be saved for a while as Germany payed reparations in excess of its net trade balance by borrowing the funds abroad, mainly in the United States. Its inter-governmental reparations debt was being exchanged for the commercial debts run up by its municipalities, public agencies and corporations to foreign private lenders. These loans, spurred by high German interest rates and tight money, were converted into domestic currency for spending at home, with the Reichsbank turning the foreign exchange over to the Allies. Germany thus established a financial triangle by raising private funds in the United States and paying them out as reparations to the Allied governments, which transferred them back to the United States as payments on their war debts. (Only France received more funds in reparations than it was obliged to pay the United States and other Allies.)

This circular flow (if one can call a triangulation "circular") could continue as long as Germany's creditworthiness remained intact, and as long as German interest rates remained higher than those in the United States. The problem was that Germany was mortgaging its future to meet pressing demands that had no realistic prospect of being sustained over time. The new foreign debts had to be repaid by an increasingly impoverished and austerity-ridden German economy. Foreign borrowing thus could be only a short-term and indeed self-negating palliative, for the more Germany borrowed internationally, the more its credit rating was endangered. The higher it held its interest rates to induce its entities to borrow abroad, the more it undermined its long-term direct investment, and hence net, export prospects.

Matters were complicated by artificially low U.S. interest rates stimulating stock-market credit that pushed up securities prices, attracting a rising inflow of foreign funds and discouraging new U.S. lending abroad. Failure by the United States to recycle its inter-Ally debt receipts to Germany (either in the form of new loans or as demand for German exports) made a breakdown of reparations payments inevitable. This led to payments deficits and consequent devaluation

---

[2] Frank Taussig, "Germany's Reparations Payments," *American Economic Review*, X (March 1920, suppl.), p. 37.

for Allied currencies, a moratorium on Europe's inter-Ally debt service, a collapse of U.S. financial liquidity and stock-market prices, and a break in the chain of international and domestic payments that triggered the Great Depression and ushered in an era of militarized nationalism.

It was the American demand above all others that forced the Allies to insist on an unrealistically high level of German reparation payments. U.S. officials viewed matters in a self-righteously legalistic light. A debt was a debt, and that was that. They did not want to acknowledge the seemingly obvious fact that Germany's scheduled payments were uncollectible except at the price of higher German competition with creditor-nation industry. Such a perception would have called for winding down U.S. tariff protection, an action that Republican administrations were unwilling to take. When Germany and other debtor countries sought to earn the dollars to make their stipulated payments, the United States and other nations raised tariffs to prevent imports from threatening their domestic producers. These trade barriers limited the ability of debtor countries to run trade surpluses, no matter how far they depreciated their currencies and how low their exports fell in price.

In view of the fact that trade historically had followed the direction of international capital flows, it seemed logical that Germany's export trade would follow the course of its reparations payments. To the extent that the Allies passed these reparations on to the United States as inter-Ally debt service, German exports appeared likely to increase most sharply to North America. However, the United States blocked this solution. Specifically to thwart German competition it levied its tariffs on the basis of relatively high American selling prices rather than the foreign invoice value. "Much of the agitation in this country for higher duties and the American valuation plan," wrote John Williams concerning the American Selling Price method of computing tariffs, "has been aimed particularly against the expected flood of cheap imports from Germany; and similar legislation has been passed or is contemplated in Sweden, Denmark, Norway, Great Britain, Switzerland, Finland, Argentina, and Japan."[3] Some Allied economists (including Williams and Ohlin) speculated that Germany might re-establish its prewar trade with Russia. But this was not a viable solution in view of the Soviet Union's own isolation and limited ability to pay.

Could market forces be expected to cope with this rigged game? All parties hoped that Germany's trade balance somehow would adjust itself to finance its indemnity and thereby enable the European Allies to pay their own war debts to the United States. Yet no one was able to specify just how Germany

---

[3]   John H. Williams, "German Foreign Trade and the Reparations Payments," *Quarterly Journal of Economics*, XXXVI (May 1922), p. 483.

was to earn the required foreign exchange. This was supposed to occur automatically, and at someone's expense—but whose? No major test ever had been made of whether any limit existed to a nation's export surplus needed to finance its capital transfers, irrespective of foreign protectionism or the level of domestic productive powers.

Neither the direct recipients of German reparations (France, Britain, Belgium *et al.*) nor the United States (which received them indirectly in the form of inter-Ally debt service), nor the German people themselves faced the fact that there was no economically feasible way for the nation to meet the judgment imposed by the Treaty of Versailles. A debt was a debt even when its principal sum was unspecified and unlimited. To hold otherwise seemed to threaten the concept of private property itself, anathema to property holders in all countries.

Only a handful of dissenters anticipated the world disaster that was looming. To explain the basis for their warnings they developed a structural analysis to controvert the monetarists advocating German reparations and the feasibility of inter-Ally debts by specifying the constraints on how much Germany or other debtors could generate to service their foreign debts. John Maynard Keynes in Britain and Harold Moulton in the United States played the leading roles in distinguishing between the *domestic budgetary problem* of absorbing spendable income by taxing citizens or borrowing from them, and the *transfer problem* of converting this domestic revenue into foreign exchange. This clarification was unpopular because it implied that Germany's reparations and inter-Ally debts should be reduced, being unpayable in practical terms.

## Contrasts between structuralist and monetarist analysis

In asserting that Germany could pay its scheduled reparations, monetarists claimed that all economic activity was *fungible*. Labor and capital producing any given product or service could turn readily to produce other goods and services. All products consumed domestically could be readily exported as shifting prices and incomes made this economically attractive and as income shifts made it possible. All that was needed was for output to exceed the sum of domestic consumption and investment plus government spending. The entire difference was exportable (a neat formulation, implying that no imports had to be made at all, not even to make exports). Some monetarists went so far as to indulge in an elasticity optimism which assumed that any reduction in the demand for domestic products would free them for export at *stable or nearly stable terms of trade*. Payments equilibrium thus could be established without having to make major new investments to restructure export production. All that was needed was to reduce domestic demand—assuming output to remain stable.

Structuralists noted that Germany had certain *a priori* needs. Various categories of imports could not be reduced, such as the basic essentials needed irrespective of price, and the raw materials needed to produce German output and exports. These categories were responsive primarily to long-term trends in production, population and export volume. Other basic categories of foreign payments included travel, transport and debt service. To use Keynes's famous metaphor, these categories of international payments behave more like solids than like the fluid, elastic phenomena described by monetarists.

Monetarists and structuralists each used a vent-for-surplus approach to analyze Germany's trade potential. For structuralists, the first step was to view exports and imports *in specific product categories* as residual functions—that is, the net difference between domestic production and consumption. Monetarists struck an *overall* balance in which the value of total output exceeded (or fell short of) domestic absorption in the form of consumption, investment plus government spending. The margin of output over absorption could be increased by raising taxes or by reducing direct investment and consumption. In effect, the government could remove from domestic purchasing power a sum equal to Germany's trade balance, and could transfer it abroad dollar for dollar, so to speak.

Structuralists pointed out that even if Germany produced more than it consumed and invested, some imports still would have to be made. Domestic production required a basic level of consumption needs to be met, needs that were associated with the growth in population. Some of these essentials had to be imported. Also, investment and essential government support were needed to keep production and export functions intact, not to speak of increasing them. Some investment goods had to be imported, along with raw materials and other primary production inputs and intermediate goods. The trade balance thus depended not merely on overall domestic spending relative to income; it involved estimating import dependency for each major category of goods and services.

The next step in estimating Germany's prospective trade balance was to assign prices to its physical volume of trade. Here a complication arose, according to the structuralists: *German exports were subject to deteriorating terms of trade as their supply increased on world markets.* Monetarists were unwilling to admit just how inelastic international demand was for these exports. Much as Ricardo had done, they insisted that the payment of reparations would raise incomes in the capital receiving nations and thus create an equivalent demand for German exports, thereby supporting their terms of trade. This suggested a 100 per cent propensity to import German products with the added reparations income received from Germany. Structuralists replied that even if German exports were increased (as consumption, investment and government spending were reduced while output presumably was maintained), these experts could not be made at pre-existing international prices. Rather, increasing export volume would cause Germany's terms of trade to shift adversely. Thus, the more Germany *tried* to pay the Allies, the less would be its actual ability to pay, especially if a capital flight accompanied the decline in its terms of trade.

## Germany's import functions

According to trade theory as it stood on the eve of the 1920s, a nation's imports represented a simple function of discretionary demand, capable of being foregone if they became too costly. No import dependency was recognized, no demand for imports in the form of hoarding (for example, as inflation hedges), or even a linkage between the volume of capital goods imports and the rate of domestic investment and modernization. As Harold Moulton put it

> Our illustrations usually run in terms of wheat and cloth and seldom in terms of raw materials, factory equipment, etc. … According to the theory as thus expounded, no imports whatever are required … The truth, of course, is that something like 15 million German people under the conditions of the modern world would starve to death if food imports were cut off and that the whole German factory system would break down completely if imports of raw materials were wiped out. My purpose therefore was to show by a careful analysis of the nature of the German economic organization precisely what volume of imports constituted the indispensable minimum for national efficiency. Whatever a theory evolved before the days of international economic interdependence might imply as to import requirements, under existing conditions a very great volume of imports were indispensable.[4]

Moulton and Keynes divided Germany's imports into four major categories, each with its own distinct demand functions that existed independently of relative international prices and incomes. The first category represented absolutely necessary imports on which Germany was dependent—the minimum essential level of imported food, energy and other raw materials (including those embodied in its exports). No matter how low German incomes or the value of the mark might fall, these purchases would still be necessary. "The imports required to maintain the German population in a state of physical efficiency and to enable the German factories to operate at something like pre-war capacity," wrote Moulton, "total in value about 14 billion gold marks, as compared with actual imports in 1922 of only about 6.2 billion gold marks. German exports must therefore equal 14 billion gold marks merely for the purpose of paying for the necessary imports. In 1922 they were less than half this total."[5]

---

[4]  Harold C. Moulton, "War Debts and International Trade Theory," *American Economic Review*, XV (December 1925), p. 707.
[5]  Moulton, *ibid.*, p. 705.

Williams observed that these essential price-inelastic imports

> have been dominated by the need of raw materials for manufacture and of food products to sustain the industrial population, which has been so great as to offset the depressive effect of the depreciating mark. With reserve stocks exhausted and fixed plant and equipment deteriorated by the war, imports of this character are the necessary first step toward a return to a normal economic life … Also, the loss of farming territory to Poland adds a permanent new element of food imports, to be offset eventually by new manufactured exports; and losses of iron territory to France would make necessary, to maintain the iron and steel industry on the pre-war basis, iron-ore imports of nearly treble the pre-war figure. In 1921 raw materials and food products were 88 per cent of total imports.[6]

The volume of these basic needs tended to rise with the growth of Germany's population, income and production, unless the nation somehow could increase its domestic output of food, fuels and raw materials. This growth function represented the second category of German imports, After all, observed Williams, "no stimulus afforded by depreciating exchange rates, however powerful, could bring about a substantial increase of German exports for more than a brief period until the raw materials for their manufacture had been provided." Moulton generalized that "the theory that in a highly developed industrial country like Germany there is one group of "importing" industries and another distinct and unrelated group of "exporting" industries has been … completely refuted both in *Germany's Capacity to Pay* and in *The Reparation Plan*"[8] published under his direction. Imports formed a basic component of many German exports, and the latter could not be increased without increasing the former in a rather stable proportion.

This perception became the inspiration for Keynes's structuralist (or as it was later termed, macroeconomic) emphasis on the established propensity to import, and of the associated propensities to consume, invest and spend stable proportions of income. The volume of investment- and income- correlated imports was derived by multiplying growth in output and income ($\Delta Y$) by either a fixed or marginal propensity to import ($Im/Y$ or $\Delta Im/\Delta Y$).

A third category of imports represented the capital goods required for new German investment and the associated restructuring of productive powers. Without such imports German production hardly could be expected to increase to satisfy export demand and/or increase domestic output to displace imports. Failure to import capital goods would restrict export growth and lead the

---

[6]   Williams, "German Foreign Trade," pp. 488f.

[7]   Williams, *ibid.*, p. 488. See also Allyn A. Young, "War Debts, External and Internal," *Foreign Affairs* 2 (1923: special suppl.), p. 399.

[8]   Moulton, "War Debts," pp. 707f.

German economy to become increasingly dependent on nations that could afford to undertake higher rates of new investment and innovation. (To be sure, foreign supplier credits financed equipment imports, so that their balance-of-payments costs were deferred more readily than imports of consumer goods.)

Figure 16.1: Structuralist Analysis of German Imports

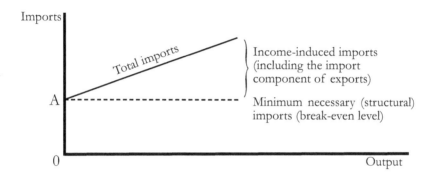

Germany attempted to shift resources to the export sector by devaluing the mark. This made sales for foreign currency (rising in value) more attractive than production for the domestic market. Also made more attractive were foreign investment inflows to purchase German land, companies and other assets. On the other hand, depreciating paper may bring about the "flight of capital," observed Taussig. "Investors may become uneasy from continued depreciation, may fear complete collapse, and may wish to place their possessions in secure form. They will buy gold exchange, sending the funds to foreign banks; or may buy foreign securities."[9]

This principle was a major reason why devaluation spurred imports and capital outflows even more than exports and capital inflows. Many Germans hoarded their savings in the form of imported commodities, especially world-class luxuries and foreign-currency investments that embodied a stable foreign-exchange value. This hoarding constituted the fourth category of German imports that not only was immune to but indeed, inversely reflected relative price shifts.

The ensuing economic collapse was not conducive to increased investment and production. It dried up the conversion of domestic savings into direct investment, the ultimate source of improving the balance of trade and payments. Instead of investing at home, Germans sought to protect themselves against

---

[9]  Taussig, *International Trade* (New York: 1927), p. 391. See also Williams, "German Foreign Trade," pp. 483, 498f.

further currency depreciation by capital flight and by hoarding hard assets. The higher import prices rose, the more motivation there was to hoard imports— just the opposite from what the price-specie flow mechanism portrayed. Imports were purchased precisely *because* their prices were rising in terms of domestic currency!

### Germany's export functions

As in the case of imports, some major components of German exports were relatively price-inelastic. Emphasis on this fact led free traders to call the structuralist approach "elasticity pessimism," a negative value-laden term. Realism is not the same thing as pessimism. It is a precondition for taking steps to escape from the kind of economic trap that produces circumstances warranting the malaise of pessimism. Only a view of international payments in terms of underlying trends and needs can explain (and hence warn) why countries often suffer even worse payments when they devalue, as did Germany in the 1920s. It also explains the even higher payments surpluses which occur when they revalue their currency upwards, as Germany would do in the 1970s and '80s.

Germany's prewar level of exports, averaging some 14 billion gold marks annually, seemed a reasonable the basis on which to project postwar trends. This sum happened to equal the estimated 14 billion marks needed for "basic" postwar imports. Hence, Germany was able to start off with a zero net trade balance once its economy revived from the war. What then had to be determined was how much of its postwar growth in output would be available for export, after meeting its substantial domestic investment needs.

As noted above, monetarists viewed Germany's exportable surplus as equaling total national product less domestic consumption. This made it appear that all that was needed to increase the export surplus (and hence Germany's capacity to pay reparations) was to minimize income by reducing consumption. But that approach neglected to take account of the new investment needed to retool Germany's economy to produce the types of products most in demand in world markets. As Keynes pointed out in his 1920 *Economic Consequences of the Peace*:

> An annual surplus available for home investment can only be converted into a surplus available for export abroad by a radical change in the kind of work performed. ... Labor can only be diverted into new channels with loss of efficiency, and a large expenditure of capital. The annual surplus which German labor can produce for capital improvements at home is no measure, either theoretically or practically, of the annual tribute which she can pay abroad.[10]

---

[10]  J. M. Keynes, *Economic Consequences of the Peace* (London: 1920), repr. in *Essays in Persuasion* [1931] (London: 1952), p. 17. See also Keynes, "The German Transfer Problem," *Economic Journal*, XXXIX (March 1929), repr. in American Economic Association, *Readings in the Theory of International Trade* (Philadelphia: 1949), pp. 161ff.

The appropriate measure of Germany's economic surplus therefore was thus equal to output minus consumption *and minus necessary direct investment*. To export the entire surplus of output less consumption would leave nothing to invest in maintaining (not to speak of building up) Germany's means of production. Moulton likewise recognized that

> the amount of expansion that can occur (in exports) represents but a small fraction of the excess of annual production over consumption. The theory that the entire excess can automatically be converted into exports ignores some of the major and controlling elements in the situation. ... If Germany could have exported each year the goods which in fact went into the development of her railroads, harbors, factories, store buildings, apartments and houses, the internal producing capacity of the nation would have been tremendously altered ... in any given year a considerable part of the excess of production over consumption—the savings of the nation—took the form of new farm buildings, ditches, and improved lands.[11]

Exportation of this output of plant, equipment and other tangible capital would have impaired Germany's capacity to produce, thereby impairing the trade balance.

The next issue, logically speaking, was what proportion of Germany's reparations payments actually would be recycled as a demand for additional German exports. Monetarists unrealistically assumed that *all* reparations payments to the European Allies (after adjusting for their own payment of war debts to the United States) would be recycled to purchase German exports. This implied a 100 per cent propensity to import specifically German goods with net reparations proceeds. Structuralists disputed this. It seemed more logical to expect German exports to respond *somewhat* to the growth of world income, but why should *all* foreign income deriving from reparations receipts be spent differently from other types of income? Keynes argued that only a portion would be spent on imports (the foreign "propensity to import") and that only a portion of this overall import spending would be used to purchase specifically German products. The overall foreign propensity to import was more like 20 per cent than 100 per cent. For income growth in the United States, which became the ultimate recipient of German reparations via the inter-Ally debt phase of the reparations triangle, the propensity to import specifically German products may have been no larger than a fraction of a percentage point. What occurred instead was that a large proportion of U.S. receipts was recycled on capital account, in the form of loans to German municipalities and firms.

The important point was that Germany's trade balance would not automatically equal its capital transfer. German exports were a function of world

---

[11]  Moulton, "War Debts," pp. 708f.

demand subject to relatively stable ratios of imports to overall income, and to a rather stable geographic distribution of international import demand. This perception inspired Keynes's approach made in his *General Theory* that the propensities to import, save and consume were fixed rather than fluidly price-responsive.

A third issue under debate concerned the extent to which German exports could increase without impairing the terms of trade, that is, without glutting world markets in the face of an increasingly satiated and inelastic demand. The postulated monetarist identity between Germany's trade balance and its balance on capital account—and thus between the transfer problem and the budgetary problem—would hold only if international *prices* (as determined by world supply and demand conditions) reflected stable underlying international *values* as measured by relative "real" production costs.

In reality the terms of trade threatened to shift adversely in response to increasing export volume. As shown in Figure 16.2, German exports would add to the nation's overall foreign exchange position as they increased toward the quantity *OA*, but they would not increase *pari passu*. The more Germany exported, the further its terms of trade would deteriorate. Beyond point *OA*, world demand for German exports was satiated and hence price-inelastic. Any attempt to make further exports actually would reduce Germany's foreign exchange position. If world demand for German exports had an elasticity of less than unity (100 per cent), Keynes concluded, then "the more she exports, the smaller will be the aggregate proceeds." The more accordions and harmonicas Germany sold abroad to raise the funds to finance its reparations payments, the lower their unit price would fall on world markers. This was basic Mill-Edgeworth offer-curve analysis.

Figure 16.2 Adverse Shifts in Terms of Trade in Response to Increasing Export Volume

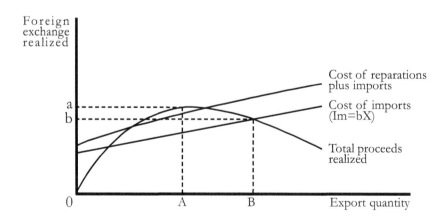

Indeed, if the world's demand for German goods has an elasticity of less than unity, there is no quantity of German-produced goods, however great in volume, which has a sufficient selling-value on the world market, so that the only expedient open to Germany would be to cut down her imports and consume home-produced substitutes, however inferior, and at an enhanced real-cost, however great.[12]

Germany's transfer problem thus existed over and above its domestic budgetary problem of generating an exportable surplus. Its international position would improve only if world demand for its exports were sufficiently elastic that increased foreign purchases more than compensated for the fall in German export prices, that is, if higher export volume more than offset the deterioration in the terms of trade. Modern economic jargon calls this the Marshall-Lerner condition, in which the demand elasticity for the exporting country's products exceeds unity. But if growth in foreign demand for German products failed to outstrip the decline in German export prices (that is, if foreign demand elasticity for German exports were less than unity), then Germany's trade balance would suffer. Its attempt to finance capital transfers by exporting more would be self-defeating.

Monetarist free traders scoffed at this notion. Haberler insisted that "there is nothing exceptional about an inelastic demand in terms of money for a particular commodity. But it is most unlikely that the elasticity of demand of a country, as shown on a Marshallian curve, will in practice be less than unity. Marshall himself considers such a case to be quite exceptional and interesting more as a *curiosum* than on account of its importance in practice."

Yet this is the state of affairs that characterized postwar Germany and many other countries in the Great Depression. It has become the norm since World War II. Haberler acknowledged Dennis Robertson's belief "that the present depression is partly due to the demand of industrial countries for foodstuffs and raw materials being inelastic. He thinks this partly explains the sharp fall in the import-prices and the accompanying depression in their export industries."

Haberler granted the possibility that "the breakdown in the export industries sets up a vicious spiral of credit contraction" akin to that which Thornton had warned about at the beginning of the nineteenth century.[13] But he hoped

---

[12] Keynes, "The German Transfer Problem," *Readings*, p. 162, and "Reply to Prof. Ohlin's Rejoinder," *Economic Journal* (September 1929), p. 405. In the function described in Figs. 16.2 and 16.3, $B=b'(L)$, the coefficient $b'$ was less than the 100 per cent that Ohlin believed. As the foreign income elasticity of demand for German exports declined, the coefficient $d'$ in $X_{Ger} = d'(Y_f)$ would fall to minimal levels and would even become negative beyond point OA.

[13] Haberler, *Theory of International Trade*, pp. 157f., citing Dennis Robertson, *Economic Fragments* (London: 1931), p. 13, *Study of Industrial Fluctuation* (pp. 131, 203ff.), and *Banking Policy and the Price Level* (London: 1926).

that matters somehow things would stabilize if only they were left alone, despite the seemingly obvious fact that they were destabilizing as the world polarized between creditor and debtor economies.

A fourth controversy arose over how large an increase in German exports could be expected in the face of foreign protectionism. As noted above, Germany's ability to export was impaired by the tariffs hastily erected by the Allies. Even Ohlin admitted that "if the policy of protection and of preference to home-made goods, which has been growing so much after the war, is intensified when German exports begin to grow, and is used consistently to prevent such exports, then the reparation payments may become virtually impossible." Under these conditions only an organized delivery of German goods-in-kind by the Allies could guarantee payment of German reparations. Ohlin admitted that "unfortunately, such a policy is outside the range of practical possibilities. The inevitable opposition of powerful American and British export industries to any such plan is one of the real obstacles, perhaps the greatest of them all, which lie in the way of an organized solution of the reparation problem."[14]

But then why persist in analyzing what *might* occur if the world were *not* so political? It might seem more beautiful and logical if matters were other than they were, but this hardly is relevant to govern economic reasoning in the real world, especially when its oversimplifications endorse policies that aggravate rather than alleviate international imbalance.

Germany finally imposed strict currency controls in the form of blocked-mark accounts, that is, payment of marks for Brazilian cotton and other imports that could be spent only on specifically earmarked German exports such as accordions and harmonicas. There certainly was nothing automatic in this principle, and it was the antithesis of the free-market ideal that Ohlin and Rueff advocated. But it was the only practical way to balance Germany's international accounts. The purchasing-power parity notion of exchange rates fell by the wayside as reparations payments caused the mark to depreciate, providing an export bounty. As Taussig observed,

> there will be a tendency for the price of foreign exchange in Germany to be kept higher than would accord with the course of commodity prices. For a long time there will be a divergence between the general [German] price level and the rates of foreign exchange. The divergence means that exporters will be in a position to profit. They can buy cheap (comparatively cheap) in Germany, sell the German goods abroad, draw on the foreign purchasers and sell the exchange to advantage at home.[15]

---

[14]  Ohlin, "Transfer Difficulties, Real and Imagined," *Economic Journal* (June 1929), pp. 177, 179.
[15]  Taussig, "Germany's Reparations Payments," p. 39. This discussion is analogous to that of gold "export points" familiar to nineteenth-century economists.

This situation illustrated Mill's principle of how the remission of capital from one country to another influenced price and currency ratios by transforming a mutual demand for commodities into an exchange of commodities for foreign currencies. Germany's foreign trade was not simply an exchange of products embodying its labor and capital for those of other countries. Rather, German exports exchanged for foreign currencies to meet reparations and debt service at falling terms of trade. The process widened the divergence of value from price, that is, of "real" cost ratios from realized export prices, imposing a terms-of-trade penalty on Germany over and above its reparations and other foreign debt obligations.

Perception of the fact that product markets operated via the intermediary of currency payments opened the way to explain how *the supply and demand situation in foreign-exchange markets tended to overwhelm comparative-cost disparities*, at least for countries paying substantial debt service. As Keynes summarized the situation:

> the process of paying the debt has the effect of causing the money in which the debt is expressed to be worth a larger quantity of German-produced goods than it was before or would have been apart from the payment of the debt; so that the population of the debtor State suffers a loss of purchasing power greater than the original equivalent of the amount of the debt.[16]

This was admitted by Taussig,[17] who hoped that "once the transition is over and the new state of equilibrium is reached, things will go smoothly." German goods would fall to whatever price was needed to balance the economy's international payments in the face of its reparations transfers. Lower export prices would mean lower real incomes for the German people, and hence less domestic absorption of output, by just enough to meet the nation's scheduled capital transfer.

## How Germany actually obtained the funds to pay reparations

Germany financed its reparations payments not through exports but by keeping domestic credit tight enough to induce its cities and companies to borrow abroad, primarily in the United States. Ohlin and Rueff claimed that this borrowing prevented the economy from becoming deflated to the point where incomes or prices would decline by enough to discourage imports and to free goods for export to settle reparations debt. "Is it not obvious," Ohlin argued, "that the buying power of a country, like that of an individual, will exceed its (his) income by the amount of gifts and loans, quite independently of any changes

---

[16]  Keynes, "Reply to Professor Ohlin's Rejoinder," *Economic Journal*, XXXIX (September 1929), p. 405.

[17]  Taussig, "Germany's Reparations Payments," p. 34.

in price levels?" Germany's foreign borrowings were twice as large as its reparations transfers, so it had "not had the "benefit" of a reduction in total buying
power, but the "disadvantage" of an increase in the amount with which borrowings have *exceeded* reparations payments. This increased buying power must have
tended to swell imports and to reduce exports."[18]

Keynes acknowledged that Germany had borrowed more from America
and other creditor nations than it had paid out in reparations, but pointed out
that these borrowings were largely for creditworthy purposes, not for consumption. They helped increase German productivity, which was the precondition for improving its balance of trade. Keynes added the legal detail that if
its foreign borrowing fell off, so would its reparations obligation, because the
Dawes Commission was obliged not to transfer funds in situations where this
would collapse the international value of the mark.[19]

The French spokesman Rueff objected to this aspect of the Dawes Plan,
claiming that it suspended the income adjustment mechanism. "The rate of
exchange for foreign currencies is determined artificially as a result of these
foreign credits." All that was necessary to promote German reparations was to
suspend international lending to Germany, for

> nothing can prevent the restoration or the maintenance of equilibrium in
> balance of payments, not even the highest tariffs ... *since transfer possibilities*
> *precisely materialize at every point of time into actual transfers.* In these circum-
> stances, suspension of a transfer on the grounds that one does not find in the
> exchange market the means necessary for effecting it simply amounts to a
> deliberate renunciation of the only measure that can make it feasible.[20]

According to Rueff the problem was that the international financial
managers appointed by the Dawes Commission in 1924 (and later by the Young
Commission in 1929) took it upon themselves to decide that Germany could
not service its reparations debt at the scheduled rate. They permitted German
borrowing and debt rescheduling to suspend the classical price adjustment
mechanisms. Rueff demanded that Germany tax its citizens by the full amount
necessary to pay its reparations, thereby abstracting an equivalent amount of
domestic purchasing power without borrowing or creating any offsetting credit
at home. "If those products which cannot be sold domestically find a foreign
purchaser immediately, balance-of-payments equilibrium will be restored. If not,
prices will tend to fall in the deficit country [Germany] until they reach the level

[18]  Ohlin, "A Rejoinder," pp. 403f.
[19]  Ohlin, "Transfer Difficulties, Real and Imagined," pp. 172f., and Keynes's reply, p. 180.
[20]  Jacques Rueff, *Balance of Payments: Proposals for the Resolution of the Most Pressing World
Economic Problem of Our Time* (New York: 1967), pp. 95, 98.

where an equivalent part of the national product is exported,"[21] irrespective of foreign trade barriers or shifts in the terms of trade and demand elasticities.

Rueff thus denied Keynes's "notion of a 'natural' level of exports" and other structural inelasticities. "The trade balance has always been, in all circumstances, what it had to be for the balance of payments to be in equilibrium." Not only did countries making capital transfers experience deflations, but those receiving this capital were supposed to experience credit inflations—a view that ignored the practice of gold sterilization by the U.S. Federal Reserve System Sterilization occurred when the Fed borrowed enough money to "absorb" the balance-of-payments inflow. It followed that "a balance of payments can only be in lasting deficit if the monetary factors that tend to correct it have been eliminated or made inoperative." This was his "principle of the conservation of purchasing power," which "simply states that never in the course of the various economic transformations that occur is purchasing power lost or created, but that it always remains constant. The result is that in all cases one man's loss is another man's gain …" The implication was that German prices need not be affected by its capital transfers, "since the purchasing power of which the population has been deprived will be transferred to the sellers of foreign exchange and utilized by them."[22] Money paid abroad by the German government and other debtors would be returned to Germany in the form of foreign purchases of its exports. But foreign borrowing by Germany would reduce its trade balance by the direct equivalent.

This "hydraulic" income-demand theory of capital transfers viewed international shifts of purchasing power in terms of a steady-state system. The more income Germany transferred abroad, the more spending power foreign countries would have. Assuming that this spending power found no response in investment, output or saving, it would have nowhere to go except to be recycled to buy German exports. The reduction and transfer of German purchasing power (by taxes on German consumers and businesses, turned over by the Reichsbank to foreign central banks as reparations) would reflect itself directly in higher exports or reduced German imports. Thus, if Germany levied the equivalent of $100 million in domestic taxes, and if its propensity to import were 20 per cent, then its imports would fall by $20 million, while demand for domestic output would be reduced by a further $80 million. Unless German residents borrowed offsetting amounts abroad, this output would be exported without impairing the terms of trade or exchange rates. If foreigners spent all their receipts of German debt service and reparations to purchase German goods, they would recycle the

---

[21] Rueff, *ibid.*, p. 134.
[22] Rueff, *ibid.*, pp. 12, 126, and "Mr. Keynes' Views on the Transfer Problem," *Economic Journal*, XXXIX (September 1929), pp. 389f.

money to Germany, supporting its prices just as if the money had remained all
the time within the domestic economy! But German international borrowing or
domestic credit creation would *reduce* the nation's trade balance by an equivalent
amount. It followed that Germany should impose economic austerity.

However, Moulton pointed out, "those who contend that an increase of
taxes will lower prices, have apparently forgotten their taxation theory. Customs
duties, excise taxes, and numerous other types of levies enter into the cost of
production and can be added to the price of commodities." Furthermore, "as a
result of the virtual destruction of the liquid capital supply of the country,
German industries now have to borrow the bulk of their working capital at very
high rates of interest. According to good economic doctrine, interest is an
element in the cost of production, and consequently enters into the selling price
of commodities."[23]

## Summary: The impact of economic austerity

The monetarist approach to Germany's transfer problem was deflationary in
urging the government to increase taxes, reduce spending and restrict German
credit creation and borrowing abroad. It seemed incredible to Keynes that the
resulting reduction in purchasing power (that is, income) was supposed to
reduce imports and/or increase exports white leaving output and the terms of
trade unaffected. "It is the essence of my argument," he observed,

> that the prices of home-produced goods in Germany should fall relatively to the
> prices of imports. For it is not simply a case of changing the value of money all
> round, but of changing the terms of international trade in a direction
> unfavourable to Germany, so that a larger quantity of exports than before will
> have to be offered for a given quantity of imports.[24]

Germany's purchasing power would be reduced by the deterioration in its
terms of trade and the change in its physical export volume.

Keynes further criticized monetarism for overlooking the sector-by-sector
and input-output aspect of matters. As he summarized matters,

> Those who think that the Transfer Problem is secondary argue thus: The
> German people receives its income in return for its current output of goods and
> services. If an appropriate part of this income is sequestered there will be no
> buyers for a corresponding amount of goods, which will therefore be available
> (in addition to what would be available otherwise) to expand exports or in
> diminution of imports.[25]

[23]  Moulton, "War Debts," pp. 714f.
[24]  Keynes, "A Reply," p. 405.
[25]  Keynes, "The German Transfer Problem," p. 161.

Once it was recognized that new investment was needed to sustain a changeover in Germany's production patterns from one concrete form (based on satisfying domestic needs) to another (that of satisfying foreign demand), it became apparent that not all the economic surplus over and above consumption was available to pay reparations. A tradeoff thus existed between the short run and the long run, between higher investment now but lower rates of reparations transfer, and a stripping of Germany's investable surplus leaving it less and less able to pay reparations over time.

According to Rueff and Ohlin, if Germany's domestic taxes were increased to *da* in Figure 16.3, the level of German real wages (disposable personal income) plus necessary investment would be reduced to level *Ad*. This would leave the volume *da* available for export and hence for payment of reparations. Moulton cited the Chase National Bank's monetary economist B. M. Anderson's contention

> that there is … a close mathematical connection between the amount of the budget surplus and the amount of the export surplus, and he scouts the idea of any trade difficulties. Mr. [Benjamin] Graham observes that "far from causing any revolutionary disturbance in industry this process can go on almost insensibly." … he contends that tariffs will not prevent the receipt of reparations; for they also are automatically gotten around as a result of international price changes.[26]

Rueff cited France's postwar experience to justify the assumption that Germany's overall rate of output would not be affected adversely by the processes of taxation and currency depreciation. Keynes retorted that "The violent social disturbances, the enormous redistribution of fortunes, and the wholesale disappointment of pre-existing contracts, which attended the prolonged and disastrous story of the depreciation of the franc to a fifth of its previous value, hardly afford a happy example of the ease of adjusting things."[27] Moulton added that "postwar European experience has repeatedly demonstrated [that] continual pressure upon the exchanges gives rise to other tendencies which shortly not only engulf the trade tendency but lead to a disorganization of the entire financial and economic system of the country."

Monetarists were simplistic, he concluded, in assuming that

> taking 2.5 billions of funds away from the German people would deprive them of the means of purchasing 2.5 billions of domestic purchasing power, would have no effect whatever on the volume of production and that this 2.5 billions of unpurchased goods would be in exportable form. No evidence has, however, been presented to show that production would remain unaffected by high taxes and declining prices.[28]

---

[26] Moulton, "War Debts," p. 703.

[27] Keynes, "A Reply," p. 406.

[28] Moulton, "War Debts," pp, 716, 714.

Monetarists viewed Germany's tax surplus and payment of reparations—that is, the working out of its budgetary and transfer problems respectively—as reducing the money supply, and hence Germany's price or income level, by enough to augment German exports, reduce imports and thereby balance its international payments. Ohlin's belief that a tax increase for reparations purposes would lower German prices was "based on the assumption that the payment of reparations will reduce the currency supply of the country."

But there was a limit to this process, Keynes observed. If Germany had sufficient gold to turn over to Allied central banks, it "could set the ball rolling by exporting sufficiently large quantities of gold to have an appreciable effect on world prices" via the price-specie flow mechanism. However, he pointed out, "Professor Ohlin's analogy of capital movements between two districts with the

Figure 16.3. The Effect of Increasing Germany's Domestic Taxes

## According to Rueff and Ohlin

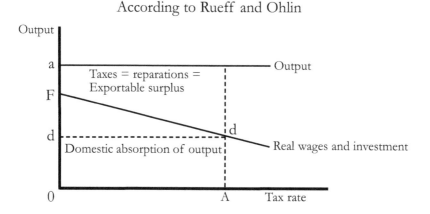

## According to Keynes and Moulton

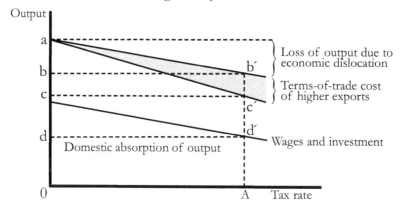

same currency system would only apply if Germany were in a position to export enough gold to make a measurable difference to demand conditions in the rest of the world." But this clearly was not the case, for the Versailles Treaty had stripped Germany of its gold. Furthermore, prices would fall in countries whose exports were displaced by those of Germany, "So we are … brought back to the … crucial question of the extent of the elasticity of the world demand for German exports."[29]

Keynes pointed out that austerity could not be expected to leave Germany's production functions untouched. Moulton agreed. "Any attempt to force a vast reorganization of German industry and trade" by diverting German capital to pay reparations "would result in less rather than more reparation payments over time."[30] German austerity would prevent the nation from upgrading its physical and human capital. If there were to be any hope of increasing Germany's export production, new investment would have to occur on an expanding scale. This meant a lower level of capital transfers to foreign countries in the short run. A federal budget surplus would impair the evolution of German productivity by discouraging government investment in necessary public infrastructure such as roads, transport, education and economic subsidies. Austerity would impair the rates of domestic investment and saving, interfering with the production process and the state of the currency.

As matters turned out, Germany was forced to transfer payments beyond its "structural" ability, stripping the economy of the resources needed to increase its productive powers at competitive world rates. This resulted in a number of unstable mechanisms as the attempt to overtax German workers and industrialists thus left financial and economic wreckage in its path. The reduction in German wage levels eroded labor productivity, induced strikes and emigration (especially of skilled labor) and prevented young Germans from pursuing the technical and higher education that had enabled them to be so productive prior to the war. Meanwhile, falling profitability—resulting from high tax and interest rates, and a shrinking domestic market—deterred new capital formation. Austerity meant bankruptcy for many firms.

What Haberler acknowledged to be a "vicious spiral of credit contraction" occurred as the need to make capital transfers stripped credit markets of their liquidity, pushed up interest rates, reduced new investment and slowed the growth of output. Discouragement of domestic investment historically has made capital-paying countries more commercially dependent on wealthier capital-recipient nations. This situation tends to become chronic rather than curing itself, increasing import dependency and thus impairing the trade balance of debtor countries, aggravated by an accelerating capital flight.

---

[29] Keynes, "A Reply," pp. 407f.     [30] Moulton, "War Debts," p. 714.

Is there something familiar in all this? Is it not what has happened to Third World countries in recent years? As domestic production falls off, the debtor economy's import needs and contractual debt service become so large that currency depreciation has little effect in reducing these payments. International accounts can be balanced only by further borrowing, on increasingly onerous economic and political terms.

The vital questions posed in this debate are still relevant. What proportion of capital transfers (reparations and debt service) would be "recycled" in the form of a demand for additional German exports? How large a volume of these exports could be made without glutting world markets in the face of an increasingly inelastic demand and rising tariff barriers by the creditor nations? To what extent would they be spurred by rising foreign income? What was the economy's maximum ability to produce a net export surplus to convert into foreign exchange under world market conditions? What was its minimum level of necessary imports? By how much could it reduce domestic consumption and investment without impairing its long-term evolution of productivity and hence its ability to generate future trade surpluses? These questions are similar to those confronting Third World countries today.

# 17

## Keynesian Income Approaches to the Balance of Payments

In explaining why Germany could not afford to pay its scheduled reparations, Keynes viewed necessary imports of food, energy and replacement parts, as more or less stable ratios of national income. His 1936 *General Theory of Employment, Interest and Money* extended this idea to map national income in terms of fairly stable "propensities" to consume, import, invest, save and export. This macroeconomic view of the economy's structural proportions made it unnecessary to view saving, investment and consumption in terms of a myriad of microeconomic price-responsive decisions by individuals and companies.

These stable trend ratios left government spending and taxation as the major variables. Fiscal policies could be shifted while private-sector ratios remained fixed. Income, investment and foreign-trade effects could be estimated in advance as the economy expanded or contracted in proportion to net injections of purchasing power in the form of government spending, private investment or export earnings. Conversely, national income would be diminished by leakages from the spending stream in the form of taxes, savings, and payments to foreigners for imports or to make capital transfers.

What Keynes called the "multiplier" was a ratio indicating the income enhancing effect of injections of purchasing power. Keynes defined it as the ratio by which aggregate income (Y) would increase for every dollar of new investment (I) or other increase in purchasing power ($\Delta Y/\Delta I$). This ratio was defined as the reciprocal of the marginal propensity to save ($\frac{1}{\Delta S/\Delta Y}$) or what was the same thing, ($\frac{1}{1-mpc}$), with *mpc* representing the marginal propensity to consume ($\Delta C/\Delta Y$). Assuming an 80 per cent marginal propensity to consume, the domestic multiplier would be $\frac{1}{1-0.8}$, or 5.

Imports and other payments to foreigners would reduce the multiplier. If imports account for 20 per cent of consumption (equal to 16 per cent of national income as a whole in the above example), then the multiplier would be reduced to $\frac{1}{1-(0.8-0.16)}$, that is, $\frac{1}{1-0.64}$, for a value of 3.33+. Thus, wrote Keynes,

> a given fluctuation of investment will be associated with a much less violent fluctuation of employment in a country in which foreign trade plays a large part and unemployment relief is financed on a larger scale out of borrowing (as was

the case, e.g., in Great Britain in 1931), than in a country in which these factors are less important (as in the United States in 1932).[1]

As income expands, so will imports $(\Delta Im/\Delta Y)$ in a more or less stable proportion. This "leakage" would become a source of demand for the exports of *other* countries, multiplying their incomes accordingly:

> In an open system with foreign-trade relations, some part of the multiplier of the increased investment will accrue to the benefit of employment in foreign countries, since a proportion of the increased consumption will diminish our own country's favourable foreign balance; so that, if we consider only the effect on domestic employment as distinct from world employment, we must diminish the full figure of the multiplier. On the other hand our own country may recover a portion of this leakage through favourable repercussions due to the action of the multiplier in the foreign country in increasing its economic activity.[2]

The result would be a reciprocal stimulation of growth within the international economy. Countries experiencing a demand for their exports would enjoy economic expansion by the ratio $\Delta Y/\Delta Ex$, which would behave in the same way as the domestic investment multiplier. As countries with substantial unemployment exported more, their incomes would rise by a multiple of their net export growth. And some portion of this higher income growth would be spent on imports, stimulating foreign economies.

To Keynes, injections or leakages of purchasing power in the form of imports, exports and capital movements would be multiplied in keeping with each economy's spending stream and credit superstructure. Keynes's income multiplier found its counterpart in the banking system's credit-creation multiplier (the reciprocal of its reserve requirement ratio under the fractional reserve system of banking). If banks had to hold, say, 20 per cent of their deposits in the form of reserves, then the banking system as a whole could create and lend out credit on a multiple of five to one. A country's income multiplier thus might be increased by reducing reserve requirements for the banking system or otherwise leveraging the credit superstructure. (However, Keynes himself did not draw this parallelism.)

Recognizing the tendency for structural ratios to shift over time, Keynes feared that the marginal propensity to consume would decline as incomes rose. "The marginal propensity to consume is not constant for all levels of employment, and it is probable that there will be, as a rule, a tendency for it to diminish as employment increases ..."[3] This threatened to reduce the multiplier over time, leading to secular stagnation as a result of over-saving.

---

[1]   J. M. Keynes, *General Theory of Employment, Interest and Money* (London, 1936), pp. 120ff. See also Fritz Machlup, *International Trade and the National Income Multiplier* (Philadelphia: 1943), p. 8.

[2]   Keynes, *General Theory*, p. 120.                [3]   Keynes, *General Theory*, p. 120.

This acknowledgement of a shifting multiplier value was critical, but neither Keynes nor his followers could pursue it without confusing the applied mathematics of their analysis. If government spending had *varying* effects on the body politic, precise calculation of the impact of increased purchasing power would become less knowable. To be sure, its changes might occur et a predictable rate within historically established parameters. Hoping to use multiplier analysis as a predictive tool to guide public policy, Keynesians downplayed the idea of shifting multiplier values. "If multiplier theory is to have any predictive values," admitted Fritz Machlup in his 1943 text on *International Trade and the National Income Multiplier*, "propensities must either be stable or their rules of change must be known." This created "a vested interest in stable marginal propensities."[4]

The essence of business cycle analysis is to trace the shifting shape of economic activity. It has long been apparent that during the course of the business cycle the foreign-trade multiplier (like the multiplier itself) falls as employment approaches full capacity and a growing proportion of income is spent on imports. As the economy encounters capacity constraints its operative ratios shift, producing trade deficits. However, the *General Theory* concentrated on the depression phase of the cycle. This was what made it only a special theory. Keynes's followers—of whom Machlup occupies a paramount position with respect to trade theory—reasoned *as if* marginal propensities are equal to average propensities, so that economic growth appears linear. Machlup acknowledged that in view of the practical difficulty of predicting changes in the multiplier, it could not really be used as a planning tool. It was merely an expository device to trace spending streams through the economy under certain assumptions. What it "predicted" was more the outcome of an academic exercise than of reality.

But in the depression-ridden 1930s, cyclical or long-term changes in propensities and multiplier values were not a major concern, nor was inflation. In postulating depression conditions and large-scale unemployment, this theorizing neglected price effects, as well as terms-of-trade effects resulting from changing levels of imports and exports.

With regard to the pricing and terms-of-trade effects of exports and capital transfers, Keynes found little reason in his *General Theory* to review what he had elaborated in his writings on German reparations and his *Treatise on Money*. In the boom conditions of the late 1920s he had cited investment and productivity as the major long-term determinant of Germany's economic position. But the task of his *General Theory* was to focus on those aspects of foreign trade that

---

[4]　Machlup, *International Trade and the National Income Multiplier*, pp. 19f., 198ff. For a discussion of how the multiplier might vary over the course of the business cycle see Haberler, *Prosperity and Depression* (3rd ed.), pp. 228–31.

could be addressed by multiplier theory regarding income and spending processes, without reference to price adjustments. The "new economics" was a doctrine
of how industrial economies might overcome depression conditions by reflating
purchasing power. It did not deal with labor constraints or the impact of spending on price changes and interest rates, or with the problem faced by raw-
materials exporters as a result of the collapse of world prices.

As full-capacity operations were approached, Machlup acknowledged, "an
analysis based on the assumption of full employment must be more, or almost
exclusively, interested in relative price changes and in the barter terms of trade."[5]
What was important was to trace the impact of government deficit spending
and new investment on the economy's spending stream and employment.

### Some shortcomings of multiplier analysis

Two sets of problems stood in the way of statistically verifying the multiplier.
Domestically, it was volatile over the course of the business cycle. Also, new
investment was assumed to occur at existing capital/output and labor/output
ratios rather than being labor-displacing (that is, increasing productivity).
Internationally, foreign trade played "a double role in ... multiplier theory: Once
as multiplicand, and secondly as one of the determinants of the multiplier."
Exports represented an injection of income, and higher overall income led to
higher imports, making the net trade balance highly complex to estimate. "This
double role of foreign trade," noted Machlup, along with the problem of segre-
gating "autonomous" from income-induced shifts in foreign trade, "is likely to
defeat every attempt at statistical verification of foreign-trade multiplier theory."
But to drop Keynes's static assumptions dismissing the effects of foreign trade
on prices, interest rates and productivity would render "the job of theorizing ...
rather horrible. And the results would hardly be worth the sacrifice of simplicity."[6] The alternative—to be more realistic—would render multiplier theory
inappropriate as an economic planning tool. Despite these limiting assumptions,
contended Machlup, "the explanatory and pedagogic value of the theory may
be considerable even if its predictive value is small."[7]

Machlup suggested extending the foreign trade multiplier to include a
catchall category called "foreign repercussions of domestic income changes,"

---

5   Machlup, *International Trade*, p.207.
6   Machlup, *ibid.*, p. 209. See also pp, 33, 13,
7   Machlup, *ibid.*, p. 9 See also pp. 59 and 199: "Despite the artificiality of the assumptions,"
    Machlup concludes, "the real purpose of the formulas is not to 'know' what, for example,
    an additional meat export will do to Argentina's income, but ... to exhibit certain relation-
    ships between independent and dependent variables, to show whether they are positively or
    negatively correlated, to tell whether it is their magnitude or their proportions which matter,
    to indicate which ones are more important and which less."

including autonomous capital transfers. This required extending the multiplier from $(\frac{1}{s})$ to $(\frac{1}{s+m+f})$. (In this equation $s$ represents the propensity to save, $m$ the propensity to import, and $f$ the foreign repercussions factor.)[8] Leakages resulting from imports, foreign investment or other spending would mute the multiplier ratio. Hence, Keynes granted, the multiplier effect would be lowest in countries with the highest ratios of foreign trade to national income—for example, European countries, in contrast to the United States.

While the U.S. economy had a lower proportion of foreign trade to national income, and hence fewer leakages abroad, it also exhibited the world's highest ratio of debt to equity investment and economic activity. Financially, it was more seriously affected by the Great Depression than any other industrial economy. The problem was not only a high income multiplier (working in reverse on the downswing) but the fact that the nation was much more financially leveraged in using checking accounts and bank credit. This pyramiding brought its financial life tumbling down in the face of world economic breakdown.

Debt leveraging was most apparent in the stock market. To a growing degree in the 1920s, more money was to be made by financial speculation (largely with borrowed funds) than through new direct investment in plant and equipment. This led Keynes to oppose the stock market in general. But by and large the *General Theory*'s adherents ignored financial considerations.

This theoretical framework for income analysis became rigidified and conservative as it became a new orthodoxy. Each country's structural ratios were depicted as being unchanging "propensities" akin to what earlier generations called "natural." Yet of all the major ratios, imports and exports show the sharpest variations over the course of the business cycle. Furthermore, much trade is financed on credit. In such cases no money actually changes hands. The export surplus is offset by a bookkeeping entry for a foreign investment "outflow" (defined as an increase in claims on foreigners for the money due for the export). Putting this financial claim on capital account in the national income and product tables gives the impression that there has been a cash export sale and an autonomous foreign loan. The national income accounting format thus diverges from reality.

Multiplier analysis agrees with most existing trade theory in suggesting that exports tend to promote imports and vice versa. The expansion of economic activity resulting from an export-induced multiplier effect leads to an increase in imports which tended to reach a new equilibrium position. "Fortunately," commented Machlup wryly, "nobody has as yet tried to make imports by definition equal to exports" in the sense that Keynes defined savings as being equal

---

[8]    Machlup, *ibid.*, p. 330. See also p. 76.

to investment.[9] In contrast to the price-specie flow mechanism, equilibrium at higher income levels is not restored by exports declining as a result of rising prices, but by imports rising and foreign incomes multiplying. This is perhaps the major doctrinal impact of the theory of the foreign-trade multiplier.

On the other hand, multiplier analysis did not recognize tendencies toward chronic ("autonomous") trade and payments imbalance. Although U.S. expansion increased the economy's imports after World War II, its other activities offset this tendency to expand world demand. Much of the nation's rising income was invested in the stock market, pushing up securities prices and attracting funds from countries already suffering trade deficits and downward pressure on their currencies. Such countries tended to suffer negative "foreign repercussions" factors in direct proportion to their trade deficits.

On balance, of course, the balance of payments must "balance." That is why it technically is called the "balance of international transactions." Either the export multiplier and propensity to import are exactly balanced by the foreign factor $f$ (which in this case would be so general as not to be much help), or a balancing item is still necessary to "finance the deficit (surplus)." This balancing item typically consists of net growth in foreign debt (or claims) or, net loss (growth) in international reserves.

### Inapplicability of multiplier analysis to "dual economies"

The analysis of Third World monocultures is complicated by the fact that their saving and investment are concentrated in their export sectors, which tend to be dominated by foreign investors who remit most of their export proceeds abroad rather than reinvesting them domestically. To use Machlup's terminology, the foreign repercussions factor offsets the foreign trade multiplier. Domestically, these dual economies and/or economically small countries produce only a narrow range of commodities, and hence have a high propensity to import. Although this may be low for the domestic subsistence sector as a result of its low income levels and lack of access to foreign exchange, it is especially high in the export sector. In conjunction with the "foreign repercussions effect," it may approach unity, that is, a 100 percent leakage when flight capital is taken into account. This repercussions factor reflects the foreign-ownership leakage, coupled with the "demonstration effect," an emulation of foreign consumption habits by individuals who can afford luxury imports.

Foreign owners of mines and plantations may transfer abroad as much as a third of the gross export income of Third World countries. Chile's foreign trade multiplier turns out to be negligible in view of the fact that most of its

---

[9]  Machlup, *ibid.*, p. 33.

export earnings are remitted in the form of profits, interest and depreciation, or used to pay for the imported machinery, fuel, management and other imports needed to produce the nation's minerals exports. Most of the export proceeds retained at home are paid as taxes to the government, which itself has nearly a 100 per cent propensity to spend this foreign exchange abroad as debt service or military spending. The remaining foreign exchange is converted into local currency to pay labor, but most hard currency is used to import necessities such as food. Throughout Latin America and Africa a few high-income recipients obtain most of the scarce foreign exchange, which they tend to hoard abroad in the form of flight capital. The fact that only a small portion of export income finds its way to the domestic sector for spending on local goods and services renders domestic multiplier analysis all but irrelevant.

Keynes denied that the multiplier could have a negative value. But if the terms-of-trade penalty that often accompanies a rising export volume offsets the income effects, its effective value becomes negative. Countries actually may worsen their position by increasing their export production. Machlup contends that it is merely "a matter of taste whether we drop the assumption that prices are unchanged," pointing to the fact that supply curves are more elastic in depression periods, resulting in an absence of inflation in response to increased demand. But demand for exports of raw materials is price-inelastic. What promises at first glance to be positive income effects from rising export volume may be offset by negative price effects when these exports are thrown onto world markets. The pretended advantage turns out to be merely that of (over)simplicity.

The terms of trade will deteriorate when increased export output faces a relatively inelastic world demand. This has characterized raw materials exports since the 1930s. Yet Machlup writes that "This probability [of price inelastic exports] is not great," and adds that "The advantages of provisionally ruling out all these complications by the stable-price assumption are certainty great."[10] This oversimplification suggests wrongheaded economic policies for heavily indebted raw-materials exporters with major foreign investment, coupled with serious capital flight.

Machlup suggests that an imperialistic interpretation of the theory of the multiplier" may lie in its use "as an argument for generous foreign tending."[11] Most U.S. "aid loans" are tied to export promotion and hence spur domestic income growth. In addition, much foreign investment turns out to be cost-free for creditor nations. Much of takes the form of retained earnings used to build up investment, or of tangible goods shipped from the United States or other

[10]  Machlup, *ibid.*, pp. 183, 205, and Haberler, *Prosperity and Depression*, p. 6.
[11]  Machlup, *ibid.*, p. 216.

hard-currency nations. Foreign investment usually has a rapid payback period, especially in balance-of-payments terms as foreign income results in higher purchases from (or payments to) the nation making the investment. This reverberatory export demand, remitted profits and depreciation spurs domestic income growth in the investing nation.

From the Third World's vantage point, multiplier analysis is overly optimistic in stressing only the gross favorable impact of exports and foreign investment. Since 1951, foreign investment in Third World countries has contributed to deteriorating terms of trade for raw materials without having much positive effect on local economies, which have become increasingly dependent on imports of food and other necessities, and hence on new loans resulting in even higher debt service. The result has been economic austerity and a deepening loss of control over their domestic economies, along with an unsustainable debt burden that has stripped them of the fiscal resources needed to improve their economic position.

### Political implications of multiplier analysis

After World War II, Keynesian income theory endorsed a policy of economic expansion, tax cuts and deficit spending, and lower trade barriers to ward off depression. The level of investment, spurred by public works programs but discouraged by taxation, was held to determine the course of the business cycle. In the 1970s, U.S. officials demanded that Europe and Japan reduce their unemployment and inflate their economies by running federal budget deficits, easing bank credit and lowering their tariffs to spur imports, especially from the United States—which itself is now running the largest budget and balance-of-payments deficits in history. U.S. officials claim that this spurs world expansion as an "engine of growth" from the demand side of the supply-and-demand equation. A byproduct has been to bid up the price of Third World raw materials in what seems to be a global trickle-down process.

Multiplier analysis is optimistic in holding any nation's income expansion to be in the interest of all others in their capacity of exporters. But Malthus drew attention in his *Principles of Political Economy* to the competitive potential of such expansion, posing the question of just what *kind* of growth or development is most desirable:

> It is for instance, a just and general rule in political economy, that the wealth of a particular nation is increased by the increasing wealth and prosperity of surrounding states; and unquestionably there cannot be a more obvious truth than that, if these states are not successful competitors in those branches of trade in which the particular nation had excelled, their increasing wealth must tend to increase the demand for its products, and call forth more effectively its

resources, But if this rule be repeatedly insisted upon without noticing the above most important limitation, how is the student in political economy to account for some of the most prominent and best attested facts in the history of commerce. How is he to account for the rapid failure of the resources of Venice under the increasing wealth of Portugal and the rest of Europe, after the discovery of a passage to India by the Cape of Good Hope; the stagnation of the industry of Holland, when the surrounding nations grew sufficiently rich to undertake their own carrying trades, the increasing trade and wealth of Great Britain, during the war of the French Revolution, under the diminishing trade and increasing poverty of the greatest part of Europe, and the comparative distress of America, when other states were enabled to participate in those trades, which as a neutral she had carried on during a great part of the late war with such signal success. ... It is surely much better that such a rule should be laid down at first with its limitations. Nothing can tend so strongly to bring theories and general principles into discredit as the occurrence of consequences, from particular premises, which have not been foreseen ... and with the mass of mankind this will pass for an impeachment of general principles, and of the knowledge or good faith of those who are in the habit of inculcating them.12

While Keynesian analysis viewed foreign expansion as favoring the United States after World War II to the extent that foreign economies developed as export markets, U.S. foreign-aid policies and international lending thwarted their evolution as industrial and agricultural competitors. Meanwhile, the favorable depiction of export sales as such, irrespective of their developmental consequences, has hindered the development of Third World countries by promoting their export monoculture syndrome.

In the 1950s two types of Latin American economists developed trade theories based on structural balance-of-payments analysis. Both schools analyzed Latin America's trade in terms of "the weakness in commodity markets, the population boom, and rising economic ambitions."13 But taking existing economic structures for granted, a conservative school sought to accommodate

---

12 Malthus, *Principles of Political Economy*, pp. 10f.
13 Dudley Seers, "A Theory of Inflation and Growth m Under-Developed Economies Based on the Experience of Latin America," *Oxford Economic Papers*, XIV (June 1962), p. 192. This paper contains a bibliography of the Latin American structuralist school. As Seers describes the dichotomy between its left and right wings, both refer to the "structures" of income, demand, output, industry, exports, imports, administration, politics, society, etc. Broadly speaking the more leftists mean by the word [structures] all these things, because each of them is considered in some way an impediment to economic growth and the achievement of a more equalitarian society. The conclusion may be drawn that social revolution is a necessary condition for an adequate rate of economic growth. On the other hand, the more conservative adherents usually put the main, if not the exclusive, emphasis on the structures of production and trade, since they are naturally less inclined to stress the need for social change. (In Marxist terms they are "commodity fetishists.")

international trade and investment to the inequitable status quo and its rigidities ("structures") rather than modernizing economic institutions to increase productive powers. A more reformist school sought to transform Latin American social and economic institutions along more productive lines. Left-wing structuralists pointed to institutional and economic rigidities limiting agricultural and industrial development.

### The Chilean experience

Structuralist analysis was inspired largely by the need to take account of the impact of foreign ownership of Latin America's export sectors. It hardly is an accident that Chile became the home of most structuralist literature. Its export monoculture is divided into two disparate sectors: a foreign-owned mining industry that for many years accounted for some 80 percent of Chilean exports, and a much less capital-intensive domestic economy.

The country's exports are dominated by copper, which for many decades was mined primarily by three large companies (Anaconda, Kennecott and Cerro), which were "Chileanized" by the Frei administration in the late 1960s when the government purchased ownership of the Chilean mines from their U.S. parents. Chile's nitrate and iodine sectors also are mostly foreign owned. The result is that when Chile exports copper, nitrates or iodine, about a third of the proceeds are retained abroad in the form of profits and interest, payment for non-Chilean capital goods and other production inputs, shipping charges, payments to parent companies for managerial services and related fees, and in recent years the Chilean government's payment for the mines it bought from their U.S. owners. Subsequent remittances to pay for the official buyouts represent funds previously retained in Chile as tax revenues on export sales.

These export-sector transactions were segregated from those of the domestic economy by Chile's central bank in its annual balance-of-payments accounts, in recognition of the functionally different variables at work. Net balance-of-payments revenues of the export sector could be rendered on a per-ton or per-pound basis for copper, or projected as economic trends in themselves where appropriate. Macroeconomic ratios had little relevance as far as multiplier effects are concerned.

The remaining two-thirds of the nominal export value remains within the Chilean economy in two forms: wage payments to domestic labor (converted into local currency by the central bank) and tax payments by the mining companies to the Chilean government. Wage payments to labor involved in copper production form only a minor proportion of the total income generated by this capital-intensive sector. The fact that the ore is mined in high Andean regions, distant from Chile's other economic activity, means that wage payments do not automatically rise when copper-export prices increase. As for the government's tax revenues and profit-sharing, this foreign exchange is recycled abroad as the central bank pays foreign debts and buys arms, food and other imports (and of course, the usual capital flight by Mr. Pinochet and his military junta during their years in power). There thus is barely any foreign-trade multiplier effect on domestic economic activity from Chilean exports, as virtually all the foreign exchange earned on Chile's raw materials is transferred abroad? Viewed in its institutional context, Chile suffered virtually a 100 per cent "leakage" of the export revenues deriving from its mining sector.

Much of the country's food was imported on credit (including U.S. foreign aid loans), while its arms were financed largely by inter-governmental military credit. Inter-governmental institutions, led by the IMF, coordinated a growing portion of Chile's foreign borrowing and import financing. This politicized the entire debt process, as well as the trade patterns sustained by this international lending. Like other countries, Chile was obliged to service its debts to foreign creditors and maintain an open environment to international investors in order to obtain IMF and World Bank loans. To the extent that debtor economies are obligated to the IMF, the World Bank, the U.S. Government and private creditors, they are obliged to use their export proceeds to amortize their outstanding debts rather than to invest these funds domestically. In this respect the "foreign repercussions" and income effects of rising exports are nowhere near as favorable as they might have been in 1945 before these countries fell into chronic debtor status and import dependency. They have been obliged to let foreigners appropriate their leading sectors and natural resources, duly remitting abroad the profits and depreciation on such investments.

It thus would be quixotic to abstract the analysis of Latin America's trade patterns from the concrete behavioral system imposed by today's international financial institutions and world diplomacy. A precondition for most countries receiving U.S. food aid has been that they refrain from modernizing their agriculture, on the logic that this would threaten export sales by U.S. farmers. American officials have considered land reform to be associated with a left-wing political shift deemed adverse to U.S. interests, When Chile balked at North American interference under its Allende regime, the domestic economy was destabilized, its leaders murdered and a police state installed. Its Social Security saving was turned over to U.S. and other foreign money managers, who siphoned off the lion's share of account earnings as management fees, while Mr. Pinochet built up a nice U.S. bank account of his own. But such unpleasant realities are not the kind of phenomena that are incorporated into most trade and investment theorizing.

One of the most pernicious effects of export monocultures has been that the saving and investment functions normally associated with production have become part of the U.S. and other creditor economies rather than a domestic part of the exporting economies. The income benefits "normally" associated with export growth are muted, despite the existence of relatively high unemployment rates in Latin America and other monoculture regions. The essence of monocultures is that "full" production capacity may be associated with as much as a 30 per cent rate of domestic unemployment given th typical shortages of specific types of labor, materials, capital and management. Such structural bottlenecks suggest that higher export earnings are likely to result in inflationary pressures rather than in expanding domestic employment and incomes.

To sum up, political leverage is more responsible than strictly market-oriented factors for the international adjustment process imposed on Chile and other Third World countries. To obtain multinational financing for infra-structure projects, debtor countries are obliged to encourage export production, not domestic self-sufficiency. As president of the World Bank, Robert McNamara directed debtor countries to take active steps to retard their rates of population growth and curtail growth in the domestic consumption of their own raw materials, presumably making a larger volume of these commodities available for export. Such political realities cannot be made explicit and "endogenous" as long as economic theorizing confines itself to analyzing only private-sector market forces. Such theorizing is politically conservative at the expense of economic realism.

### Summary: The failure of multiplier and trickle-down prescriptions

Almost regardless of world price and cost functions, two macroeconomics functions were supposed to help less developed economies expand in keeping with the industrial nations following World War II. First, expansion of national income was supposed to lead automatically to higher imports on a *pro rata* basis from supplier countries. General economic expansion in North America and Europe was projected as increasing the demand for imports, including Third World raw materials. Thanks to relatively stable propensities to import, the world economy was supposed to expand or contract so that rising fortunes in the United States and Europe would be a "demand engine" calling forth corresponding expansion in the periphery. The U.S. Baker and Brady plans claimed that Third World debt problems would be solved simply by the United States and other industrial nations expanding rapidly enough to create a thriving market for the exports of debtor countries.

This line of argument is the same approach that holds that U.S. unemployment among, say, black urban teenagers can be reduced simply by economic recovery. Experience has shown how overly optimistic this liberal view is. It has become obvious that no such fixed propensities to spend a given proportion of income on imports are at work. The international trickle-down theory is a false model. Expansion in the high-technology center tends to occur independently of progress in the less developed periphery, and even at the latter's expense and deepening economic obsolescence.

A second factor promising to catalyze the development of less developed countries was the tendency the industrial nations to invest more abroad as their incomes rose. This was supposed to provide productive capital to less developed countries, helping to bid up the relatively low wage levels and cheap land and mineral resources that made them attractive to international investors. Not acknowledged was the tendency for investment to underdevelop host economies, warping them into monocultures while aggravating their food deficits. Foreign investment led to an export-oriented pattern of growth rather than domestic diversification to achieve self-sufficiency through import displacement.

The Third World's growing international dependency and inability to escape from its debt trap stems ultimately from limited production capacity. This in turn may be traced to such bottlenecks as agricultural rigidities stemming from backward institutions of land tenure, and lack of adequate rural infrastructure. In the face of this institutional backwardness, increased consumption resulting from population growth and higher wage levels results in higher imports of food, fuels and other essentials. In the most rigidified economies this results in nearly a 100 per cent propensity to import. Such a situation (in which no multiplier exists at all) should not be accepted as a normal state of affairs. More income will not spur output or achieve balance in the international accounts unless existing bottlenecks are alleviated and social-economic life is restructured in less polarized and less debt-ridden ways.

# 18

## How Monetarist Austerity Perpetuates Debt Peonage

After World War II the world seemed to have learned its lesson from the previous war and its transfer problems. Neither allies nor enemies were burdened with postwar arms and reparations debts. Marshall Plan aid to Europe took the form of direct transfers of money, not loans. In the realm of economic theory, Keynesian income analysis urged the world to avert postwar depression by following expansionary rather than deflationary policies. Instead of deflating currencies and prices back to prewar levels as had been done following past wars, central banks sought currency parities. When taxes were raised, it was held desirable to levy them as much as possible on the wealthy, on special interests and on windfall gains. Governments committed themselves to use deficit spending when necessary to promote full employment, and monetary supply also supported this aim.

This was the golden age of Keynesian economics. It was made possible largely by the fact that nations emerged from the war with abundant resources of purchasing power (savings accumulated during the war with few consumer goods to buy), skilled labor, productive plant—and relatively little debt. The postwar expansion rode a wave of credit-financed spending by consumers, business and government.

National economies were to be integrated with each other on the foundation of mutual growth in demand. Postwar recovery in the industrial nations was envisioned as providing a market for Third World raw materials, while the ensuing multiplication of incomes in less developed countries would (it was hoped) sustain the purchase of industrial-nation exports in a self-expanding process. Meanwhile, the United States took the lead in using foreign aid as a diplomatic lever to deter the kind of protectionism that had fragmented the world in the 1930s.

This internationalist optimism assumed that the elasticities of demand for raw materials and low-wage exports would be sufficiently high to maintain generally balanced trade. It also assumed that backward economic institutions in Europe's former colonies would modernize themselves under the stimulus of political independence and freedom. After all, social reform had occurred naturally enough in the industrial nations. It had been a struggle, but the liberal fight was won in country after country.

However, equivalent political momentum and infrastructure was lacking in the less developed countries, above all Africa and Latin America. Their social and technological transformation was further discouraged by the Obsolescence Syndrome. Rising productivity in the industrial nations rendered much Third World labor and small-scale capital uncompetitive. By foreclosing opportunities for Europe's former colonies to compete in many high technology areas, free trade suspended the normal feedback process between economic development and political restructuring. This is why these countries were called "backward" after World War II. The patronizing term "developing" would come later, as if they were hurrying to catch up rather than succumbing to underdevelopment.

Most raw-materials producers even stopped growing the food needed to sustain their expanding populations, white not creating sufficient industry to employ them. Relatively few farmers were ready to become urban entrepreneurs as had been the case in Europe and the United States. Agriculture was not family-owned and operated but was organized on the latifundia plantation system in conjunction with microfundia. Mineral and plantation monocultures were associated with widening food deficits and mounting foreign debts.

The upshot was that productive powers and incomes polarized between rich and poor countries as a result of factors not touched on by the *General Theory*. Keynes had focused on Britain's domestic problems of the 1930s, not those of its colonies or other less developed regions. High on the list of problems underplayed by the *General Theory* was the growth of international dependency and structural payments deficits leading to a growing debt overhead.

Expansionary income policies and democratic egalitarianism in the industrial nations thus went hand-in-hand with international inequality. Poor countries supplied raw materials at prices that did not reflect long-term replacement costs (for depletable resources) or ecological damage, while low-wage products were priced too low to support adequate levels of social spending to educate the population and in other ways modernize their societies. This was the dark reverse side of the coin of postwar industrial-nation prosperity. Raw materials were supplied by a backward periphery that has been unable to sustain its demand for industrial-nation exports. Its cumulative payments deficits have been financed by foreign borrowing, requiring a rising flow of debt service to be paid in a process that is mathematically unsustainable, and collapsed in 1982 with Mexico's insolvency.

These problems were most serious in less developed countries, but Keynesianism became discredited primarily in the industrial nations, especially in the United States during the Vietnam War years. Largely in a reaction against inflationary demand and its associated payments deficits, monetarism made its comeback. The new generation of monetarists retained from Keynesianism its macroeconomic point of reference in terms of aggregate income variables, but administered them in a downward rather than upward direction.

## Meade's marginalist approach to the balance of payments

The British economist James Meade was a major figure in narrowing the scope of international trade theory. On the one hand he referred to macroeconomic income variables in tracing marginal adjustments under restrictive academic assumptions typical of the then popular Hicks-Harrod-Domar models of domestic economic balance. However, Meade ignored structural problems and opposed statism and direct economic controls. He argued that price and wage flexibility (by which he meant wage reductions and austerity) under free trade might balance international payments in the context of full employment, primarily by currency devaluation. The first volume of Meade's *Theory of International Economic Policy*, entitled *The Balance of Payments* (1951), argued that

> the price adjustment mechanism of variable exchange rates or of flexible wage rates must be used to adjust the balance of payments, so that the balance of payments is put into equilibrium without any movement away from the modified free trade position.[1]

Of course, this would not be the case if devaluation had the effect of reducing foreign exchange receipts, as occurs in cases where demand for a country's exports is price inelastic, or where falling incomes had adverse effects on productivity. And as Harry Johnson has aptly criticized, Meade's free-trade case further assumed "the pursuit of appropriate internal control policies by the Government, without investigating what happens if the Government is not successful in maintaining knife-edge full employment with stable prices."[2] This assumption of a simplistic full-employment price level enabled Meade to conclude that *dirigiste* policies such as credit allocation, subsidies or related societal planning were unnecessary.

Meade's second volume, *Trade and Welfare* (1955), wedded Keynesianism and marginalism by using the methodology of comparative stories to argue that the world's real income would be maximized by a slightly modified system of free trade rather than by protectionism or other statist policies. As in his earlier volume, he assumed technological production functions to be given as independent facts of life. This fatal assumption ruled out what hitherto had been the most important objective of protectionist policy: to bring about dynamic changes in productivity.

[1] James E. Meade, *The Theory of International Economic Policy*. Volume One: *The Balance of Payments* (Oxford: 1951), p. 329.
[2] Harry G. Johnson, *Money, Trade and Economic Growth: Survey Lectures in Economic Theory* (Cambridge: 1962) p. 17.

In assuming full employment and optimum technology to be "givens" for each country, Meade dealt with optimum tariff levels and exchange rates under severely limiting assumptions: no feedback was acknowledged to exist between income levels and productivity, and no institutional restructuring or modernization was deemed necessary. Trade and domestic spending was supposed to be conducted on a cash rather than a credit basis. If the resulting distribution of world income was felt to be inequitable, Meade suggested, the wealthy nations might elect to subsidize the poorer countries, but need not help modernize them and should not condone their protectionism and debt renegotiation. It was better for the rich nations to do what they were best at doing—earning as much money as possible—and then to share this surplus with poorer countries—alms for the poor, as it were.

Meade acknowledged that using foreign aid to compensate for free trade's reinforcement of an inequitable status quo probably was utopian, given the fact that international diplomacy operates on the adversary system of competing national self-interest. If the industrial nations really wanted to help enrich the poorer countries, they would not engage in such strong domestic protectionism and financial nationalism promoted as the Washington Consensus has promoted since the 1990s. Perhaps it might have been more helpful to have written a book on policy describing how industrial nations in fact use protectionist tax incentives and other controls—as well as bilateral and multilateral foreign aid—to strengthen their international position and thereby contribute to international polarization. But such *Realpolitik* was not Meade's objective.

Like all definitions of equilibrium, Johnson notes, Meade's is "by nature ideological." It is an abstract ideal consisting of "the absence of all controls and restrictions on trade." Any use of active policy is characterized by another value-laden term: "unnatural," disparaging the naturalness of policies aimed at stabilizing the balance of payments or exchange rates by active government policy. In holding that balance-of-payments equilibrium could be achieved simply by shifts in exchange rates, prices and general wage levels, Meade used macroeconomics for an anti-government argument against sectoral planning and technological upgrading.

The conclusion (to quote Harry Johnson's summary) was that "a country must employ *both* some means of control over its aggregate expenditure *and* some means of control (the exchange rate or trade restrictions) over its international trade. … for each policy objective you need a policy instrument." But the instrument is blunt and broad rather than sharp, for Meade has cooked the books in advance. He defines payments disequilibrium not merely in terms of how much accommodating finance actually is made necessary by the payments deficit (by how much gold or foreign exchange the central bank must sell or borrow abroad), but by the amount of accommodating finance which it *would have been necessary* to provide in any period in order to avoid any depreciation in the exchange rate *without the employment* of exchange controls, import restrictions or other governmental measures especially devised to restrict the demand for foreign currencies.

The question thus becomes one of how large the payments deficit would have been if the government did not do what governments are supposed to do—to use controls and related policy instruments.

As matters turn out, Meade's definition "is so constructed that only a price-level or exchange-rate adjustment can eliminate balance-of-payments disequilibrium—any other method of eliminating an 'actual' disequilibrium would create a 'potential' disequilibrium."[3] This hypothetical reasoning in terms of what a country's balance of payments would be if governments did not enact policies made the even more serious assumption that no such policies would be wielded by *foreign* governments. But where does such reasoning lead? Why reason as if the real world were not one in which the United States protects its agriculture with quotas and unilaterally demands "orderly marketing agreements" for textiles and other industries? We are drawn into a just-pretend Cloud-cuckoo-land of speculation far removed from the actual behavior of nations in the modern adversarial system of self-interested diplomacy. And how curious it is for a book purporting to be on policy to hold that direct controls over imports and credit, subsidies, special taxes and all other special government policies are unnatural.

The result is a rather narrow-minded erudition. In the mathematical supplement to his work Meade "shows that his model allows 28,781,143,379 possible 'policy combinations.'"[4] But nowhere among these marginalist policies are to

---

[3]  Johnson, *Money, Trade and Economic Growth*, p. 16, and "The Taxonomic Approach to Economic Policy," *Economic Journal*, 61 (December 1951), pp. 812ff., citing Meade, *The Balance of Payments*, p. 15 (italics added). See also p. 823, citing Meade, p. 296 for an example of his opposition to direct controls. Instead of endorsing exchange controls "as a means of dealing with hot-money movements … Meade prefers counter-speculation by the authorities," assuming that the latter are able to out-guess the market. (On balance, as George Soros showed in his 1992 raid on sterling, official intervention usually ends up subsidizing speculation, not penalizing it.) Meade admits "that controls may not be in the world interest if nominal yields do not correspond to 'real productivity'." But this normally *is* the case! It would be more reasonable to admit at the outset that interest rates are held high for balance-of-payments reasons *not* reflecting the "real rate of productivity," and then to examine controls from a realistic point of view. But Meade's laissez faire prejudice leads him to assume a simplistic utopian world.

[4]  Johnson, "The Taxonomic Approach," p. 830, citing Meade's *Mathematical Supplement*. He adds that "in order to choose between the impossible number of alternatives with which even a relatively simple analytical problem confronts him, the theorist is strongly tempted to eliminate some of the cases by prejudging the results of measurements he does not and perhaps could not make." Meade distils these combinations down to a menu of 399 preferred cases.

be found strategies to modernize production or achieve structural transform-ation! There is no discussion of government strategies to renegotiate its foreign debts (for instance, on the ground that it is unable to service them without cutting its own throat over the long term). There is merely a bald assertion that governments should devalue(marginally) to earn the foreign exchange to pay (marginally) rising levels of debt service. Existing social and economic institu-tions, however backward, inequitable, unprogressive, corrupt or self-defeating they may be, may be *subsidized* to help maintain employment, but are not to be changed. One therefore suspects that all of Meade's nearly 29 billion policy combi-nations are merely just so many grains of sand to throw in the eyes of observers wishing to know what governments in the dynamic real world can in fact do about their payments deficits and the structural problems underlying them.

Johnson aptly has warned that "the theorist is strongly tempted to simplify his problems to the point at which his results cannot be applied at all to practical problems. Thus Professor Meade conducts most of his analysis in terms of a world of two countries, each of which produces only one good—an assumption which … corresponds to no practical problem in international economics whatsoever." If four goods were produced instead of two (a single export good and a domestic good in each country), the result would be "a string of clumsy determinants without any very obvious conclusions to be drawn from them."[5] In other words, even this small dose of realism would produce a dross of unquantifiable, over-elaborated mathematics and geometrics.

Another pitfall of Meade's basic line of reasoning is his use of "propen-sities" as fixed ratios taken to be causal in themselves rather than merely accommodating. The most questionable fixed propensity is that of foreign lending. The implication—which goes much further than Keynes went—is that an economy lends or invests a fixed proportion of its savings abroad, presum-ably because it has got into the habit of doing so over the years. In reality, foreign investment is a volatile function depending on relative international interest rates, profit opportunities, military and economic destabilization spurring flight capital, tax dodging, criminal activities and so forth. Meade's neat analysis acknowledges none of these intrusions of ugly reality. Johnson notes that he also "assumes that domestic expenditure is affected by the home rate of interest but not by the foreign rate of interest, though the difference between the two affects the amount of foreign lending; it would seem more reasonable

---

5   Johnson, "The Taxonomic Approach," p. 827, citing Meade's *Mathematical Supplement*, p. 46. He adds (p. 828) that "This temptation [to oversimplify] is particularly dangerous when questions of economic policy are involved, because then the desire for simplicity may be reinforced by personal preferences in prompting the exclusion of possible cases." Elasticity pessimism is the usual case ignored by free traders, who also neglect foreign reactions and other responses cited in the balance of this chapter.

to assume that the foreign rate of interest will have some influence on domestic saving if residents can in fact lend their savings abroad."[6]

I have cited Johnson's criticisms at such length because he later became one of Meade's supporters, having perceived that Meade had grasped the last remaining available straws to defend free-trade policies.

## Alexander's absorption approach encourages devaluation

While Meade was constructing his models in the early 1950s, the IMF economist Sidney Alexander developed crude macroeconomic formulae to suggest how devaluation might cure payments deficits via its impact on domestic income and expenditure. This remains the foundation for IMF programs and condition-alities ever since. The idea is that by reducing real wages and direct investment— that is, domestic "absorption" of current output—devaluation is supposed to free output for export.

The theory borrows its categories from Keynesian macroeconomics, but its spirit is that of the monetarism that Keynes controverted in the German reparations debate. Keynes viewed hoarding—that is, non-spending—as the major threat to prosperity, and hence to direct investment, and by logical exten-sion to the trade balance, inasmuch as the latter is a function of the economy's productive powers. Alexander's model recommends policies to maximize rather than minimize hoarding, in the hope that this will minimize wages and con-

---

[6] Johnson, *ibid.*, pp. 816, 829, citing Meade's *Mathematical Supplement*, p. 10. Johnson further points out (p. 817) that Meade assumes that a country's total domestic expenditure and gross foreign lending or investment are "affected by the price of its export goods but not by the price of its imports (or of its 'home-trade' goods, where these are dealt with)." This assumption is made ostensibly "for simplification," but when such simplifications are at odds with reality (not to speak of common sense) they are more accurately a distraction. Real income falls when the terms of trade decline as import prices rise (for example, for grains and oil over the past decade). This suggests not only less domestic saving but also flight capital—a problem that Meade does not address.

Johnson cites a number of studies indicating that the proportion of income saved declines as the terms of trade deteriorate. (See the 1949 United Nations report on *Inflationary and Deflationary Tendencies, 1946–48*, pp. 5–14, and Arnold C. Harberger, "Currency Depre-ciation, Income, and the Balance of Trade," *Journal of Political Economy*, 58 [Feb. 1950], pp. 47–60.) Pointing out that such narrow assumptions produce irrelevant results, Johnson concludes (p. 826) that he "does not … believe that much assistance could be rendered to practical economic policy by further development along the lines laid down."

In any case, Meade's theoretical categories do not lend themselves to statistical measure-ment. To cite a glaring example, his measure of exports is net of all import content. This becomes a statistical nightmare to quantify. In the case of machine tools or other products made of steel in economies producing some iron and steel, how should one define the import content—on a *pro rata* basis (imputing an *average* mix of domestic and foreign steel), or on the basis of actual imports? What of the fuels used in production, or the foreign financing involved?

sumption. His objective is not full employment. In fact, he states that his model only will work where substantial unemployment exists.

The absorption model defines a country's net trade balance (*B*) as a residual function, equal to the difference between total goods and services produced in that country (*Y*) and the value taken off the market domestically." The latter "absorption" (*A*) is equal to consumption plus investment (*C+I*), with investment being defined to include inventories. Machlup has pointed out that the government sector (*G*) should also be recognized as a distinct function, so that *C+I+G=A*. However, *G* may be negative if the government runs a budget surplus, which is called hoarding (*H*). In either case the government budget appears only as a net item. The key to success for austerity programs is the tendency for devaluation to reduce domestic absorption *by increasing hoarding*, that is, *Y–A*.

This approach is reminiscent of the Ohlin-Rueff monetarism of the 1920s. In monetarist terminology, to solve the budgetary problem is to solve the transfer problem. Cutting back domestic income reduces consumption and investment, *thereby freeing an equivalent value of output for export*. By absorbing purchasing power, the government sector is supposed to free this output for export. As noted earlier, this approach makes the fatal assumptions that output is not affected by declining income, and that there is no adverse terms-of-trade effect. Falling wages and profits are not supposed to push the federal budget into deficit, because taxes are to be raised while expenditures are cut. The budget surplus replaces direct investment as the major variable, in the context of a contracting rather than expanding domestic economy.

Economic contraction is the consequence in practice, but the pretense is that less domestic demand "frees" more goods for export. As Alexander puts matters: "If a devaluation is to affect the foreign balance, it can do so in only two ways (1) it can lead to a change in the production of goods and services in the country," specifically a shift from home-market goods to exports by making the latter more profitable in domestic-currency terms; or (2) the devaluation may change the amount of real absorption associated with any given level of real income,"[7] that is, by reducing employment and investment while making imported capital goods more expensive. To be sure, devaluation cannot employ

[7]  Sidney S. Alexander, "Effect of a Devaluation on a Trade Balance," IMF Staff Papers, 2 (April 1952), pp. 264f., 268f., and M. O. Clement, Richard L. Pfister and Kenneth J. Rothwell, *Theoretical Issues in International Economics* (Boston: 1967), p. 307. The clearest discussion of Alexander's formulas that I have been able to find is Machlup's "Relative Prices and Aggregate Spending in the Analysis of Devaluation," *American Economic Review*, 45 (June 1955), pp. 255–78 (esp. p. 258 for the formulae in question). It is no coincidence that the working assumptions of bad theories are laid out more clearly by their antagonists than by their originators. If the proponent of a self-defeating theory had expressed himself

resources more fully or better, because it discourages domestic investment. Its efficacy in rectifying balance-of-payments deficits thus works solely via short-term price and income influences at the cost of longer term export and import-displacing capacity.

Alexander's analysis, like that of Meade, portrays devaluation as reducing the demand for foreign exchange without using the direct controls so hated by free traders. One reason why such controls are deemed unnecessary is the assumption that no autonomous capital movements take place—that is, no capital flight occurs as a result of the ongoing devaluation. Yet this is what occurs in practice. As Machlup has remarked: "These restricting conditions serve to present the problem in splendid isolation from certain very realistic conditions."[8]

As the absorption theory stands, even though total output normally declines under the austerity conditions associated with chronic devaluation, purchasing power is supposed to fall even more sharply, enabling more output to be exported. "As long as the demand for imports is not perfectly inelastic," that is, an abso-lute dependency established without respect for income and price levels, "the quantity of imports purchased falls." Devaluation makes imports more costly, reducing overall income.[9] Labor and capital are shifted from the domestic sector (where prices are relatively low and falling) to the export sector, where prices and hence profit incentives are rising, at least until domestic productivity declines in response to falling incomes.

Austerity models do not recognize this adverse productivity effect. Yet it seems obvious enough that falling incomes impede countries from investing capital in their agriculture and industry. This will aggravate their long-term

more clearly, he would have seen his own contradictions. Muddiness of expression usually results from shying away from perceiving the problem directly.

Stated arithmetically, and letting $Y$ represent real output (somewhat confusingly called "income") while $H$ represents the domestic budget surplus (identical with "hoarding" or "non-absorption"), it follows that

$$Y = C + I [+G] + (X-M)$$
$$(X-M) = Y - (C + I [+G])$$
$$B = Y - A = H$$
$$\Delta B = \Delta Y - \Delta A = \Delta H$$

The trade balance $B$ is defined as being equal to the budget surplus $H$ (domestic non-absorption of output). Breaking out $G$ separately helps focus on certain fixed categories of government spending. They may be called structural. In the 1984 *U.S. Economic Report of the President* (Washington: 1984), pp. 35–39, these structural federal expenditures include entitlements and other non-discretionary government programs that Congress has no authority to cut back. Omitting $G$, as Alexander does, neglects the established momentum of such expenditures. It thus may be unconstitutional—which perhaps explains why the theory can be applied better in dictatorships than in democracies.

8  Clement, Pfister and Rothwell, *Theoretical Issues*, p. 307, and Machlup, "Analysis of Devaluation," p. 255.

import dependency, even if the trade balance shows a temporary improvement as production is diverted to export markets.

In addition to overlooking the adverse investment effects of devaluation and austerity, absorption models neglect social factors such as the disruption resulting from strikes and what have become known as IMF riots. Capital flight occurs as individuals and firms save abroad in the form of hard currencies. *The hoarding at which Alexander aims thus tends to take the form of a balance-of-payments drain*, not an improvement. Yet he excludes this phenomenon from his model.

### The cash-balance effect

To reduce domestic absorption of output, it is necessary to increase the propensity to save, but not in the form of flight capital. (This in itself presupposes capital controls and a vigilant federal police, both of which IMF financial philosophy discourage.) The objective is to spur hoarding, not dishoarding. This is difficult to achieve, because the inflationary impact of devaluation reduces "the future value of savings and hence the incentive to save."[10] If savings are spent on consumer goods, the economy will have fewer goods left to export, while its demand for imports increases.

Alexander suggests that if people aim to hold a given purchasing power in the form of cash balances (within the country, not abroad) rather than maintaining their consumption levels, they will have to increase their *rate* of saving in the face of falling post-devaluation real incomes.

If the money supply is inflexible, and if money-holders desire to maintain cash holdings of a certain real value, they must, as prices rise, accumulate more cash. This will require a reduction in their real expenditures relative to their real incomes ... as long as the banking system or government does not create more money, except to the extent that goods or services may be sold abroad and the domestic money supply thereby increased.[11]

By reducing the purchasing power of bank deposits, devaluation forces savers (including businesses) to set aside more income if they are to maintain the same amount of purchasing power in their savings account and cash balance. Higher saving obliges them to reduce current consumption (or investment). But contra Alexander, subsequent statistical studies have confirmed what Milton

9    *Ibid.*, p. 300. The terms-of-trade effect will be equal to zero only if devaluation either does not alter the terms of trade or if its initial and secondary effects precisely offset each other. (See Machlup, "Analysis of Devaluation," pp. 261f.)

10   Johnson, *International Trade and Economic Growth: Studies in Pure Theory* [1958], (Cambridge: 1967), p. 163. Machlup (p. 264) calls this the "price expectations effect": individuals and firms may rush to increase their inventories before prices rise yet more.

11   Alexander, "Effect of a Devaluation on a Trade Balance," p. 271.

Friedman postulated in his 1957 *Theory of the Consumption Function*: As inflation rises, people save *less* and move into commodities as a hedge—often small portable valuable objects such as gold or luxury cars. Alexander thus is on shaky ground in calling the "cash-balance impact" of devaluation "the best known of the indirect effects," supposedly increasing $S/Y$ rather than $C/Y$ as depreciating currency pushes up import prices, and hence overall domestic prices.

The reality is that few people choose to increase their cash balances to maintain a constant sum of liquid purchasing power in inflationary situations. Friedman, Philip Cagan and other monetarists have traced how people reduce the proportion of income kept in the form of cash balances. The velocity of monetary turnover increases as the rate of inflation accelerates. Savers move out of cash balances and capital-market instruments into commodities, or keep their balances in hard currencies abroad, or shift their savings into "hard assets" of international purchasing power such as fine arts, gold, foreign automobiles and the like. The most typical response is for investors to shift their funds to capital markets in the industrial nations whose securities prices or other asset prices are rising. Yet Alexander baldly states that "Capital movements are ruled out here; if they were allowed they might change or eliminate the cash-balance effect."[12] Capital flight has become an overriding factor in the balance of payments of most Third World and post-Soviet economies. To acknowledge this would interfere with Alexander's laissez faire conclusions. By neglecting capital flight to the creditor nations, his IMF plan imposes a blind spot that becomes fatal for client Third World countries. Hoarding in countries with chronically depreciating currencies does not consist of directly productive assets, and thus does not bring new wealth into being.

Alexander points out that raising cash by selling securities will depress their prices, thereby pushing up interest rates. This is true, all other things equal, but that is irrelevant because interest rates in Third World countries have become primarily a function of central bank policy in response to balance-of-payments considerations under chronic crisis conditions. In 1990 these rates were over 40 percent annually—in dollarized terms—in Argentina and Brazil, and over 20 percent in Mexico. It was these high rates that depressed asset prices in debtor countries that were turned into financial tributaries. Debt service was paid not only to creditors in hard-currency nations but also to the financial elites of the debtor countries themselves, typically operating out of offshore banking enclaves.

Alexander and the IMF ignore the fact that while high interest rates attract foreign short-term capital to stabilize the balance of payments, they destabilize the domestic economy and aggravate international dependency by discouraging

---

[12]  Alexander, *ibid.*, p.271.

new direct investment. As Machlup points out: "The offer of assets and debt securities at reduced prices would attract foreign buyers—which would greatly help matters [at least in the short run]—but we have excluded any autonomous capital movements from our analysis." In any event, foreign investment inflows entail future outflows of remitted profits, thereby undercutting the balance of payments over time. Also, banks are ruled out as buyers of these securities "because we have excluded additional credit creation."[13]

If local residents and businesses hoard their funds or buy the financial assets thrown onto the market, *it is in preference to undertaking new direct investment.* This is supposed to help matters by reducing domestic absorption: But how can this be expected to improve the trade balance over time? Without investment, purchasing new equipment and hiring new workers how can modernization take place and the economy produce more exports or import substitutes? It would seem that the long run is being sacrificed to scrape by in the short run. The capital flight that Alexander excludes from his analysis, and the reduced investment which he praises as if it helps rather than impairs matters, make the allegedly positive effects of devaluation appear doubtful, and in fact, counter-effective. The objective seems to be for the IMF to strip debtor-country assets to pay foreign bondholders, banks and other creditors, not to help the poor client countries.

### How wage lags erode living standards

In contrast to Friedman's simple monetarism which assumes that all prices change at the same rate, Alexander focuses on the long-known tendency for wage payments to lag behind the general rate of inflation, squeezing consumption accordingly.

> There may be a long lag of wages behind prices, and profits might therefore gain at the expense of wages as a result of the devaluation. ... Taxes, at least in the advanced countries, can be expected to take a larger share of given real income when the price level is higher. To the extent that income is shifted from those

---

[13]  Machlup, "Analysis of Devaluation," p. 273.
[14]  Alexander, "Effect of a Devaluation," p. 273. On the logic that raising taxes will reduce overall purchasing power, presumably "freeing" output for export, Alexander concludes: "The government can, in advanced countries, usually be expected to have a low marginal propensity so absorb." However, governments in Third World countries have a notoriously large international leakage. They use their revenues largely to repay foreign debts and import arms and food. Governments thus may have an even higher "propensity" to turn over income to foreigners than does the private sector, especially in dictatorships such as Mobutu's Zaire, the Marcos's Philippines and the Shah's Iran. A budgetary surplus may result in *more* foreign exchange transferred abroad, and perhaps even more imports made than would be the case if more were left in the hands of the domestic subsistence sector.

with a high marginal propensity to absorb [that is, to spend] to those with a low propensity, the foreign balance will be improved by the devaluation.[14]

And this foreign balance really is all that the IMF cares about. Devaluation (and its consequent inflation) is supposed to redistribute income from wage earners and fixed-income (local-currency) recipients to profit recipients (employers) and above all to hard-currency creditors, that is "largely to people richer and thriftier than … fixed-salary workers, and pensioners."[15] This is not supposed to increase investment, nor are governments supposed to use their higher tax revenue to import more arms, food or infrastructure-investment goods. The major impact occurs as real incomes decline for wage earners, especially as the government reduces subsidies for food and other essentials.

This line of analysis was anticipated already at the beginning of the nineteenth century. No less an economic historian than Marx traced the genesis of Cantillon's two-sector analysis of economic activity—recognizing differential rates of inflation in the business and consumer sectors—through John Barton's 1817 analysis of the role played by foreign trade in the evolution of prices, wages and profits. Emphasizing how the profitability of investment may be enhanced by inflation, Barton put his finger on why employers favored the price inflation that typically accompanied currency depreciation:

> The remarkable increase of population which has taken place, not only in England, but in almost every European state, during the last fifty or sixty years, has perhaps proceeded chiefly from the increased productiveness of the American mines. An increased abundance of the precious metals raises the price of commodities in a greater proportion than the price of labour; it depresses the condition of the labourer, and at the same time increases the gains of his employer, who is thus induced to enlarge his circulating capital to the utmost of his ability, to hire as many hands as he has the means to pay;—and it has been seen that this is precisely the state of things most favourable to the increase of people. That a fall in the value of money lowers the recompense of labour has been incidentally pointed out by several late writers.[16]

This passage expresses the distinction (later emphasized by Keynes) between a profit inflation and an income or wage inflation. As Marx elaborated the monetary impact of the trade balance (and its consequent gold inflows creating inflationary pressures),

> the rise in wages was not proportionate to the rise in the price of commodities; (real) wages, therefore, fell and there followed an increase in relative surplus labour and consequently in the rate of profit, not because the labourers were become more productive but because there had been a decline in absolute wages, that is, in the sum of the

15 Machlup, "Analysis of Devaluation," p. 263.
16 John Barton, *Observations on the Circumstances which Influence the Condition of the Labouring Classes of Society* (London: 1817), pp. 29ff.
17 Marx commenting on the above passage, in *A History of Economic Theories: From the Physiocrats to Adam Smith* (New York: 1952), p. 196. (This is Terence McCarthy's translation of Marx's *Theories of Surplus Value*, the first English-language translation of that work.)

Table 18.1: Balance-of-Payments Impact of Devaluation and Austerity

| POSITIVE EFFECTS | NEGATIVE EFFECTS |
|---|---|
| INFALTION-ASSOCIATED EFFECTS, as devaluation increases import prices and domestic prices ||
| 1. According to the REAL-BALANCE EFFECT, people increase their saving rate (S/Y) in order to maintain a constant purchasing power of their liquid savings. This lowers the consumption rate (C/Y), leaving more output available for export. | In the face of falling real incomes (or slower growth) people try to maintain consumption standards by living off their saving (Friedman's "Permanent Income Hypothesis"). This reduces the rate of saving and investment, leaving less available for export. |
| 2. Devaluation makes imports more expensive, discouraging them (and spurring exports). | Depreciation and inflation leads to hoarding of luxury imports and, most important, to capital flight. |
| 3. Wage lags redistribute income away from workers (the "Barton effect"), freeing more output for export—assuming no adverse productivity effects of falling real income. | Falling living standards lead to strikes and political instability, interrupting economic activity, reducing output, and leading to bankruptcy of marginal firms. |
| PRODUCTIVITY EFFECTS ||
| 4. No productivity impact recognized. | Slower growth in the domestic market leads to less investment, hence slower productivity growth and capital formation. Over time this increases import dependency. Even in the short run it leads to investment outflows to more thriving markets abroad. |
| EFFECTS OF FINANCIAL AUSTERITY AND TIGHTENING BANK CREDIT ||
| 5. Lower spending leaves more output to be exported. Higher interest rates lead people to borrow abroad. | Less bank credit means less export credit, in a world where export competitiveness has become largely a function of the credit-terms of exports. Foreign borrowing builds in future debt-service costs, which come to dominate the balance of payments. High interest rates also encourage foreign takeovers as domestic firms lack competitive financing. |
| EFFECT OF FISCAL AUSTERITY ||
| 6. Higher taxes reduce domestic demand, freeing an equivalent value of output for export (assuming no transfer problem). | Devaluation increases government needs to service foreign currency debt. This displaces government spending on economic infrastructure, or it increases tax rates, which mean higher operating and production costs. |
| TERMS-OF-TRADE EFFECT ||
| 7. Devaluation rewards labor and capital employed in the export sector more than that used to produce domestic output. Hence, resources are shifted to export production—presumably at steady terms of trade. | More exports reduce the terms of trade. This makes the transfer problem more complex than the merely domestic budgetary problem. |

means of subsistence given to the labourer; because, in short, the position of the workingman had deteriorated. In such countries, labour in reality, had become more productive for its employers.[17]

And also more productive of a trade surplus as well as profits, Alexander would add. But in Barton's day the modern phenomenon of capital flight had not appeared.

In sum, lower wage levels are supposed to free an equivalent value of output for export, or perhaps spur direct investment by increasing profits by the amount of wages cut back (adjusted for business losses resulting from the devaluation). By contrast, as Chapter 9 has traced, the Economy of High Wages principle finds high wages to be a precondition for achieving high productivity, while low wages are associated with low productivity and economic obsolescence. The result is capital flight and deepening foreign-currency debt.

## *The money illusion*

Alexander acknowledges that the income-transfer effect of currency devaluation requires continual depreciation. That is, it depends "on dynamic movements, on rising prices rather than on high prices." Matters turn on consumer and business anticipations and the willingness of workers to be fooled by the money illusion as they are preoccupied with their nominal money wages, not with the actual purchasing power of these wages. "A small devaluation may take advantage of the money illusion, or impart a dynamic momentum to the wage inertia, or lead to modification of tax rates, etc."[18] As long as people can be confused by illusion they may refrain from engaging in the strikes and riots that erode the trade balance by rendering resources idle.

But it is axiomatic among practical trade analysts that the only way substantially to improve in the trade balance is to devalue *to excess*. A quantum leap is necessary to alter trade patterns and win new markets. This is why the United States devalued the dollar by nearly 40 percent in 1933—hardly a marginal amount.

## *Redeployment and investment effects of devaluation*

Devaluation's direct effect on absorption is defined as the switch from domestic to export production or the production of import substitutes. This switching, notes Machlup, "will depend chiefly on how the economy responds to price incentives," as well as on the mobility and flexibility of its labor and capital.[19] But as noted earlier, for resources to shift into export production, some retooling is necessary. This is particularly the case in Third World economies

---

[18]   Alexander, "Effect of a Devaluation," p. 274.
[19]   Machlup, "Analysis of Devaluation," pp. 260, 262.

whose export sectors are much more capital intensive than their domestic subsistence sectors. Government efforts to build up the export infrastructure may be needed—hardly giving much hope for running a domestic budget surplus. Furthermore, labor displaced from domestic industries probably will be unable immediately to find work producing exports. This idling of resources and of new investment is likely to impair the trade balance at least in the short run—something fatal for a theory whose time frame in any event is only short-term.

If the capital goods required for retooling the economy must be imported, the trade balance will be eroded. Machlup points to "the high cost of investment effect" following devaluation, that is, "the discouragement which increased cost of imported investment goods may cause to investors. ... Investment in imported labor-saving machinery, very profitable at predevaluation exchange rates, turned out to be too expensive relative to domestic labor once the exchange rates were corrected."[20] Devaluation thus impedes technological modernization. It often involves selling ownership of resources and public enterprises to foreigners, setting the stage for transferring profits, interest charges and other fees abroad in years to come.

The efficacy of devaluation, like that of monetary inflation in mercantilist doctrine, boils down to the "idle resources effect." By making domestic products cheaper on world markets, devaluation is supposed to spur employment in the export sector and possibly in sectors producing import substitutes. The reality is that by lowering real incomes it reduces demand, shrinks markets and contributes to unemployment in the domestic sector. If this labor receives unemployment insurance or other transfer payments, absorption will *not* fall by as much as output, so that the trade balance will be eroded. Even so, the IMF holds that a state of unemployment is best suited to making the absorption approach work. Its logic is that resources are unlikely to be switched to the export sector as long as full-employment conditions persist. Alexander concludes that countries whose labor is fully employed should prefer monetary stringency and tight credit to devaluation as a means to improve their trade balance.

### *Adverse effect of devaluation on the foreign debt burden*

A devaluation obliges government and private businesses that have borrowed in foreign currencies to use more local income to service these debts. When Canada's dollar fell in value from US$1.06 to $0.86 during 1978-79, its domestic-currency costs of servicing foreign debt denominated in U.S. dollars, German marks, Swiss francs and Japanese yen increased proportionally. The national government

---

[20]  Machlup, *ibid.*, pp. 264f.

and provincial borrowers had to increase taxes to cover their higher debt servicing costs, or reduce spending in other areas such as development infrastructure.

Higher taxes added to domestic cost structures while reducing the private
sector's purchasing power. The resulting cost squeeze threatened to drive marginal
businesses into bankruptcy, leading to a write-off of their capital. This is how
debtor economies are stripped of their ability to promote long-term capital
formation.

Also aggravating inflation and impairing capital formation is the instability associated with austerity programs. Output is reduced by the strikes and
political disturbances noted earlier, by adding to costs through crime and urban
decay, and by impairing the investment climate generally. Governments imposing such "stabilization" plans often are able to stay in power only by suspending
the democratic process and overriding the institutions of parliamentary democracy.
As the political situation polarizes, the economic structure ossifies. The class war
is back in business, imposed at the international margin as a consequence of the
foreign-debt quandary.

### *False assumption that budgetary saving will produce a 1:1 trade improvement*

The critique of monetarist austerity models focuses on their unwarranted
assumption that the trade balance will improve by increasing exports or
reducing imports by the full amount of domestic austerity imposed. Instead of
viewing spending on imports as a more or less fixed structural proportion of
income (a propensity to import of between 3 percent for the United States, and
25 per cent for much of Europe and many Third World countries), the absorption approach assumes that all income reduction will either cut imports or free
a corresponding value of output for export on a 100 percent basis. This is the
equivalent of assuming a one-to-one ("unitary") marginal propensity to import.

As such, it represents a throwback to the theories of Ohlin and Rueff in
the 1920s. Like their theories, it recognizes no linkages such as the need to
import raw materials in order to produce industrial exports, or even to import
capital equipment to produce more raw-materials exports. Also ignored is the
fact that export prices probably must decline in order for the economy to win
more foreign markets. Yet if the terms of trade decline, the foreign exchange
earned by diverting domestic resources to export production will turn out to be
*less* than the cutback of domestic incomes.

Whether export volume rises by enough, while imports fall by enough to
stabilize the balance of payments depends on (1) their relative elasticities of
demand, and (2) the degree to which falling incomes will depress new direct
investment in agriculture and industry below the rate needed to sustain the

devaluing country's growing population and maintain competitive production functions with other economies. If the country has fallen into international dependency—that is, if its trade is price- and income-inelastic—and if IMF and World Bank austerity programs deprive it of the resources and incentives needed to modernize productivity in keeping with world rates, then *austerity will aggravate international dependency, impair the balance of payments and exacerbate capital flight.*

### Additional shortcomings of the absorption approach

Keynes hoped that devaluation would inflate the economy and spur employment via the multiplier process resulting from higher export sales. By contrast, the IMF's motive is to cut back domestic demand, including direct investment. A shrinking income is to be redistributed from the domestic to the export sector, and from wage earners to employers. Such investment as does occur is to concentrate on producing exports rather than satisfying domestic demand. There is little question of competitive beggar-my-neighbor policy for Third World debtor economies engaging in such devaluations, because their major exports are raw materials priced in world currencies (dollars or sterling) and non-competing low-wage products.

   In cases where meaningful export competition actually *is* achieved with industries in the industrial nations, the latter are liable to retaliate. This is how the United States responded to Brazilian exports in the 1980s. When Brazil sought to promote its exports in an attempt to service its nearly unmanageable foreign debt, it achieved a $2.4 billion trade surplus with the United States in 1983. It announced hopes to increase that amount in 1984 as part of its planned $9 billion worldwide trade surplus deemed necessary to service its foreign debts. But the United States government brought dumping charges against Brazil,[21] creating problems for Brazilian exports of alcohol, textiles, auto parts, shoes and tobacco. Brazil became the only major Third World sugar exporter subjected to U.S. import duties. U.S. antidumping claims obliged Brazil to levy a 27 per cent export tax on its steel, undercutting the nominal advantages of its currency devaluation. Yet the academic and IMF devaluation models look narrowly at countries being subjected to austerity, not foreign responses of this sort. The usual response is that an export-price war breaks out among debtor-country products, benefiting the industrial nations that dominate the IMF.

   A government tax surplus is demanded despite the need for Third World countries to create more domestic infrastructure to modernize their economies. Rather than broadening their economic base to build up self-dependency, this

---

[21] See for instance "Brazil Says Sanctions Imperil Trade," *The New York Times*, March 19, 1984.

pushes debtor countries to become raw-materials monocultures. By discouraging new direct investment and infrastructure not associated with the export trade, by shrinking the domestic market and exacerbating capital flight, the fiscal surplus contributes to high unemployment rates which, in the industrial nations, would inspire chronic budget deficits to reflate the economy. Austerity programs end up making debtor countries more dependent on imports as the economy is choked by a lack of credit, rising taxes and falling government subsidies.

To summarize the above criticisms, the absorption formulas neglect the wide range of factors that actually shape international economic behavior. They select a few hypothetical relationships—largely unrealistic—while neglecting the institutional rigidities that impair the balance of trade, such as the absence of land reform or failure to upgrade the quality and productivity of labor. Finally, it should be added, such models ignore the correlation between low wage levels and high rates of population growth.

## *The absorption approach slips into monetarism*

The resurgent monetarism since the 1970s absorbed Keynesian macroeconomics by representing income and production functions as essentially monetary in character. The essence of IMF austerity programs since their inception has been that the trade balance cannot improve unless the central bank imposes monetary stringency, preferably in conjunction with a federal budget surplus.[22]

Whereas Keynesian analysis and multiplier theory trace how full employment may be achieved by expanding income and investment, monetarism aims to achieve balance by shrinking the money supply. The phenomenon in which its advocates are most interested is not full employment or economic modernization but price stability and international payments equilibrium sufficient to keep paying foreign creditors. Foreign debt service and basic capital-flight trends to the creditor nations are to be sustained by belt-tightening, not by raising income and production levels.

Alexander added that if people saved more in inflationary situations in order to maintain a constant liquid purchasing power in the form of bank deposits, this would enable the banking system to increase its credit. Under the fractional reserve principle of banking, this would produce a multiplier effect for deposit growth (assuming no leakages). In order not to undo the "favorable"

---

[22] "An ideal line of policy," wrote Alexander in an update of his theorizing, "is to, with one hand guide the money supply so as to maintain full employment without inflation, and with the other hand set the exchange rate for foreign balance. Any change in the exchange rate would thus require a correlative change in the money supply." ("Effects of a Devaluation: A Simplified Synthesis of the Elasticities and Absorption Approaches," *American Economic Review*, 49 [March 1959], p. 25.)

income reduction resulting from the devaluation, he recommended that the central bank should sterilize any such buildup of cash balances. This is reminiscent of the demands made by Ohlin and Rueff in the 1920s that Germany not be permitted to borrow abroad, on the ground that this would offset the positive deflationary effects of its reparations transfers. The problem with a tight money policy of this sort is that increasing interest rates push up capital costs, thereby reducing investment and potential output.

As long as trade theory remains couched in terms of short-term adjustments, it seems unnecessary to work on the production factors underlying the deficit. Everything depends on monetary policy. As Machlup recognized, "Nothing can be said about the effects of a devaluation unless exact specifications are made regarding the supply of money and credit and the fiscal policy of the government."[23] On the other hand, there is no way of knowing in advance just how severe the currency depreciation must be, given the rigidities and inelasticities of much world trade.

Harry Johnson was an important transitional figure in converting Alexander's absorption formulas into a monetarist format. Claiming to isolate "the initiating causes of disequilibrium" so that "the most appropriate type of remedial policy can be followed," he sought to "illuminate the monetary aspects of balance-of-payments disequilibrium" by pointing out that the balance of payments may be viewed as equivalent to "the difference between aggregate receipts by residents and aggregate payments by residents."[24] But he did not distinguish between underlying long-term causes of payments deficits and their monetary preconditions in the form of accommodating financing. Demand management was given preference over restructuring production. A policy of tightening the money supply was preferred to the longer-term strategy of enhancing productivity through land reform, anticorruption moves or better education and upgrading of the labor force.

Johnson excludes production functions from consideration by insisting that "balance-of-payments problems are fundamentally monetary phenomena. ... it is an obvious proposition, but one which is often overlooked."[25] Shifts in imports and exports are viewed as resulting only from changes in purchasing power. "It is evident that a balance-of-payments problem is monetary in nature and that it is fundamentally related to the fact that the banking system can create credit."[26] The monetary *dimension* of the balance-of-payments deficits thus is

---

[23]   Machlup, "Analysis of Devaluation," pp. 272ff.
[24]   Johnson, *International Trade and Economic Growth*, pp. 156, 158. See also p. 162.
[25]   Johnson, *ibid.*, p. 167, and *Money, Trade and Economic Growth*, p. 19.
[26]   Johnson, *International Trade and Economic Growth*, p. 18.

viewed as their ultimate *cause*, calling for a solely monetary and financial cure—
which ends up bleeding the patient to death.

Monetarists assume that if the money supply can be kept tight enough,
prices will fall. In essence, the Chicago School's slogan "Money matters" means
that it can be *made* to matter by using it as a financial constraint. True, you cannot
"push on a string" and expect monetary *expansion* automatically to spur production. But the monetary authorities can *pull* on a string to reduce income and
prices. So we are back to the price-specie flow mechanism with a macroeconomic face, imposed by government fiat under the direction of IMF central
planners.

Attempts were made to head off this aggressive kind of monetarism even
before Johnson published his balance-of-payments analysis. Machlup warned
that tackling only the monetary aspects might merely exacerbate production
problems:

> If … reduction in absorption causes a net decline in employment (instead of the
> desired transfer of resources), a sequence of secondary nonspending will cut
> down consumption and investment even further, depending on the propensity
> to absorb; and if the transfer of resources should still fail to take place, at least
> the purchase of imports will be reduced, with a definitely positive effect on the
> trade balance. Needless to say, no government would want to have the
> improvement of the trade balance take this form, but it is only fair to mention
> that it can happen.[27]

It is exactly what has happened as a result of monetarism's Third World
austerity programs.

## Summary: Believing is seeing

General equilibrium analysis assumes no policy at all, a laissez faire world subject
only to inertia. The monetarist version deems only *automatic* responses to be
purely "economic" in character, except for policy decisions concerning the
money supply. The theory is now widely seen to be outmoded, and never was

---

[27] Machlup, "Analysis of Devaluation," pp. 271f. He points out (p. 268) that "The argument
underlying the aggregate-spending approach has been developed from a "fundamental
equation" which represents more definitions. Such equations usually serve a useful purpose
in aiding the organization of the analysis. But this may easily tempt an analyst into "implicit
theorizing," illegitimately deducing causal relationships, and overlooking the shifting
meanings of terms in different contexts." He singles out Alexander's absorption formulas
for making this error. For instance (p. 275), much government expenditure "is not a function
of income but an independent variable that can be administered in a direction opposite to
that of changes in income.

very relevant in the first place. Central banks today focus on interest rates, and on loosening financial regulations so as to spur asset-price inflation in ways that shift income from employees to *rentiers*. The latter are euphemized as "wealth-holders" so that the process can be called "wealth creation" rather than a process of debt peonage.

Keynes wanted to subordinate creditor interests to the goal of full employment and direct investment. Monetarists sacrifice economic progress and prosperity on the altar of international debt. Keynes did not deny that to the extent that income expansion became inflationary, it would erode the purchasing power of society's debt overhead, but he viewed these debts as being economic dead-weight in any event. Monetarism has as its alpha and omega the preservation of the domestic and international debt overhead in at least steady (preferably rising) purchasing power. This makes it the economic doctrine of the banking and financial sectors, and of creditor nations vis-à-vis debtor economies. Growth in investment and living standards is to be permitted only to the extent that it honors the legacy of debt claims on society's wealth and income—literally the "dead hand" (mortgage) of the past weighing on the present.

These financial claims tend to grow at compound interest, that is, at rates in excess of going rates of profit and economic surplus-creation. The spirit of monetarism thus asserts the prerogatives of past financial property distribution even at the cost of mass unemployment, foregone development and the imposition of economic paralysis and political autocracy.

What macroeconomic income-oriented approaches share in common with monetarism is a disregard for the need to upgrade productivity and hence wage levels to achieve international balance. Both approaches accept as given facts of nature the existing technological, financial, social and political environment. They thus have become two sides of the same coin. When monetarism insists that shrinking incomes can rectify payments deficits, it assumes that this will lower production costs and/or free erstwhile domestic consumer output (haircuts, groceries, etc.) for export. Instead of viewing labor and business as production inputs subject to modernization, they treat them only as sources of demand, as recipients of income who will go on doing their job without their productivity being adversely affected by falling income levels.

In preaching austerity rather than prosperity, monetarism sees the road to stability and wealth as entailing a deflation of purchasing power, impoverishing the domestic market—while accusing government planning of paving the road to serfdom by trying to regulate or constrain finance. The problem with monetarist debt peonage is that to reduce wages requires sufficient unemployment to depress the general demand for labor. This wastes resources rather than utilizing the population and capital better. A trade surplus is to be created sufficient to pay a country's exponential growth in foreign debt and capital flight. "Balance" in international payments is supposed to be achieved at the cost of chronic impoverishment of the labor market. Falling wage levels are assumed to cut costs proportionally, not recognizing any adverse productivity feedback.

Medieval doctors bled patients, imagining that this helped restore a healthy balance. But it weakened them. Today, we think of these physicians as well-meaning fools. But at least in medieval times, patients were not forced to go to such doctors. That has not been the case with IMF and World Bank practitioners. And there is less excuse for their imposition of monetarist austerity plans, because the identical assumptions that underlaid them were controverted in England's bullion debate in the early 1800s, in the German reparations debate in the 1920s, and during the half-century that IMF advice has created poverty and dependency. The IMF's monetarist models have been maintained only by the most rigorous censorship of the history of economic thought, making the institution closer to the medieval Inquisition than to medicine.

By the mid-1980s many debtor countries reached the point where debt service had come to absorb *all* their net export proceeds left after foreign direct investors had retained their profits abroad, along with the foreign-currency costs of export production. The debt reductions that began with Mexico under the Brady Plan of 1989, followed by Venezuela in 1990, are only the preliminary acknowledgement that there is little realistic hope for these countries to export their way out of debt. They have been subjected for too many decades to austerity programs that sacrificed hopes for long-term growth. The high interest rates and credit constraints imposed by austerity disallow technology to be applied economically on *financial* grounds (the high cost of capital, and limited domestic market) as distinct from the direct production and operating costs on which most orthodox trade theory focuses. The concluding chapter turns to this problem, which has received little analysis since the eighteenth century.

This completes the review of economic orthodoxy concerning "real" and financial aspects of international polarization and convergence. Part II stressed the interaction between trade and development. It showed how laggard countries tend to collapse in an Economy of Low Wages Syndrome rather than experience the normal feedback processes of rising wages and technological modernization. Part III has traced the interaction between international finance and development. It has shown how countries that fall into foreign debt are obliged to support their interest rates for balance-of-payments reasons at the cost of direct investment in the home market.

# PART IV

## Toward the Future

… the most fatally unpractical thing in the world is to go on reaching methods by results which take every factor into account except the one upon which the whole result ultimately depends.

R. L. Nettleship, *The Theory of Education in Plato's Republic* (1880), p. 27.

# 19

## The Lessons of History

These lectures place the history of international economics in the context of the policy debates that have shaped theories of trade and investment with regard to the nature of competitive advantage, productivity differences among nations, the achievement of technological and financial leads, the determination of international prices and gains from trade, the migration of labor and capital, and the impact on exchange rates of debt service, military spending and other "capital transfers."

From the English mercantilists through early free traders, and from protectionists among English landowners to American and German industrialists, the most important policy inspiration has been the desire to understand the world's polarization tendencies—how nations pull ahead of others or get left behind in a position of economic and financial dependency. The aim has been either to put dynamics in place to consolidate one's lead, or to catch up by nurturing domestic technology and credit. From either perspective the basic task of international economics is to explain how rich nations may achieve widening productivity and cost advantages for their industry and agriculture, compared to how the colonial and post-colonial periphery has been malformed by what I call the Monoculture Syndrome with its economically and politically obsolete labor, agriculture, capital and oligarchic governments.

Placing the polarization vs. convergence debate in this historical and policy setting shows how its breadth of scope widens as we look further back in time. Early observers perceived with remarkable clarity the political context and positive feedback character of England's industrial head start, as did subsequent protectionists in America and continental Europe in mapping out their own long-term national strategy. From the outset, English mercantilism and subsequent protectionism, traced the positive feedback and obsolescence processes that shape market relations, and extended the analysis of trade and development into the political and social sphere. Most of these perceptions were voiced by men well placed in the political leadership of their times.

The subsequent narrowing of scope—away from long-term development to short-term market analysis, away from the monetary and financial context of trade to a "barter" theory, and away from a government policy-oriented focus to one of laissez faire—has been politically dictated by the success of England, the United States and subsequent lead nations in achieving dominant intellectual as well as economic status. It seems ironic that the more successful a nation becomes, the narrower and more short-term tends to be the scope of its international economic theorizing—almost as if it would pull up the policy ladder behind it. The aim is to impose a superficial trade theory and financial austerity on the less developed periphery, treating their resources as "endowments" dealt out by nature rather than fostered actively by national policy.

To place this narrowing of intellectual scope in perspective, it is appropriate in this final chapter to summarize my overall argument. Central to almost all ethical discussion about trade has been the distinction between value and price, starting with how the thirteenth-century Schoolmen rationalized the benefits of trade. Their efforts show how invariant certain concerns have remained through the centuries. Ultimately at issue is the exchange of labor for commodities, whether domestically or internationally. But the charging of interest on loans to finance this trade—or for war debts, for that matter—is independent of the labor process. Interest is an element that enters into price without involving value in the classical sense of being ultimately reducible to the cost of labor.

It took nearly five centuries for medieval concerns to culminate in Ricardian value theory, which based itself on an objective and universal standard by expressing all costs in terms of labor-time equivalents. This approach left little room for what subsequently was called the Economy of High Wages principle involving labor productivity and capital productivity, or how shifts in the supply and demand for labor and its products affected wage levels and international prices. The usual Malthusian assumption was that if wage levels rose, the working population would increase to a point where wages would fall back near subsistence levels. This was held to be an international as well as a domestic principle. Countries with rising wage levels might price themselves out of world markets, resulting in trade deficits, monetary outflows and unemployment that would return wages to basic subsistence levels.

At the root of price and value theorizing, including measures of the terms of trade, has been the question of what constitutes fair value. What was held to be "unfair" was a divergence of prices from underlying costs. This occurred most notably in the case of land rent, the "unearned increment" that landlords on well-situated fertile soils received by being able to produce crops at a lower price than farmers on less fertile soils, whose relatively high production costs tended to establish market prices. Applying this idea to international trade in agricultural and mineral products, there seemed little reason to suspect that the terms of trade would shift in favor of the most densely populated nations. If any set of countries would reap monopoly gains or "unearned increments," it was held to be the raw-materials producers. The flow of world labor was to these regions as emigrants sought to better their lot. Capital also flowed to the periphery in search of higher returns than could be earned at home. As a result of this labor and capital migration, it was widely assumed that the world economy would become more homogeneous.

One phenomenon threatening this trend was the ability of industrial nations to monopolize high-technology capital and charge high prices to dependent and increasingly indebted economies. Over time this monopoly rent accruing to industrial-nation labor and capital has grown to exceed the economic rent of raw-materials producers that Ricardians feared would result from diminishing returns. High-productivity labor and capital exchange for relatively low-paid labor and capital in the periphery, while many raw materials have been supplied at the low-cost rather than high-cost margin of production.

To estimate "fair value" in international trade, the double factoral terms of trade adjusts import and export prices for the return to the labor going into their production. An equitable parity of exchange often is held to be that which would compensate the labor of all trading parties equally.

But how is such a balance to be brought into being in a world of differential labor and capital productivity, investment per worker, population density and specialization patterns? Is it fair that high-productivity labor should earn no more than low-productivity labor? How should one treat the return to capital, especially when the latter is financed by borrowing? And is it "fair" for debt service and other capital transfer payments to impair the terms of trade?

In view of the self-transforming nature of the industrial, agricultural and financial revolutions, the main task of trade theory should be to enquire into the extent to which international trade and investment contribute to the equitable long-term development of the active trading parties and their "host economies." Much of Part II, culminating in Chapters 8, 9 and 10, therefore deals with the developmental aspect of trade in the context of foreign investment, debt service and technological modernization.

The key issue is not merely one of values for goods and services as if they were being bartered, but what kinds of exports, investment and borrowing best develop a national economy over time. Fortunately, it is not necessary to reinvent the wheel in making this inquiry. At least for policymakers in the world's leading industrial nations, these concerns played a critical role in the tariff and trade theorizing in the nineteenth century. Technologically minded economists took into account the various types of indirect or "off the balance-sheet" costs suffered by monocultures. These costs ranged from soil and mineral depletion to the entrenchment of oligarchies such as still characterize many of today's raw-materials exporters.

It seems obvious that historical experience—headed by the history of policy—should be the starting point for theorizing about international development. A number of fairly recent studies describe the historical setting for world economic evolution. Immanuel Wallerstein has treated the modern (post-medieval) economy as a global economic system polarizing between the center and its periphery.[1] Archaeologists such as Phil Kohl and Carl Lamberg-Karlovsky have extended this world-system approach back to the inception of bulk long-distance commerce in the fourth and third millennia BC, when the Sumerians took the lead in developing a raw-materials periphery from Asia Minor to the Iranian highlands.[2] Even in these Bronze Age millennia it was the industrial center that took the lead in developing a foreign capacity to supply metals, stone, wood and other geographically specific products not found at home.

It is significant that Bronze Age Mesopotamian industry was developed initially in public hands (the temples and palaces), later passing into private hands. The privatization of industry and policy tends to follow its public inception, being viable only when public enterprise and policy have done their jobs successfully by providing a basic economic and institutional structure.

What has been central to explaining world economic evolution is not just national development as such, but how national prices and incomes, exchange rates and investment patterns are determined, how this development relates to the world economy as a whole, and strategies to shape it. Chapter 2 paves the way for this world-historical mode of analysis by showing that leading elements of international cost structures and trade patterns are not inherently natural but have long historical and political roots. The good news in this lesson is that just as the success of many national economies has been the result of active government policy to shape markets rather than passively to acquiesce to the dictates of nature, so poverty also is a result of policy. Today's poorer countries may ameliorate their condition by doing what England, the United States, Europe and Japan have done, and take control of their destiny. This involves shaping their market relations to promote greater self-reliance and upgrade the quality of their labor, land and capital.

The bad news is that the world's leading economies have spent generations reinforcing their head start, beginning with their policy of high-wage industrialization and capped by an array of international diplomacy and "foreign aid" programs. The World Bank and International Monetary Fund now act as the

---

[1]  Immanuel Wallerstein, *The Modern World-System: Capitalist Agriculture and the Origins of the European World-Economy in the Sixteenth Century* (New York: 1974), and *The Capitalist World Economy* (Cambridge: 1979).

[2]  Phil Kohl, "The Use and Abuse of World Systems Theory: The case of the 'pristine' West Asian state," in Carl Lamberg-Karlovsky, ed., *Archaeological Thought in America* (Cambridge: 1989).

board of directors for industrial creditor nations to deal with less developed debtor countries. They have lent money for governments to provide infrastructure only along lines that have fed into European, North American and now East Asian development. The result has been to subsidize international polarization while indebting client Third World economies.

The economic and political feedback processes that our modern world of increasing returns has put in place imply that the longer a maldeveloping economy defers agricultural and industrial modernization, the higher will be the lost-opportunity cost of living in the free-trade present. For too many centuries these countries have maximized short-term Ricardian gains from trade rather than pursuing long-term objectives. The costs of undoing this policy are now falling due.

The cost of overcoming the existing international system of social, economic and technological lags involves government subsidies whose expenses will raise costs in the short run. In the case of agrarian reform, modernization may reduce short-term output. To achieve international competitiveness in the types of goods that help countries upgrade the quality of their labor force probably requires tariffs and subsidies much like those which the United States has provided since its Civil War. These policies entail government spending—just the opposite of what austerity programs impose.

International economics logically needs to start with the failure of peripheral economies to achieve parity with the metropolitan center, which almost always has pioneered raw-materials development. In an attempt to become self-sufficient centers, Europe's imperial powers carved out colonial spheres of influence and endowed them with African slaves and other "factors of production" concentrated in the export sector. The objective was to monopolize the world's productive capital and skilled labor, and hence silver and gold, and to deprive rivals of these resources. To promote the production of plantation crops, the imperial nations gave land grants to favored aristocratic families, establishing a latifundia/microfundia pattern of large export-oriented estates and subsistence smallholdings. This helped foster the industrialization of England and France while their colonies specialized in low-wage raw-materials exports, usually under entrenched oligarchic political systems. Colonial regimes typically were controlled to ensure that the periphery's development would conform to the international and domestic market mechanisms shaped by the mother countries. The development of competing industries was banned throughout colonial North and South America, India and other parts of Asia and Africa, highlighted by bans on iron and textile manufacturing. By the time these regions obtained their nominal political freedom—in the early nineteenth century for Latin America and after World War II for much of Africa and Asia—market forces (reinforced by debt relationships) sufficed by themselves to ensure continuation of these production and trade patterns.

International economics should begin with the failure of peripheral economies to achieve parity with the metropolitan center—with the notable exception of the United States, followed by Japan. Chapters 3 and 4 review early theorizing with regard to the economic, monetary, demographic, social and cultural feedback processes that have reinforced the industrial and technological head start achieved by lead nations. Countervailing centrifugal tendencies come into play only with a change of policy—protective tariffs by the periphery, or as the mercantilists warned, decay in the industrial center. East Asia's economies have modernized their policies, but those of Latin America and Africa have protected or subsidized their industry or agriculture mainly to benefit foreign-owned export enclaves, whose remission of earnings reinforces the head start achieved by the United States and Europe.

A running theme throughout this book has been how the international mobility of labor and capital—the brain drain to the world's high-wage, politically free economies, and the international investment protected by industrial-nation diplomacy from local regulatory efforts by host countries—has helped polarize the world economy. In today's increasingly capital-intensive world, financial cost advantages reinforce productivity and cost advantages. An important aspect of financial advantage has been flight capital from the periphery to the industrial center. Much of this capital has been reinvested in lead-nation industry, while some has been re-lent to Third World borrowers at relatively high interest rates.

Chapter 3 provides a basis for tracing the role of money in financing the investment and infrastructure necessary to provide industrial-nation labor with growing complements of physical and human capital. Hume's price-specie flow mechanism, voiced in 1752 and promptly controverted by Tucker, Steuart and others (and accordingly amended by Hume himself, at least in his private correspondence), was trotted out in later decades to claim that any country trying to run a sustained trade surplus would suffer a monetary and price inflation which would undercut its export prices and restore balance-of-payments equilibrium. But most economists of the 1750–75 generation understood that the opposite was often more likely to be the case. Countries receiving monetary inflows would be able to increase employment, investment and hence productivity, enhancing their balance-of-payments position.

Chapter 4 shows how early economic observers such as Berkeley, Steuart and Tucker perceived the extent to which rising wage levels might become self-justifying to the extent that they reflected themselves in even higher productivity gains. The upshot was a doctrine of how free trade would throw a growing economic advantage to the most advanced nations rather than to the poorest countries.

From the vantage point of England and other imperial nations, the most serious threat was that a high level of military and related colonial spending might dissipate their resources. The best way to avoid this problem was to give America and other colonies their political independence. Nominal American independence would free England from having to provide for the colonies' costly military defense spending, while relying on market forces to maintain their dependency on the metropolitan center, which would concentrate its economic surplus on directly productive investment.

It was with this idea in mind that during the century 1750–1848, England adopted free trade. This policy promised to achieve the same objective at which mercantilism earlier had aimed. Thanks to its head start, England could under-sell foreign producers and thus monopolize the world's monetary bullion and the gains from trade without having to bear the direct military expenses of overt colonialism. The free-trade Methuen treaty with Portugal and the Eden Treaty with France enabled English industry to vanquish native competition in these markets. Would it not be much easier to do this in its sparsely populated colonies and those of other European powers?

Rather than inflating prices, the money England drew in was used to increase investment and employment. This expanded its export production. Only the cost of warfare threatened to drain England's balance of payments. Recognition of this fact by liberal policymakers spurred a drive to create a peaceful cosmopolitan world order as an arena in which England could compete better than on the battlefield. An informal empire of free trade thus became the nation's ultimate project of state.

Having established free trade at home over the course of a century, England's strategic problem became one of how to export laissez faire ideology as a means to deter foreign protectionism and thereby keep foreign markets open to English industrial exports. The last thing called for in this ideological initiative was to repeat the arguments that had won over England's own Parliament, namely that free trade would uniquely benefit England as the leading industrial power at the expense of poorer economies. Henceforth free trade was supposed to make countries more equal and, in the process, to increase the resources of all trading "partners." But once hitherto protectionist countries opt for free trade, it usually is to close off advantageous lines of investment for less developed countries.

Contrasting theories of international economic convergence with the reality of world polarization, Part II shows how more realistic assumptions can be introduced to modify the wine and cloth models of Ricardo, Mill and their followers. It explains the polarization tendency resulting from the international specialization defended by free-trade doctrine, headed by the theory of comparative costs and the factor-price equalization theorem (Chapters 5 and 6). Chapter 5 shows how Ricardo's analytic format may be made more dynamic by recognizing factor mobility, increasing returns and the adverse unemployment and environmental depletion effects of over-specialization, as contrasted to diversification, basic self-sufficiency and balanced growth that characterized economies on the eve of the Industrial Revolution. What promised to improve Portugal's position under free trade turned out to result in a net loss of its cloth-making labor and capital, depriving it of the opportunity to participate in rising industrial productivity over time. The Ricardian model is unable to explain this impact.

Ricardian theory depicts each country as having some production lines in which it is gifted at producing *relatively* less expensively than others. If all trade were barter and there were no common *absolute* costs, each country might gain from free trade, at least in the short run. The implication is that there are sufficient markets for the economy to specialize entirely, save for the usual local niches. This would increase the division of world labor in keeping with Adam Smith's description of the virtues of specialization and its economies of scale. Protectionists replied that the laissez faire argument was unable to explain how the Industrial Revolution was transforming the character of world production, including labor and even agriculture, providing industrial nations with agricultural productivity advantages and also industrial substitutes for many raw materials. Agricultural productivity rose with population density, reflecting the proximity of urban industry.

Ricardo's theory did not touch upon the effect of productivity shifting over time. The reality is that countries that forego industrialization and tech-nological modernization became part of a specialization of world production in which "market forces" induce skilled labor and capital to emigrate from the peripheral economies that fail to protect and nurture their own industry and food production.

Ricardo's assumption of diminishing returns in agriculture denied the positive effects of substituting capital for land, and even ignored the consequences of increasing returns in industry. He did not acknowledge how industrialization and its associated revolution in agricultural productivity tended to be a positive feedback process that accelerates the rate of innovation in the industrial nations, and therefore widens international cost differentials. To the extent that such cost differentials increase, the gains from trade were supposed to rise accord-ingly. But Ricardo did not deal with how agricultural and raw-materials specialization led to the Monoculture Syndrome and mineral depletion, unequal wealth and income distribution, and a tendency toward oligarchic control of the colonial periphery. These consequences of the world division of labor all but foreclosed industrialization in the periphery along the same lines as in the lead nations. For agricultural and raw-materials producers, the question was one of how to break out of the poverty syndrome.

International prices and income levels diverged from Ricardo's labor-time theory of value. And contrary to Malthusian population theory, high income levels have been associated with lower rather than increased fertility rates. Populations have grown most rapidly in the raw-materials producing periphery. More producers, coupled with a sharply rising "entry price" to industrialization, threaten a chronic world oversupply of certain raw materials relative to manufactures and food grains.

To trace the influence of shifting supply and demand on international pricing, John Stuart Mill developed a terms-of-trade analysis to show where the terms of trade might settle. As Chapter 6 describes, international prices are determined not only by direct production costs but by supply and demand— including monopoly power, achieved mainly by "head-start" nations. Their strategy under free trade retained the mercantilist aim of achieving monopoly power for their high-technology manufacturing and, especially since World War II, for basic food grains thanks to rising agricultural productivity. As the agricultural protectionist Malthus had claimed against the free-trade Ricardians, price supports for farm income and import quotas have led to the substitution of capital for farmland with increasing productivity benefits.

Mill's analysis of international pricing (mathematically represented by Edgeworth and refined by Alfred Marshall) showed what happens to economies for whose exports world demand is not elastic. Under conditions of relative world oversupply, continued export efforts by raw-materials producers and low-wage manufacturers are self-defeating. The more such countries export, the less overall foreign exchange they earn. The leading industrial nations work up low-priced raw-materials imports into relatively high-priced industrial exports. These conditions call for economic diversification and import substitution in the periphery, not further specialization in export industries. Production for the home market would create a circular flow of income and reciprocity of demand that is absent from export markets.

Mill and Edgeworth doubted that such economic malformations would become a frequent case. It certainly seemed reasonable that domestic policy-makers would not let such a situation continue for long. Few nineteenth-century economists reckoned with the effective loss of self-determination found throughout much of today's Southern Hemisphere. Free-trade models downplay the prospect of "elasticity pessimism," yet it has become increasingly serious in today's real world. The industrial nations have gained the market for products in strong ("elastic") world demand, while former colonies are left only with what "nature" provided, subject to restrictions dating from the colonial period steering them to produce raw materials in relatively inelastic demand, earning less as world markets become glutted.

Few free-trade economists have analyzed the economic consequences and preconditions of technology. Chapter 7 traces how the economic analysis of technology was left mainly to protectionists, whose doctrines emphasized potential future cost reductions and capital accumulation rather than the short-term benefits of adhering to technological dependency. Technological leadership has long been an objective of national policy-making, using protective tariffs and subsidies to encourage investment in desirable sectors.

Chapters 7, 8 and 9 describe why shifting terms of trade are inherent in the economics of industrial and agricultural technology. Increasing returns have been the norm in every sector. Steam-powered (and later electrified) capital has replaced manual labor in production, just as agricultural capital and the application of agricultural chemistry and artificial fertilizers have transformed the allegedly inherent powers of the soil. Skilled high-wage labor working with sophisticated capital is able to undersell low-wage manual labor, much as Tucker and Steuart foresaw in the eighteenth century. Most industrial nations satisfy their own food needs rather than becoming more dependent on peripheral, less densely populated countries as Ricardo feared would be the case. The world is not characterized by diminishing returns in either industry or agriculture, or by an immobility of labor. Increasing returns have concentrated the gains from trade and international investment in the most industrialized nations. Poor countries are in danger of becoming technologically obsolete, their labor and land unable to compete equitably with that of the more balanced industrial economies.

Instead of attributing competitive advantage to productivity differentials (as had Ricardo, his predecessors and the sophisticated protectionists), post-classical orthodoxy at the hands of Eli Heckscher, Bertil Ohlin, Paul Samuelson and their followers focuses on wage and profit variations, which are traced simply to their raw quantitative "factor proportions" (Chapter 8). Countries with much capital relative to labor are supposed to have low profits (not necessarily more productive capital or labor!), giving them an advantage in capital-intensive products. Much labor means cheap labor *ipso facto*, and this is held to be an economic advantage, on the premise that labor is equally productive throughout the world. The inference is that economies suffering balance-of-payments deficits need lower wages and financial austerity, headed by cutbacks in public spending. But unfortunately, this policy is counterproductive. Enforced poverty makes it even more difficult for less developed countries to install the economic infrastructure and educational systems required to upgrade their labor, agriculture and industry to world-class standards.

Protectionist analysis showed that theories of international convergence rested on a number of anachronistic assumptions. For starters, there are no inherently labor- or even land-intensive goods. Capital competes with labor, land and even mineral resources with increasing efficiency. Meanwhile, the need to introduce newer and more productive machinery spurs the demand for machine-building labor in the industrial nations, but not in the less capital-intensive periphery.

Another assumption made by free-trade doctrine is that lower-priced factors of production (labor, land and low-interest capital) improve an economy's competitive advantage *pari passu*. The Economy of High Wages doctrine demonstrates that rising money wages tend to be associated with even larger increases in labor productivity. The corollary of this principle is the Economy of Low Wages syndrome: Low wages and living standards tend to be associated with productivity shortfalls stemming from inadequate investment in education and other "human" capital and skills, and from a general subculture of poverty over time. Economic modernization requires rising levels of investment per worker by individuals, businesses and government.

Acknowledgment of these trends should discourage theorizing along the lines of the factor-price equalization theorem. What really is brought into contact via trade is industrial-nation capital and more poorly remunerated Third World labor and land. To the extent that the products of high-wage labor compete with those of low-wage labor, it is more likely the latter that ends up unemployed. Low-wage manual labor may face the problem of becoming economically and culturally obsolete as investment in capital and educational skills is substituted for economically and culturally unskilled labor and raw land with growing efficiency. Recognition of this economic imperative to upgrade the productivity of factor inputs converts the factor price equalization theorem into the kind of factor-price *disparity* mechanism posited by mid-nineteenth-century U.S. protectionists in particular, with antecedents in the writings of Tucker and Steuart in the 1750–75 generation.

Chapters 8 and 9 suggest that the lower an economy's wages are, the greater its productivity lag tends to be. *Unit* labor costs often are highest in low-wage countries than in high-wage economies using skill-intensive professional labor with high levels of capital per worker. This explains why nations with high living standards and active government educational programs to train labor have been able to undersell low-wage economies.

Another aspect of world polarization between a high-wage industrial center and a low-wage periphery producing primary commodities has been the emigration of skilled labor emphasized throughout Parts I and II. Historically, many professionals have preferred to remain in their traditional occupations even when this has involved moving abroad, rather than suffering wage cuts or shifting to low-wage sectors at home. Meanwhile, the population explosion spurred by poverty leads to high fertility rates, and hence a heavy overhead of children not in the labor force. Poor economies lack the money to employ these individuals as they mature and enter the labor force, or to train them along modern lines, or provide the necessary complement of private and public-sector capital needed to set them to work in competition with the labor of higher-income nations.

A final point that should discourage all barter theories of international convergence based simply on ratios and comparative rather than absolute costs is the existence of numerous common denominators in international cost structures. These common denominators—energy and raw materials, food, capital goods, some types of skilled labor, and so forth—plug comparative-cost ratios into a single worldwide absolute-cost system.

Under conditions of increasing returns the world economy does not form an analogy to thermodynamic entropy. Wealth flows from poor (economically "cold") economies to wealthy ("hot") ones, not the other way around. The path to wealth is via prosperity and capital accumulation, not austerity. Economies that let their income levels fall below the rates needed to sustain technological modernization run the danger of leaving their labor, land and capital economically obsolete. Chapter 9 therefore summarizes how economic polarization results from economic negentropy, that is positive feedback, in contrast to the entropy-type "equilibrium" theorizing that underpins most international convergence theories. Once increasing returns are recognized as being the norm, a basic economic question becomes one of deciding what rates of private and public investment are needed to upgrade labor, land and capital to keep economies internationally competitive. This kind of projection may be done on an industry-by-industry basis for important new technologies, as the Japanese and other East Asians have recognized in the case of computer and electronic technology.

A corollary is that once economies fall into a state of economic obsolescence, the level of curative "catch-up" investment tends to grow geometrically. Yet poorer countries have less and less ability to generate the requisite investment surplus. The adverse political and cultural by-products of economic polarization tend to lock in existing specialization patterns, largely by entrenching domestic oligarchies whose behavior is more in the character of a cosmopolitan class than the kind of nationalism found in eighteenth-century, mercantilist Europe or nineteenth-century America.

Under such conditions even industrial and agricultural protectionism tends to be warped into the kind of monopolistic favoritism that led to the rejection of mercantilist statism in Enlightenment Europe and to the anti-trust legislation at the turn of the twentieth century in the United States. Today, privatization of Latin American public utilities is being put forth as a radical anti-oligarchic policy opposed to the excesses of corrupt protectionism.

Most writers until quite recently believed that each economy would evolve through basically the same set of "stages of development" (Chapter 10). Not anticipated were the various economic, political and even cultural formations that have blocked economies from emulating the path taken by England, the United States and other lead nations that have progressed through these stages. Development strategies based on enhancing the domestic market have been rejected in favor of export-oriented specialization.

Early writers seem to have expected that if England or any other nation succeeded in conquering the world economy, it would help industrialize less developed countries by example, and by foreign investment. A cosmopolitan homogeneity seemed likely, much as Rome established a common body of law and culture throughout its empire. But until recently, economic observers did not foresee that an increasingly industrialized center would use market forces and government diplomacy to shape a malformed periphery ruled by client oligarchies in Latin America, Africa and parts of Asia. The principles of national self-determination were assumed to prevent this. Countries would adopt the most successful model before them. But in reality the lead nations have disturbed the development of the less developed countries, creating the phenomenon of institutionalized backwardness.

Chapter 11 deals with the narrowing scope and unrealistic methodology of international trade theory over the past two hundred years. Free-trade histories of international economics reflect the degree to which manipulating the history of ideas may become a ploy to maintain the status quo. As George Orwell observed, whoever controls the past controls the present, and hence the future. The history of international trade and financial theory has fallen prey to the censorial spirit of free-trade ideology blocking knowledge of the development of rival theories. Protectionism for its part has relied more on political lobbying than on academic theorizing, leaving the field of international economics as a preserve for laissez faire advocates who brand alternative views as lying outside the subject matter of the discipline they have narrowly re-defined.

Only a few writers on the outskirts of international economics have developed an alternative view.[3] A large part of the problem stems from trying to make economics a "natural science," treating society in much the same way one might view physical nature. We must beware of writers who use the term

---

[3] Andre Gunder Frank, *Capitalism and Underdevelopment in Latin America* (New York, 1967), *World Accumulation. 1492–1789* (New York: 1978), *Dependent Accumulation and Underdevelopment* (New York: 1979), and *Critique and Anti-Critique* (New York: 1984).

"nature" (as in natural endowments) as a code word for the status quo. To follow nature has meant to acquiesce in the existing division of labor between lead nations and poor countries. This commitment to defend the status quo has led free-trade theory to treat international trade in isolation from finance, technology, demography, ecology, politics and the military dimension.

Chapter 12 describes why international investment has not reversed the polarizing tendencies of the commodity trade and emigration described in Part II. Laissez faire economists hold that if industrial nations gain wealth relative to less developed countries, they will invest their trade surpluses in the latter, with the salutary effect of helping these countries catch up. Economists from Adam Smith through Marx traced how the industrial nations moved to avoid bottle-necks by ensuring a smooth supply of raw materials from abroad. The problem has been that rather than being dispersed across the economic spectrum, foreign investment was concentrated in insulated export enclaves, creating "dual economies" whose capital-intensive production enclaves stand in sharp contrast to relatively backward or malformed subsistence sectors.

This pattern of international investment has the further effect of holding down the terms of trade for raw materials, while backward systems of land tenure inherited from the colonial epochs retard food production throughout the Southern Hemisphere. These rigid institutions were adverse to optimum technological modes of production, but have been reinforced by world diplomacy working to entrench the status quo, underdeveloping Third World economies. Loans ("indirect investment") have subsidized unprogressive governments or concentrated on public infrastructure to support export production, thereby undercutting the long-term trade and payments position of debtor countries.

Part III analyzes the impact of debt service, military spending and other capital transfers. From the Bullion Debate during the Napoleonic Wars through the German reparations debate a century later, theories of international finance polarized between two irreconcilable approaches. Monetarists claimed that no real transfer problem existed. Indebted countries or others running payments deficits would experience monetary austerity automatically, reducing consumption and investment. Today this effect is achieved by governments tightening the money supply under IMF direction. For countries with inconvertible paper currencies, depreciation serves to divert domestic output for export. Although economists possessing a broader scope and more realistic principles refuted this creditor-oriented extremism, the bullionist-monetarist "hard money" view has risen to the status of academic orthodoxy.

Chapter 13 compares the debate between monetarism and structuralism regarding international polarization tendencies in the financial sphere to those in commodity trade. The modern theory of capital transfers starts with England's bullion debate over whether payments deficits were self-curing or not (Chapter 14). Would England's transfer of military subsidies to its continental allies pay for themselves" by making exports less expensive and imports more costly, as implied by the price-specie flow mechanism? Would the adjustment involve income effects as capital transferred abroad became a reciprocal demand for English exports? To what degree would capital transfers distort international values and hence investment decisions?

In answering these questions monetarists (the bullionists, led by Ricardo) emphasized marginal income adjustments, while the anti-bullionists (Thornton *et al.*) asked what happened when certain limits were bypassed. The "hard money" party urged the Bank of England to roll back the money supply until the sterling price of gold fell to its prewar 1797 level—as if stability could not be achieved just as well at the postwar level. (This would not have benefited bondholders by as much, because the purchasing power of their capital and interest would be less than would be the case under the deflationary policies called for by the stockbroker Ricardo.) Their anti-bullionist adversaries pointed out that the rise in the price of gold was caused not so much by domestic inflation as by England's military payments abroad and its need to import grain during two years of crop failure.

Much as Chapter 14, dealing with Ricardo and the bullion debate, corresponds to Chapter 5 which reviewed his theory of comparative costs, so Chapter 15 (dealing with the effect of capital transfers on the terms of trade as analyzed by Mill and his successors) forms a natural extension of the supply and demand principles discussed in Chapter 6. The common denominator is Mill's qualification of Ricardian analysis by introducing market considerations of supply and demand. In addition to the shifting supply and demand of commodities, international prices diverged from underlying direct labor and capital values because of autonomous demand for foreign exchange. The demand for monetary gold, for instance, had far-reaching effects via inflationary or deflationary leads and lags. Prices do not change equally, but distort existing relationships between labor, capital and land, and for debt and savings vis-à-vis current output and the valuation of assets. Import and export prices are overlayered by capital transfers that distort domestic monetary relations as well as international exchange.

The "elasticity pessimism" posed by Mill and Edgeworth with respect to commodity trade finds its counterpart in the price inelastic demand for foreign exchange. Here again Chapters 6 and 15 run along similar lines. At issue is whether monetary inflation or deflation resulting from capital transfers can be cured simply by reducing or increasing the money supply, or whether the underlying problem is non-monetary and hence structural. Mill's "offer" curves show the extent to which payment for imports and exports is just one part of the supply and demand for foreign exchange. The need to make capital transfers, above all those involving debt and military payments is a price-inelastic phenomenon that threatens to lead to a deteriorating economic spiral. Debt service works to depreciate the currency, and hence the price of the indebted country's exports and assets.

The first effect of monetary inflation or deflation is felt in the capital markets, and only later spills over into the goods markets. A booming stock and real estate market may pull in yet *more* foreign funds seeking to ride the inflationary investment wave in hopes of earning capital gains, thereby counteracting the alleged price specie-flow mechanism.[4]

Balance-of-payments stabilization usually is achieved not by commodity-price shifts leading to adjustments in exports and imports, but by the much faster-working policy of interest rate adjustments. Countries running deficits raise their interest rates to attract foreign capital. The problem is that by deterring the new direct investment needed to increase exports and displace imports, this financial response undercuts the long-term trade position.

Such capital-account problems did not become critical until the 1920s, when the aftermath of World War I saw the German and French hyperinflations warp economic life to a degree far beyond anything hitherto experienced. As in the case of most hyperinflations until quite recently, those of the 1920s stemmed from capital transfers—German reparations and inter-Ally debts. The typical pattern was for foreign exchange to depreciate by more than domestic prices rose, and for the inflation rate to outstrip growth in the domestic money supply.

During the German reparations debate Allied economists (Ohlin, Rueff *et al.*) put forth the Ricardian idea that to the extent that rising taxes could extract demand from the domestic market, they free an equivalent value of goods for export. Anti-monetarists (led by Keynes and Moulton) pointed out that higher taxes increase production and distribution costs, as do the higher interest rates that resulted from inflation and/or tight money. Even when more output is exported, therefore, the added volume may worsen the terms of trade—and foreign countries may defend against such exports by increasing their own protectionism, as the United States did in the 1920s.

Foreign borrowing served as a balancing item in international payments to stabilize exchange rates in the nineteenth century. But foreign debt relation-

---

[4]  There is some anticipation of this counter-intuitive possibility in commodity price theory. Lead-nation exports such as prestige cars and other consumer goods often find markets precisely because they are more expensive and indeed, denominated in appreciating currencies that promise to increase their (resale) value. This hedge effect spurred German Volkswagen sales in the United States during the 1950s and 1960s, and sales of Mercedes-Benzes and BMWs in the 1970s and 1980s.

ships lead to financial dependency, polarizing the world economy between creditor and debtor nations—a counterpart to the trade dependency discussed in Parts I and II of this book.

Creditor-nation economists argued that Germany's ability to pay reparations was not constrained by any limits to its balance-of-payments position, even though foreign economies were raising their tariffs against German exports. Germany could pay its reparation debts by imposing domestic monetary and fiscal austerity. It was not held necessary to upgrade the economy's productive powers (export-earning or import-displacing capacity), or to get creditor nations to change their policies so as to accept more exports from the debtor economy. These assumptions rationalized the policies that helped bring on the world financial crash of 1929 and the ensuing Great Depression. As Chapter 18 shows, these same monetarist assumptions are still being used to impose austerity programs that impair investment and income growth in Third World debtor countries, contributing to their economic and technological obsolescence.

Structuralists pointed out that price and income changes in themselves cannot discourage many types of international payments. Debts must be paid to foreigners regardless of cost ratios or currency parities. Based on this structural imperative, along with military spending and imports of food and other essentials, Keynes and Moulton in the 1920s and 1930s warned that the scheduled German reparations and inter-Ally debts could not be paid without bankrupting debtor economies countries and bringing down the world economic system.

Economists agreed that what is needed to finance capital transfers ultimately is to improve the trade balance. This presupposes new direct investment, which often involves imported capital goods, as well as energy and other raw materials to produce the added exports (or displace the imports). These expenditures threaten to aggravate the trade deficit in the short run. Foreign credits burden the long-term balance-of-payments deficit as interest accrues on unpaid debt balances, requiring yet more borrowing on increasingly onerous terms.

For many decades Latin American economies such as Argentina (emulated by the United States after 1971) sought to avoid the deflationary discipline of gold by moving onto an inconvertible paper standard. Their floating (*i.e.*, sinking) currency was intended to devalue the economy's exports by enough to spur exports and discourage imports to the degree needed to finance the requisite capital transfer. But this impaired the debtor economies' long-term position as rising interest rates deterred domestic investment, and also increased the carrying charges of foreign debt. Hyperinflations spurred capital flight, and also political instability. Currency depreciation made debtor-country assets cheaper to foreign investors, whose purchases laid the basis for future remittances of earnings and dividends.

Matters are complicated by the fact that much industry in the debtor economies is owned either by foreigners or by local oligarchies that block social investment in education and other infrastructure necessary to bring a modern labor force into being. Foreign investors are not much interested in allocating their assets in keeping with domestic needs and self-sufficiency. As noted earlier, they tend to invest in the export sector to provide raw materials for the industrial creditor-nation economies. This creates dual economies in the periphery, and concentrates mines and landholdings in export enclaves. Land use is shifted away from local subsistence production to export production. This is especially harmful for food production, an area in which indebted countries have become more dependent on the industrial nations. The result is a set of dual economies less able to feed and otherwise support themselves—just the opposite from what Ricardian analysis forecast—while unable to generate sufficient trade surpluses to carry their foreign debts. The need to borrow the interest that falls due locks these countries into the economic diplomacy that the creditor nations impose by the IMF and World Bank, which have evolved into the world's new centralized planning institutions.

Economywide ratios are not very helpful in analyzing dual economies whose export enclaves reflect the capital-per-worker ratios of the creditor nations rather than those of the host countries. Chapters 7 and 8 examine capital/labor ratios with high-wage vs. low-wage labor in light of the theory of factor endowments and factor-price equalization. The same issue arises with the so-called Leontief paradox, much as the contrast between investment and savings functions in the export sector vis-à-vis the domestic sector complicate the application of Keynesian-type macroeconomic ratios to trade theory.

Modern structural models rightly begin with macroeconomic relationships. But it is necessary to make these functions specific rather than overly abstract, for example, as in failing to recognize that an economy's industrial profile is composed of numerous sectors, each having its own average ratio of investment and saving (or profit) to output, employment and sales revenue. The criticisms made in Chapter 8 with regard to the factor proportions theory and the Leontief paradox (as being too general and abstract in their various economy-wide ratios) therefore apply also to Keynesian and monetarist macroeconomics discussed in Chapter 17.

Falling into debt dependency typically leads to a loss of domestic control over foreign-owned sectors. This phenomenon may be supplemented by covert political intervention to support free-trade cosmopolitan parties against nationalistic ones. The German-American support for Chile's Social Democrats in the 1970s as against the socialists is a case in point, as are nominally popularist regimes that actually serve foreign interests in the most critical areas, for instance the Peronist party in Argentina at various times.

A further problem in applying multiplier analysis to international trade and investment is that it tends to be the creditor economies whose incomes are "multiplied" by revenue inflows from indebted raw-materials exporters. Remitted earnings and debt service are supplemented by enormous sums of flight capital, so that exports from dual economies do not multiply local income. In general, Third World economies have been warped so that when they grow, it is not as rivals but mainly as export markets for North America and Europe (and now Asia). Foreign aid and a broad array of diplomatic pressures bolster market forces in steering them into this cul-de-sac—much the same objective towards which mercantilist policy aimed in the eighteenth century.

With regard to determining where the world should go from here, Part III shows that living in the short run hurts financially, much as the trade-structure considerations discussed in Part II impaired long-term development. Debtor economies are obliged to keep their interest rates high, depreciate their currencies, cut back spending on public infrastructure (and even privatize it since the 1980s), and let foreigners take control of their natural resources and other assets at distress prices.

Inflation in the industrial creditor nations has pushed up prices that often improve their terms of trade (as noted by Prebisch). Their monetary inflation becomes further self-justifying to the extent that it spills over into the stock market and property market, drawing in foreign funds and thus further polarizing world exchange rates.

The failure to recognize the characteristics of today's capital-transfer problems detailed in Chapter 18 suggests that the IMF and World Bank are so doctrinaire as to be incapable of reform. Their lending policies reflect a narrow-minded lack of realism in pursuit of deflationary creditor-oriented policies which, since Ricardo's day, have gone hand in hand with an over-specialization of labor and growing international dependency.

Whenever we find so great a degree of unreality to characterize a theory that backs an economic doctrine and its applied models, we should suspect special interests to be at work. It hardly is surprising that the ideology of today's global orthodoxy reflects the self-interest of the industrial creditor nations. The great riddle is why Third World countries have been so willing to accept this self-serving body of international economics.

The key lies in the class relations of Latin America and Africa. (Even England, known for its industrial antagonisms for the past two centuries, never had anything like the death squads found throughout Latin America.) When currency depreciation works to transfer resources from the domestic to the export sector, it favors foreign investors and large exporters relative to those who produce food for the home market. Inflation in Third World countries tends to impoverish workers as wages lag behind the rising cost of living. Unionizing does not help much, because currency depreciation causes a price inflation that wipes out domestic-currency wage gains. Local inflation also spurs capital flight, discouraging domestic saving and investment—except where governments pay local real interest rates of nearly 50 per cent annually, as Brazil and Argentina did in 1989–90, and Russia soon thereafter.

Currency depreciation and its associated hyperinflation facilitates tax dodging by the wealthy classes in countries with weak fiscal regimes, enhancing the position of Third World elites. The result has been to favor a financial layer lording it over the rest of society, especially as balance-of-payments deficits require high interest rates, much to the benefit of the creditor class. Meanwhile, low prices for many Third World exports are blamed on foreigners rather than on the local magnates who find that their interest lies with the polarizing world trade and financial arrangements sponsored by the IMF and World Bank doctrines of financial and technological dependency.

Today's international economic methodology pretends that free trade and capital markets under these arrangements promote economic convergence rather than polarization. This doctrinaire theorizing supports policies that serve today's vested interests. In the past, countries being exploited juxtaposed an alternative economic canon. The fact that this has not occurred today reflects the success of monetarist free-trade theory in censoring the history of economic thought to conceal the degree to which sponsorship of official economic policy—and the academic theory mustered to support it—reflects these vested policy interests.

# 20. Debt Peonage and the Neoliberal Road to Serfdom

Trade theory has not made much advance since this book was published in 1992. Indeed, little has changed since 1969–72 when I gave the lectures on which it is based. The guardians of orthodoxy who author today's textbooks cover their eyes with blinders against any hint of the logic that underlay the protectionist policies by which England and America endowed themselves with capital prior to adopting free trade. Simplistic assumptions are retained even though long since controverted, with little acknowledgement of the more realistic alternatives that have long been known.

If insanity is doing the same thing over and over again in the expectation of a different result, then neoliberal trade theorists are at best useful lunatics for international predators. The usual term is "useful idiots," but it takes great intelligence to persist in wrongheaded, counter-productive policies in the face of consistent failure. The problem is learned ignorance, which typically goes hand in hand with an almost religious faith in ideological labels. "Nothing is so passionate as a vested interest disguised as an intellectual conviction," explained the main character in Sean O'Casey's play *The White Plague*.

In the preface to his *Foundations of Economic Analysis*, Paul Samuelson wrote that "a scholar in economics who is fundamentally confused concerning the relationship of definition, tautology, logical implication, empirical hypothesis, and factual refutation may spend a lifetime shadow-boxing with reality."[1] Nowhere is this more the case than in his own factor-price equalization theorem. Like the circular reasoning of most general equilibrium theorizing, it treats the status quo as natural and implies that government policies which "interfere with free markets" are ineffective in promoting long-term goals. A major shortcoming of such trade theorizing is the failure to recognize that if less prosperous economies *are* to raise their productivity and living standards to world levels, it can only be through national policies involving structural reform, not merely by marginal adjustments.

By the same token, economies that protect their industry, agriculture and public domain from foreign takeover and steer clear of foreign debt will benefit when foreign governments accept neoliberal theory that depicts selling off the public domain and adopting free trade and capital movements as promoting

---

[1]   Paul Samuelson, *Foundations of Economic Analysis* (Atheneum, 1964), p. ix.

efficiency and prosperity, not dependency. That kind of naïve wrong-headedness and living for short-term gains is a prescription for disaster.

Failure to protect, regulate and subsidize key sectors leads to a shut-down of manufacturing industry and impoverishment of agriculture. The pretense that government action to promote better employment, productivity and living standards is synonymous with paving the road to serfdom has become a myth that encourages financial, trade and technological dependency. It ends up locking countries into debt service and chronic balance-of-payments drains to pay for imports and foreign loans.

It should be clear by now that the financial sector is the last interest group from which to expect greater realism. Attributing the relative value of commodities to labor and productivity alone, for example, Ricardo diverted attention away from the role of debt service in determining international prices, on the ground that debt was not a direct production cost. He also dropped from view the burden of taxes to carry the public debt. Recognizing that what is not analyzed is less likely to be criticized and regulated, the financial sector has embraced this narrow approach of leaving the financial dimension out of account. Also ignored is the fact that to the extent that foreign borrowing and speculation finances a real estate and stock-market bubble, speculators and even normal buyers will find their interest to lie in borrowing abroad in the hope of making capital gains, but leave the economy more highly indebted. The temples of high finance promote this as the path to progress rather than debt peonage.

To explain how nations have achieved or lost an economic lead requires a political and above all financial explanation of why international incomes and wealth are polarizing rather than equalizing. Take for example the population plunge and emigration suffered by the former Soviet economies since the dismantling of their industry after 1991. Such demographic phenomena once were placed at the core of economic theory, as was the debt overhead. Yet most trade theorists fail to take into account the *rentier* charges imposed by financial claims, or how economic polarization leads to social shrinkage. By treating financial and population dynamics as exogenous, economists relinquish analysis of the real world to journalists and lobbyists.

Trade theory will encourage warped policies if it is dominated by special-interest pleading. The guiding principle for lobbyists is that of trial lawyers: Find the best-credentialed experts willing to back your argument, and then build up their prestige all the more. Nobel Prizes help. Such maneuvering turns trade theorists wittingly or unwittingly into policy lobbyists, providing slogans and nostrums for short sound bites. Instead of seeking to describe how the real world is evolving, sponsors of the policies at issue ignore whatever evidence does not advance the policies being promoted. Economic logic thus becomes turned into something more in the character of fiction than a map of reality.

Today's economic orthodoxy starts with a policy prescription opposing protective tariffs and capital controls, and then reasons backward to select the assumptions, definitions and concepts that will rationalize it. The narrow scope of this theorizing makes it difficult to see how protectionism may increase productivity and spur growth, increase employment and self-sufficiency (especially in food production) and hence reduce dependency. In a similar manner, mainstream IMF-style monetarists neglect how paying foreign debts depresses the currency and the terms of trade in the way that J. S. Mill described, or how financial protectionism may protect against global lending whose effect is to inflate property prices and push up exchange rates. A rising debt overhead inflates the carrying charges for real estate and industry, raising the cost of living and doing business. Yet so thoroughly has this policy been embraced that asset-price inflation is welcomed as "wealth creation," as if it were not simultaneously debt creation entailing future payment of debt service that puts downward pressure on exchange rates.

When the currency falls, import prices rise, adding to domestic price pressures. Central banks may respond by raising interest rates to stabilize the exchange rate. But high interest rates increase prices all the more. Keynes called this Gibson's Paradox, which is not paradoxical at all when one realizes that interest charges are as much a cost of doing business as are taxes. Ricardian trade theory and the labor theory of value divert attention from this problem, and Keynesian macroeconomics is not of much more helpful in today's world in which rising indebtedness and the tax shift off property onto labor threaten to add as much to the economy's price structure as technological progress lowers direct pro-duction costs.

Ricardo's Bullionist school insisted that international debt service was self-financing. This early version of monetarism was controverted already in the 1810s, as Chapter 14 has described. The logical failings of subsequent monetarists were exposed a century later when John Maynard Keynes in England and Harold Moulton in the United States analyzed how Inter-Ally war debts and German reparations led to the world financial crisis that brought on the Great Depression in the 1930s (Chapter 16). But only the monetarist side of this debate is reported today. Pro-creditor historians of economic thought fail to include alternative logic and evidence when writing their narratives. A similar censorship has occurred with the arguments between protectionists and free traders over whether the global economy tends to polarize or converge in the absence of countervailing government policy to shape markets to promote or drain the wealth of nations.

### Requirements for a modern theory of trade and finance

Theories of international trade and payments are built on concepts of how domestic economies operate. Most trade theory still focuses on direct production costs, but corporate, personal and public debt has become more important. A relevant theory therefore needs to take account of the fact that non-production costs have risen. Ricardo's depiction of comparative costs in terms of the labor theory of value seemed plausible enough in an epoch when food represented the major element in the worker's budget. Most outlays were for consumer goods whose prices could be resolved into labor costs. But today, housing costs (mainly for mortgage debt) and personal debt charges may amount to 40 percent of the budgets of many families. Property prices are determined largely by the supply of mortgage credit to finance their purchase. Charges for personal bank loans, credit-card debt and auto debt, plus forced savings for Social Security, pension-fund contributions and health insurance typically push non-commodity costs to over half the basic budget for labor.

For employers, whereas Ricardo viewed the cost of capital in terms of the labor time needed for its production, the credit terms on which it is financed—in terms of interest rates, debt/equity ratios and differing national tax treatment—make it appropriate to recognize the degree to which financial and property charges have risen to dominate commodity export prices and hence the terms of trade. Across the board, debt service accounts for a rising share of capital and labor costs. Interest and principal payments on education loans, home mortgages, medical debts, health insurance, and forced saving for retirement pensions are overshadowing nominal wage payments and labor productivity in determining international competitiveness. The cost of medical care in the United States, for instance, falls on individuals and their employers rather than being absorbed by the public sector.

Governments throughout the world are shifting the tax burden off finance and property onto labor and industry. The effect is to promote financial and real estate bubbles in which debt-financed purchases overshadow new capital investment. These developments make the concept of "cost of production" much more complex today than it was during the formative centuries of trade theory. In the balance of payments, property and financial transactions have come to overshadow commodity exports and imports in determining exchange rates.

Analyzing trade in terms of raw labor/capital ratios is like formulating military strategy based on the polite eighteenth-century rules of warfare that pit infantries against each other on the open field where cannon and cavalry were only a supplement to hand-to-hand combat. Modern economic rivalry has become as capital-intensive as warfare. Technology is embodied more in capital equipment and patented rent-yielding "intellectual property rights" than in workers and their on-the-job skills as was the case when Adam Smith and Ricardo wrote. The major cost differentials in goods and services traded among nations derive from the financing of their physical capital, *e.g.*, via interest rates, debt/equity ratios and tax treatment. As for the cost of labor, as noted above, housing now plays the role that food did in earlier times. The important difference is that whereas crops are traded at a common world price, housing reflects a combination of domestic debt creation and tax favoritism for property owners.

The debt overhead grows at compound rates of interest, outstripping the real economy's ability to increase production and consumption. The basic principle is that coined by U.S. President Nixon's economic advisor Herbert Stein: "A trend that can't go on forever, won't." Interest and other carrying charges divert income from the circular flow of payments between producers and consumers. This debt service is a form of financial and fiscal leakage.[2]

The problem is that although finance has become the critical element in production, most credit today is extractive, not productive. Analyzing its carrying charges requires an updated conceptual framework to distinguish between direct investment (capital formation) and speculation in already-existing property and financial securities in search of capital gains (asset-price inflation).

### Prices, incomes and exchange rates in a financialized world

The purchasing-power parity theory asserts that exchange rates tend to reflect commodity prices. The classical economists focused on grain prices as proxies for wages and hence for exchange rates. (Today, McDonald's hamburgers provide a familiar measure.) Mill's *Essays on some Unsettled Questions of Political Economy* qualified this commodity-trade approach by showing how military spending and debt service affected exchange rates. Although there was still a tendency to treat the capital account and its associated flow of interest and dividends as marginal complications, most countries now find their balance of payments dominated by foreign investment in stocks, bonds and real estate. The analysis of exchange rates thus must take into account interest rates, foreign lending, and international rates of asset-price inflation for real estate, stocks and bonds.

Take the case of McDonald's as a company. An attempt was made in 2005 to raid it and separate its real estate from its hamburger business. The idea was to mortgage its property and pay out the loan proceeds as dividends in order to raise its stock price. This would have built interest charges into the next generation

---

[2]  I describe the problem in "Saving, Asset-Price Inflation, and Debt-Induced Deflation," in L. Randall Wray and Matthew Forstater, eds., *Money, Financial Instability and Stabilization Policy* (Edward Elgar, 2006), pp. 104–24.

of hamburger prices. The raid failed, but across the economic spectrum an un-precedented layer of non-material production costs is growing.

The easing of credit in the United States and other countries since 1980 has fueled bond-market and stock market bubbles, followed by a global real estate bubble capitalizing economic rent for real estate, monopoly rent and intellectual property rights at rising debt/equity ratios. Asset-price inflation ("capital gains") has loaded global assets and incomes with debt, without necessarily spurring new direct investment.

Global financialization turns many traditional principles upside down. Commodity-price inflation erodes competitiveness for imports and exports, but asset-price inflation attracts global funds into the stock, bond and real estate markets. As economies become more financialized, rising rent, property and debt charges tend to offset wage advantages. One result is that instead of labor migrating to earn higher money wages to spend on goods and services having a fairly uniform global price, employees seek lower housing costs and less financial overhead. A rising number of programmers and other information-technology professionals from Silicon Valley, for instance, have come to realize that housing costs and taxes in California absorb so much of their paychecks that they can do better by moving back to India, buying land and hiring household servants for a fraction of what it would cost in the United States. A debt-and-property theory of commodity pricing and competitive advantage among nations is needed to take account of the non-production costs that form a growing component of prices and of national income.

In contrast to material technology, which is fairly universal across national boundaries, debt, finance, taxes and property law are institutional characteristics. As such, they vary from one nation to another. It follows that international economics should emphasize the degree to which prices are shaped by govern-ment policy, not merely by material technology itself. An asymmetrical world calls for an institutional analysis of finance and debt to replace the symmetrical world of classical trade theory based on common production functions and labor costs.

By treating the institutional context of finance and property as "exogenous" and lying more in the realm of sociology than economics, the neoclassical main-stream rules out what should be the very essence of the evolving character of competitive advantage among nations. By linking the world economy financially, the world's globalization since 1945 has linked what Ricardo analyzed as com-parative advantage into an absolute global cost schedule—in a world where the way to achieve prosperity and wealth is to borrow as much as one can to invest in assets that whose prices are rising more rapidly than the rate of interest so as to maximize "total returns." The result is a race into debt and highly financialized pricing that turns Adam Smith's concept of the wealth of nations upside down.

Economies polarize between creditors and debtors as the degree of financialization increases, even as technology raises productivity to lessen the materially necessary costs of production. The debt and property overhead tends to grow exponentially as interest payments accrue to savings and are recycled in the form of new loans against property already in place rather than being invested in new means of production. Interest charges and economic rents are extracted from the economy, shrinking the market for goods and services and thus reducing the incentive for new direct investment. Economies become financially "top-heavy," polarizing between savers and debtors as the production-and-consumption economy becomes increasingly indebted to the finance-and-property shell.

Under these conditions there is little growth in net saving as measured in the national income accounts. The Keynesian multiplier becomes nearly infinite as banking systems break free of their tie to the precious metals. The foreign-trade multiplier loses all functional meaning as the trade balance is decoupled from domestic credit creation. This is the brave new world that a realistic modern-day theory of the international economy must analyze.

## Settling trade deficits in government debt, payable and unpayable

The world that classical trade theorists analyzed was one of universally available technology and fairly standard consumption patterns. Gold and silver were the universal backing for banking and currency systems, as had been the case since classical antiquity. But since the U.S. dollar replaced gold as the "money of the world," and especially since American war spending in Southeast Asia drove the dollar off gold in August 1971, turning it into a fiat currency. Central bank reserves now take the form mainly of loans to the U.S. Treasury.

This world has become increasingly unipolar, bolstered by the tendency to concentrate the world's savings in U.S. bond and stock markets and real estate. Oil-exporting countries from Saudi Arabia to Norway are especially noteworthy for investing their trade surpluses more in U.S. stocks than in building up domestic infrastructure.

What blocks economic theorizing from basing itself on these perceptions is its retreat from addressing the *rentier* overhead of financial, property and monopoly claims. The international economy is made largely extractive by a combination of asset stripping and the right of key-currency countries (headed by the United States) to import goods and buy out foreign companies with

[3]  I have explained the principles of dollar hegemony in *Super Imperialism* (1972; 2nd ed., 2002) and *Global Fracture* (1977, 2nd ed., 2004).

paper IOUs whose prospect of repayment is of questionable quality.[3] Dollar hegemony enables America to pay for its imports, foreign military adventures and the buyout of foreign assets simply with government bonds without limit. When the United States runs a trade and payments deficit, the dollars that its consumers pay for imports—and its investors pay to buy stocks, bonds and entire companies—end up in local central banks as dollar recipients exchange them for domestic currency.

By accepting these dollars, countries exchange tangible exports and enterprises for mere paper—the government bonds (that is, almost forced loans to the U.S. treasuries) in which central bank reserves now consist. If countries do not recycle their dollar inflows in this way, their currency will soar, hurting their exporters in dollarized world markets. Central banks feel that they have little option but to turn around and send the dollars back to the United States by buying its Treasury bills. *In effect, America's balance-of-payments deficit finances its federal budget deficit with foreign countries' export proceeds.*

Why should a nation want to earn dollars under these conditions? Under the gold standard, export surpluses provided the backing for an expansion of domestic currency and credit, and consequently for economic growth. The larger a nation's gold and hard-currency reserves, the longer its central bank could avoid raising interest rates to protect these reserves when incomes rose and led to higher imports in business-cycle upturns. But domestic money and credit no longer relies on gold and silver bullion backing. The fact that trade surpluses are settled in IOUs of the U.S. Treasury casts doubt on the benefit of producing for export, especially as these U.S. Government debts seem categorically unpayable since they passed the trillion-dollar mark in 2006. The dollar no longer is a hard currency as traditionally defined. No longer able to muster a balance-of-payment surplus, America's hollowed-out economy is obliged to rely on diplomatic arm-twisting, backed ultimately by military power and more covert operations.

International economic theory never before has been called on to deal with such a situation. Removal of the gold backing to settle balance-of-payments deficits leaves no constraint on domestic credit creation, and hence opens the door to unprecedented asset-price inflation. A major effect is to raise property prices relative to wages. This has the unfortunate consequence of making gains in property prices (that is, riding the wave of asset-price inflation) the focus of investment. The effect is to divert savings away from creating wealth by investing in real capital that increases productive capacity. This is happening now on a global scale, not just domestically. Meanwhile, the United States is turning other nations into financial and fiscal satellites.

China affords the most successful example of a country using trade and foreign investment to accelerate its development. This success came with problems, however, because of foreign investment in its export-driven manufacturing sector.

What was China to do with the resulting dollars, and how could it best replace foreign markets by developing a more prosperous domestic market?

China's response has been to use its trade surplus to buy property rights to assure a supply of raw materials for the future. These investments have been mainly in countries that seek dollars to service foreign debts they have accumulated by following orthodox trade theory and running trade deficits for decades. For such countries the textbook gains from trade have been swamped by the losses on debt service and the terms-of-trade penalty resulting from foreign dependency.

China's maneuvering shows how much more complex today's global economy is than the old free-market models portray. International relations no longer are primarily an exchange of goods by the most efficient producers as Ricardian trade theory described, nor do exporters receive gold for their trade surpluses. The precondition for industrial power is control of fuel, minerals and other basic raw materials and monopolized technology. Ownership of such resources now plays the role that national gold stocks did in times past.

Ultimately at issue is how trade and investment are transforming world geopolitics. Structural analysis of the global economy requires a more empirically accurate vision of how institutional behavior in the future will differ from today's world. For hundreds of years the aim of trade and investment was to upgrade economies from primary production (food and raw materials) to manufacturing. But since 1991 a major objective of neoliberal trade and investment policy has been to convince the former members of the Soviet Union to reverse direction by dismantling their manufacturing and higher education, sending their skilled workers abroad and exporting fuels and minerals to pay for imported manufactures. Remarkably, the governing elites in these economies accepted this caricature of trade-oriented development as a reasonable application of comparative advantage. The problem was that the new narrowed-down trade rules gave them no advantage except (for Russia) raw-materials production and armaments, not manufacturing. What they did have were capital assets, headed by real estate and public infrastructure unencumbered with debt. This enabled trade deficits to be financed by real-estate borrowing and property sell-offs to foreigners. The tradeoff was not one kind of exports for another, but property and financial claims for commodities.

## *A manual of economic malpractice*

In the name of introducing more efficient free markets, application of the Washington Consensus devastated the former Soviet Union. By ending public enterprise and regulation, the policy managed to de-industrialize the world's former #2 superpower. Given a freer hand in Russia than in any other country, neoliberal planners endowed a narrow *rentier* class drawn mainly from the former nomenklatura bureaucracy. Instead of planning a self-reliant economy, their objective changed to one of squeezing out an export or financial surplus that could be transferred abroad. A remarkably similar experience occurred in nearly all the post-Soviet countries, from the Baltics to Central Asia.

The aim of uprooting the industry of centrally planned economies was announced clearly enough. On December 19, 1990, the IMF and World Bank, the Organization for Economic Cooperation and Development (OECD) and the European Bank for Reconstruction and Development (EBRD) produced a joint report on *The Economy of the USSR. A study undertaken to a request by the Houston Summit.* Published by the IMF and reflecting its doctrinal leadership, the report's recommendations played much the same role for the Soviet Union that Versailles had done for Germany. Like that treaty, the plan delivered the *coup de grace* that settled a great war, in this case the Cold War that had lasted over forty years. But unlike Versailles and earlier military conquests that had parceled out the land and natural resources of Europe's feudal kingdoms, the Houston plan was not imposed by force. Promising to deliver prosperity, an extremist version of free-market ideology persuaded the post-Gorbachev "reformers" to relinquish what had been the public domain to a new elite in a quick give-away. Government enterprises were carved up into ownership rights and sold off in due course to foreign buyers.

Under Communist planning Russia had little market feedback to guide production. Its bureaucracy was inefficient at best, corrupt at worst, but at least the economy functioned without a propertied *rentier* class taking rent and interest. This changed as Boris Yeltsin's "family" of supporters—mainly the old *nomenklatura* of former Communist Party members and its Komsomol youth groups—dismantled industrial planning in favor of free-market monetarism.

In this remarkable conquest by ideology, free-market rhetoric played the role that religious authority had done in earlier times. Promoted first at gunpoint in Chile and later exported from the United States with heavy financial subsidy to Russia and other countries, the neoliberal mantra held that public enterprise and even government regulation were wasteful. "There is no example of a successful modern centrally planned economy," the IMF report asserted. It foreclosed discussion of ways "to enhance performance under the old system" by claiming that government planning had "proved to be counterproductive." A mixed economy would not work, not even one with checks and balances of the sort found in the United States, Britain, Scandinavia, Germany or France. The report in fact read much like right-wing Republican campaign editorials attacking Roosevelt's New Deal programs. Unsuccessful in the United States, the neoliberals did succeed in wiping out pension security and related social support systems throughout the former Soviet bloc, and persuading its members to adopt a flat tax on earnings—with almost no property taxation.

The report's policy proposals show that the dismantling of Russian industry was not an accidental result of bad administration. It was planned, by free-market fundamentalists whom Russian critics called Market Bolsheviks for their policy of uprooting existing connections and support systems. Reflecting today's received wisdom of trade and investment theory, the policy applications since 1991 reveal how dangerous its theoretical shortcomings can be in practice.

Anticipating what the American advisor Jeffrey Sachs called shock therapy, the report claimed not to know of any "path of gradual reform … which would minimize economic disturbance and lead to an early harvesting of the fruits of economic efficiency." Only a radical Pinochet-type shock would do the trick. As in Chile, therapy took the form of endowing an oligarchy of insiders with privatized public enterprises, virtually for free. The expectation was that the new owners would find their interest to lie in selling off their ownership rights to Western buyers, who would become the decisive players in the transition to market conditions, not employees or government agencies. Revenue from privatized enterprises would be remitted abroad, requiring Russia either to borrow the money to make the capital transfer or to sell off even more public enterprises, mineral rights and real estate to foreigners so as to subsidize its economic shrinkage program. In such circumstances it is more appropriate to speak of the losses from trade and investment than the tautological "gains from trade."

At issue is the degree to which theoretical models reflect how the real world actually works. Reacting against more than seventy years of bureaucratic planning, Russia was so ideologically dispirited that its politicians and indeed, the population at large accepted the notion that anything not Communism had to be capitalism. They did not realize how many kinds of markets exist, and hence how wide their policy choice really was. The distinction between industrial capitalism and finance capitalism did not become a topic for discussion.

Envying Western consumerism, most Russians had long deemed America to be the paradigm of efficient capitalism. Their hope was that the advisors it supplied through the Agency for Economic Development (AID) and the Harvard Institute for International Development (HIID) would help Russia emulate the U.S. mode of prosperity. As the Cold War gave way to peace, Russia presumably would be able to shift from military to consumer production. But as matters turned out, the notion of free enterprise being applied was so extreme as to exclude even the most basic principles of civil law.

The moral is that misrepresentation of the real world's economic dynamics poses as great a danger to countries today as military conquest did in times past. The Norman Conquest created the landed aristocracy that has governed England for a thousand years by controlling the power of the land and its rental income. Spain's conquest of the New World created the land tenure arrangements that shaped the oligarchies that emerged in Latin America, and English colonialism shaped the Slave South of the United States. In a similar way today, the future of Russia and other post-Soviet states threatens to be determined by the inequitable way in which its land, mineral resources and public enterprises are being privatized.

IMF planners promoted the model designed some forty years earlier (described above in Chapter 18) to squeeze debt service out of Third World countries. The guiding idea is to shrink the domestic market by taxing labor and industry heavily, in the expectation that this will free output for export. The reality is that such austerity programs discourage new capital formation, and erode educational and living standards. This increases dependency on foreign suppliers and creditors, impairing rather than helping the balance of payments.

On the pretext of helping Russia's balance of payments by freeing output for export—and also "freeing" property ownership for sale to foreigners—the IMF report callously dismissed "the overhang problem," that is, purchasing power represented by the savings of individual citizens. Urging that an optimum market economy "must be accompanied by rapid and comprehensive price liberalization," it called for a wipeout of existing savings by hyperinflation. The idea was that reducing the population's purchasing power would leave more output to be exported, while rising prices would cure shortages by eliciting more output. What actually happened was that Russia's industry was closed down.

Opposing Russian proposals to democratize ownership by creating Yugo-slav-style worker-management of enterprises, the IMF warned that "workers' ownership in enterprises … would run counter to the desired objectives of enterprise reform." There were to be no employee constraints on management, much less employee stock ownership on any scale that would provide managerial rights. Instead of permitting domestic savers to buy into former state enterprises, the IMF advisors rejected proposals to let people use their savings to buy shares in the industries being sold by the government, claiming that giving away state property to insiders would lead to greater efficiency.[4] Public enterprises,

---

[4]   The best general review to date is *The Tragedy of Russia's Reforms: Market Bolshevism Against Democracy*, by Peter Reddaway and Dmitri Glinski (Washington D.C.: 2001). Commenting on the fact that the IMF report "opposed privatization measures that would give large numbers of citizens a real stake in ownership, because that would 'result in widely scattered ownership' and 'ineffective monitoring and control of enterprise managers,'" the authors note (p. 179) that "Because the separation of ownership from management is typical of many American corporations, this reasoning is hard to follow."

mineral rights and the rest of the public domain accordingly were sold off to foreigners on premise that foreign management would make Russian companies more competitive, enabling rising productivity and earnings to provide more foreign exchange to buy imports. Encouraged by U.S. and World Bank advisors who presented a radical anti-government philosophy as if it were the height of scientific wisdom, Russian officials transferred hundreds of billions of dollars worth of oil, gas, minerals and public utilities to insiders at little or no cost, simply to have it privately administered by supporters of the Yeltsin regime.

By insisting that managers operate free of worker control and even from public regulation, the IMF and World Bank accused government rules to prevent managerial abuses of interfering with "free markets." Their advisors encouraged privatization and voucher programs that deprived workers and minority share-holders from having a voice in company management. The new managers were permitted to bleed their enterprises and make capital gains by selling them—at rates that still were cheap by Western standards—and to transfer their takings abroad. An unprecedented looting of enterprises was tolerated on the premise that Russia's most important need was to create a vested capitalist class of insiders loyal to the reformers. The word "reform" soon took on a negative connotation to most Russians.

Instead of creating a class of entrepreneurs who managed companies effi-ciently, the IMF-Washington plan created client oligarchies that found their interest to lie in stripping the former Soviet Union's assets and selling their ownership rights to U.S. and other Western financial investors. Privatizers were no exception to the rule that the narrower an oligarchy in control of a nation's mineral resources, land and real estate, industry and monopolies, the more cosmopolitan its members will behave and hence the larger the capital flight in which they will engage. They indulged in an estimated $25 billion in annual capital flight from Russia alone throughout the 1990s. This raises the obvious question of whether the government might have generated as much by operating these enterprises itself. What is larger: the overhead cost of a bureaucratic state, or that of servicing a huge debt, largely denominated in foreign currency?

Once given property, according to the doctrine of privatization, the new oligarchy would be motivated to run business along economically rational lines. But the new owners found it most rational to trade their ownership rights for holdings in the U.S. and European economies, or simply to close down factories and sell them for scrap. Industrial output and employment plummeted, as did living standards for the vast majority of the population when the IMF's austerity program led to inflationary shortages. Many buildings were gentrified into luxury housing as the former Soviet Union experienced the largest real estate bubble in modern history. The new housing, office buildings, stores and hotels were built for foreigners, however, not for the population at large.

Post-Soviet regimes cut back social programs while taxing money away from labor, and raising foreign exchange by selling public assets to global investors. The IMF's Cold War planners seem to have recognized that as wealth distribution became more unequal, the upper layer would become more cosmopolitan. The more easily this privileged class could gain a free lunch via privatization, the more eager its members would be to exchange their shares for North American and European assets, if only to avoid the clutches of domestic tax collectors and criminal prosecutors when the inevitable political backlash occurred.

When the dust cleared, the monetarist policies subsidized by U.S. support, euphemistically called foreign aid, had dismantled Soviet industry and left the economy dependent on imports. The Soviet Union was subjected to a hyper-inflationary austerity similar to that which the IMF had imposed on Latin America and Africa for over thirty years. Capital flight crashed the ruble's exchange rate, making imports more expensive. A Western-oriented elite benefited at the expense of workers and pensioners as the IMF's demand to restrict the money supply shrank production and employment. Also shrinking was the population as health standards fell and AIDS spread from the classic response to poverty: a combination of drug addiction and prostitution.

Generalizing the strategy, neoliberal policy has become the capstone of a U.S.-centered world order whose effect is to indebt economies, transfer ownership of their commanding heights first to a domestic oligarchy and then to Western (especially U.S.) investors, and then let the host economies collapse under the added financial and fiscal cost burden. This policy involves a ten-step process entailing

(1) privatization to remove assets from the public domain. The path of least resistance is to transfer basic infrastructure to political insiders, with the understanding that they will find their interest to lie in turning around and selling their shares to partners in the United States and Western Europe at prices that still leave substantial leeway for capital gains for institutional investors in these countries;

(2) an absence of domestic regulation, permitting owners to extract monopoly rent ("super-profits") and transfer the proceeds abroad in capital flight to London, Switzerland and New York;

(3) dependency on foreign banks to create domestic-currency credit that in principle could be created at home without entailing foreign-exchange outflows in years to come;

(4) denomination of domestic debt in foreign currencies (euros, dollars or Swiss francs), creating a debt burden that will grow as the domestic currency depreciates;

(5) a regressive flat tax that falls on labor, increasing its cost and effectively pricing it out of European and other markets – and even the domestic home market;

(6) merely nominal taxes on real estate and other property, promoting "free lunch" speculation by inverting the classical principle of progressive taxation;

(7) a property bubble that sharply raises access prices to housing and commercial space;

(8) de-industrialization, euphemized as progress into a postindustrial "service" economy;

(9) rising trade dependency and a deepening structural deficit in international payments as a result of rising foreign debt; and

(10) capital flight and emigration of labor.

This free-market package is anti-democratic, seeking to reverse the Progressive reform agenda formulated by the late 19th century and implemented in the first half of the 20th century in Western social democracies. Its effect is to polarize economies between property-owning *rentiers* and increasingly indebted populations. In this respect it represents an economic Counter-Reformation mounted by financial and property interests.

## A Baltic Miracle or neoliberal debt trap?

Upon receiving their political independence in 1991, members of the former Soviet Union possessed land, subsoil resources, and public industrial enterprises. They also had social strictures designed ostensibly to protect and benefit the working class. These were denigrated as a dead hand restraining economic progress as compared to the visions of Western-style consumer prosperity to be achieved through free markets and tariff-free importation. Acting on Western advice, governments in these countries abolished the vestiges of their former systems and adopted the world's highest and most anti-labor flat tax regime, with only minimal taxation of property and its price gains, although generations of Russian domination left them without the modern infrastructure found in the West, their governments were blocked from raising the money or creating the public credit to finance such infrastructure.

This created the conditions favorable to the world's fastest-growing property bubbles as speculators saw an opportunity for almost tax-free gains by borrowing from the leading creditor nations and their bank branches in these countries to buy land and buildings. Many economists applauded this as a sign of genuine prosperity. Global and domestic investors found debt-financed speculation in real estate and public enterprises (*i.e.*, capital already in place) so lucrative that little credit has gone into financing new means of production.

Rising property prices have become the badge of Western-style prosperity, but they differ from classical wealth creation. Failure to distinguish between tangible capital formation and a bubble economy based on debt-financed asset-price inflation has led to an extractive finance capitalism rather than industrial capitalism. Instead of modernizing moribund industry throughout the former Soviet Bloc, free-market forces shut it down. Rising import dependency was financed by foreign investment flowing into these countries to buy their real estate or extend mortgage loans against it, as well as to buy the public enterprises and mineral rights being sold off.

What variables were at work that would have enabled labor and industry in the Baltic States, for instance, to compete with Scandinavia and China? How could they handle their rising foreign debt and exchange-rate pressures if they could not find exports to finance their imports? Rather than addressing these questions, Baltic governments simply wrung their hands without even asking how long the accelerating emigration of working-age labor could persist. Latvia, for instance, long bore a great resentment against Russia for the fact that in the 1950s Stalin deported some 50,000 middle-class Latvians as part of his Russification program. But its adoption of Washington Consensus policies is driving between 50,000 and 100,000 Latvians abroad every year without incurring a nationalist backlash, so powerful are neoliberal preconceptions compared to objective reality in determining national economic policy.

Instead of serving as a guide to national development, today's neoliberal doctrine is a how-to-do-it manual for stripping away the wealth of nations. Trade and investment ideology is mobilized to turn theory and practice into a cheerleading exercise for economic shrinkage at the hands of high finance. The geopolitical game is to convince as many countries as possible to act as raw-materials providers to the wealthiest, most militarily powerful creditor nations. The main arena has become the brains and ideological leanings of national leaders and their administrative bureaucracies. Economic theory is trivialized into a rhetorical device rather than a blueprint of now nations actually may gain from international trade and investment. The reality is that international finance has become an exercise in asset stripping, while freely created credit gives the United States a free ride.

## Conclusion

Academically, the objective of mainstream economic theorizing is to see who can draw the most beautiful picture of how a parallel universe might operate fairly if all nations only could benefit from each other's good fortune. The neoliberal program of free trade and free capital movement (that is, capital flight) and shifting the tax burden off property and finance onto labor shuns political or historical considerations as "exogenous," and thus ignores the reality of exploitative trade and finance. Attempts to reform economics to make the discipline more realistic by including the dynamics of property, credit and debt led a century ago to the development of sociology as a distinct field apart from economics as such. This cut off the trunk of mainstream economics from its political, financial, environmental and even technological context. Instead of aiming at scientific explanation, it has become an ideological and rhetorical net to capture the hearts and minds of voters and lawmakers.

Is it reasonable to speak of the Ricardian gains from trade resulting from specialization of international production when this leads to debt peonage for much of the Southern Hemisphere and the post-Soviet bloc? Is the attempt to pay debts by imposing austerity plans counter-effective beyond a certain point? If so, where does this point lie?

The IMF report on the USSR idealizes the positive effects of foreign ownership of rent-yielding resources—mineral rights and property. The practical implication is that most of the planet is to live in debt peonage to *rentiers* in the United States and Western Europe, whose receipt of interest, profits and capital gains will finance their nations' imports of fuels, raw materials and low-wage manufactures. If possible, the resulting geoeconomic relationship will not involve military conflict (although many *rentier* economies will maintain a potentially coercive military umbrella), but will rely on "free markets" as defined by financialized ownership patterns. Third World client oligarchies are to behave in a cosmopolitan manner that dovetails into existing trade and financial dependency patterns.

What needs to be recognized is the extent to which national diplomacy backs academic theory in the interest of finance just as intensively as it promotes international trade negotiations in the interests of local industry and agriculture. The more special the interest, the less virtue it finds in broadening the scope of understanding to deal with the financial and property dimensions of trade and investment. The Chicago Boys in Pinochet's Chile and the Harvard Boys in Yeltsin's Russia based their careers on supporting doctrinaire IMF and World Bank policies that devastated the countries they ostensibly were supposed to help. Their promotion to positions of executive authority followed a vetting process to ensure that their ideology reflected the interests of their institutional employers with regard to planning foreign economies.

All economies are planned, and all markets are structured. The key to understanding their dynamics is to ask who is doing the planning and structuring, and in whose interest countries will place decision-making. Will it be in the hands of elected officials with a clear empirical knowledge of reality to guide their national economic laws, or in those of academics serving special interests as they turn theories of international trade, lending and debt into a disinformation system?

# INDEX

Printed in the USA
CPSIA information can be obtained
at www.ICGtesting.com
LVHW071612160124
769011LV00008B/66

9 783949 546013